FIGHTERS

of WORLD
WAR II

FIGHTERS

of WORLD
WAR II

Edited by David Donald

MetroBooks

MetroBooks

An imprint of Friedman/Fairfax Publishers

Copyright © 1998 Orbis Publishing Ltd
Copyright © 1998 Aerospace Publishing

This material was previously published in 1990 as part of
the reference set *Airplane*.

Library of Congress Cataloging-in-Publication data available upon request.

ISBN: 1-56799-684-1

Editorial and design by
Brown Packaging Books Ltd
Bradley's Close
74–77 White Lion Street
London N1 9PF

Picture credits
TRH Pictures: 6, 37, 69, 122, 130, 190

Printed in the Czech Republic

10 9 8 7 6 5 4 3 2 1

For bulk purchases and special sales, please contact:
Friedman/Fairfax Publishers
Attention: Sales Department
15 West 26th Street
New York, NY 10010
212/685-6610 FAX 212/685-1307

Visit our website:
http://www.metrobooks.com

Contents

Messerschmitt Bf 109

Willy Messerschmitt's Bf 109 was the Luftwaffe's benchmark fighter throughout World War II. It was the mount of the vast majority of the German aces and scored more kills than any other Axis aircraft. After 1945 it continued to serve with several air forces and even went back to war with Israel.

The birth of the Bf 109 was the outcome of political feuding between Erhard Milch and Willy Messerschmitt, which threatened extinction of the private Bayerische Flugzeugwerke, a situation only averted when the company negotiated to supply a Romanian cartel with a new transport aircraft in 1933. Infuriated by Messerschmitt's attitude of independence, officials at the Reichsluftfahrtministerium (RLM, or State Ministry of Aviation) drew from Messerschmitt the retort that he had been obliged to seek business elsewhere because of the lack of support from Berlin itself. Stung by this accusation, the RLM awarded fighter development contracts to Arado, BFW, Focke-Wulf and Heinkel, it being confidently expected that Messerschmitt's lack of experience in high-speed aircraft design would mean that his contender would stand no chance of success.

Employing features of his excellent Bf 108 Taifun four-seat tourer, Messerschmitt's design emerged as a small angular low-wing monoplane with retractable landing gear, leading-edge slats and enclosed cockpit. It was intended to use the new Junkers Jumo 210A engine, but this was not available for the Bf 109 V1 prototype so an imported Rolls-Royce Kestrel VI of 518 kW (695 hp) was used, the aircraft being rolled out and flown in September 1935.

When flown in competition with the Ar 80 V1, Fw 159 V1 and He 112 V1, at the Travemünde trials, the Bf 109 V1 performed well despite minor problems and, amid general surprise, was rewarded by a contract for 10 prototype development aircraft (although it was not in fact declared the outright winner, 10 Heinkel aircraft also being ordered).

Three further prototypes (the Bf 109 V2 registered D-IUDE, Bf 109 V3 D-IHNY and Bf 109 V4 D-IOQY) were flown in 1936, powered by Jumo 210A engines and with provision for two synchronised MG 17 machine-guns in the nose decking. However, rumours abounded that the British Hawker Hurricane and Supermarine Spitfire were to be armed with four guns, so that by the time the Bf 109 V4 prototype flew a third MG 17 was planned to fire through the propeller hub.

The proposed two-gun Bf 109A production version did not therefore materialise, and the first pre-production Bf 109B-0 examples were flown early in 1937, at the same time as the Bf 109 V5, Bf 109 V6 and Bf 109 V7 prototypes. Considerable operational experience was gained by three Staffeln of Jagdgruppe 88, which were equipped with production examples of the Bf 109B-1, Bf 109B-2 and Bf 109C-1 versions during the Spanish Civil War, experience that not only assisted in the development of the aircraft itself but of air combat in general; for it was largely through men such as Werner Mölders and Adolf Galland (the former arguably the finest fighter pilot of all time, and the latter to become Germany's General of Fighters during World War II), who fought in Spain with the Bf 109, that there came to be evolved the basic air fighting tactics which were to last until the end of the era of gun fighting combat.

By the beginning of World War II in September 1939, the Luftwaffe had standardised its fighter equipment with the Bf 109. The Bf 109D series, although produced in fairly large numbers and still in service, was giving place to the Bf 109E (widely known as the 'Emil'). Ten pre-production Bf 109E-0s appeared late in 1938 with two nose-mounted MG 17 machine-guns and two in the wings, and powered by the 821-kW (1,100-hp) DB 601A engine. Production Bf 109E-1s started leaving the Augsburg factory at the beginning of 1939 with alternative provision for two 20-mm MG FF cannon in place of the wing machine-guns. Maximum speed was 570 km/h (354 mph) at 3750 m (12,305 ft) and service ceiling 11000 m (36,090 ft), performance figures which helped the Bf 109E to eclipse all of its opponents in the first eight months of the war. A sub-variant, the Bf 109E-1/B, introduced soon after, was a fighter-bomber capable of carrying a 250-kg (551-lb) bomb under the fuselage.

Production of the Emil was shifted from Augsburg to Regensburg in 1939 (to make way for the Bf 110 twin-engined fighter) as a massive subcontract programme was undertaken by Ago, Arado, Erla and WNF, 1,540 aircraft being delivered that year. On the eve of the invasion of Poland the Jagdverband comprised 12 Gruppen flying 850 Bf 109E-1s and Bf 109E-1/Bs and one with Ar 68s. Some 235 Bf 109D-1s were still serving with the Zerstörergeschwader. The first occasion on which Bf 109s fought the RAF was during the

One of the earliest known air-to-air photographs of a Bf 109, this November 1936 picture shows the Bf 109 V4 (no. 4 prototype), with Jumo 210A engine and armament of three MG 17 machine-guns, each with 500 rounds. The similarity to later production Bf 109 versions is strikingly apparent.

To speed production by an as-yet small industry the Bf 109 was licensed in 1937 to Fieseler and in 1938 to Focke-Wulf and Erla. This photograph was taken at Bremen in August 1938 and shows the first 10 Bf 109C-2s completed by Focke-Wulf. The C-2 was the final Jumo-engined version, with five MG 17s.

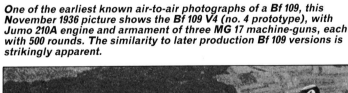

daylight raid by 24 unescorted Vickers Wellingtons on Wilhelms-haven on 18 December 1939, 12 of the bombers being destroyed for the loss of two Bf 109Es of JG 77.

In 1940 production of the Emil increased to 1,868 aircraft, the D-series being almost entirely discarded from front-line use. Principal sub-variants produced that year were the Bf 109E-2, Bf 109E-3 (with two MG 17s in the nose and two in the wings, plus an MG FF/M firing through the propeller shaft) and the Bf 109E-4 (with two nose MG 17s and two wing MG FF cannon). All these versions saw widespread action during the great daylight battles over southern England in the Battle of Britain. When employed in the 'free chase' tactic they proved deadly, being generally superior to the Hurricane and well matched with the Spitfire. However, as is now well known, the capabilities of the Bf 109E were frequently squandered when the aircraft were too often tied to close escort of bomber formations, a role in which the Bf 109Es were deprived of their greatest assets, speed and manoeuvrability. Later in the Battle of Britain they were also employed as fighter-bombers (the Bf 109E-4/B). Other variants, which appeared soon after the Battle of Britain, included the Bf 109E-5 and Bf 109E-6 reconnaissance fighters, the latter with DB 601N engine, the Bf 109E-7 with provision for belly drop-tank, and the Bf 109E-7/Z with GM-1 nitrous oxide engine boost.

Early in 1941 the Emil was beginning to appear in the Mediterranean theatre, tropicalised versions of the above sub-variants serving with JG 27 in North Africa. However, by the time Germany opened its great attack on the Soviet Union in June 1941, the Bf 109F series was beginning to join the front-line fighter squadrons, although the Emil continued to serve for a long time yet.

Testing the skill of the pilots

Powered by the 895-kW (1,200-hp) DB 601E, the Bf 109F was generally regarded as the most attractive of the entire Bf 109 family, introducing extended and rounded wingtips and enlarged spinner, while Frise ailerons and plain flaps replaced the Emil's slotted flaps. A fully retractable tailwheel superseded the earlier fixed type, and a cantilever tailplane was introduced. In the matter of gun armament, however, the Bf 109F was widely criticised, for it reverted to the hub cannon and two nose decking MG 17s. While this tended to satisfy the German *Experten* (aces) as benefitting the aircraft's performance, it was pointed out that the majority of Luftwaffe fighter pilots needed a heavier armament with which to achieve a 'kill'.

Pre-production Bf 109F-0s were evaluated by the Luftwaffe during the second half of 1940, and Bf 109F-1s were delivered early the following year. A number of accidents indicated that removal of the tailplane struts left the entire tail unit vulnerable to sympathetic vibration at certain oscillating frequencies of the engine, and

strengthening modifications were quickly put in hand. After the Bf 109F-2 (with 15-mm MG 151 replacing the 20-mm MG FF) came the principal version, the Bf 109F-3, early in 1942 with a top speed of 628 km/h (390 mph) at 6700 m (21,980 ft).

Bf 109Fs had joined the Geschwaderstab and III Gruppe of Adolf Galland's JG 26 'Schlageter' early in 1941 on the Channel coast, and during the early stages of Operation Barbarossa in the East this version equipped Major Günther Lützow's JG 3 'Udet', Werner Mölders' JG 51, Major Günther von Maltzahn's JG 53 'Pik As' and Major Johannes Trautloft's JG 54. The superiority of the new fighter (even over the Spitfire Mk V in the West) quickly became apparent as the German fighter pilots' victory tallies soared.

The Bf 109F underwent progressive improvement and development: the Bf 109F-4 had an MG 151 rebarrelled to 20-mm, the Bf 109F-4/R1 could be fitted with *Rüstsatz* (field conversion kit) comprising two 20-mm MG 151 guns in underwing packs for the bomber-destroyer role, the Bf 109F-4/B fighter-bomber was capable of

Messerschmitt Bf 109G-14/U4 cutaway drawing key

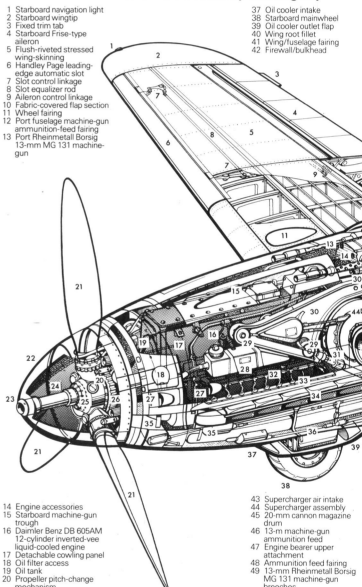

1 Starboard navigation light
2 Starboard wingtip
3 Fixed trim tab
4 Starboard Frise-type aileron
5 Flush-riveted stressed wing-skinning
6 Handley Page leading-edge automatic slot
7 Slot control linkage
8 Slot equalizer rod
9 Aileron control linkage
10 Fabric-covered flap section
11 Wheel fairing
12 Port fuselage machine-gun ammunition-feed fairing
13 Port Rheinmetall Borsig 13-mm MG 131 machine-gun
14 Engine accessories
15 Starboard machine-gun trough
16 Daimler Benz DB 605AM 12-cylinder inverted-vee liquid-cooled engine
17 Detachable cowling panel
18 Oil filter access
19 Oil tank
20 Propeller pitch-change mechanism
21 VDM electrically-operated constant-speed propeller
22 Spinner
23 Engine-mounted cannon muzzle
24 Blast tube
25 Propeller hub
26 Spinner back plate
27 Auxiliary cooling intakes
28 Cooling header tank
29 Anti-vibration rubber engine-mounting pads
30 Elektron forged engine bearer
31 Engine bearer support strut attachment
32 Plug leads
33 Exhaust manifold fairing strip
34 Ejector exhausts
35 Cowling fasteners
36 Oil cooler
37 Oil cooler intake
38 Starboard mainwheel
39 Oil cooler outlet flap
40 Wing root fillet
41 Wing/fuselage fairing
42 Firewall/bulkhead
43 Supercharger air intake
44 Supercharger assembly
45 20-mm cannon magazine drum
46 13-m machine-gun ammunition feed
47 Engine bearer upper attachment
48 Ammunition feed fairing
49 13-mm Rheinmetall Borsig MG 131 machine-gun breeches
50 Instrument panel
51 20-mm Mauser MG 151/20 cannon breech
52 Heelrests
53 Rudder pedals
54 Undercarriage emergency retraction cables
55 Fuselage frame
56 Wing/fuselage fairing
57 Undercarriage emergency retraction handwheel (outboard)

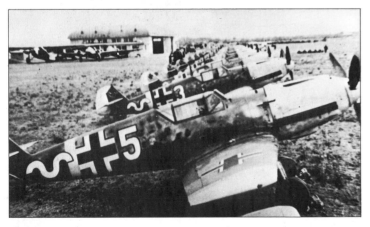

Pictured at Schiphol, Netherlands, in the summer of 1940, these Bf 109E-1s equipped 7./JG 52 and were one of the expertly flown units that established total air superiority in the race to the Channel in May of that year. Note KLM Fokker and Lockheed transports in the background. JG 52 gained 10,000 air victories by September 1944.

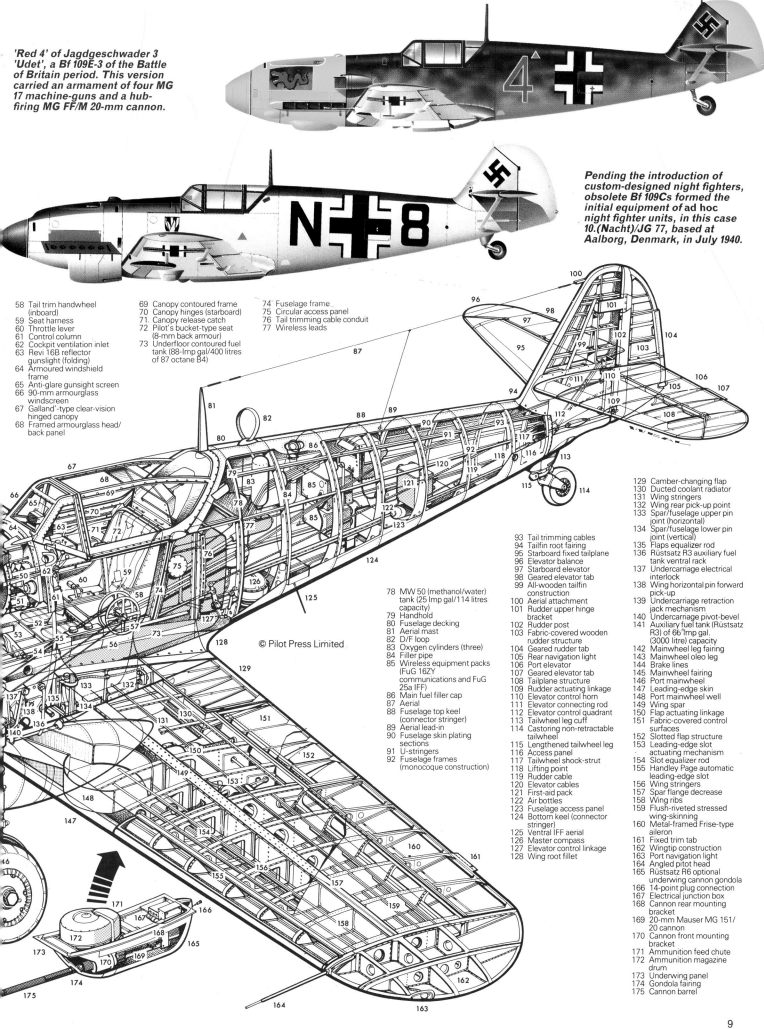

'Red 4' of Jagdgeschwader 3 'Udet', a Bf 109E-3 of the Battle of Britain period. This version carried an armament of four MG 17 machine-guns and a hub-firing MG FF/M 20-mm cannon.

Pending the introduction of custom-designed night fighters, obsolete Bf 109Cs formed the initial equipment of ad hoc night fighter units, in this case 10.(Nacht)/JG 77, based at Aalborg, Denmark, in July 1940.

58 Tail trim handwheel (inboard)
59 Seat harness
60 Throttle lever
61 Control column
62 Cockpit ventilation inlet
63 Revi 16B reflector gunsight (folding)
64 Armoured windshield frame
65 Anti-glare gunsight screen
66 90-mm armourglass windscreen
67 Galland'-type clear-vision hinged canopy
68 Framed armourglass head/back panel
69 Canopy contoured frame
70 Canopy hinges (starboard)
71 Canopy release catch
72 Pilot's bucket-type seat (8-mm back armour)
73 Underfloor contoured fuel tank (88-Imp gal/400 litres of 87 octane B4)
74 Fuselage frame
75 Circular access panel
76 Tail trimming cable conduit
77 Wireless leads

78 MW 50 (methanol/water) tank (25 Imp gal/114 litres capacity)
79 Handhold
80 Fuselage decking
81 Aerial mast
82 D/F loop
83 Oxygen cylinders (three)
84 Filler pipe
85 Wireless equipment packs (FuG 16ZY communications and FuG 25a IFF)
86 Main fuel filler cap
87 Aerial
88 Fuselage top keel (connector stringer)
89 Aerial lead-in
90 Fuselage skin plating sections
91 U-stringers
92 Fuselage frames (monocoque construction)

93 Tail trimming cables
94 Tailfin root fairing
95 Starboard fixed tailplane
96 Elevator balance
97 Starboard elevator
98 Geared elevator tab
99 All-wooden tailfin construction
100 Aerial attachment
101 Rudder upper hinge bracket
102 Rudder post
103 Fabric-covered wooden rudder structure
104 Geared rudder tab
105 Rear navigation light
106 Port elevator
107 Geared elevator tab
108 Tailplane structure
109 Rudder actuating linkage
110 Elevator control horn
111 Elevator connecting rod
112 Elevator control quadrant
113 Tailwheel leg cuff
114 Castoring non-retractable tailwheel
115 Lengthened tailwheel leg
116 Access panel
117 Tailwheel shock-strut
118 Lifting point
119 Rudder cable
120 Elevator cables
121 First-aid pack
122 Air bottles
123 Fuselage access panel
124 Bottom keel (connector stringer)
125 Ventral IFF aerial
126 Master compass
127 Elevator control linkage
128 Wing root fillet

129 Camber-changing flap
130 Ducted coolant radiator
131 Wing stringers
132 Wing rear pick-up point
133 Spar/fuselage upper pin joint (horizontal)
134 Spar/fuselage lower pin joint (vertical)
135 Flaps equalizer rod
136 Rüstsatz R3 auxiliary fuel tank ventral rack
137 Undercarriage electrical interlock
138 Wing horizontal pin forward pick-up
139 Undercarriage retraction jack mechanism
140 Undercarriage pivot-bevel
141 Auxiliary fuel tank (Rüstsatz R3) of 66 Imp gal. (3000 litre) capacity
142 Mainwheel leg fairing
143 Mainwheel oleo leg
144 Brake lines
145 Mainwheel fairing
146 Port mainwheel
147 Leading-edge skin
148 Port mainwheel well
149 Wing spar
150 Flap actuating linkage
151 Fabric-covered control surfaces
152 Slotted flap structure
153 Leading-edge slot actuating mechanism
154 Slot equalizer rod
155 Handley Page automatic leading-edge slot
156 Wing stringers
157 Spar flange decrease
158 Wing ribs
159 Flush-riveted stressed wing-skinning
160 Metal-framed Frise-type aileron
161 Fixed trim tab
162 Wingtip construction
163 Port navigation light
164 Angled pitot head
165 Rüstsatz R6 optional underwing cannon gondola
166 14-point plug connection
167 Electrical junction box
168 Cannon rear mounting bracket
169 20-mm Mauser MG 151/20 cannon
170 Cannon front mounting bracket
171 Ammunition feed chute
172 Ammunition magazine drum
173 Underwing panel
174 Gondola fairing
175 Cannon barrel

© Pilot Press Limited

Introduced into Luftwaffe service midway through the **Battle of Britain in August 1940**, the **Messerschmitt Bf 109E-7** featured a modified fuel system and attachments for a ventral drop tank. Being equipped to carry the extra fuel, the new aircraft were able to provide effective escort for the big daylight raids over **London in September 1940**. 'Red 2' (no. 2058), depicted here, was being flown by **Unteroffizier Klick** of 3./**LG 2** when it was shot down by **RAF** fighters in the famous raids on London of 15 September.

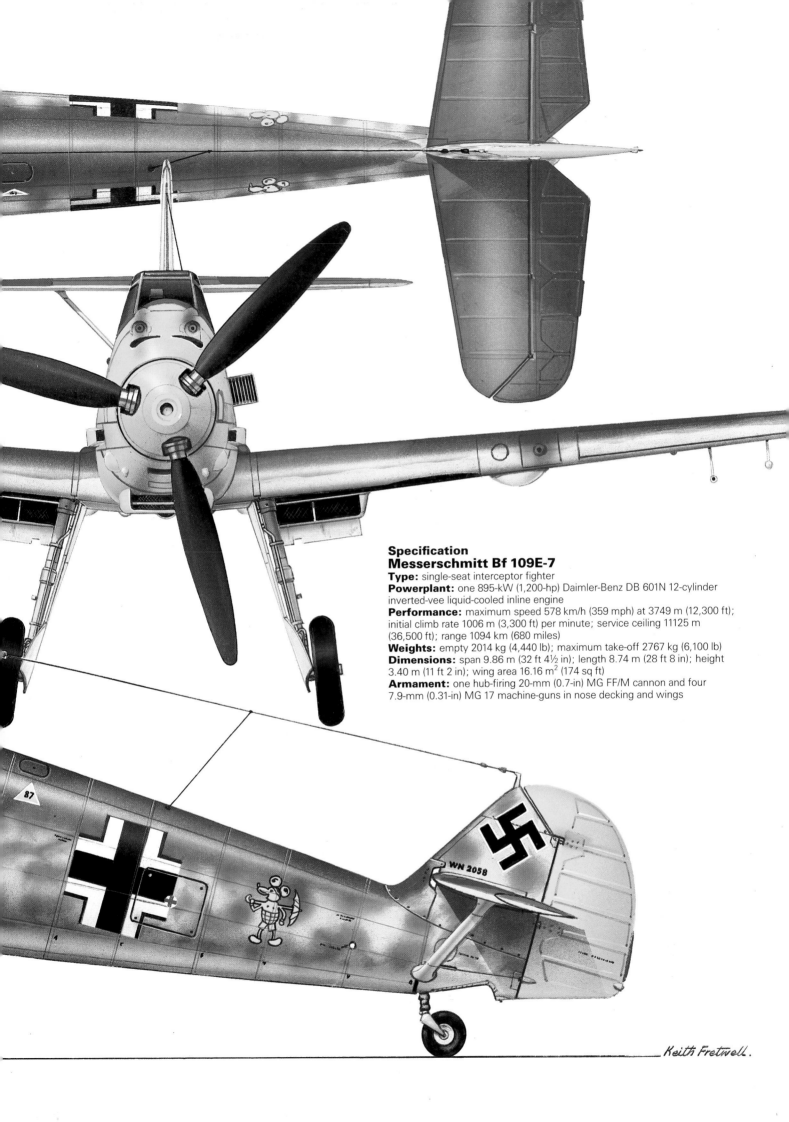

Specification
Messerschmitt Bf 109E-7
Type: single-seat interceptor fighter
Powerplant: one 895-kW (1,200-hp) Daimler-Benz DB 601N 12-cylinder inverted-vee liquid-cooled inline engine
Performance: maximum speed 578 km/h (359 mph) at 3749 m (12,300 ft); initial climb rate 1006 m (3,300 ft) per minute; service ceiling 11125 m (36,500 ft); range 1094 km (680 miles)
Weights: empty 2014 kg (4,440 lb); maximum take-off 2767 kg (6,100 lb)
Dimensions: span 9.86 m (32 ft 4½ in); length 8.74 m (28 ft 8 in); height 3.40 m (11 ft 2 in); wing area 16.16 m² (174 sq ft)
Armament: one hub-firing 20-mm (0.7-in) MG FF/M cannon and four 7.9-mm (0.31-in) MG 17 machine-guns in nose decking and wings

Keith Fretwell.

Messerschmitt Bf 109

Wearing the insignia of the Gruppen-Kommandeur, I. Gruppe, of a Jagdgeschwader in 1939, the Bf 109D was powered by the DB 600A and was in effect the production version developed from the V10 prototype. It carried an armament of one hub-firing MG FF cannon and two MG 17s and its performance was in most respects better than a Spitfire I.

The Bf 109 V10 flown by Ernst Udet in July 1937 at the Zurich International Flying Meeting. Despite demonstrating an excellent performance, Udet crashed the aircraft during the Circuit of the Alps race after failure of the DB 600 engine.

carrying up to 500 kg (1,102 lb) of bombs, and the Bf 109F-5 and Bf 109F-6 reconnaissance fighters were introduced later in 1942. It was principally in the tropicalised Bf 109F-4 that the 22-year-old Oberleutnant Hans-Joachim Marseille became the highest-scoring Luftwaffe fighter pilot in the West with 158 air victories, although he died bailing out from a Bf 109G-2 on 30 September 1942 in North Africa.

'Gustav', the universal soldier

The Bf 109G (dubbed the 'Gustav' by German pilots) was introduced into service in the late summer of 1942 and came to be built in larger numbers than any other version. It was powered by the 1100-kW (1,475-hp) DB 605A, although pre-production Bf 109G-0s retained the DB 601E. Basic armament remained two nose-mounted MG 17s and hub-firing 20-mm MG 151/20 cannon. The Bf 109G-1, with pressure cabin, was powered by the DB 605A-1 with GM-1 power boosting, and the tropical version, the Bf 109G-1/Trop, carried 13-mm (0.51-in) MG 131s in place of the MG 17s, necessitating larger breech blocks and giving rise to the nickname Beule (bump) on account of the raised fairings forward of the windscreen. The Bf 109G-2 dispensed with the pressure cabin and the Bf 109G-2/R1 was a fighter-bomber; the Bf 109G-3 was similar to the Bf 109G-1 but with FuG 16Z radio, and the Bf 109G-4 was an unpressurised version of the Bf 109G-3. The Bf 109G-5 introduced the DB 605D engine with MW-50 water-methanol power-boosting (making possible a maximum power of 1343 kW/1,800 hp for combat bursts), while the Bf 109G-5/R2 featured a taller rudder and lengthened tailwheel leg in an effort to counter the aircraft's swing on take-off.

Most important of all the 'Gustavs' was the Bf 109G-6 which, in various sub-variants, was powered by AM, AS, ASB, ASD or ASM versions of the DB 605 engine; basic armament was the hub-firing 30-mm MK 108 cannon, two nose MG 131s and two underwing 20-mm MG 151/20 guns. Numerous Rüstsatz kits were produced including those to produce the Bf 109G-6/R1 fighter-bomber with a bomb load of up to 500 kg (1,102 lb), and the Bf 109G-6/R2 bomber-destroyer with two 21-cm (8.27-in) WGr 210 'Dodel' rockets replacing the underwing cannon. The Bf 109G-6/U4 (with an Umrüst-Bausatz or factory conversion set) was armed with two 30-mm MK 108 underwing cannon, and the Bf 109G-6/U4N night-fighter carried radar. Tropicalised versions of most of these were also produced. The Bf 109G-7 was not built, but the Bf 109G-8 reconnaissance fighter formed part of the equipment of Nahaufklärungsgruppe 13 late in 1943 on the Channel coast. Fastest of all 'Gustavs' was the Bf 109G-10 with the DB 605D with MW-50 and bulged cockpit canopy (known as the 'Galland hood'); top speed was 690 km/h (429 mph) at 7400 m (24,280 ft); the Bf 109G-10/R2 and R6 possessed the revised tail and tailwheel assembly of the Bf 109G-5/R2 and were equipped with FuG 25a IFF equipment; the Bf 109G-10/U4 had provision for a belly gun pack containing two MK 108 30-mm guns, but this could be replaced by a non-jettisonable fuel tank known as the Irmer Behalter. The Bf 109G-12 was a two-seat trainer, field-modified from the Bf 109G-1 to provide conversion training on the Schulejagdgeschwader, notably JG 101, 102, 104, 106, 107 and 108 in 1944. Last operational version was the 'universal' Bf 109G-14 with lightened fixed armament but with provision for external guns, WGr 210 rockets or bombs. The Bf 109G-16 heavily armoured ground-attack fighter-bomber entered production before Germany's surrender but did not see operational service.

Development of the Bf 109H high-altitude fighter started in 1943, being a progression from the F-series with increased wing span and the GM-1 boosted DB 601E. Maximum speed was 750 km/h

J-310 was the first Bf 109 to serve with Switzerland's Fliegertruppe, delivered on 17 December 1938. Powered by a 507-kW (680-hp) Jumo 210Da engine (like the German Bf 109B), it had an armament of four MG 17 machine-guns (as fitted to the Bf 109C). The Swiss used Bf 109s until the end of 1949, some being assembled locally.

Called 'tripala' by the Spanish (the earlier models had a two-bladed propeller), the Bf 109E-1 was by far the best fighter in Spain in early 1939, when this picture was taken at a Légion Kóndor base. Armament was two cannon and two MG 17 machine-guns. The Légion transferred 40 Bf 109s to Spain, which built other models post-war.

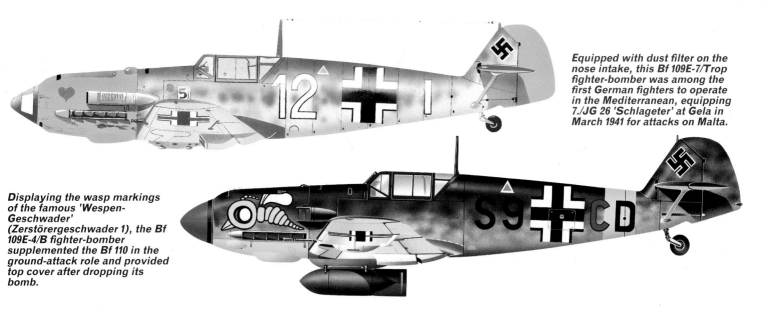

Equipped with dust filter on the nose intake, this Bf 109E-7/Trop fighter-bomber was among the first German fighters to operate in the Mediterranean, equipping 7./JG 26 'Schlageter' at Gela in March 1941 for attacks on Malta.

Displaying the wasp markings of the famous 'Wespen-Geschwader' (Zerstörergeschwader 1), the Bf 109E-4/B fighter-bomber supplemented the Bf 110 in the ground-attack role and provided top cover after dropping its bomb.

(466 mph) at 10100 m (33,135 ft). Pre-production aircraft were evaluated operationally in France and a few sorties were flown by production Bf 109H-1s, but wing flutter problems caused the H-series to be abandoned, although projects included the Bf 109H-2 with Jumo 213E, and the Bf 109H-5 with DB 605 engines.

Last main operational version of the Bf 109 was the K-series, developed directly from the Gustav; indeed the Bf 109K-0 pre-production aircraft were converted G-series airframes. The Bf 109K-2 and Bf 109K-4 (pressurised) were powered by MW-50 boosted 1492-kW (2,000-hp) DB 605 ASCM/DCM engines and armed with one 30-mm MK 103 or MK 108 cannon and two 15-mm (0.59-in) MG 151 heavy machine-guns, and the Bf 109K-6 had provision for two underwing 30-mm MK 103s. Only two Bf 109K-14s (DB 605L with MW-50 and a top speed of 725 km/h; 450 mph) saw action before the end of the war, being delivered to Major Wilhelm Batz's Gruppenstab, II./JG 52, in April 1945.

Trials and experiments

With the Focke-Wulf Fw 190 reaching full operational status only after two years of war, the Bf 109 provided the backbone of the Luftwaffe's fighter arm throughout World War II: with more than 30,000 examples produced (because of confusion caused by bombing of factories, an accurate production total could not be arrived at, but only the Russian Ilyushin Il-2 had a higher figure, with 36,163 models built), it was natural that experiments and projects abounded.

For example, among the more bizarre trials were those conducted on Bf 109Es to carry a parachutist in an over-wing 'paracapsule'. Another (in the Starr-Schlepp programme) involved the mounting of

a Bf 109E on a DFS 230 troop-carrying glider as a means of delivering airborne forces; this experiment was followed later in the war by the well-known *Beethoven-Gerät* composite weapon system involving the use of Bf 109s and Fw 190s mounted atop unmanned Junkers Ju 88s loaded with explosives. A number of radical operational tactics were pioneered by Bf 109 units, including the aerial bombing of American bomber formations with 250-kg (551-lb) bombs dropped from Bf 109Gs (pioneered by JG 1 in 1943), and the use by JG 300 of day fighters for freelance night combat against night bombers, known as *wilde Sau* tactics.

A development of the Emil was the Bf 109T carrierborne fighter, intended for deployment aboard the German carrier *Graf Zeppelin*. Featuring folding wings, arrester hook and catapult spools, 10 pre-production Bf 109T-0s and 60 Bf 109T-1s were produced between 1939 and 1941, but when the carrier's construction was abandoned most of these aircraft were delivered to the Luftwaffe for land-based operation.

Perhaps the most ambitious of all projects was the Bf 109Z *Zwilling*, involving the union of two Bf 109F airframes and outer wing panels by means of new wing and tail sections; the pilot was to have been accommodated in the port fuselage and two versions were proposed, a *Zerstörer* with five 30-mm guns and a fighter-bomber with a 1000-kg (2,205-lb) bomb load. A prototype was built but this was never flown.

Bf 109s were supplied to numerous foreign air forces from 1939 onwards, and considerable licence-production of the 'Gustav' was undertaken by Avia at Prague and IAR at Brasov in Romania. The most successful of the foreign air arms with Bf 109s was the Finnish

Aircraft VK+AB was Bf 109 V24 (prototype no. 24), works number 5604. It was built in 1940 alongside V23 (CE+BP) as the third and fourth development aircraft for the Bf 109F, with round wingtips, a better-streamlined engine installation and other changes. The Bf 109F was the nicest of all 109s to fly.

JG 54 Grünherz (green heart) moved from northern France to the Soviet Union in 1941, and this picture was taken on the Leningrad front in summer 1942. These Bf 109-G2s bear the badges of II./JG 54 (left) and III.JG 54 (right). The G-2 was the first 'Gustav' to enter service, in late April 1942.

Messerschmitt Bf 109

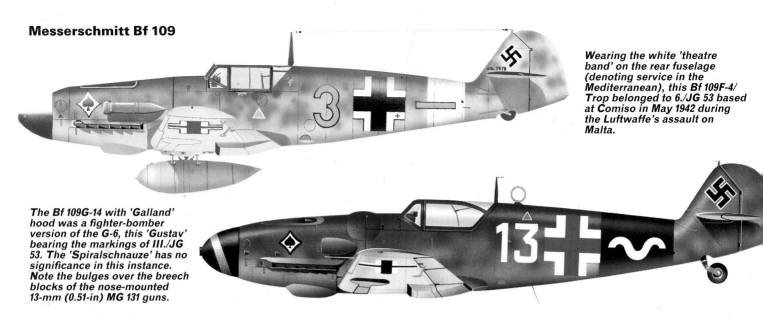

Wearing the white 'theatre band' on the rear fuselage (denoting service in the Mediterranean), this Bf 109F-4/Trop belonged to 6./JG 53 based at Comiso in May 1942 during the Luftwaffe's assault on Malta.

The Bf 109G-14 with 'Galland' hood was a fighter-bomber version of the G-6, this 'Gustav' bearing the markings of III./JG 53. The 'Spiralschnauze' has no significance in this instance. Note the bulges over the breech blocks of the nose-mounted 13-mm (0.51-in) MG 131 guns.

air force, its highest-scoring pilot, Lentomestari Eino Juutilainen, achieving 94 victories, of which 59 were scored in 'Gustavs'; he was the highest-scoring non-German/Austrian fighter pilot of all time and his aircraft were never once hit in combat.

Spain undertook licence assembly of the Bf 109 during and after World War II using the Hispano-Suiza 12-Z-89 and 12-Z-17 engines in German-supplied airframes, and later the Rolls-Royce Merlin; these aircraft, termed Hispano HAS 1109-J1L, HA 1110-K1L (two-seater) and HA 1112-K1L, remained in service until the 1960s. Other postwar use of the Bf 109 included a number of C-210 'Mezec' (Czech-built Jumo 211F-powered 'Gustavs') flown by Israel against the Egyptian air force in 1948.

The Bf 109 was widely supplied to German satellite states in World War II, and was also used by neutral countries such as Spain and Switzerland. Total Bf 109 production amounted to over 30,000 plus 24 prototypes.

Messerschmitt Bf 109 variants

Bf 109a (later Bf109 VI): D-IABI, first prototype; 518-kW (695-hp) Rolls-Royce Kestrel V engine; first flight in September 1935 **Bf 109 V2, V3 and V4:** three prototypes (D-IUDE, D-IHNY and D-IOQY); Jumo 210A engines **Bf 109B:** pre-production **Bf 109B-0** with Jumo 210B; **Bf 109B-1** with Jumo 210D; **Bf 109B-2** with Jumo 210E and later, 210G engines **Bf 109 V10 and V13:** two prototypes (D-ISLU and D-IPKY); Daimler-Benz DB 600 engines **Bf 109C:** developed from **Bf 109 V8** prototype; **Bf 109C-0** and **Bf 109C-1** with four MG 17s; **Bf 109C-2** with five MG 17s **Bf 109 V13:** modified with boosted DB 601 engine; world speed record of 610.54 km/h (379.38 mph) on 11 November 1937 **Bf 109D:** developed from Bf 109 V10 and V13 prototypes; **Bf 109D-0** with DB 600Aa and armament of two 20-mm and two 7.92-mm (0.31-in) guns; **Bf 109D-1** similar; **Bf 109D-2** with two wing MG 17s; **Bf 109D-3** with two MG FFs in wings **Bf 109 V14:** prototype (D-IRTT); fuel injection DB 601A engine; two 20-mm and two

7.92-mm (0.31-in) guns; **Bf 109 V15** (D-IPHR) similar but one 20-mm gun **Bf 109E: Bf109E-0** with four 7.92-mm (0.31-in) guns; **Bf 109E-1** (and **Bf 109E-1/B** bomber) similar; **Bf 109E-2** with two 20-mm and two 7.92-mm (0.31-in) guns; **Bf 109E-3** with one hub 20-mm and four 7.92-mm (0.31-in) guns; **Bf 109E-4** (also **Bf 109E-4/B** and **Bf 109E-4/Trop**) similar to Bf 109E-3 but no hub gun; **Bf 109E-4/N** with DB 601N engine; **Bf 109E-5** and **Bf 109E-6** reconnaissance fighters with two 7.92-mm (0.31-in) guns; **Bf 109E-7** similar to Bf 109E-4/N with provision for belly tank (**Bf 109E-7/U2** ground attack sub-variant); **Bf 109E-7/Z** with GM-1 boost; **Bf 109E-8** with DB 601E engine; **Bf 109E-9** reconnaissance fighter **Bf 109F: Bf 109F-0** from E-airframes with DB 601N engine; **Bf 109F-1** with one 20-mm and two 7.92-mm (0.31-in) guns; **Bf 109F-2** with one 15-mm and two 7.92-mm (0.31-in) guns (**Bf 109F-2/Z** with GM-1); **Bf 109F-3** with DB 601E engine; **Bf 109F-4** (and **Bf 109F-4/B**) with one 20-mm and two 7.92-mm (0.31-in) guns and DB 601E; **Bf 109F-5** and **Bf 109F-6** reconnaissance fighters with two 7.92-mm (0.31-in) guns; trials aircraft included one with BMW 801 radial, one with Jumo 213,

one with butterfly tail and one with wing fences **Bf 109G: Bf 109G-0** with DB 601E engine; **Bf 109G-1** with DB 605A-1 and GM-1; **Bf 109G-1/Trop** with one 20-mm and two 15-mm guns (*Beule*); **Bf 109G-2** was unpressurised version of Bf 109G-1 (also **Bf 109G-2/R1** fighter-bomber); **Bf 109G-3** with FuG 16Z radio; **Bf 109G-4** unpressurised version of Bf 109G-3; **Bf 109G-5** with enlarged rudder had DB.605D with MW-50; **Bf 109G-6** with variations of DB 605 (see text) and two 13-mm (0.51-in), one 30-mm and two underwing 20-mm guns (also R and U subvariants, see text); **Bf 109G-8** reconnaissance fighter; **Bf 109G-10** with DB 605G and MW-50; **Bf 109G-12** was two-seat trainer; **Bf 109G-14** with one 20-mm and two 15-mm guns plus provision for underwing guns or rockets; **Bf 109G-16** ground-attack fighter **Bf 109H:** high-altitude fighter developed from F-series; **Bf 109H-0** pre-production; **Bf 109H-1** with DB 601E; **Bf 109H-2** and **Bf 109H-3** with Jumo 213; **Bf 109H-5** with DB 605L **Bf 109J:** proposed Spanish licence-built version; not proceeded with **Bf 109K:** development from Bf 109G-10; **Bf 109K-0** with DB 605D and GM-1; **Bf 109K-2** and **Bf 109K-4** (pressurised) with DB 605ASCM/DCM and MW-50, and one 30-mm and two 15-mm guns; **Bf 109K-6** with three

30-mm and two 15-mm guns; **Bf 109K-14** with DB 605L and MW-50 **Bf 109L:** proposed version with Jumo 213E engine; maximum estimated speed 763 km/h (474 mph); not built **Bf 109S:** proposed version with blown flaps; not built **Bf 109T:** carrierborne version of Bf 109E for carrier *Graf Zeppelin*; 10 **Bf 109T-0** converted by Fieseler; 60 **Bf 109K-1** with DB 601N; **Bf 109T-2** was conversion of T-1 with deck gear removed **Bf 109TL:** project based on near-standard Bf 109 with two underwing Jumo 109-004B turbojets; abandoned in 1943 **Bf 109Z Zwilling:** twin Bf 109F airframes with single pilot and five 30-mm guns (**Bf 109Z-1**); **Bf 109Z-2** with two 30-mm guns and 1000-kg (2,205-lb) bomb load; **Bf 109Z-3** and **Bf 109Z-4** conversion of Bf 109Z-1 and Bf109Z-2 respectively with Jumo 213 engines; one prototype built but not flown; led to Me 609 project **Me 209 V1, V2, V3 and V4:** D-INJR, D-IWAH, D-IVFP and D-IRND; high-speed prototypes developed for speed records **Me 309 V1, V2, V3 and V4:** GE-CU, GE-CV, GE-CW and GE-CX; high-speed, high-altitude fighter prototypes intended to replace Bf 109F **Me 609:** projected development of Bf 109Z *Zwilling* twin Bf 109; abandoned

Despite the absence of unit markings it is known that this Bf 109 was serving in autumn 1943 with II./JG 26, one of the crack fighter units in northern France. It is a G-6/R6, the R6 modification adding the pair of 20-mm MG151 cannon and ammunition in underwing gondolas. The slats are clearly visible here.

Taken in 1944, when many Bf 109s were being used in the anti-bomber role with heavy rocket mortars, this photograph shows a pair of G-6/R2s with the most common of these weapons, the Wfr Gr 21 which lobbed 21-cm rockets from the tubes under the wings. They were called Pulk Zerstörer (formation destroyer).

Mitsubishi Ki-46 'Dinah'

In keeping with the predilection for hillbilly names shown by early members of the Allied Air Technical Intelligence Unit, the Ki-46 was assigned the codename 'Dinah'. Apart from being one of Japan's most attractive aircraft designs, it was also an impressive warplane.

In 1937, within two months of the entry into service of the Mitsubishi Ki-15, a clean two-seat single-engined reconnaissance monoplane with spatted landing gear (later given the Allied codename 'Babs'), the Technical Branch of the Koku Hombu (air headquarters) began to draft preliminary specifications for its successor. Aware that fighter aircraft in service in Europe were capable of exceeding with ease the 480-km/h (298-mph) speed of the Ki-15 and that comparable fighters were under development in the Soviet Union and the United States, Major Yuzo Fujita and engineers Ando and Tanaka stressed speed as the main requirement for the new aircraft, with long endurance as the next most important demand. Indeed, the specified top speed of 600 km/h (373 mph) at 4000 m (13,123 ft) appeared exceedingly sanguine, as the fastest Japanese aircraft then was the Kawasaki Ki-28 fighter prototype which had reached only 485 km/h (301 mph) at that altitude. The required endurance was six hours at a speed of 400 km/h (249 mph) between 4000 m and 6000 m (13,123 ft and 19,685 ft). Fortunately, other usual requirements were waived and the designers were free to select either a single- or twin-engined configuration using radial engines in the 589.1-kW to 708.4-kW (790-hp to 950-hp) class (Nakajima Ha-20-Otsu or Ha-25, or Mitsubishi Ha-26).

As Mitsubishi Jukogyo K.K. (Mitsubishi Heavy Industries Co. Ltd) was already working on a high-performance reconnaissance aircraft, the Ki-40 derived from its proposed Ki-39 twin-engined fighter, the company was awarded the contract for the new aircraft on a sole-source basis on 12 December 1937. The design team, led by Tomio Kubo and Joji Hattori, concluded almost immediately that the Ki-40 would not be able to meet the speed requirements imposed by the Koku Hombu. Work on the Ki-40 was terminated and a brand-new design, retaining the fully retractable landing gear and twin-engine configuration of the earlier design but characterised by its narrow fuselage, was undertaken. Bearing the Kitai (experimental airframe) designation Ki-46, this aircraft also featured thin-section wings with a single main spar and two auxiliary spars. The two-man crew was to be accommodated in separate cockpits, the main fuel tank being placed between these two cockpits.

Even though the Nakajima Ha-25 radial engine was both lighter and more powerful than the Ha-26, Mitsubishi stuck to its policy of powering its aircraft with engines of its own manufacture and selected a pair of 671.1-kW (900-hp) Ha-26-Ko units for the Ki-46. Nevertheless, by using close-fitting cowlings (which were designed in co-operation with the Aeronautical Research Institute of the University of Tokyo), constant-speed propellers and large spinners, the Mitsubishi design team hoped that the performance requirements could be met. Flight trials, which began at Kagamigahara in late 1939, unfortunately proved that the designers had been overly optimistic; the maximum speed attained by the Ki-46 prototypes was 540 km/h (335.5 mph) at 4000 m (13,123 ft). However, as the Ha-26-powered machine proved highly satisfactory in all other respects, the Koku Hombu ordered it placed in production as the Army Type 100 Command Reconnaissance Aircraft Model 1 (Ki-46-I) and instructed Mitsubishi to proceed at once with the development of a

The Ki-46-II was the most widely used version of the type 100 Command Reconnaissance Aircraft, with production continuing well into 1944. Many served in mixed equipment units alongside the later-production Ki-46-III in the Pacific conflict. Note the prominent landing light in the underside of the nose and the direction-finding antenna in the pod above the fuselage. This version was also fitted with extra fuel tankage in the wings.

Mitsubishi Ki-46 'Dinah'

This Ki-46-III of the 3rd Chutai, 81st Sentai, based on the island of Java in 1944, displays the original brown primer as the upper camouflage. With excellent performance, particularly between 8000 m (26,250 ft) and 10000 m (32,810 ft), it could watch enemy airfields with impunity.

more powerful version, the Ki-46-II. Meanwhile, as the Ki-46-I was going to be slower than required, and thus could be intercepted by the most recent fighters in service with Japan's potential enemies, a trainable 7.7-mm (0.303-in) machine-gun was added to provide token rear defence.

In addition to work for the Imperial Japanese Navy, Mitsubishi was then producing Ki-15-II 'Babs' reconnaissance aircraft, Ki-21-I and Ki-21-II 'Sally' twin-engined bombers, Ki-30 'Ann' single-engined bombers, Ki-51 'Sonia' ground-attack and tactical reconnaissance aircraft, and Ki-57 'Topsy' twin-engined transports for the Imperial Japanese Army, and its plant facilities and production personnel were already working at full capacity. Consequently, the production of Ki-46s-Is was slow to gain momentum, the first few aircraft being assigned for service evaluation during the spring of 1940. As more Ki-46-Is became available, crew training began at the Shimoshizu Rikugun Hikogakuko (Shimoshizu Army Flying School) in anticipation of the Ki-46-II service debut.

By the spring of 1941 no fewer than 368 Ki-46s had been ordered by the Imperial Japanese Army, but the production rate remained at the dismal level of only four aircraft per month. Improvements were on the way, as Mitsubishi had been instructed to terminate production of the Ki-15s and Ki-30s in 1940 and to reassign personnel and facilities to Ki-46 production. The results of this decision were felt almost immediately; the production rate reached 10 units in November 1941 and steadily increased thereafter until a peak of 75 Ki-46s were produced in March 1944.

New version

While Mitsubishi production staff were feverishly reorganising plant layout and work flow to step up manufacturing rates, their colleagues in the engineering department had proceeded with the development of the Ki-46-II. To power this version, Mitsubishi selected its new Ha-102 radial, a derivative of the Ha-26 fitted with

two-speed supercharger and rated at 805.4 kW (1,080 hp) for take-off and 786.7 kW (1,055 hp) at 2800 m (9,186 ft), and thus avoided the need to redesign the close-fitting cowlings, as the Ha-102 retained the overall diameter of the earlier engine. This proved to be a wise selection, as the Ki-46-II, first flown in March 1941, slightly exceeded the top speed initially required by the Koku Hombu by attaining 604 km/h (375 mph) at 5800 m (19,029 ft). With the Ki-46-II production assured at a satisfactory rate and its performance meeting requirements, the Imperial Japanese Army was able to form operational units in mid-1941 and then turn its attention to solving minor teething problems.

During initial service trials vapour locks had occurred frequently under hot and humid weather conditions. To find a solution to this problem, which affected both the Ha-26-Ko and Ha-102 versions of the aircraft, hot-weather trials were conducted in Formosa during June 1940 using a Ki-46-I, and in June 1941 with a Ki-46-II. Relocation of fuel lines around the engines and a switch from 87-octane to 92-octane petrol satisfactorily corrected the condition. Less easily solved was an inherent weakness in the main landing gear legs, which tended to collapse during heavy landings. Partial correction was provided by fitting a stronger auxiliary rear strut, but this weakness was never fully eliminated. Other shortcomings noted by service trial crews were of a minor nature and did not prevent the type from being rushed to operational units to undertake covert mapping and intelligence gathering in preparation for Japanese operations in South East Asia.

Whereas the Allies had been forced to use jury-rigged aircraft for their pre-war covert operations (e.g. the Lockheed 12 transport

The Luftwaffe made vain attempts to acquire a manufacturing licence for the Ki-46 under the Japanese-German Technical Exchange Programme. This example was tested by the USAAF after capture at the end of the Pacific conflict, impressing pilots with its high-altitude speed and endurance.

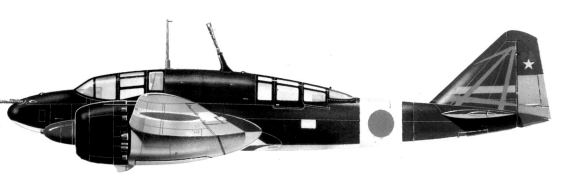

The twin 20-mm Ho-5 nose cannon and the obliquely-mounted, forward-firing 37-mm Ho-203 cannon identify this as a Ki-46-III Kai, a high-altitude interceptor derivative of the Ki-46-III. Approximately 200 were produced to counter the USAAF B-29 bombers, this example serving with the 17th Independent Fighter Company.

used by the British and French in 1939-40 to photograph military facilities in Germany and Italy, and the Consolidated LB-30 adapted by the Americans to fly over Japanese islands in the western Pacific), the Imperial Japanese Army had had the foresight to order the Ki-46, a specialised strategic reconnaissance aircraft with performance rendering it virtually immune to interception by the obsolete fighters then fielded by the Allies. Assigned to seven Dokuritsu Dai Shijugo Chutais (independent companies) during the summer of 1941, Ki-46-IIs obtained thorough coverage of the areas which Japan planned to attack at the onset of the Pacific war. Notably, flying from Cambodia in October 1941, these aircraft reconnoitred the sites for the planned amphibious landings in Malaya. Then, as fighting was about to start, small detachments of the 50th, 51st and 81st Dokuritsu Dai Shijugo Chutais were assigned to the 3rd Hikoshidan (air division) for operations against Commonwealth forces in Malaya, while detachments of the 8th Sentai (regiment) and 76th Dokoritsu Dai Shijugo Chutai went to the 5th Hikoshidan for operations against the Philippines. Other Ki-46-II companies provided support for operations in China as new units were being formed in Japan.

Beginning in December 1941, Japanese forces rapidly swept through Malaya, the Philippines and the Dutch East Indies, and, moving forward, their Ki-46s soon appeared over a far-flung area. In particular, operating from Timor, they flew regular missions over northern Australia and, from bases in Burma and the Andaman Islands, reconnoitred portions of India. 'Dinah' crews, faced with

A design that never quite lived up to expectations, the Ki-46-III Kai did not lack firepower, with 200 rounds per nose-mounted cannon and eight 25-round magazines for the oblique cannon, but an unexceptional climb rate and degree of agility worked against the type in the high-altitude interceptor role.

nothing better than Hawker Hurricanes and Curtiss P-40Es, had little to fear at that time, and provided the Japanese high command with much valuable photographic coverage of Allied installations. As long as Allied radar coverage in the theatre remained spotty, even the appearance of newer fighters, such as the Supermarine Spitfire and Lockheed P-38F, could not markedly change this situation.

Increased capability

Nevertheless, anticipating stiffer opposition, in May 1942 the Koku Hombu had instructed Mitsubishi to initiate the design of an improved Ki-46 version. Characterised externally by a redesigned forward fuselage to provide a new canopy over the pilot's seat without the step between the nose and the top of the fuselage, the first of two Ki-46-III prototypes flew in December 1942. Powered by two Ha-112-II engines rated at 932.1 kW (1,250 hp) at 5800 m (19,029 ft), the Ki-46-III reached a top speed of 630 km/h (391 mph) at that altitude. Placed in production alongside the Ki-46-II (slow deliveries of Ha-112-II engines prevented a full switch to the newer version), the Ki-46-III extended the type's immunity to interception. However, with increased availability of radar and better fighters, by the end of 1943 the Allies began to achieve greater success against the 'Dinah'. Unfortunately for its Japanese crews, a more advanced version (the Ki-46-IV with turbocharged engines, which had first flown in February 1944) was not placed in production as by then priority was being given by the Japanese to the production of fighters urgently required for the defence of the homeland. Losses increased markedly, but the Ki-46-IIIs, and even the obsolescent Ki-46-IIs, remained active throughout the Philippines campaign in 1944-45 and went on to keep a tab on Boeing B-29 bases in the Marianas until the end of the war.

When Japan was forced on the defensive, the Imperial staff realised the urgency of fielding heavily-armed interceptors to defend the home islands against Allied bombers. Accordingly, as the Ki-46-III was 83 km/h (52 mph) faster than the then-standard twin-engined fighter of the Imperial Japanese Army, the Kawasaki Ki-45 Kai-Ko, the Rikugun Kokugijutsu Kenkyujo (Army Aerotechnical Research Institute) was given the task of developing a stopgap high-altitude interceptor fighter using the airframe of the fast reconnaissance aircraft. Design work on this version began in June 1943, modifications entailing the removal of the photographic equipment and the installation of two forward-firing 20-mm cannon in the nose and one 37-mm cannon in the centre fuselage firing upward and forward. Modified on an assembly line at the Tachikawa Dai-Ichi Rikugun Kenkyujo (First Army Air Arsenal at Tachikawa), the interceptor version received the Kitai designation Ki-46-III Kai and the service designation Army Type 100 Air Defence Fighter. This version entered service in October 1944 and subsequently served with the 28th and 106th Sentais, the 16th Dokuritsu Hikotai (independent wing), and the 4th, 16th, 81st, 82nd and 83rd Dokuritsu Dai Shijugo Chutais. Against B-29 daylight raids the Ki-46-III Kai proved disappointing, as its climb rate was insufficient for an interceptor, and as it was an easy prey for the Superfortress gunners because of its lack of armour and self-sealing tanks. Moreover, not being fitted with AI-radar, the type lost even its limited usefulness when the B-29s began operating at night.

Ultimate value

Also dictated by the changing military situation, the Ki-46-III Otsu, Ki-46-III Hei and Ki-46-IV Otsu were proposed ground-attack versions using modified Ki-46-III and Ki-46-IV airframes. However, the lack of crew and fuel tank protection ill-suited the Ki-46-III Otsu to this type of operations and only a few were obtained late in the war. Conversely, the earlier modification of Ki-46-II airframes into three-seat Ki-46-II Kai trainers had proved more successful, and a few of these aircraft served alongside standard Ki-46-Is and Ki-46-IIs at the Shimoshizu Rikugun Hikogakuko.

If, in its fighter and ground-attack versions, the Ki-46 failed to meet expectations, the Imperial Japanese Army had good reason to be pleased with the performance of the reconnaissance models. That this was the case is evidenced by the fact that no serious efforts were made to place in production either of the Ki-46's intended successors, the Tachikawa Ki-70 and the Mitsubishi Ki-95. As for the Allies, the high opinion in which they held 'Dinah' was confirmed by the thorough evaluation given to captured aircraft, with pilots from the Air Technical Intelligence Unit commenting favourably on its performance and handling characteristics. Most certainly, these are tributes to Major Fujita's foresight in demanding, back in 1937, that the aircraft be capable of exceeding by 25 per cent the speed then achieved by the fastest Japanese aircraft. Production amounted to 1,742 aircraft, all built at Nagoya by Mitsubishi.

Mitsubishi Ki-46 Hei cutaway drawing key

1 Starboard navigation light
2 Starboard wingtip
3 Wing front spar
4 Main spar
5 Auxiliary rear spar
6 Starboard aileron
7 Aileron hinges
8 Aileron actuating hinge fairing
9 Aileron fixed tab
10 Access plates
11 Control rods
12 Leading-edge fuel tank
13 Filler/access points
14 Rib station
15 Centre spar
16 Centre fuel tank
17 Aft fuel tank
18 Flap profile
19 Starboard flap outer section
20 Starboard nacelle aft fairing
21 Wing inner aft fuel tank
22 Wing inner centre fuel tank
23 Nacelle panels
24 Access
25 Engine bearer ring support
26 Cooling gills
27 Exhaust slots
28 Cowling inner ring
29 Intake trunking
30 Intake slot
31 Spinner
32 Three-blade propeller
33 Starter dog
34 Propeller hub
35 Reduction gear housing
36 Cowling nose ring
37 Mitsubishi Ha-112 Otsu radial engine
38 Exhaust manifold
39 Unstepped nose glazing
40 Inner coaming
41 Fixed frame
42 Nose panels
43 Nose landing lamp
44 Starboard mainwheel
45 Nose access/(optional) camera hatch
46 Nose (optional) fuel tank
47 Fuselage forward frame
48 Rudder pedal assembly
49 Control column
50 Throttle quadrant
51 Seat adjustment lever
52 Control horn
53 Compass housing
54 Starboard electrics panel
55 Canopy sliding section
56 Pilot's headrest
57 Pilot's 13-mm back armour
58 Pilot's seat and harness
59 Oxygen hose
60 Seat support frame
61 Control rod linkage
62 Wing root fillet
63 Wing front spar/fuselage frame
64 Main spar centre-section carry-through
65 Wing control surface actuating rods
66 Canopy track
67 Canopy fixed aft glazing
68 Armoured headrest support
69 Aerial mast
70 Dorsal decking
71 Fuselage main (contoured cut-out) fuel tank
72 Spring-loaded hand/entry grips
73 Cockpit former longeron
74 Fuel feed lines
75 Centre-section camera mounting rings
76 Ventral sliding hatch
77 Hatch actuating lever
78 Ventral glazing
79 Centre-section compartment
80 Centre-section camera stowage
81 Support frame
82 Fuselage structure
83 Dorsal identification light
84 Aerial
85 Aerial lead-in
86 Radio installation
87 Anti-vibration mountings
88 Centre-section side window
89 Main reconnaissance camera installation
90 Aft cockpit
91 Fixed glazing
92 Canopy sliding section
93 Canopy frames
94 Aft bulkhead
95 Canopy track
96 Dorsal gun stowage trough (deleted)
97 Canopy end glazing
98 Fuselage panelling
99 Fuselage structure
100 Fuselage frames
101 Tail surface control lines
102 Lifting tube
103 Tailfin root fairing
104 Starboard tailplane
105 Elevator balance

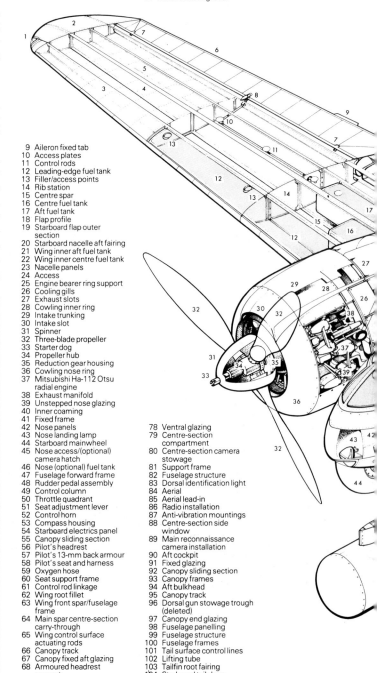

Mitsubishi Ki-46 variants

Ki-46: prototypes of a two-seat reconnaissance aircraft powered by two Mitsubishi Ha-26-Ko 14-cylinder radial engines, rated at 581.6 kW (680 hp) for take-off and 671.1 kW (900 hp) at 3600 m (11,811 ft), and driving three-bladed constant-speed propellers
Ki-46-I: pre-series aircraft produced as the **Army Type 100 Command Reconnaissance Aircraft Model 1**; with the exception of minor equipment changes these aircraft were essentially identical to the prototypes; a single rear-firing 7.7-mm (0.303-in) Type 89 machine-gun on a trainable mount was manned by the radio operator; Ki-46 and Ki-46-I production was 34 aircraft
Ki-46-II: main production version, the **Army Type 100 Command Reconnaissance Aircraft Model 2** differed from the Model 1 in being powered by more powerful engines and in having its fuel capacity increased from 1490 to 1675 litres (328 to 365 Imp gal) by adding tanks in the wing leading edges; the engines were Mitsubishi Ha-102s rated at 805.4 kW (1,080 hp) for take-off and 786.7 kW (1,055 hp) at 2800 m (9,186 ft); improvements progressively introduced during the course of production included a switch from 87-octane to 92-octane fuel and strengthening of the main landing gear; production was 1,093 aircraft
Ki-46-II Kai: Kitai designation given to a small number of Ki-46-IIs which were modified to serve in the conversion training role; the main fuel tank between the pilot and radio operator was reduced in size and capacity to provide space for a raised cockpit and stepped windscreen for the instructor; designated **Army Type 100 Operations Trainer**
Ki-46-III: following the testing of two prototypes, this improved version was placed in production as the **Army Type 100 Command Reconnaissance Aircraft Model 3**; it was powered by two Mitsubishi Ha-112-II direct fuel-injection radial engines

rated at 1118.6 kW (1,500 hp) for take-off and 932.1 kW (1,250 hp) at 5800 m (19,029 ft); major modifications incorporated in this model included a redesigned windscreen with unbroken curve, an internal fuel capacity increased to 1895 litres (417 Imp gal), provision for a 460-litre (101.2-Imp gal) ventral drop tank, and deletion of the rear-firing trainable gun; late-production aircraft also featured individual exhaust stacks; 609 production aircraft were built
Ki-46-III Kai: fighter conversion of the Ki-46-III with two forward-firing 20-mm Ho-5 cannon in the nose and one obliquely-mounted forward-firing 37-mm Ho-203 cannon above the reduced capacity centre fuselage fuel tank; this modification was developed by the Rikugun Kokugijutsu Kenkyujo, with production modification as the **Army Type 100 Air Defence Fighter** was entrusted to the Tachikawa Dai-Ichi Rikugun Kokusho
Ki-46-III Otsu and Hei: conversion of Ki-46-III airframes to obtain ground-attack aircraft needed for use in the anti-invasion role; two forward-firing 20-mm Ho-5 cannon in the nose, with the Hei version being further modified to carry bombs externally; only a few Ki-46-III Otsu were obtained and designated **Army Type 100 Ground Attack Aircraft**; the Ki-46-III Hei remained on the drawing board
Ki-46-IV: final development of the reconnaissance model powered by turbocharged Mitsubishi Ha-112 Otsu-Ru engines maintaining their military rating of 932.1 kW (1,250 hp) up to 8200 m (26,903 ft); four prototypes were tested but production of the Ki-46-IV as the **Army Type 100 Command Reconnaissance Aircraft Model 4** was not implemented; likewise, proposed interceptor and ground-attack versions, with armament patterned after that of the Ki-46-III Kai and Ki-46-III Hei respectively, were not realised

The beautifully streamlined and extended forward canopy was the most noticeable feature of of the Ki-46-III, a version with improved performance and an endurance of six hours through increased fuel capacity. Production was at Nagoya and Toyama, this example displaying the individual exhaust stacks fitted to augment thrust.

106 Starboard elevator
107 Elevator hinge
108 Tailfin leading-edge
109 Tailfin forward spar
110 Tailfin structure
111 Aerial attachment
112 Rudder balance
113 Rudder upper hinge
114 Rudder frame
115 Rudder trim tab
116 Rudder actuating hinge
117 Rudder tab hinge fairing
118 Rudder post
119 Rudder contoured lower section
120 Tail navigation light
121 Elevator trim tab
122 Tab actuating hinge
123 Elevator frame
124 Elevator hinge
125 Elevator balance
126 Tailplane structure
127 Tailplane front spar
128 Control cables
129 Ribs
130 Tailplane tailfin front spar/ fuselage integral member

131 Tailwheel retraction guide track
132 Shock absorber strut
133 Tailwheel retraction strut
134 Support frame
135 Retractable tailwheel
136 Tailwheel doors
137 Fuselage ventral panelling
138 Lower longeron
139 First-aid/access
140 Inspection/access panel
141 Fuselage skinning
142 Retractable crew entry step
143 Wing root fillet
144 Port flap inner structure
145 Port nacelle aft fairing
146 Port flap outer section
147 Flap profile
148 Aileron hinges
149 Aileron fixed tab
150 Port aileron frame

151 Aileron actuating hinge fairing
152 Port wingtip structure
153 Port navigation light
154 Front spar
155 Pitot tube
156 Wing ribs
157 Wing structure
158 Access panels
159 Wing main spar
160 Leading-edge fuel tank
161 Filler/access
162 Centre fuel tank
163 Aft fuel tank
164 Nacelle formers

165 Bulkhead frame
166 Engine bearer ring support attachment
167 Port nacelle oil tank
168 Exhaust slots
169 Wing inner centre fuel tank
170 Wing inner aft fuel tank
171 Wing main spar attachment

172 Wing front spar attachment
173 Leading-edge ribs
174 Cowling frame
175 Cowling inner frame
176 Engine bearer ring
177 Undercarriage retraction strut
178 Cooling gills
179 Mainwheel leg pivot
180 Engine bearer ring lower support strut
181 Exhaust
182 Mainwheel door
183 Mainwheel leg

184 Port mainwheel
185 Axle
186 Brake line
187 Torque links
188 Shock strut
189 Lower intake
190 Engine cowling nose ring
191 Inner ring
192 Gear housing
193 Three-blade Sumitomo propeller
194 Spinner
195 Starter dog
196 Propeller hub
197 Intake trunking
198 Intake slot
199 Ventral (centre-line) tank pylon
200 Auxiliary ventral fuel tank (101 Imp gal/460 litre capacity)

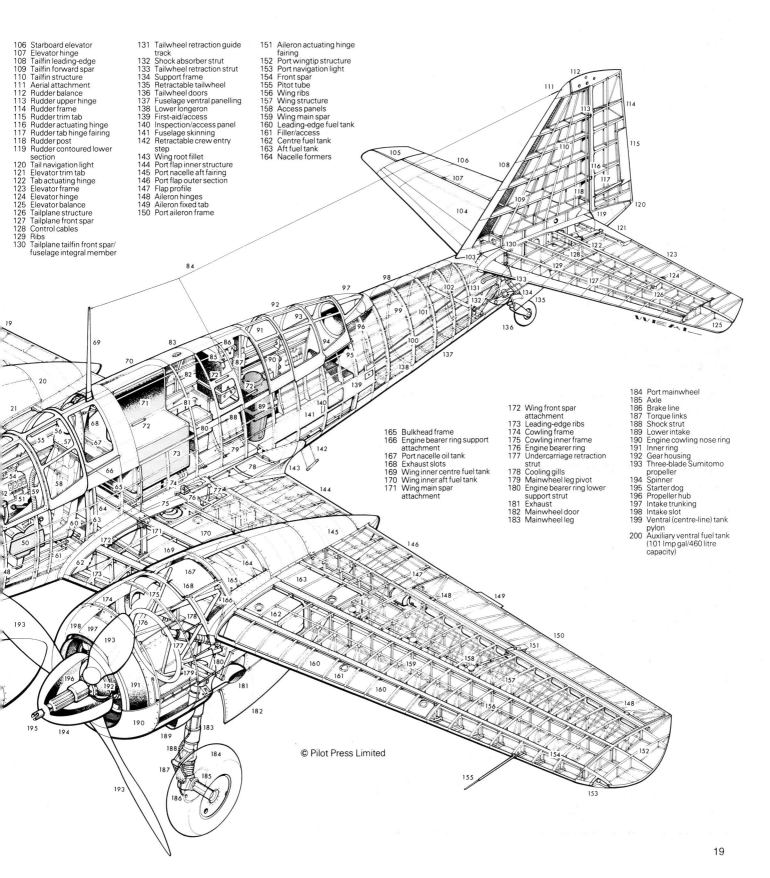

© Pilot Press Limited

19

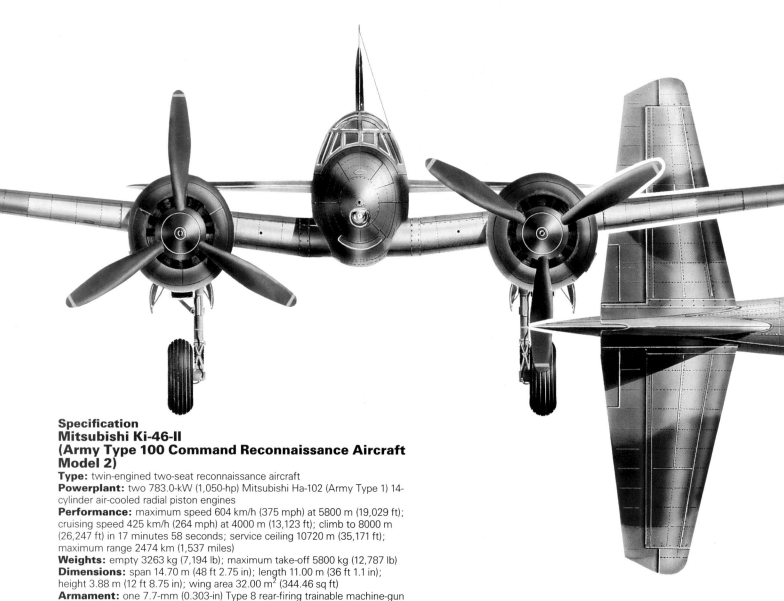

Specification
Mitsubishi Ki-46-II
(Army Type 100 Command Reconnaissance Aircraft Model 2)

Type: twin-engined two-seat reconnaissance aircraft
Powerplant: two 783.0-kW (1,050-hp) Mitsubishi Ha-102 (Army Type 1) 14-cylinder air-cooled radial piston engines
Performance: maximum speed 604 km/h (375 mph) at 5800 m (19,029 ft); cruising speed 425 km/h (264 mph) at 4000 m (13,123 ft); climb to 8000 m (26,247 ft) in 17 minutes 58 seconds; service ceiling 10720 m (35,171 ft); maximum range 2474 km (1,537 miles)
Weights: empty 3263 kg (7,194 lb); maximum take-off 5800 kg (12,787 lb)
Dimensions: span 14.70 m (48 ft 2.75 in); length 11.00 m (36 ft 1.1 in); height 3.88 m (12 ft 8.75 in); wing area 32.00 m² (344.46 sq ft)
Armament: one 7.7-mm (0.303-in) Type 8 rear-firing trainable machine-gun

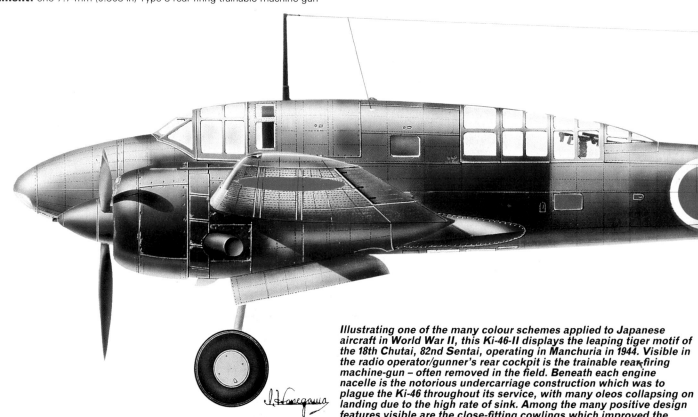

Illustrating one of the many colour schemes applied to Japanese aircraft in World War II, this Ki-46-II displays the leaping tiger motif of the 18th Chutai, 82nd Sentai, operating in Manchuria in 1944. Visible in the radio operator/gunner's rear cockpit is the trainable rear-firing machine-gun – often removed in the field. Beneath each engine nacelle is the notorious undercarriage construction which was to plague the Ki-46 throughout its service, with many oleos collapsing on landing due to the high rate of sink. Among the many positive design features visible are the close-fitting cowlings which improved the pilot's sideways vision, and the thin wing section – a major factor in the type's excellent overall performance.

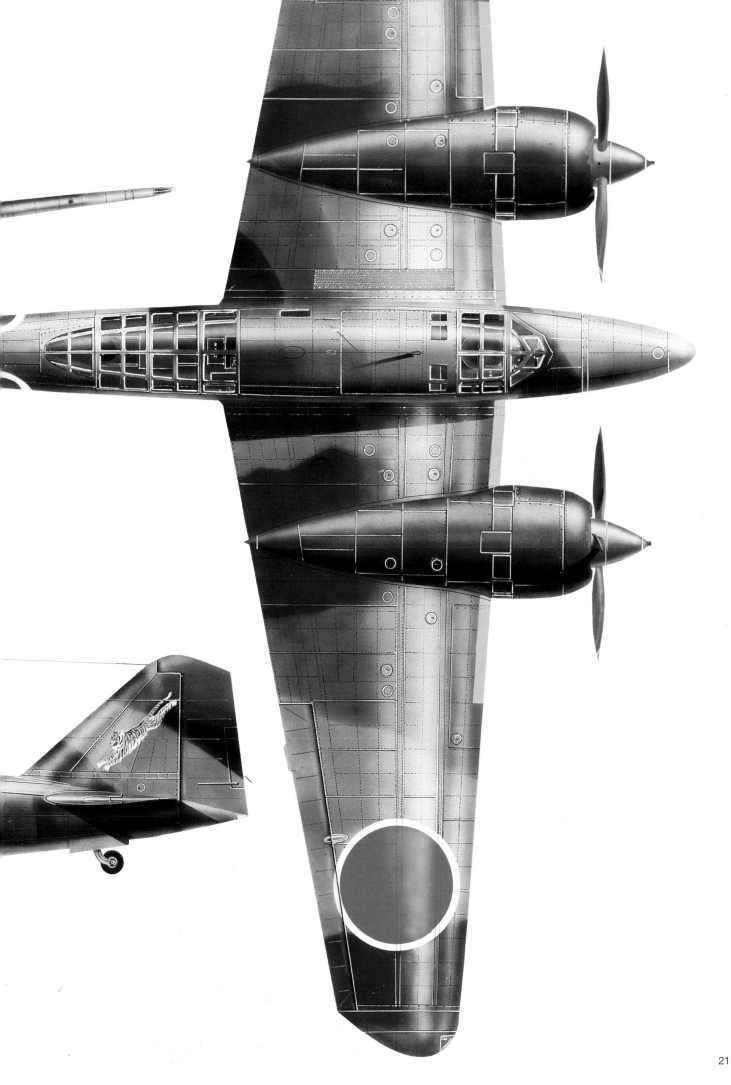

P-47 Thunderbolt:
Fighter-Bomber Supreme

Built in larger numbers than any other US fighter in history, the P-47 Thunderbolt was at first thought to be clumsy and overlarge. Later the 'Jug' did as much to win World War II as any other Allied aircraft, proving ideal for the ground-attack role and more than adequate in air combat.

Built in larger numbers than any other fighter in American history, the mighty P-47 – popularly called the Jug, short for Juggernaut – was the exact opposite of the Russian philosophy of making fighters small and agile. Today even the smallest fighters make the P-47 look like a midget, but in World War II it was a monster. RAF pilots said the driver of a P-47 could escape enemy fire by running about in the cockpit, and the shock its laden weight of 6124 kg (13,500 lb) provoked would have been turned to amazement had people then (1942) known that by 1945 later versions would turn

Five of the first P-47s to be delivered to a fighting unit. The unit, of course, was the 56th Fighter Group; the aircraft in the background were with the 61st FS, led by the Group CO. Still equipped with early P-47Bs, this group (under the famed Colonel Hubert Zemke) arrived in England at the end of 1942 to prove the P-47 in combat.

the scales at 9390 kg (20,700 lb) – considerably heavier than a loaded Dornier Do 17 bomber! One can argue indefinitely about small and large fighters, but the 'T-bolt' was to prove itself one of the most useful Allied aircraft, in all theatres.

Certainly the question of small or large fighters was far from resolved in the US Army Air Corps in 1940. One of its chief fighter builders, Republic Aviation Corporation (successor to Seversky Aircraft) had a heritage of rotund radial-engined fighters with elliptical wings and tails, and was in production with the P-35 and about to produce the P-43 Lancer with inward-retracting landing gear and a turbocharged Twin Wasp engine. For the future there were various AP-4 projects with the 1044-kW (1,400-hp) R-2180 or the massive new 1380-kW (1,850-hp) R-2800 Double Wasp, as well as the lightweight AP-10 with liquid-cooled Allison engine and two 12.7-mm

(0.5-in) machine-guns. Combat reports from Europe suggested none would make the grade, and on 12 June 1940 chief engineer Alex Kartveli submitted a dramatically more formidable machine which technically was probably the most advanced then in existence. It was quickly accepted by the worried Army Air Corps and allotted the designation XP-47B, the original XP-47 and XP-47A having been versions of the totally different AP-10.

Big-engined inspiration

The new fighter was an exceptionally severe challenge. For a start, the engine installation was so complex Kartveli designed this first, and then schemed the rest around it! The chosen engine, the big 18-cylinder R-2800, was supplied by a turbocharger which, for various aerodynamic and efficiency reasons, was mounted under the rear fuselage instead of close to the engine. The multiple exhausts were grouped into two monster pipes, which at their upstream ends glowed red-hot at full power and which led back beneath the wing to the turbocharger itself. Here a variable valve system called a waste gate either expelled the hot gas to the atmosphere or, as altitude was increased, diverted it to drive the turbine. The latter spun a centrifugal compressor at some 60,000 rpm to feed high-pressure air to the engine via even larger ducts which incorporated intercoolers to increase the density of the air, and thus give further-enhanced engine power. The mass of large pipes and ducts made the fuselage deep, and put the wing well above its bottom.

This was just what Kartveli did not want, because the great power of the engine needed an enormous propeller: even with the novel use of four blades in a constant-speed Curtiss electric propeller, the diameter had to be no less than 3.71 m (12 ft 2 in). To provide safe clearance between the tips and the ground on take-off, the landing gear had to be exceptionally long, especially because the wing was

not in the low position and had to have dihedral. Long landing gears are not only very heavy (if they are not to get a reputation for breaking) but also need long spaces in the wings when retracted. Again, this was just what Kartveli did not want, because he proposed to use the phenomenal armament of not two but eight of the big 12.7-mm (0.5-in) Browning guns, all in the wings outboard of the landing gear legs. It was a technical triumph to design main gears which on retraction shortened by 22.86 cm (9 in) to fit into normal-size bays in the wing between the spars. Immediately outboard of the landing gears were four guns in each wing, staggered so that the four bulky ammunition belts (each of at least 350 rounds) could lie in boxes side-by-side extending very nearly to the tip of the wing.

Distinct shape in the sky

The bluff nose cowl was not circular but extended below into a pear shape to accommodate the ducts for left and right oil coolers and for the bulky intercooler air which was then discharged through a large rectangular valve on each side of the rear fuselage. It was then necessary to find somewhere to put an exceptionally large fuel capacity, and main and auxiliary tanks for 776 and 379 litres (205 and 100 US gal), both of self-sealing construction, were installed above the wing between the supercharger air ducts and in the rear fuselage

Of 15,683 P-47s just two had liquid-cooled engines. Two P-47D-15-RAs were held back to serve as testbeds for the Chrysler XIV-2200-1, a remarkable 1865-kW (2,500-hp) unit comprising front and rear halves each made up of four inverted-vee twins (16 cylinders in all) with drive gears in the centre. Note the radiator/turbo duct.

First of the Thunderbolts, the XP-47B is seen here shortly after being rolled out on to the Farmingdale field late in April 1941. It had a canopy that hinged open sideways. After ground testing it was flown by Lowry L. Brabham on 6 May. Leaking gas from the exhaust ducts almost forced Brabham to bale out.

under the cockpit. The cockpit was extremely well equipped: it was packed with controls for systems and devices not then found in other fighters, such as electric fuel-contents transmitters, cabin air-conditioning, variable gun-bay heating and anti-icing by an Eclipse pump. There was a deep Vee windscreen, upward-hinged canopy and sharp upper line to the rear fuselage which caused all early P-47s later to be called 'razorbacks'.

Completely unpainted, the prototype XP-47B flew on 6 May 1941, exactly eight months after it was ordered. It was clearly a potential world-beater, but gave a lot of trouble. Handicapped by its sheer size and weight, it suffered problems with fabric-covered flight-control surfaces, canopies which jammed, and snags with the guns, fuel system and engine installation. Despite agonised misgivings, the US Army ordered 171 of the new fighters and soon followed with orders for 602 of an improved model, designated P-47C. The first production P-47B left the assembly line at Farmingdale, Long Island, in March 1942. This had a sliding canopy with jettison system, metal-skinned control surfaces (not yet standard), sloping radio mast mounted farther aft, blunt-nose ailerons, balance/trim rudder tab and production R-2800-21 engine. The first deliveries went to the 56th Fighter Group of what by this time was the US Army Air Force. After suffering severely from control problems, tyre bursts and other difficulties, the 56th FG went on to become the top-scoring fighter group in all US forces, with a final air-combat score of 674½. With the 78th FG, the 56th joined the 8th Air Force in England and flew its first escort mission on 13 April 1943. With 1155 litres (305 US gal), the big fighters could not accompany the bombers very far, and they found life tough in close combat with the smaller Messerschmitt Bf 109s and Focke-Wulf Fw 190s. The unmatched diving speed of the P-47 meant they could always break off, but that after all was not the basic objective, which was to shoot down the Luftwaffe.

Recognition problems

The last P-47B had a pressurised cockpit and was designated XP-47E. The 172nd was the first P-47C, with a fundamental problem of balance removed by mounting the engine nearly 0.305 m (1 ft) further forward and for the first time fitted with an attachment under the fuselage for a 227-kg (500-lb) bomb or a 757-litre (200-US gal) drop tank, a most important addition. Externally the most obvious change was the shorter vertical radio mast. Recognising the P-47 should have presented no problem, but in the European theatre standards of recognition were so poor that the first Thunderbolts (which were painted olive-drab overall) were given white bands across the tail surfaces, and a white nose, so they would not be shot down by mistake for the totally different Fw 190. (The equally different British Typhoon was likewise given distinctive markings very

Four more aircraft of the 56th FG pictured in the Connecticut/Long Island area in mid-1942 whilst in the painful process of ironing out the remaining 'bugs' in this potentially great fighter. This photograph emphasises the sharp dorsal spine which led to these early models of Thunderbolt becoming known as 'razorbacks'.

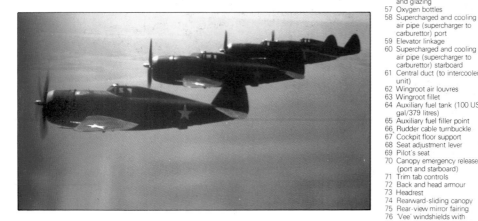

Republic P-47D-10 Thunderbolt cutaway drawing key

1 Rudder upper hinge
2 Aerial attachment
3 Fin flanged ribs
4 Rudder post/fin aft spar
5 Fin front spar
6 Rudder trim tab worm and screw actuating mechanism (chain driven)
7 Rudder centre hinge
8 Rudder trim tab
9 Rudder structure
10 Tail navigation light
11 Elevator fixed tab
12 Elevator trim tab
13 Starboard elevator structure
14 Elevator outboard hinge
15 Elevator torque tube
16 Elevator trim tab worm and screw actuating mechanism
17 Chain drive
18 Starboard tailplane
19 Tail jacking point
20 Rudder control cables
21 Elevator control rod and linkage
22 Fin spar/fuselage attachment points
23 Port elevator
24 Aerial
25 Port tailplane structure (two spars and flanged ribs)
26 Tailwheel retraction worm gear
27 Tailwheel anti-shimmy damper
28 Tailwheel oleo
29 Tailwheel doors
30 Retractable and steerable tailwheel
31 Tailwheel fork
32 Tailwheel mount and pivot
33 Rudder cables
34 Rudder and elevator trim control cables
35 Lifting tube
36 Elevator rod linkage
37 Semi-monocoque all-metal fuselage construction
38 Fuselage dorsal 'razorback' profile

39 Aerial lead-in
40 Fuselage stringers
41 Supercharger air filter
42 Supercharger
43 Turbine casing
44 Turbosupercharger compartment air vent
45 Turbosupercharger exhaust hood fairing (stainless steel)
46 Outlet louvres
47 Intercooler exhaust doors (port and starboard)
48 Exhaust pipes
49 Cooling air ducts
50 Intercooler unit (cooling and supercharged air)
51 Radio transmitter and receiver packs (Detrola)
52 Canopy track
53 Elevator rod linkage
54 Aerial mast
55 Formation light
56 Rearward-vision frame cut-out and glazing
57 Oxygen bottles
58 Supercharged and cooling air pipe (supercharger to carburettor) port
59 Elevator linkage
60 Supercharged and cooling air pipe (supercharger to carburettor) starboard
61 Central duct (to intercooler unit)
62 Wingroot air louvres
63 Wingroot fillet
64 Auxiliary fuel tank (100 US gal/379 litres)
65 Auxiliary fuel filler point
66 Rudder cable turnbuckle
67 Cockpit floor support
68 Seat adjustment lever
69 Pilot's seat
70 Canopy emergency release (port and starboard)
71 Trim tab controls
72 Back and head armour
73 Headrest
74 Rearward-sliding canopy
75 Rear-view mirror fairing
76 'Vee' windshields with central pillar
77 Internal bulletproof glass screen

78 Gunsight
79 Engine control quadrant (cockpit port wall)
80 Control column
81 Rudder pedals
82 Oxygen regulator
83 Underfloor elevator control quadrant
84 Rudder cable linkage
85 Wing rear spar/fuselage attachment (tapered bolts/bushings)
86 Wing supporting lower bulkhead section
87 Main fuel tank (205 US gal/776 litres)
88 Fuselage forward structure
89 Stainless steel/Alclad firewall bulkhead
90 Cowl flap valve
91 Main fuel filler point
92 Anti-freeze fluid tank
93 Hydraulic reservoir
94 Aileron control rod
95 Aileron trim tab control cables
96 Aileron hinge access panels
97 Aileron and tab control linkage

98 Aileron trim tab (port wing only)
99 Frise-type aileron
100 Wing rear (No. 2) spar
101 Port navigation light
102 Pitot head
103 Wing front (No. 1) spar
104 Wing stressed skin
105 Four-gun ammunition troughs (individual bays)
106 Staggered gun barrels
107 Removable panel
108 Inter-spar gun bay access panel
109 Forward gunsight bead
110 Oil feed pipes
111 Oil tank (28.6 US gal/108 litres)
112 Hydraulic pressure line
113 Engine upper bearers
114 Engine control correlating cam
115 Eclipse pump (anti-icing)
116 Fuel level transmitter
117 Generator
118 Battery junction box
119 Storage battery
120 Exhaust collector ring
121 Cowl flap actuating cylinder
122 Exhaust outlets to collector ring
123 Cowl flaps
124 Supercharged and cooling air ducts to carburettor (port and starboard)
125 Exhaust upper outlets
126 Cowling frame
127 Pratt & Whitney R-2800-59 18-cylinder twin-row engine
128 Cowling nose panel
129 Magnetos
130 Propeller governor
131 Propeller hub
132 Reduction gear casing
133 Spinner
134 Propeller cuffs
135 Four-blade Curtiss constant-speed electric propeller
136 Oil cooler intakes (port and starboard)

137 Supercharger intercooler (central) air intake
138 Ducting
139 Oil cooler feed pipes
140 Starboard oil cooler
141 Engine lower bearers
142 Oil cooler exhaust variable shutter
143 Fixed deflector
144 Excess exhaust gas vent
145 Belly stores/weapons shackles
146 Metal auxiliary drop tank (75 US gal/284 litres)
147 Inboard mainwheel well door
148 Mainwheel well door actuating cylinder
149 Camera gun port
150 Cabin air-conditioning intake (starboard wing only)
151 Wingroot fairing
152 Wing front spar/fuselage attachment (tapered bolts/bushings)
153 Wing inboard rib mainwheel well recess
154 Wing front (No. 1) spar
155 Undercarriage pivot point
156 Hydraulic retraction cylinder
157 Auxiliary (undercarriage mounting) wing spar
158 Gun bay warm air flexible duct
159 Wing rear (No. 2) spar
160 Landing flap inboard hinge
161 Auxiliary (No. 3) wing spar inboard section (flap mounting)

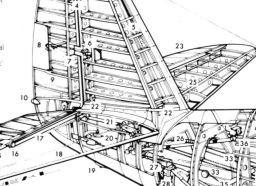

PILOT PRESS
COPYRIGHT
DRAWING

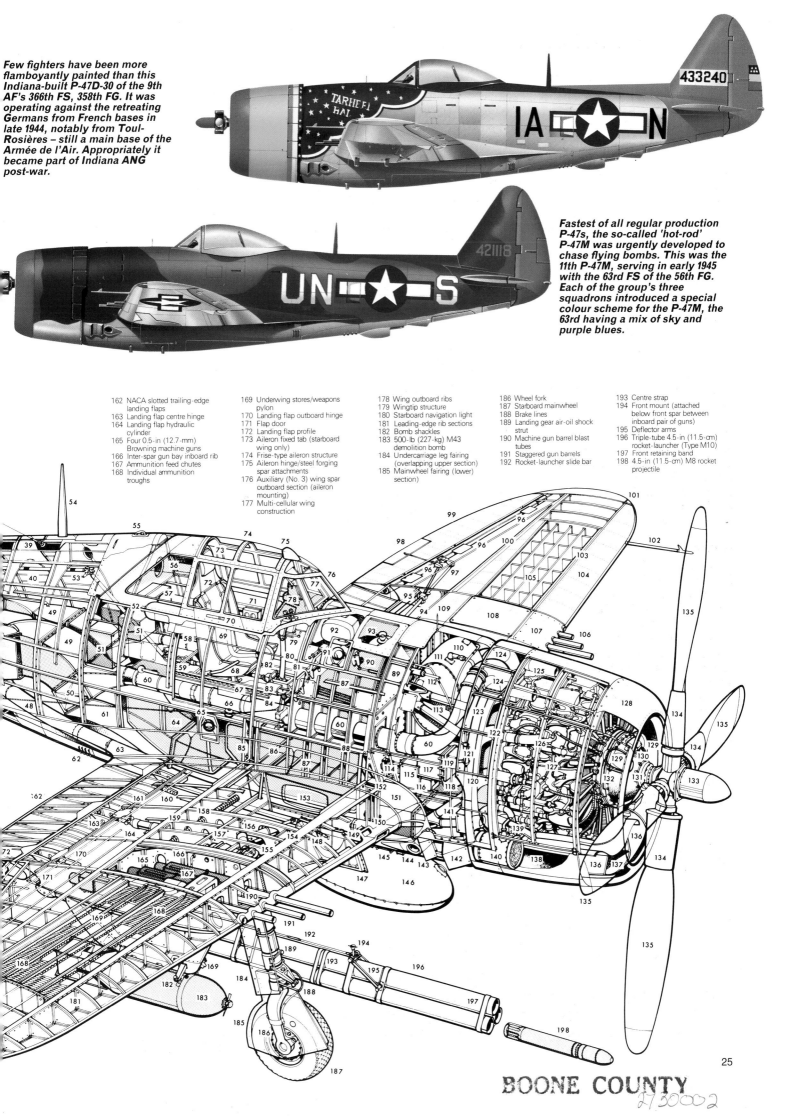

Few fighters have been more flamboyantly painted than this Indiana-built P-47D-30 of the 9th AF's 366th FS, 358th FG. It was operating against the retreating Germans from French bases in late 1944, notably from Toul-Rosières – still a main base of the Armée de l'Air. Appropriately it became part of Indiana ANG post-war.

Fastest of all regular production P-47s, the so-called 'hot-rod' P-47M was urgently developed to chase flying bombs. This was the 11th P-47M, serving in early 1945 with the 63rd FS of the 56th FG. Each of the group's three squadrons introduced a special colour scheme for the P-47M, the 63rd having a mix of sky and purple blues.

162 NACA slotted trailing-edge landing flaps
163 Landing flap centre hinge
164 Landing flap hydraulic cylinder
165 Four 0.5-in (12.7-mm) Browning machine guns
166 Inter-spar gun bay inboard rib
167 Ammunition feed chutes
168 Individual ammunition troughs

169 Underwing stores/weapons pylon
170 Landing flap outboard hinge
171 Flap door
172 Landing flap profile
173 Aileron fixed tab (starboard wing only)
174 Frise-type aileron structure
175 Aileron hinge/steel forging spar attachments
176 Auxiliary (No. 3) wing spar outboard section (aileron mounting)
177 Multi-cellular wing construction

178 Wing outboard ribs
179 Wingtip structure
180 Starboard navigation light
181 Leading-edge rib sections
182 Bomb shackles
183 500-lb (227-kg) M43 demolition bomb
184 Undercarriage leg fairing (overlapping upper section)
185 Mainwheel fairing (lower section)

186 Wheel fork
187 Starboard mainwheel
188 Brake lines
189 Landing gear air-oil shock strut
190 Machine gun barrel blast tubes
191 Staggered gun barrels
192 Rocket-launcher slide bar

193 Centre strap
194 Front mount (attached below front spar between inboard pair of guns)
195 Deflector arms
196 Triple-tube 4.5-in (11.5-cm) rocket-launcher (Type M10)
197 Front retaining band
198 4.5-in (11.5-cm) M8 rocket projectile

BOONE COUNTY

25

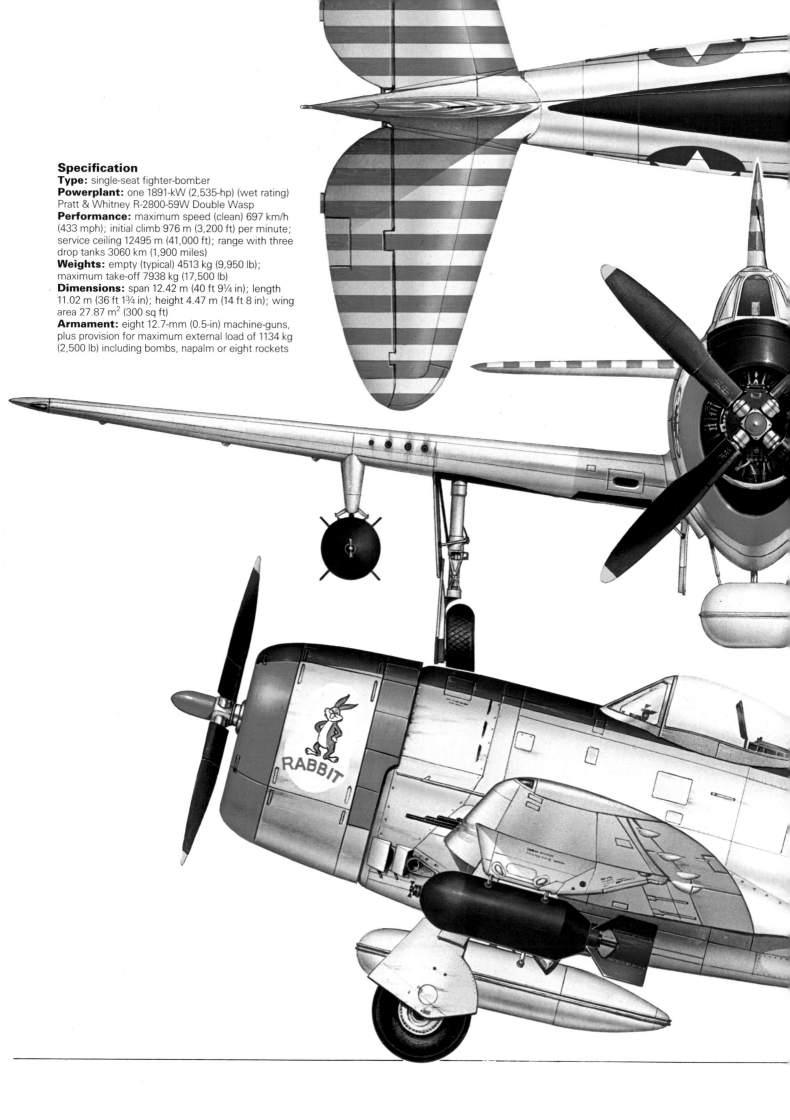

Specification
Type: single-seat fighter-bomber
Powerplant: one 1891-kW (2,535-hp) (wet rating)
Pratt & Whitney R-2800-59W Double Wasp
Performance: maximum speed (clean) 697 km/h
(433 mph); initial climb 976 m (3,200 ft) per minute;
service ceiling 12495 m (41,000 ft); range with three
drop tanks 3060 km (1,900 miles)
Weights: empty (typical) 4513 kg (9,950 lb);
maximum take-off 7938 kg (17,500 lb)
Dimensions: span 12.42 m (40 ft 9¼ in); length
11.02 m (36 ft 1¾ in); height 4.47 m (14 ft 8 in); wing
area 27.87 m² (300 sq ft)
Armament: eight 12.7-mm (0.5-in) machine-guns,
plus provision for maximum external load of 1134 kg
(2,500 lb) including bombs, napalm or eight rockets

RABBIT

Fighter-bomber par excellence, the P-47D is seen here with bombs of the 454-kg (1,000-lb) size hung under the wing pylons and one of the nine types of drop tank and napalm carried on the centreline. This particular aircraft, a P-47D-25-RE, served with the 527th Fighter Squadron of the 86th Fighter Group. This was one of the leading fighter groups in the Mediterranean theatre; it fought its way from North Africa through Sicily into Italy, and equipped with P-47Ds in 1944. It then operated intensively not only in ground attack on Kesselring's retreating forces in Italy but also over the Balkans and on long-range escort duties of B-24s (occasionally other bombers) as far as Berlin. The principal home base for 'Rabbit' was Pisa. Note that the stripes of the 86th FG have obliterated the USAAF tail number.

P-47 Thunderbolt: Fighter-Bomber Supreme

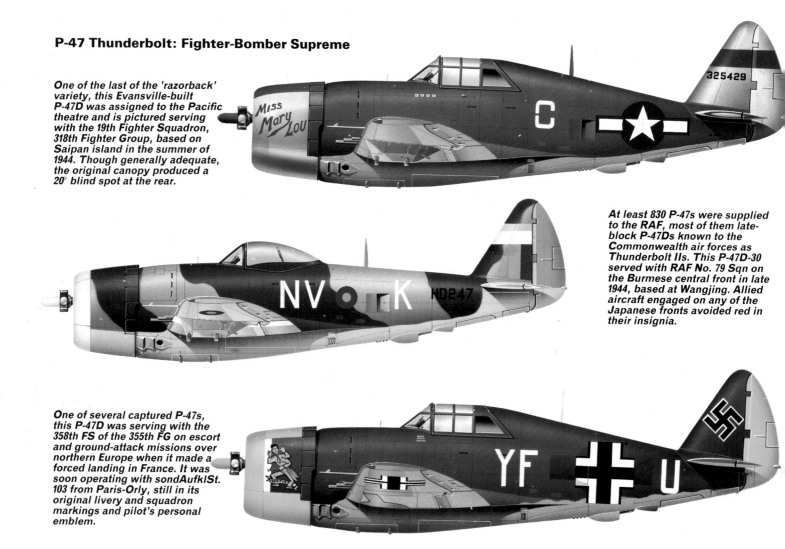

One of the last of the 'razorback' variety, this Evansville-built P-47D was assigned to the Pacific theatre and is pictured serving with the 19th Fighter Squadron, 318th Fighter Group, based on Saipan island in the summer of 1944. Though generally adequate, the original canopy produced a 20° blind spot at the rear.

At least 830 P-47s were supplied to the RAF, most of them late-block P-47Ds known to the Commonwealth air forces as Thunderbolt IIs. This P-47D-30 served with RAF No. 79 Sqn on the Burmese central front in late 1944, based at Wangjing. Allied aircraft engaged on any of the Japanese fronts avoided red in their insignia.

One of several captured P-47s, this P-47D was serving with the 358th FS of the 355th FG on escort and ground-attack missions over northern Europe when it made a forced landing in France. It was soon operating with sondAufklSt. 103 from Paris-Orly, still in its original livery and squadron markings and pilot's personal emblem.

like the 'invasion stripes' painted on all Allied machines a year later.) By mid-1943, when the first of the P-47D models reached front-line units, everyone had come to respect the P-47's great strength, which often enabled it to limp home with severe damage and to effect a self-destructive belly landing without injury to the pilot.

Most prolific version

Though the first order for the P-47D was placed on 13 October 1941, before the United States entered the war, it was mid-1943 before the flood of production had much effect. Eventually no fewer than 12,602 of this version were built, far more than of any other US fighter, and including output from a new factory at Evansville, Indiana. A further 354 identical machines were made by Curtiss-Wright as the P-47G. Basically the P-47D grouped a whole package of improvements, such as a refined engine with water injection for emergency combat boost, a better turbocharger installation, improved pilot armour, and multi-ply tyres (also retrofitted to earlier

P-47s) which did not burst even on rough strips when the aircraft was carrying bombs and tanks. The ability to carry both loads together came with the P-47D-20 (and counterparts at the Evansville plant), which introduced a 'universal' wing having pylons for 454-kg (1,000-lb) bombs on each side or a 568-litre (150-US gal) tank, as well as the load on the centreline. With three tanks the P-47 could escort bombers deep into Germany, going all the way on most missions; on the return journey it became common practice to use unexpended ammunition shooting up targets of opportunity on the ground, and the P-47D became the chief ground-attack aircraft of the Allied air forces in Europe in the final year of war, as well as serving in large numbers in the Pacific and with the RAF (825, mainly in Burma), Soviet Union, Brazil and Mexico (and many other air forces post-war).

In July 1943 one aircraft was given a cut-down rear fuselage and the clear-view bubble canopy from a Typhoon. This XP-47K was so popular the new hood was immediately introduced to production, starting with the P-47D-25-RE and Evansville's P-47D-26-RA. Previously Farmingdale had delivered 3,962 P-47Ds and the Indiana plant 1,461; from the Dash-25 onwards the two factories produced 2,547 and 4,632. By this time the aircraft were being delivered unpainted, which slightly enhanced performance. Despite the great increase in weight (to some 7938 kg/17,500 lb), the boosted engine improved performance, which gained a further fillip (such as 122 m/400 ft per minute extra climb) as a result of the fitting of a broad paddle-blade propeller especially useful at high altitude. The lower rear fuselage caused slight loss in directional stability and from the D-27-RE batch the fin area was increased by a shallow dorsal

Last of the Thunderbolts, the P-47N was the largest and heaviest, with a new long-span wing with tankage tailored to the vast Pacific theatre. The prototype N was 42-27387, originally built as a D. These two are N-5-REs from the middle of the 1,667 built at Farmingdale. The dorsal fin was larger than that on the late P-47D.

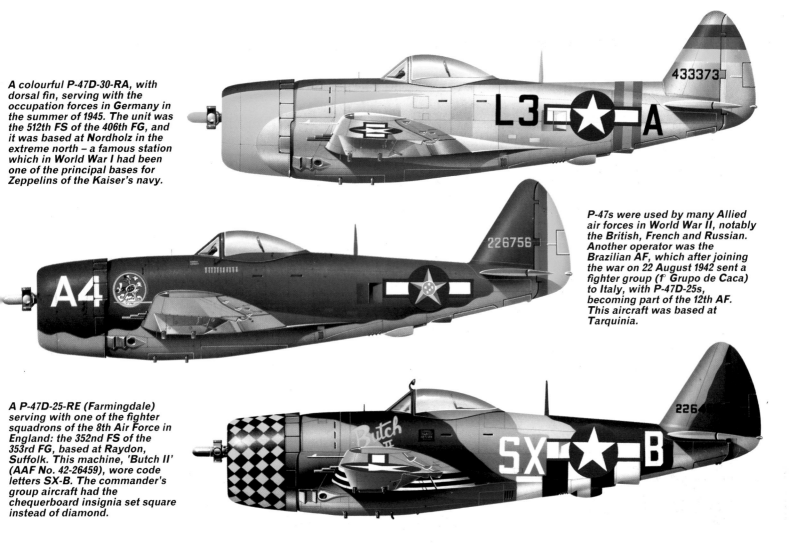

A colourful P-47D-30-RA, with dorsal fin, serving with the occupation forces in Germany in the summer of 1945. The unit was the 512th FS of the 406th FG, and it was based at Nordholz in the extreme north – a famous station which in World War I had been one of the principal bases for Zeppelins of the Kaiser's navy.

P-47s were used by many Allied air forces in World War II, notably the British, French and Russian. Another operator was the Brazilian AF, which after joining the war on 22 August 1942 sent a fighter group (1º Grupo de Caça) to Italy, with P-47D-25s, becoming part of the 12th AF. This aircraft was based at Tarquinia.

A P-47D-25-RE (Farmingdale) serving with one of the fighter squadrons of the 8th Air Force in England: the 352nd FS of the 353rd FG, based at Raydon, Suffolk. This machine, 'Butch II' (AAF No. 42-26459), wore code letters SX-B. The commander's group aircraft had the chequerboard insignia set square instead of diamond.

spine stretching most of the way to the canopy. From the D-35-RA block each wing was given zero-length attachments for five 12.7-cm (5-in) rocket projectiles on each side.

The only other service variants were the 'hot-rod' P-47M and the very long-range P-47N. The P-47M was quickly produced in the summer of 1944 to counter the menace of the 'V-1' flying bomb, which ordinary P-47s were hard-pressed to catch, and the various German jet and rocket fighters. Basically a late-model P-47D, the P-47M had the extra-powerful R-2800-57(C) engine with uprated CH-5 turbocharger which had previously been fitted to the experimental XP-47J to make it the fastest piston-engined fighter of all at 811 km/h (504 mph). The only other significant change was the fitting of airbrakes to the wings to assist slowing down behind slower aircraft before opening fire.

Pacific fighter

The P-47N, however, was almost a new aircraft because it had a long-span wing of totally new design which not only was tailored to much increased gross weights but also for the first time contained fuel. A 352-litre (93-US gal) tank was fitted in each, so that with external tanks no less than 4792 litres (1,266 US gal) could be carried. This resulted in a really capable long-range fighter for the Pacific war, though the loaded weight of up to 9616 kg (21,200 lb) required a strengthened landing gear and fairly good long airstrip. Features of the production P-47N included the Dash-77 engine, enlarged ailerons and square-tipped wings for rapid roll, and zero-length rocket launchers. Farmingdale built 1,667, Evansville also managing to deliver the first 149 of an order for 5,934. Farmingdale completed the last of the P-47N series not to be cancelled in December 1945, bringing the grand total of all versions to 15,683.

In typical US style, plenty of information was published not only about the 'Jug' but also about its accomplishments. P-47s flew 546,000 combat sorties between March 1943 and VJ-Day in August

1945. They had an outstanding combat record of only 0.7 per cent losses per mission, with 4.6 enemy aircraft destroyed for each P-47 lost. They dropped 119750 tonnes (132,000 US tons) of bombs, many thousands of gallons of napalm and fired 132 million rounds of 'fifty calibre' and over 60,000 rockets. They burned 774129000 litres (204,504,000 US gal) of fuel in 1,934,000 operational flight hours. The claims for ground targets knocked out were astronomic, but even more important were the European (excluding Italian front) claim of 3,752 aircraft destroyed in air combat and a further 3,315 on the ground. These losses to the Luftwaffe bled it white; they could not be replaced.

Republic P-47 Thunderbolt variants

XP-47B: prototype, first flown on 6 May 1941; powered by 1380-kW/1,850-hp (later 1492-kW/2,000-hp) XR-2800 radial; maximum weight 5482 kg (12,086 lb) and maximum speed 663 km/h (412 mph) (total 1)

P-47B: first production version, initial aircraft being flown in March 1942; 1492-kW (2,000-hp) R-2800-21 radial; sliding hood and metal-skinned control surfaces; maximum weight 6060 kg (13,360 lb) and maximum speed 674 km/h (419 mph) (total 171)

P-47C: revised production model, first flown in September 1942; initially same engine as P-47B, then (from P-47C-5-RE onwards) powered by 1716-kW (2,300-hp) R-2800-59; longer forward fuselage, and provision for belly/bomb tank; maximum weight 6770 kg (14,925 lb) and maximum speed 697 km/h (433 mph) (total 602)

P-47D: major production model, the first example being flown in December 1942; 1716-kW (2,300-hp) R-2800-21W or 1891-kW (2,535-hp) R-2800-59W water-injected radial; numerous modifications in various blocks; maximum weight 7938 kg (17,500 lb) and maximum speed, clean 697 km/h (433 mph) (total 12,602)

XP-47E: experimental 1943 version of P-47D with pressurised cockpit (total 1)

XP-47F: experimental 1943 version of P-47B with so-called laminar-flow wings (total 1)

P-47G: designation of P-47D razorback-model built by Curtiss-Wright (total 354)

XP-47H: experimental development of P-47D with 1716-kW (2,300-hp) Chrysler XIV-2220-1

liquid-cooled 16-cylinder inverted-Vee engine; totally different in appearance to other P-47 models; length 11.94 m (39 ft 2 in); and maximum speed 789 km/h (490 mph) (total 2)

XP-47J: experimental development based on the P-47D with lightened structure and special 2089-kW (2,800-hp) R-2800-57(C) radial with CH-5 turbocharger; fitted with six 12.7-mm (0.5-in) machine-guns; first flown in November 1943 and in August 1944 reached an instrumented level speed of 811 km/h (504 mph); maximum weight 6056 kg (13,350 lb) (total 1)

XP-47K: developed P-47D with clearview teardrop hood from a Hawker Typhoon; first flown on 3 July 1943 (total 1)

XP-47L: developed P-47D-20-RE with larger fuselage fuel tanks increasing standard capacity from 1155 to 1401 litres (305 to 370 US gal) (total 1)

P-47M: 'sprint' model based on P-47D but with 2089-kW (2,800-hp) R-2800-57(C) and CH-5 turbocharger; first flown in mid-1944; sometimes fitted with only six 12.7-mm (0.5-in) machine-guns; maximum weight 7031 kg (15,500 lb) and maximum speed 756 km/h (470 mph) (total 133, including 3 prototypes)

P-47N: long-range model for Pacific theatre; fitted with new wing with fuel tanks, broad ailerons and square-cut tips; stronger landing gear and other modifications; 2089-kW (2,800-hp) R-2800-57(C) radial; maximum weight up to 9616 kg (21,200 lb), maximum speed 740 km/h (460 mph) and maximum range 3540 km (2,200 miles) (total 1,816)

Hawker Hurricane

One of the most important aircraft of all time, the Hurricane has always had to settle for second place to the Spitfire in the mythology of aviation. It was Hurricanes which saved the nation in the Battle of Britain, and they went on to fight alongside Allied troops in huge numbers, in every theatre of the war.

Stemming from efforts to accelerate fighter development with the F.7/30 specification, which itself failed to produce radical technological advance, the Hawker Hurricane originated in 1933 as an attempt to produce a monoplane adaptation of the successful Hawker Fury biplane – and therein lay the design anachronism that effectively placed it a whole generation behind the Spitfire for, while Mitchell advanced into monocoque construction throughout, Camm's design lay firmly in the realm of fabric-over-frame. Yet in the hectic months of 1939 and 1940, when RAF fighters were required to fight and fly in desperately primitive operating conditions, it was the very simplicity of the Hurricane's structure that enabled it to survive severe battle damage and undergo effective repair.

The first Hurricane (K5083) was flown from Brooklands on 6 November 1935 by Group Captain P.W.S. Bulman. Powered by a 764-kW (1,025-hp) Rolls-Royce Merlin 'C' 12-cylinder liquid-cooled inline engine, developed from the private-venture PV-12, the prototype weighed 2460 kg (5,420 lb) all-up and featured a two-bladed wooden Watts propeller; its top speed was 507 km/h (315 mph) at 4575 m (15,000 ft).

As production of the first 600 Hurricanes, ordered in June 1936, built up during 1937 (albeit somewhat delayed by abandonment of the Merlin I in favour of the Merlin II, necessitating alterations to the nose contours), the wing-mounted eight-Browning gun battery was confirmed and minor alterations were made to the airframe, including an improved radiator bath, a strengthened hood canopy and the discarding of tailplane struts.

Initial service deliveries were made to No. 111 (Fighter) Squadron at Northolt before the end of 1937, and the next year Nos 3 and 56 Squadrons followed suit. Early spinning trials disclosed a need to increase keel area, provided by a ventral fairing added forward of the fixed tailwheel, and by a 7.62-cm (3-in) downward extension of the rudder.

Within the limitations imposed by the basic airframe structure and by the desperate need to accelerate production in the threatening international climate, little could be done initially to improve the Hur-

ricane I before the outbreak of war. However, the fixed-pitch wooden propeller was replaced by a two-position, three-bladed de Havilland metal propeller, and later by a Rotol constant-speed propeller – the latter bestowing much improved climb and performance at altitude. These alterations were made possible by the arrival of the 768-kW (1,030-hp) Merlin III with universal propeller shaft. Metal-covered wings also appeared in production by 1939.

By the outbreak of war a total of 497 Hurricane Is had been completed for the RAF, and 18 home-based fighter squadrons had taken deliveries. Some export orders had been authorised to friendly nations, these including Yugoslavia (12, plus licence production), South Africa (7), Romania (12), Canada (20), Persia (2), Poland (1), Belgium (20, plus licence production) and Turkey (15). Plans were well advanced to create another production line at the Gloster Aircraft Company, and tooling up to produce Hurricanes at the Canadian Car and Foundry Company at Montreal was under way (a total of 1,451 Hurricanes was built in Canada during the war). In 1941 the Austin Motor Company, Longbridge, also produced 300 Hurricanes.

Into successful action

Four Hurricane I squadrons (Nos 1, 73, 85 and 87) accompanied the RAF to France in September 1939, and it was to Pilot Officer P.W.O. Mould of No. 1 Squadron that the first German aircraft, a Dornier Do 17, fell on 30 October. The Hurricane proved able to cope with the primitive airfield conditions in France, principally on account of its sturdy, wide-track landing gear – while the Spitfire was held at home to meet any threat to the British Isles.

By 1940 Hurricane Is were beginning to roll off the Gloster production line, as well as from the new Hawker factory at Langley, Bucks. A Hurricane squadron, No. 46, served at Narvik during the last days of the Norwegian campaign but all its aircraft were lost

Amid the dust and sand of the Western Desert, which not only reduced visibility but caused severe wear to aircraft engines, these Hurricane IID anti-tank fighters of No. 6 Squadron taxi out for take-off at Sidi Bu Amud in January 1943 during the rout of the Afrika Korps which followed the 2nd Battle of Alamein.

Hawker Hurricane

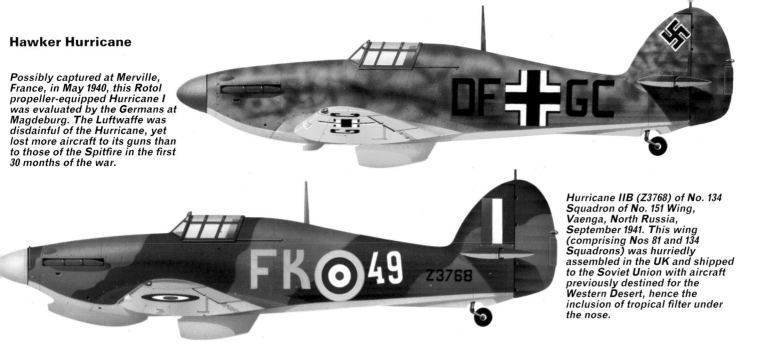

Possibly captured at Merville, France, in May 1940, this Rotol propeller-equipped Hurricane I was evaluated by the Germans at Magdeburg. The Luftwaffe was disdainful of the Hurricane, yet lost more aircraft to its guns than to those of the Spitfire in the first 30 months of the war.

Hurricane IIB (Z3768) of No. 134 Squadron of No. 151 Wing, Vaenga, North Russia, September 1941. This wing (comprising Nos 81 and 134 Squadrons) was hurriedly assembled in the UK and shipped to the Soviet Union with aircraft previously destined for the Western Desert, hence the inclusion of tropical filter under the nose.

when the carrier HMS *Glorious* was sunk while bringing them home. Over Dunkirk, and in the closing stages of the Battle of France, Hurricanes were in constant action against the Luftwaffe, although those of the Belgian air force suffered almost total destruction.

Saviour of the nation

The Hurricane I provided Fighter Command's mainstay in the Battle of Britain, equipping a maximum of 32 squadrons (compared with 18½ of Spitfires) between July and October 1940, no fewer than 2,309 having been delivered by 7 August. Top speed of the Rotol-equipped Hurricane I was 528 km/h (328 mph) at 5030 m (16,500 ft), a performance which fell far short of that of the superlative Messerschmitt Bf 109E, and it was this shortfall that caused it to be committed – whenever possible – against enemy bombers rather than the German single-seaters. The Hurricane proved to be exceptionally popular among its pilots as a highly manoeuvrable dogfighter with rock-steady gun-aiming properties and the tightest of turning radii, which helped to make the type particularly effective against the Messerschmitt Bf 110 heavy fighter. It was, however, the extraordinary teamwork between the various elements of the air defences that won the great battle.

In September 1940, when the battle was still at its height, the first Hurricane Mk IIs were beginning to appear with the 883-kW (1,185-hp) two-stage supercharged Merlin XX with Rotol propeller and slightly lengthened nose. Still armed with eight Browning guns in the Mk IIA Series I version, this Hurricane possessed a top speed of 550 km/h (342 mph). The Mk IIA Series 2 introduced pick-up points for a 'universal' wing capable of mounting 200-litre (44-Imp gal)

Hurricane IIC night-fighter of No. 87 (Fighter) Squadron being flown by Sqdn Ldr D.G. Smallwood, DSO, DFC; note the CO's pennant aft of the exhaust glare shield. No. 87 Squadron, which flew Hurricane IICs from June 1941 until March 1944, was one of the longest-serving Hurricane night-fighter squadrons in the RAF.

underwing fuel tanks; this variant was originally developed to enable Hurricanes to be supplied by air to the Middle East, but the fall of France ended this venture after fewer than a dozen aircraft had attempted the flight. Hurricane IIAs were also capable of carrying a pair of 113-kg (250-lb) bombs under the wings and were flown on offensive sweeps across the English Channel early in 1941.

Maximum firepower

The Hurricane IIB introduced a new 12-Browning gun wing (as well as retaining the bomb shackles) and came to be known as the Hurribomber, while the Mk IIC featured an armament of four 20-mm Oerlikon/Hispano cannon – at that time (mid-1941) still regarded as an extraordinary armament for a single-seater (although one such Hurricane had been fought experimentally in the Battle of Britain with limited success). These two sub-variants equipped no fewer than 96 RAF squadrons during 1941-44 and saw continuous action in northern Europe, North Africa and the Far East, being employed principally in the ground attack role. They also played a significant part in the Greek, Iraqi, Syrian and Malayan campaigns. Last of the Merlin XX-powered Hurricanes was the Mk IID, introduced in 1942, with a 40-mm Vickers or Rolls-Royce anti-tank gun under each wing. Atlhough a small number of this variant remained home-based, the majority was shipped to the Western Desert (where the type played a major part in the Battle of Bir Hakeim) and later to Burma. Following early experience in the Western Desert, whose abrasive dust and sand wrought havoc with aero engines, all Hurricanes supplied to the Middle and Far Eastern theatres were fitted with Vokes air filters over their carburettor intakes, an ungainly but necessary modification which reduced performance by some 8 per cent.

The Hurricane II remained the principal variant in service during the war, eventually providing the major ground-attack element of the RAF in the Far East. A total of 2,952 Hurricanes was supplied to the Soviet Union, of which all but about 30 were Mk IIs or their Canadian-built equivalents. The majority was shipped as deck cargo on the North Cape convoys (and suffered heavy losses accordingly), though many were also supplied from Middle East stocks. Another important duty undertaken by the Mk II was night fighting, at one time participating in the almost fruitless Turbinlite venture over the UK but also serving as night intruders over France and Belgium during 1941 and 1942 until this task was taken over almost exclusively by the Bristol Beaufighter and de Havilland Mosquito.

Final variant for the RAF was the Hurricane IV (the Mk III was an unbuilt project intended to introduce the Packard-built Merlin 28 into the Hawker production line). This version, originally termed the Mk IIE, featured the 954-kW (1,280-hp) Merlin 24 or 27 and a new universal wing capable of mounting anti-tank guns, rocket projectiles or other external stores. Owing to the need for only limited airframe

Hawker Hurricane

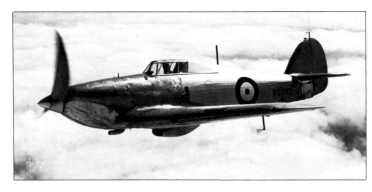

The Hurricane prototype (K5083) in a relatively late photograph of the aircraft being flown by P.G. Lucas in 1937 after removal of tailplane struts, installation of gunsight, modification to the radiator bath and with additional strengthening members on the cockpit canopy.

Hawker Sea Hurricane II cutaway drawing key

1 Fabric-covered rudder construction
2 Tail navigation light
3 Rudder tab
4 Elevator tab
5 Fabric covered elevator construction
6 Elevator horn balance
7 Tailplane construction
8 Rudder control horn
9 Elevator hinge control
10 Sternpost
11 Tailfin construction
12 Fabric covering
13 Rear aerial mast
14 Rudder balance weight
15 Aerial cable
16 Tailfin aluminium leading edge
17 Port tailplane

31 Aluminium alloy fuselage frames
32 Bolted joint fuselage tubular construction
33 Deck arrest hook
34 Arresting hook pivot point
35 Bottom longeron
36 Arresting hook damper
37 Wooden dorsal fairing formers
38 Aerial mast
39 Upper identification light
40 Upward firing recognition flare launcher
41 Tailplane control cables
42 Fuselage access panel

54 Battery
55 Oxygen bottle
56 Hydraulic system equipment
57 Dinghy stowage
58 Seat back armour plate
59 Head armour
60 Rearward sliding canopy cover
61 Canopy framework
62 Safety harness
63 Pilot's seat
64 Seat adjusting lever
65 Fuselage/wing spar attachment joint
66 Ventral oil and coolant radiator
67 Position of flap hydraulic jack (fitted on port side only)

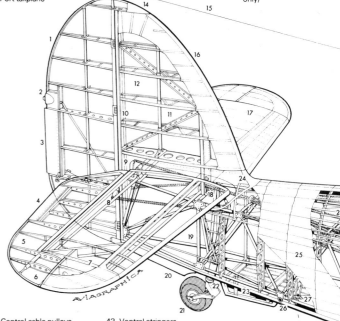

modifications, many Mk IIs were converted to accommodate the new wing and, with new engine, remained in service with the RAF until after the war. The final Hurricane built for the RAF, a Mk IIC (LF363), was delivered to No. 309 (Polish) Squadron in February 1944, while the last of all to be built (also a Mk IIC, PZ865), was purchased by the manufacturers and survives to this day. Total production of the Hurricane amounted to 14,231, including those produced in Canada. In addition the extensive repair organisation, created in 1939, returned 4,537 repaired Hurricanes to the RAF.

Sea Hurricanes

Loss of the French Atlantic seaboard in 1940 exposed the vital British convoys to increasing action by long-range German bombers such as the Heinkel He 111 and Focke-Wulf Fw 200, and it was decided to adapt the Hurricane I for catapulting from merchant ships (CAM-ships) to provide some measure of protection against this menace. The first such variant, the Sea Hurricane IA, was a simple adaptation of ex-RAF Hurricane Is to feature catapult spools. Limited success attended these operations in 1941, for it was intended that, once launched, the 'Hurricat' pilot had no alternative after action but to ditch his aircraft or make a forlorn search for land.

The next venture was to convert a number of merchantmen (MACs) to provide a small flight deck from which Sea Hurricane Mk IBs might operate, and these aircraft featured an arrester hook. A third version, the Sea Hurricane Mk IC, carried the four-cannon armament but was still powered by the Merlin III. It was followed by

18 Control cable pulleys
19 Port access panel to tailplane controls
20 Ventral fin
21 Tailwheel
22 Dowty shock absorber tailwheel strut
23 Fin framework
24 Fin/tailplane root fillet
25 Fuselage fabric covering
26 Lifting bar socket
27 Arresting hook latches
28 Dorsal stringers
29 Fuselage diagonal wire bracing
30 Upper longeron

43 Ventral stringers
44 Trailing edge wing root fillet
45 Downward identification light
46 Radio racks
47 Radio equipment (R3002 and R3108)
48 Parachute flare launch tube
49 Sliding canopy track
50 Canopy rear fairing construction
51 Turn-over crash pylon struts
52 Radio equipment (TR1196 and R1304)
53 Radio equipment (TR1143 and TR1133)

68 Gun heater air duct
69 Inboard flap housing
70 Trailing edge ribs
71 Outer wing panel rear spar joint
72 Breech-block access covers
73 Cannon breech-blocks
74 Outboard flap housing
75 Rear spar
76 Aluminium aileron construction
77 Fabric covered starboard aileron
78 Aileron control gear
79 Wing tip construction
80 Starboard navigation light
81 Intermediate wing spars
82 Aluminium wing ribs
83 Front spar
84 Leading edge nose ribs
85 Starboard landing lamp
86 Wing stringer construction
87 Ammunition feed drums
88 Ammunition boxes (total 364 rounds)
89 Main undercarriage swivelling joint
90 Hispano 20-mm cannon
91 Starboard wing cannon bays
92 Cannon barrel front mounting

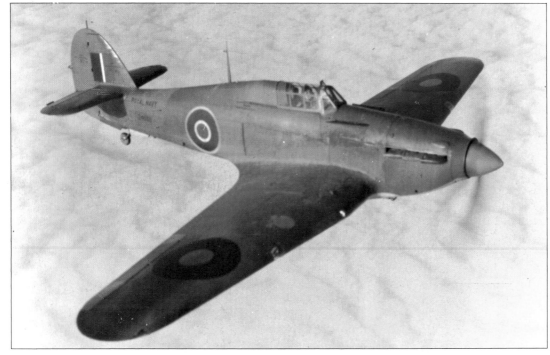

The Sea Hurricane IB was a conversion of the RAF's Mk 1, and this Fleet Air Arm version featured catapult spools, arrester hook and naval radio. The Gloster-built aircraft shown here features exhaust glare shields forward of the windscreen. Sea Hurricanes were in constant action in the Mediterranean, particularly in 1942.

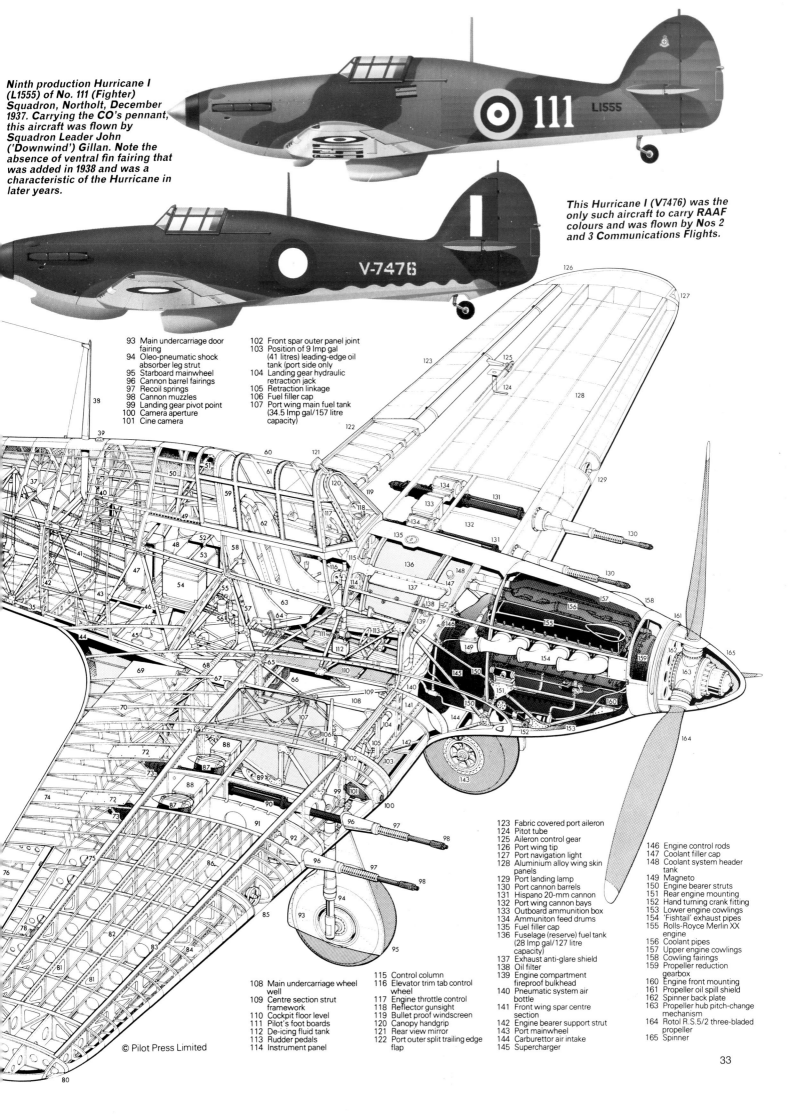

Ninth production Hurricane I (L1555) of No. 111 (Fighter) Squadron, Northolt, December 1937. Carrying the CO's pennant, this aircraft was flown by Squadron Leader John ('Downwind') Gillan. Note the absence of ventral fin fairing that was added in 1938 and was a characteristic of the Hurricane in later years.

111   LI555

This Hurricane I (V7476) was the only such aircraft to carry RAAF colours and was flown by Nos 2 and 3 Communications Flights.

V-7476

93 Main undercarriage door fairing
94 Oleo-pneumatic shock absorber leg strut
95 Starboard mainwheel
96 Cannon barrel fairings
97 Recoil springs
98 Cannon muzzles
99 Landing gear pivot point
100 Camera aperture
101 Cine camera

102 Front spar outer panel joint
103 Position of 9 Imp gal (41 litres) leading-edge oil tank (port side only)
104 Landing gear hydraulic retraction jack
105 Retraction linkage
106 Fuel filler cap
107 Port wing main fuel tank (34.5 Imp gal/157 litre capacity)

123 Fabric covered port aileron
124 Pitot tube
125 Aileron control gear
126 Port wing tip
127 Port navigation light
128 Aluminium alloy wing skin panels
129 Port landing lamp
130 Port cannon barrels
131 Hispano 20-mm cannon
132 Port wing cannon bays
133 Outboard ammunition box
134 Ammuniton feed drums
135 Fuel filler cap
136 Fuselage (reserve) fuel tank (28 Imp gal/127 litre capacity)
137 Exhaust anti-glare shield
138 Oil filter
139 Engine compartment fireproof bulkhead
140 Pneumatic system air bottle
141 Front wing spar centre section
142 Engine bearer support strut
143 Port mainwheel
144 Carburettor air intake
145 Supercharger

146 Engine control rods
147 Coolant filler cap
148 Coolant system header tank
149 Magneto
150 Engine bearer struts
151 Rear engine mounting
152 Hand turning crank fitting
153 Lower engine cowlings
154 'Fishtail' exhaust pipes
155 Rolls-Royce Merlin XX engine
156 Coolant pipes
157 Upper engine cowlings
158 Cowling fairings
159 Propeller reduction gearbox
160 Engine front mounting
161 Propeller oil spill shield
162 Spinner back plate
163 Propeller hub pitch-change mechanism
164 Rotol R.S.5/2 three-bladed propeller
165 Spinner

108 Main undercarriage wheel well
109 Centre section strut framework
110 Cockpit floor level
111 Pilot's foot boards
112 De-icing fluid tank
113 Rudder pedals
114 Instrument panel

115 Control column
116 Elevator trim tab control wheel
117 Engine throttle control
118 Reflector gunsight
119 Bullet proof windscreen
120 Canopy handgrip
121 Rear view mirror
122 Port outer split trailing edge flap

33

Hawker Hurricane

Specification
Hawker Hurricane Mk I

Type: single-seat interceptor fighter

Powerplant: one 768-kW (1,030-hp) Rolls-Royce Merlin III inline piston engine

Performance: maximum speed 511 km/h (318 mph) at 5500 m (18,000 ft); initial climb rate 770 m (2,520 ft) per minute; service ceiling 10970 m (36,000 ft); maximum range 740 km (460 miles)

Weights: empty 2118 kg (4,670 lb); maximum take-off 2994 kg (6,600 lb)

Dimensions: span 12.20 m (40 ft 0 in); length 9.59 m (31 ft 4 in); height 3.96 m (12 ft 11½ in); wing area 23.93 m² (257.6 sq ft)

Armament: eight 7.7-mm (0.303-in) Browning machine-guns with 2,660 rounds of ammunition

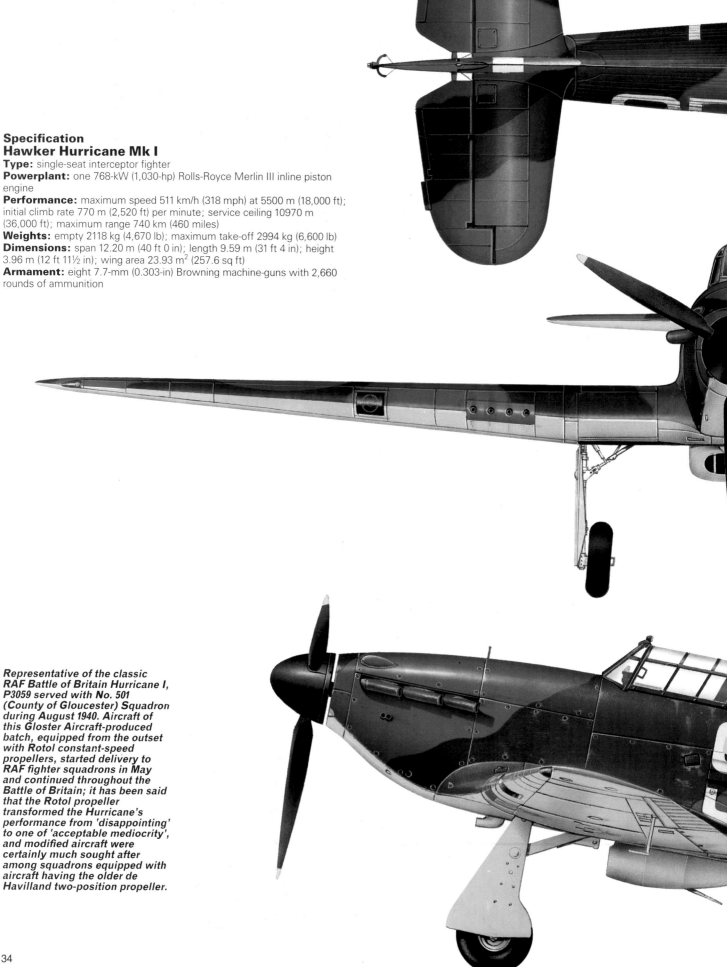

Representative of the classic RAF Battle of Britain Hurricane I, P3059 served with No. 501 (County of Gloucester) Squadron during August 1940. Aircraft of this Gloster Aircraft-produced batch, equipped from the outset with Rotol constant-speed propellers, started delivery to RAF fighter squadrons in May and continued throughout the Battle of Britain; it has been said that the Rotol propeller transformed the Hurricane's performance from 'disappointing' to one of 'acceptable mediocrity', and modified aircraft were certainly much sought after among squadrons equipped with aircraft having the older de Havilland two-position propeller.

Unofficially adorned with peacetime squadron flash, this tropicalised Hurricane IIB (BD930) was flown by No. 73 Squadron in the Western Desert in 1942. Veteran of the French campaign and Battle of Britain, No. 73 Squadron was rushed to the Middle East to meet the crisis of 1940, becoming separated from its ground crews and losing many aircraft en route.

A No. 6 Squadron Hurricane IID with 40-mm anti-tank guns, base at LG89 and LG91 in the Western Desert, July 1942. First to receiv this Hurricane version, No. 6 Squadron played a major part i destroying enemy vehicles in th desert during the months immediately prior to the decisiv 2nd Battle of Alamein.

a full conversion of the Hurricane IIC, the Sea Hurricane IIC with Merlin XX, four-cannon wing, catapult spools, arrester hook, underwing store provision and naval radio. It possessed a top speed of 512 km/h (318 mph) at 5340 m (17,500 ft), a service celing of 9300 m (30,500 ft) and a maximum range of 1710 km (1,062 miles). It was withdrawn from service at sea in October 1943.

At one time, late in 1942, the Fleet Air Arm held on charge a total of more than 600 Sea Hurricanes, and almost every fleet and escort carrier of the Royal Navy at one time or another mustered at least a partial complement of these aircraft. One of their most memorable actions was fought over the Malta convoy of August 1942 when Sea Hurricanes from HMS *Indomitable, Eagle* and *Victorious* beat off attacks by 600 Axis aircraft, destroying 39 for the loss of seven of their own number.

Although RAF Hurricanes were relegated to second-line duties at home from mid-1944 onwards, particularly in the training role and on meteorological and radar calibration work, Hurricane IIs and IVs remained in first line service in the Mediterranean and Far East theatres until 1945, providing outstanding support for the 14th Army's advance through Burma in the latter theatre.

Other careers

Many experiments were carried out on Hurricanes between 1939 and 1945, mostly aimed at increasing the theatre-reinforcement capabilities (i.e. ferry range); these experiments included the carriage of a jettisonable auxiliary upper wing (the Hillson Bi-Mono project), pickaback trials aboard a Consolidated B-24 Liberator, and towing

Dramatic dusk launch of a Sea Hurricane IA from the bow-mounted catapult of a merchant ship. Introduced to provide Allied convoys with on-the-spot fighter defence against enemy aircraft, the catapult Sea Hurricanes enjoyed limited success in 1941; with nowhere to go, the pilot was forced to bale out or ditch in the hope he would be fished out of the sea by a passing ship.

trials behind an Avro Lancaster. Other trials included the carriage of outsize rocket projectiles and the fitting of a semi-laminar flow wing. A floatplane version was proposed at the time of the 1940 Norwegian campaign, and skis were fitted to at least one Canadian Hurricane. Alternative engines were proposed from time to time although the only such project believed to have reached construction was a Yugoslav Hurricane fitted with a Daimler-Benz DB 601A in 1941.

After the war a large number of Hurricanes were declared surplus to British requirements and many of these aircraft underwent refurbishing for export. The Irish Air Corps had acquired a small number of Mk Is during the war, and 13 further aircraft were supplied during 1945-57. Hurricanes also served with the Turkish, Egyptian and South African air forces during the mid-1940s. About 50 Hurricane IIBs and IICs were delivered to Portugal (although some of these were used only to provide spares), and a delivery of 16 Hurricane IIs to Persia completed an order for 18 aircraft negotiated before the war. One other Hurricane, a unique two-seat trainer converted from a Mk IIC, was also sold to Persia in 1947.

Hawker Hurricane variants

F.36/34 prototype: one aircraft (K5083) with 764-kW (1,025-hp) Merlin C; eight-gun armament fitted later; first flown 6 November 1935

Hurricane I: original production model with 768-kW (1,030-hp) Merlin II or III, eight Browning 7.7-mm (0.303-in) guns; early aircraft with fabric-covered wings, later metal-clad (total 2,719 excluding Canadian-built; about 90 exported)

Canadian Hurricane I: built by Canadian Car and Foundry Co. in Montreal, 1940; Merlin III and DH propellers; batch included Hillson Bi-Mono slip-wing Hurricane (total 40)

Hurricane IIA Series 1: introduced 883-kW (1,185-hp) Merlin XX two-stage supercharged engine in September 1940; eight-gun wing; some converted from Mark Is

Hurricane IIA Series 2: introduced provision for wing stores on Universal wing; some converted from Mark I; included some PR Mk I Conversions and PR Mk IIA

Hurricane IIB: introduced 12-Browning gun wing and bomb-tank shackles for 227-kg (500-lb) bombs (total approximately 3,100 built by Hawker, Gloster and Austin, plus many converted from other versions; included the PR Mark IIB)

Hurricane IIC: introduced four 20-mm gun armament in 1941; bomb and drop tank provision; worldwide service; also tropicalised (total approximately 3,400 built by Hawker, Gloster and Austin, plus many conversions)

Hurricane IID: introduced pair of 40-mm Vickers or Rolls-Royce anti-tank guns plus two Brownings in 1942; many tropicalised (total approximately 800 built; plus many conversions)

Hurricane IV: introduced 954-kW (1,280-hp) Merlin 24 or 27 and Universal wing to carry alternative rockets, drop tanks, bombs or anti-tank guns in 1942; many tropicalised (total approximately 2,000 built, plus numerous conversions)

Hurricane V: two prototypes (KZ193 and NL255, converted Mk IVs) with ground-boosted Merlin 32 and four-bladed Rotol propeller

Canadian Hurricane X: Packard Merlin 28; about 100 with eight-gun wing, remainder with IIB wing; many converted to IIC wing (total 489 built in 1940-41)

Canadian Hurricane XI: 150 aircraft with 12-gun or four-cannon armament; majority shipped to Soviet Union in 1942-43

Canadian Hurricane XII: 248 aircraft with Hurricane IIC modifications; included single ski-equipped example

Canadian Hurricane XIIA and Sea Hurricane XIIA: Packard Merlin 29; 150 aircraft shipped principally to Soviet Union and Burma in 1943

Sea Hurricane IA: catapult fighter for CAM-ship operations (50 aircraft converted from Hurricane I in 1941)

Sea Hurricane IB: catapult spools and arrester hook for operations from CAM-ships or MACs (total approximately 340 converted from Hurricane IIA Series 2 in 1941-42)

Sea Hurricane IC: as Sea Hurricane IB but four-cannon armament included (total approximately 400 converted from Hurricane IIB and IIC in 1942-43)

Sea Hurricane IIC: full-standard conversions of Hurricane IIC with hook, spools and naval radio (total approximately 400 converted from Hurricane IIC); although it is possible to state the total number of Hurricanes built, no exact records exist – or were ever kept – of the number of each variant owing to *ad hoc* conversions both by the manufacturers and in the field)

SPITFIRE
Fighter Supreme

Comment on the Supermarine Spitfire is almost superfluous; this magnificent thoroughbred fighting machine is perhaps the best-known British aircraft of all time. It remained in production throughout World War II, remaining a fully competitive interceptor while also being developed into a number of other roles, such as PR platform, tactical fighter-bomber and shipboard fighter.

The Spitfire is perhaps the most famous British aircraft of all time. Though it played a minor role in the Battle of Britain compared with the less glamorous Hawker Hurricane, it was problably the most important single type of aircraft on the Allied side in World War II. It was built in larger numbers than any Allied type outside the Soviet Union, remained in production throughout the entire war, and was developed to a greater extent than any other aircraft in history. Britain was fortunate that, as a purely private venture by the chief designer with the support of his board, the nation possessed a prototype in 1936 of a fighter which was capable of being developed to much more than twice the engine power and much more than twice the laden weight in order to stay in the very forefront of the air-combat battle.

No exponents of the Spitfire deserved a greater reputation than the Free Poles, many of whom had relatives living under the Nazi yoke. This Spitfire Mk Vb was the mount of the commanding officer of No. 303 Sqn, RAF, which flew the from January 1941 until April 1945.

Had Britain relied upon official specifications, the only 1936 fighter would have been the Supermarine 224, a clumsy machine with an airframe structurally resembling the Schneider Trophy seaplanes, with a 492-kW (660-hp) Goshawk engine and armed with four machine-guns, two in the fuselage and two in the fixed 'trousered' landing gears. The designer, Reginald Mitchell, was unimpressed with his creation, went back to his drawing board and created the Type 300. This was much smaller and better streamlined, had retractable landing gear, was of all stressed-skin construction, and was intended to be powered by the new Rolls-Royce PV.12 engine of some 671 kW (900 hp). All the guns were in the wings, firing outside the disc of the propeller; and thanks to young Squadron Leader Ralph Sorley, the Air Ministry had decided that future fighters might need eight machine-guns. Moreover, the absence of a modern British gun was being made up by a licence to make the American Browning (itself a World War I gun). By late 1935 this gun in British 7.7-mm (0.303-in) calibre was being planned for production at the BSA company.

Mitchell schemed the wing of the Type 300 with a distinctive elliptical shape to accommodate all eight guns well outboard, with belt magazines quickly replenished through hatches in the skin.

It so happened that this wing, so characteristic of the Spitfire, was one of the best ever designed for a fighter of this era. The elliptical shape played no part in this, and merely made it difficult to make. But aerodynamically the profile was good for speed over 90 per cent that of sound (over Mach 0.9), and during World War II Spitfires were dived to Mach 0.92, much faster than any of the German jets. By this time Supermarine had developed a new wing, with a so-called laminar profile, fitted to the Spitfire's intended replacement, the Spiteful. It was in fact a much worse wing, and when it was later fitted to the first Supermarine jet fighter many pilots, including the chief test pilot, wished the old Spitfire wing had been used instead!

Flight test and production

Like its lifelong enemy the Messerschmitt Bf 109, the new Supermarine fighter had a narrow landing gear pivoted near the fuselage and retracting out and up into the wings. Again like the Bf 109, the Spitfire used a water/glycol engine cooling liquid which was piped to radiators under the rear part of the inner wing, though in the British aircraft an odd asymmetric arrangement was chosen, with the coolant radiator under the right wing and a slim oil-cooler radiator under the left. Other features included split flaps (worked, like the landing gear, by a hydraulic system with a hand pump in the cockpit), a comfortable cockpit with a Perspex (ICI transparent acrylic plastic) hood that the pilot could slide to the rear on runners, six plain stub exhausts on each side, a fixed tailskid and a hefty but crude two-blade wooden propeller (because none of the new variable-pitch propellers were available in the UK).

Altogether the new fighter was the most beautiful of its era. The Air Ministry had written specification F.37/34 around it and assigned the serial number K5054 (curiously, an earlier number than that of the prototype Hurricane, K5083, which was built six months earlier). The trim new prototype was flown unpainted by chief test pilot 'Mutt' Summers at Eastleigh airfield (now Southampton airport) on 5 March 1936. The aircraft handled like a dream, but such was the difficulty of training workers to make modern stressed-skin aircraft that the planned mass production was slow to get under way. The first Spitfire I reached No. 19 Squadron at Duxford in July 1938, and

only five had been delivered at the time of the Munich crisis in September that year. By 1939 the Mk I was being made more effective as the clouds of war gathered. The Merlin engine, into which the PV.12 (used in the prototype) had been developed, was being improved in more powerful versions. The first de Havilland and Rotol constant-speed three-blade propellers were at last becoming available. The cockpit was given a bulged hood providing more room and a better view, and a thick slab of Perspex and glass was added at the front to make the windscreen bulletproof. The seat and engine bulkhead were given armour, and the two rather small fuel tanks (total 386 litres/85 Imp gal) ahead of the cockpit were made armoured-plated against bullet holes. Previously the engine had been fitted with ejector exhaust stacks and a pump to work the hydraulic system, and after the outbreak of war improved radio was fitted together with IFF (identification friend or foe), an automatic radio interrogator which gave positive identification of other aircraft in the vicinity (though this did not stop many tragic mistakes).

In 1938 Joe Smith, who on Mitchell's untimely death had become chief designer, had begun a planned process of development of later marks of Spitfire. One major scheme involved a 'B' series wing with the two inboard guns on each side replaced by a large 20-mm Hispano cannon, with drum feed. In early 1940 a batch of 30 Mk IBs was delivered, but the cannon were not then reliable. The corresponding 'C' type wing removed all the machine-guns and provided the formidable armament of four cannon in close pairs. This remained relatively rare.

Spitfire variants

Spitfire I: original production model with 768-kW (1,030-hp) Merlin II, eight Browning 7.7-mm (0.303-in) guns (at first four not fitted because of short supply) or (Mk IB) two 20-mm and four 7.7-mm (0.303-in) guns (total 1,566)

Spitfire II: Castle Bromwich aircraft with small changes and 877-kW (1,175-hp) Merlin XII (total 750 IIA and 170 IIB)

Spitfire III: experimental prototype (1 only) with 955-kW (1,280-hp) Merlin XX

Spitfire IV: Griffon prototype; same mark number used for 229 PR versions of Mk V

Spitfire V: strengthened fuselage for 1103-kW (1,478-hp) Merlin 45 or 1097-kW (1,470-hp) Merlin 50; drop tank and bomb provisions; F or LF span, 'A', 'B' or 'C' armament (total 94 Mk VA, 3,923 Mk VB and 2,447 Mk VC)

Spitfire VI: high-altitude interceptor with 1056-kW (1,415-hp) Merlin 47, pressurised cockpit and HF 12.24 m (40 ft 2 in) pointed wings (total 100)

Spitfire VII: high-altitude interceptor with two-stage Merlin 61, 64 or 71, pressurised cockpit, retractable tailwheel, often broad pointed rudder (total 140)

Spitfire VIII: definitive fighter with two-stage Merlin 61, 63, 66 or 70; unpressurised; LF, F or HF wings (total 1,658)

Spitfire IX: temporary stop-gap marriage of two-stage Merlin 61, 63 or 70 with Mk V airframe; LF, F or HF wings; 'B', 'C' or 'E' armament (total 5,665)

Spitfire X: pressurised version of PR.XI; Merlin 77; one example with HF wing (total 16)

Spitfire XI: unarmed reconnaissance aircraft; Merlin 61, 63 or 70; (total 471)

Spitfire XII: low-level interceptor; single-stage Griffon II or IV of 1294-kW (1,735-hp), LF wing; 'B' guns (total 100)

Spitfire XII: low-level PR aircraft based on Mk B but with Merlin 32 (three-blade propeller, of DH type unlike other late Spitfires); four 7.7-mm (0.303-in) guns only (total 18)

Spitfire XIV: two-stage Griffon 65 or 66 of 1529 kW (2,050-hp); driving five-blade propeller and redesigned and strengthened airframe with symmetric deep radiators, broad tail and

often teardrop canopy' F or LF span; 'C' or 'E' guns (total 957)

Spitfire XVI: Mk IX with Packard Merlin 266; F or LF span; usually 'C' or 'E' guns; many with teardrop canopy (total 1,054)

Spitfire XVIII: definitive fighter with two-stage Griffon; F span; 'E' guns; teardrop canopy and extra wing fuel; FR.XVIII (post-war FR.18) with rear-fuselage reconnaissance camera (total 300)

Spitfire XIX: unarmed PR version; two-stage Griffon; most pressurised (total 225)

Spitfire XX: single prototype rebuilt from Mk IV and prototype Mk XII

Spitfire 21: redesigned airframe; mainly Griffon 61 or 64 driving five-blade propeller; four 20-mm guns (total 122)

Spitfire 22: minor changes; some with 1772-kW (2,375-hp) Griffon 85 and contraprop (total 278)

Spitfire 24: minor changes; Spiteful tail; short-barrel Mk V cannon (total 54)

Seafire IB: navalised Spitfire VB (total 166)

Seafire IIC: catapult hooks and strengthened landing gear; Merlin 32 and four-blade propeller (total 372)

Seafire III: double-folding wing; 1183-kW (1,585-hp) Merlin 55M (total 1,220)

Seafire XV: single-stage 1380-kW (1,850-hp) Griffon VI and asymmetric radiators as Spitfire XII; most with sting hook; late production teardrop canopy (total 390)

Seafire XVII or 17: as Seafire XV with teardrop canopy; often strengthened landing gear; some (FR.17) with camera in place of rear tank (total 232)

Seafire 45: same new airframe as Spitfire 21; non-folding wing; Griffon 61 (five-blade) or 85 (contraprop) (total 50)

Seafire 46: as Seafire 45; teardrop canopy; FR.46 with rear-fuselage camera (total 24)

Seafire 47: folding wing (most hydraulic); 1772-kW (2,375-hp) Griffon 87 or 88 with contraprop and carburettor air inlet just below spinner; increased fuel; late production all FR type with camera (total 140)

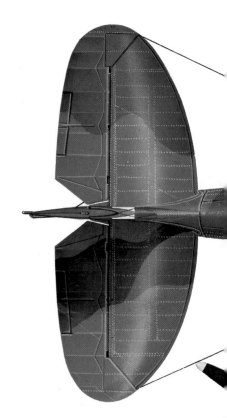

The personal aircraft of Wing Commander Douglas Bader when he commanded the Tangmere Wing in early 1941, this Mk VA was one of the last Spitfires built without cannon armament, which was distrusted by Bader. The aircraft was one of a batch of 450 Mk Is ordered from Vickers-Armstrong (Supermarine) on 22 March 1940. The order was subsequently amended to cover Mk V aircraft; most were Spitfire VBs, but a small batch of Spitfire VAs was also built. Bader was flying this aircraft, which unlike others had no provision for bomb armament, when he collided with a Messerschmitt Bf 109 over France and baled out to captivity on 7 August 1941.

Specification

Type: single-seat interceptor fighter

Powerplant: one 1103-kW (1,478-hp) Rolls-Royce Merlin 45 Vee piston engine

Performance: maximum speed 594 km/h (369 mph) at 5945 m (19,500 ft); initial climb rate 1445 m (4,740 ft) per minute; service ceiling 11125 m (36,500 ft); maximum range 1827 km (1,135 miles)

Weights: empty 2267 kg (4,998 lb); maximum take-off 2911 kg (6,417 lb)

Dimensions: span 11.23 m (36 ft 10 in); length 9.12 m (29 ft 11 in); height 3.02 m (9 ft 11 in); wing area 22.48 m^2 (242 sq ft)

Armament: eight 7.7-mm (0.303-in) Browning machine-guns with 350 rounds per gun

W3185

No. 601 (County of London) Sqn was an auxiliary unit which spent much of the war in the Mediterranean theatre. Here two of its Mk Vbs (with clipped wings) formate on their wing leader, Wing Commander I.R. Gleed, who featured personal codes on his mount.

Supermarine Spitfire IX cutaway drawing key:

1 Starboard wingtip
2 Navigation light
3 Starboard aileron
4 Browning 0.303-in (7.7-mm) machine-guns
5 Machine-gun ports (patched)
6 Ammunition boxes (350 rounds per gun)
7 Aileron control rod
8 Bellcrank hinge control
9 Starboard split trailing-edge flap
10 Aileron control cables
11 Cannon ammunition box (120 rounds)
12 Cannon 20-mm Hispano cannon
13 Ammunition feed drum
14 Cannon barrel
15 Rotol four-bladed constant speed propeller
16 Cannon barrel fairing
17 Spinner
18 Propeller hub pitch control mechanism
19 Armoured spinner backplate
20 Coolant system header tank
21 Coolant filler cap
22 Rolls-Royce Merlin 61 liquid-cooled 12-cylinder Vee piston engine
23 Exhaust stubs
24 Forward engine mounting
25 Engine bottom cowling
26 Cowling integral oil tank (5.6-Imp gal/25.5-litre capacity)
27 Extended carburettor air intake duct
28 Engine bearer struts
29 Main engine mounting member
30 Oil filter
31 Two-stage supercharger
32 Engine bearer attachment
33 Suppressor
34 Engine accessories
35 Intercooler
36 Compressor air intake scoop
37 Hydraulic reservoir
38 Hydraulic system filter
39 Armoured firewall/fuel tank bulkhead
40 Fuel filler cap
41 Top main fuel tank (48-Imp gal/218-litre capacity)
42 Back of instrument panel
43 Compass mounting
44 Fuel tank/longeron attachment fitting
45 Bottom main fuel tank (37-Imp gal/168-litre capacity)
46 Rudder pedal bar
47 Sloping fuel tank bulkhead
48 Fuel cock control
49 Chart case
50 Trim control handwheel
51 Engine throttle and propeller controls
52 Control column handgrip
53 Radio controller
54 Bullet-proof windscreen
55 Reflector gunsight
56 Pilot's rear view mirror
57 Canopy framing
58 Windscreen side panels
59 Sliding cockpit canopy cover
60 Headrest
61 Pilot's head armour
62 Safety harness
63 Pilot's seat
64 Side entry hatch
65 Back armour
66 Seat support frame
67 Pneumatic system air bottles
68 Fuselage main longeron
69 Optional long-range auxiliary fuel tank (29-Imp gal/132-litre capacity)
70 Sliding canopy rail
71 Voltage regulator
72 Cockpit aft glazing
73 IFF radio equipment
74 HF aerial mast
75 Aerial cable lead-in
76 Radio transmitter/receiver
77 Radio compartment access hatch
78 Upper identification light
79 Rear fuselage frame construction
80 Fuselage skin plating
81 Oxygen bottle
82 Signal cartridge launcher
83 IFF aerial
84 Starboard tailplane
85 Starboard elevator
86 Fin front spar (fuselage frame extension)
87 Fin rib construction
88 HF aerial cable
89 Rudder mass balance
90 Rudder construction
91 Sternpost
92 Rudder trim tab
93 Trim control jack
94 Tail navigation light
95 Elevator tab
96 Port fabric-covered elevator construction

By 1941 there had been many experimental or special variants, including the intended speed-record Speed Spitfire, two seaplanes, a part-plastic example to conserve scarce materials, a strengthened Mk III and two Mk IVs which introduced the larger Griffon engine and a four-blade propeller. Production, however, had been confined to the Mk I and the almost identical Mk II which was built at a vast 'Shadow Factory' at Castle Bromwich near Birmingham. And the next major production model, the Mk V, was not greatly different. It had a strengthened fuselage like the Mk III, a more powerful Merlin with wider blades on its three-blade propeller, provision for 'A', 'B' or 'C' wings, attachments under the belly for a 136-litre (30-Imp gal) drop tank (on occasion a much larger tank could be attached here) or a bomb of up to 227 kg (500 lb). The most common model was the Mk VB with two cannon and four machine-guns, but at the end of Mk V production the four-cannon 'C' armament became more common. Aircraft destined for the Mediterranean theatre had a dust and sand filter under the nose which spoilt both the appearance and performance. Aircraft expected to operate mainly at low level had the tips of the wings removed, which was effected by the undoing of two bolts.

The prototype Spitfire XII shows off its purposeful lines. All Mk XIIs had the clipped wings shown, suiting the type to the low-level interception role, and also introduced into production Spitfires with the larger Rolls-Royce Griffon engine, housed in a lengthened nose with 'bumps' over the tops of the cylinder banks.

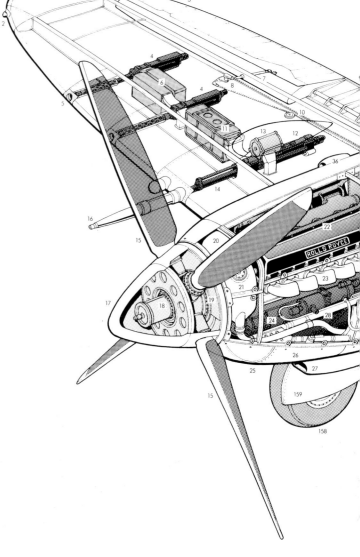

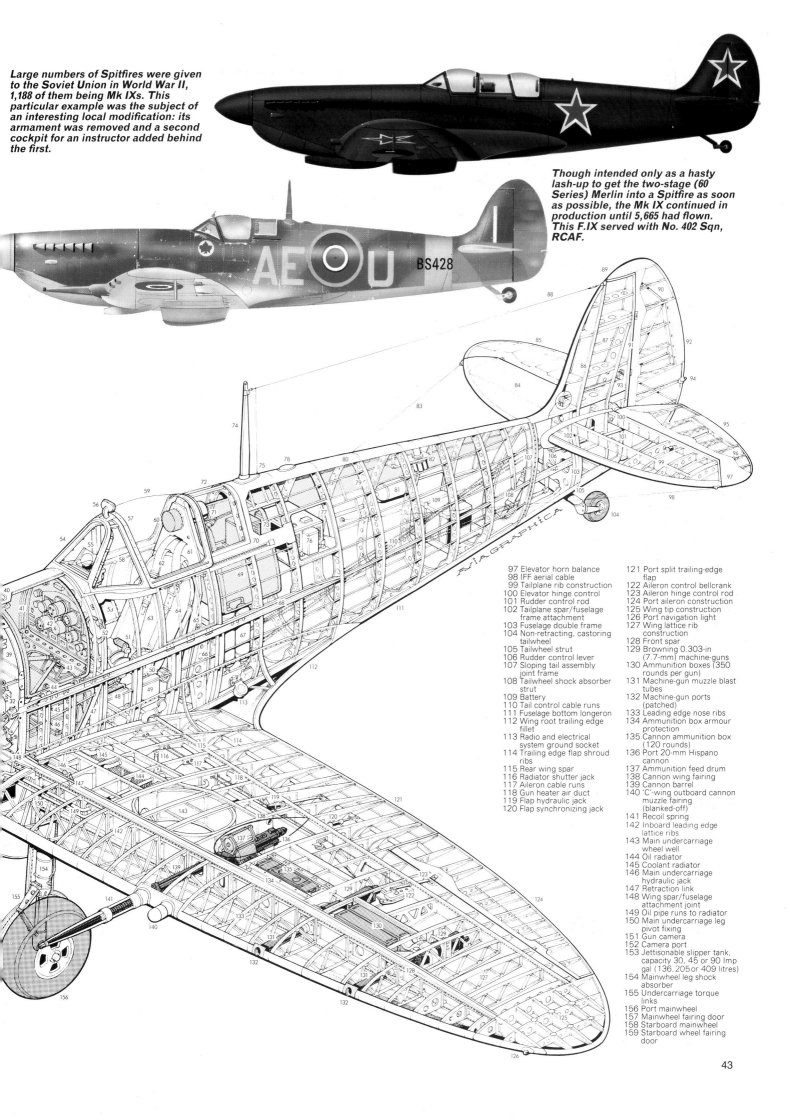

Large numbers of Spitfires were given to the Soviet Union in World War II, 1,188 of them being Mk IXs. This particular example was the subject of an interesting local modification: its armament was removed and a second cockpit for an instructor added behind the first.

Though intended only as a hasty lash-up to get the two-stage (60 Series) Merlin into a Spitfire as soon as possible, the Mk IX continued in production until 5,665 had flown. This F.IX served with No. 402 Sqn, RCAF.

AE U BS428

 97 Elevator horn balance
 98 IFF aerial cable
 99 Tailplane rib construction
100 Elevator hinge control
101 Rudder control rod
102 Tailplane spar/fuselage frame attachment
103 Fuselage double frame
104 Non-retracting, castoring tailwheel
105 Tailwheel strut
106 Rudder control lever
107 Sloping tail assembly joint frame
108 Tailwheel shock absorber strut
109 Battery
110 Tail control cable runs
111 Fuselage bottom longeron
112 Wing root trailing edge fillet
113 Radio and electrical system ground socket
114 Trailing edge flap shroud ribs
115 Rear wing spar
116 Radiator shutter jack
117 Aileron cable runs
118 Gun heater air duct
119 Flap hydraulic jack
120 Flap synchronizing jack
121 Port split trailing-edge flap
122 Aileron control bellcrank
123 Aileron hinge control rod
124 Port aileron construction
125 Wing tip construction
126 Port navigation light
127 Wing lattice rib construction
128 Front spar
129 Browning 0.303-in (7.7-mm) machine-guns
130 Ammunition boxes (350 rounds per gun)
131 Machine-gun muzzle blast tubes
132 Machine-gun ports (patched)
133 Leading edge nose ribs
134 Ammunition box armour protection
135 Cannon ammunition box (120 rounds)
136 Port 20-mm Hispano cannon
137 Ammunition feed drum
138 Cannon wing fairing
139 Cannon barrel
140 'C'-wing outboard cannon muzzle fairing (blanked-off)
141 Recoil spring
142 Inboard leading edge lattice ribs
143 Main undercarriage wheel well
144 Oil radiator
145 Coolant radiator
146 Main undercarriage hydraulic jack
147 Retraction link
148 Wing spar/fuselage attachment joint
149 Oil pipe runs to radiator
150 Main undercarriage leg pivot fixing
151 Gun camera
152 Camera port
153 Jettisonable slipper tank, capacity 30, 45 or 90 Imp gal (136, 205 or 409 litres)
154 Mainwheel leg shock absorber
155 Undercarriage torque links
156 Port mainwheel
157 Mainwheel fairing door
158 Starboard mainwheel
159 Starboard wheel fairing door

43

Spitfire: Fighter Supreme

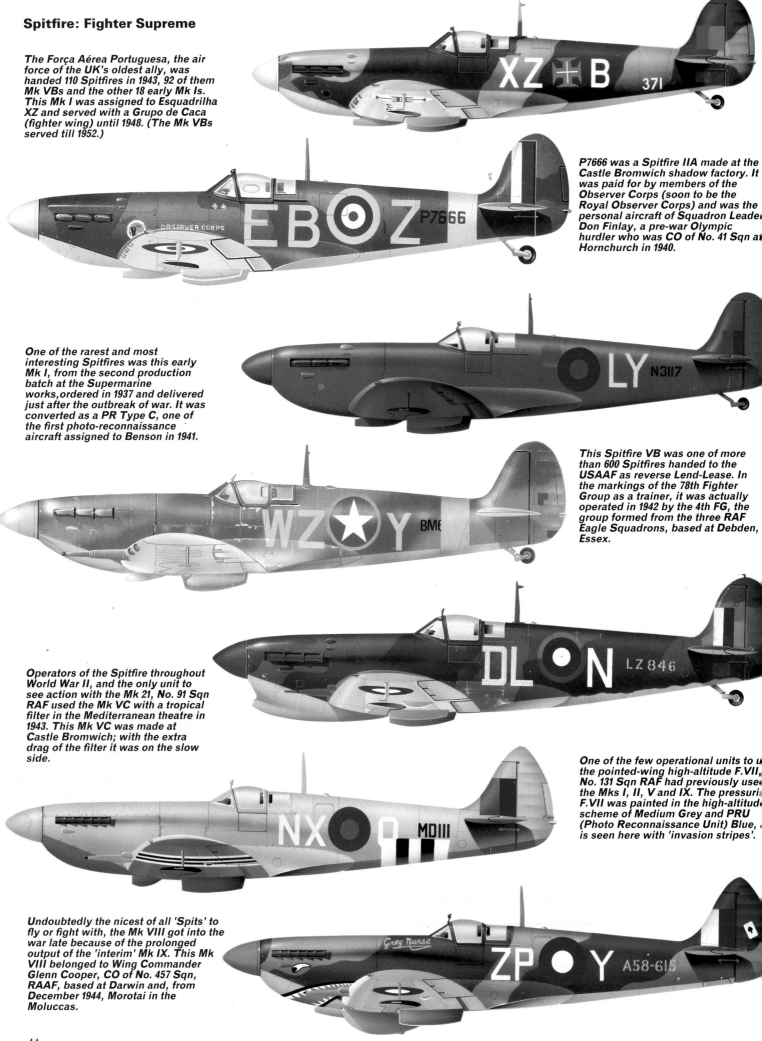

The Força Aérea Portuguesa, the air force of the UK's oldest ally, was handed 110 Spitfires in 1943, 92 of them Mk VBs and the other 18 early Mk Is. This Mk I was assigned to Esquadrilha XZ and served with a Grupo de Caca (fighter wing) until 1948. (The Mk VBs served till 1952.)

P7666 was a Spitfire IIA made at the Castle Bromwich shadow factory. It was paid for by members of the Observer Corps (soon to be the Royal Observer Corps) and was the personal aircraft of Squadron Leader Don Finlay, a pre-war Olympic hurdler who was CO of No. 41 Sqn at Hornchurch in 1940.

One of the rarest and most interesting Spitfires was this early Mk I, from the second production batch at the Supermarine works, ordered in 1937 and delivered just after the outbreak of war. It was converted as a PR Type C, one of the first photo-reconnaissance aircraft assigned to Benson in 1941.

This Spitfire VB was one of more than 600 Spitfires handed to the USAAF as reverse Lend-Lease. In the markings of the 78th Fighter Group as a trainer, it was actually operated in 1942 by the 4th FG, the group formed from the three RAF Eagle Squadrons, based at Debden, Essex.

Operators of the Spitfire throughout World War II, and the only unit to see action with the Mk 21, No. 91 Sqn RAF used the Mk VC with a tropical filter in the Mediterranean theatre in 1943. This Mk VC was made at Castle Bromwich; with the extra drag of the filter it was on the slow side.

One of the few operational units to use the pointed-wing high-altitude F.VII, No. 131 Sqn RAF had previously used the Mks I, II, V and IX. The pressurised F.VII was painted in the high-altitude scheme of Medium Grey and PRU (Photo Reconnaissance Unit) Blue, is seen here with 'invasion stripes'.

Undoubtedly the nicest of all 'Spits' to fly or fight with, the Mk VIII got into the war late because of the prolonged output of the 'interim' Mk IX. This Mk VIII belonged to Wing Commander Glenn Cooper, CO of No. 457 Sqn, RAAF, based at Darwin and, from December 1944, Morotai in the Moluccas.

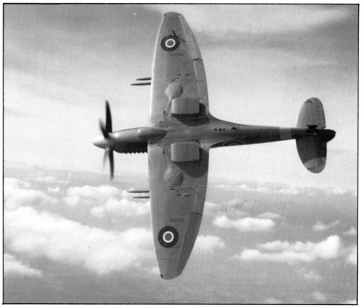

The prototype of the Spitfire 21 in flight. This last variant to enter service in World War II was powered by a Griffon 61 or 64 driving a Rotol five-blade propeller (though some examples had the Griffon 85 driving a six-blade contra-rotating propeller) and had a standard gun armament of four 20-mm Hispano cannon.

These so-called 'clipped-wing Spits' needed a slightly longer take-off and landing run and were poorer at high altitude, but at low level they were faster and even more agile. Manoeuvrability in the Mk V was in any case improved by the use of aluminium instead of fabric to skin the ailerons. No fewer than 6,479 Spitfire Vs were built, more than any other mark.

Photo-reconnaissance

A small proportion of the Mk Vs (229) were completed as photo-reconnaissance aircraft, and though this was confusing they were then designated PR.IV (there had already been the quite different Griffon-engined Mk IV). PR versions had the guns replaced by 302 litres (66½ Imp gal) of extra fuel in the leading edge of the wing. Two cameras were fitted in the rear fuselage, in a heated bay, taking photographs on either side of track with a small overlap in the centre. The pilot had extra oxygen and the engine a larger oil supply.

The Mk VI was the first high-altitude interceptor version, with a pressurised cockpit and pointed wingtips that increased span to 12.24 m (40 ft 2 in). Such aircraft were needed in 1941 to catch ultra-flying Junkers Ju 86P and 86R raiders, a problem which posed severe problems with extreme cold that iced up the windscreen and stopped guns working. An even more important advance in the high-altitude regime was being provided by Rolls-Royce with the 60-series of Merlin engines. These had two superchargers in series, with an intercooler to reduce the temperature of the air and thus increase its density still further. At altitudes of about 9145 m (30,000 ft) these engines gave twice the power of earlier Merlins, and when fitted to a Spitfire they were instantly distinguishable by a slightly longer nose, six instead of three exhaust stubs on each side, a four-blade propeller and symmetrical radiators, the oil cooler being joined by an extra cooling radiator on the left side. In combat none of these differences was obvious, so in 1942 the much more formidable Mk IX Spitfire was an unpleasant surprise that removed the previous advantage enjoyed by the Focke-Wulf Fw 190.

The definitive Spitfire VIII

The Mk IX was simply a Mk V with the new engine – in fact a hasty lash-up to get the Merlin 61 (later the 63, 66 or 70) into action quickly. The definitive model was the Mk VIII, a much better aircraft; yet the Mk IX was kept in production to the amazing total of

Deck handlers 'spot' Seafire IIC fighters at the stern of the flight deck of a Royal Navy fleet carrier in 1943. Right at the stern is a Fairey Albacore with wings folded. The Seafire IIC, the first mark built as such rather than converted from a Seafire, did not have folding wings but was a hooked Spitfire VC.

The ultimate Spitfires were the 20 series, powered by two-stage Griffon engines and featuring a much stronger wing with fully enclosed undercarriage (although this cavorting F.Mk 22 has its tailwheel doors still open). The wing finally lost the beautiful elliptical shape that had become the trademark of the wartime variants.

5,665 and was still being built in 1945! It came with a profusion of variations, including LF (9.88 m/32 ft 7 in), F (the regular 13½ m/36 ft 10 in) and HF (12.24 m/40 ft 2 in) wings, the three previous armamemt schemes plus an 'E' wing with two cannon and two 12.7-mm (0.5-in) guns, and bombs loads up to 454 kg (1,000 lb). Even more remarkably, when Spitfires were built with the American-made Packard V-1650 (Merlin 266) they were not the Mk VIII type but the lash-up Mk IX airframes, the result being designated Mk XVI. Large numbers of LF.XVIE with 'E' armament and clipped wings were used by the 2nd Tactical Air Force in 1945.

Only relatively small numbers were produced of the beautiful Mk VIII – in the opinion of most pilots, the nicest of all Spitfires to fly – and the Mk VII. The latter was a marriage of the two-stage Merlin

Spitfire: Fighter Supreme

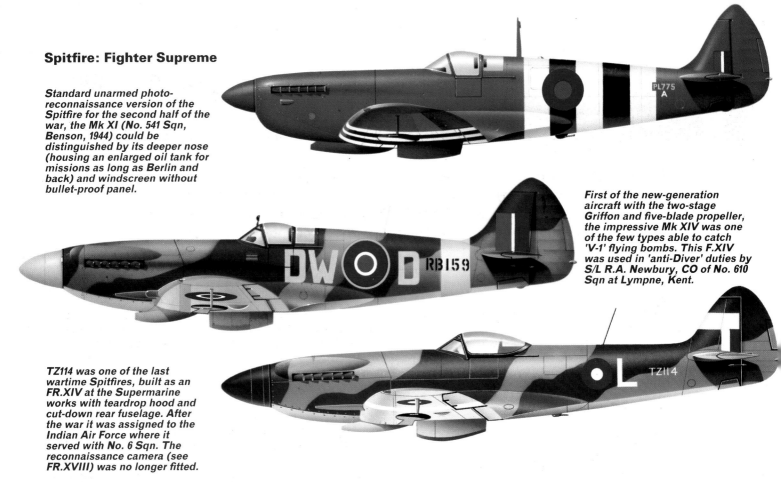

Standard unarmed photo-reconnaissance version of the Spitfire for the second half of the war, the Mk XI (No. 541 Sqn, Benson, 1944) could be distinguished by its deeper nose (housing an enlarged oil tank for missions as long as Berlin and back) and windscreen without bullet-proof panel.

First of the new-generation aircraft with the two-stage Griffon and five-blade propeller, the impressive Mk XIV was one of the few types able to catch 'V-1' flying bombs. This F.XIV was used in 'anti-Diver' duties by S/L R.A. Newbury, CO of No. 610 Sqn at Lympne, Kent.

TZ114 was one of the last wartime Spitfires, built as an FR.XIV at the Supermarine works with teardrop hood and cut-down rear fuselage. After the war it was assigned to the Indian Air Force where it served with No. 6 Sqn. The reconnaissance camera (see FR.XVIII) was no longer fitted.

engine with the pressurised cockpit of the Mk VI, with double-layer sealed canopy and a modified 'C' type wing with reduced-span ailerons. Some Mk VII aircraft had a broader rudder with pointed top, later made standard on Merlin 60-series aircraft, and another refinement was a retractable tailwheel. These were also features of the Mk VIII which in addition introduced a neat tropical filter, most of this type going to overseas theatres including the Pacific. The last of the Merlin Spitfires, the Mk XI, or PR.XI, was the most important Allied reconnaissance aircraft in the European theatre, being used by the RAF and USAAF on lone unarmed sorties from England to target areas as distant as Berlin. Most had the pointed rudder, and all a retractable tailwheel, but the one distinctive feature of this unarmed mark was the deep underside of the engine cowl, as a result of the oversize oil tank necessary on such long missions.

Apart from the original Mk IV, the first Spitfire with a Griffon engine was the Mk XII. The bigger engine resulted in a longer nose with bumps on top to accommodate the fronts of the cylinder blocks. The Mk XII was a hastily contrived low-level interceptor to catch Fw 190 hit-and-run raiders, and it reached almost 563 km/h (350 mph) at sea level, compared with 502 km/h (312 mph) for a Mk IX. A batch of 100, in two versions, was supplied to two RAF home-defence squadrons in 1942. They were totally unlike earlier Spitfires, notably in that on take-off they swung violently to the right instead of gently to the left, because the propeller rotated in the opposite direction. All had clipped wings, and some had retractable tailwheels.

More powerful engines

Predictably, Rolls-Royce fitted two-stage supercharging to the big Griffon and the result, the 65-series engine, was much more than twice as powerful as the original Merlin at all heights. It also made the Spitfire 0.91 m (3 ft) longer and gave it two deep radiators. This great engine was first used in the Mk XIV, which though to some extent a quick lash-up of 1943, was an outstanding aircraft in all respects. On the ground it could be distinguished, apart from the massive nose, by its five-blade propeller. This affected directional stability, so a larger vertical tail was fitted. Directional stability again became marginal in later F (fighter) and FR (fighter-reconnaissance, with rear-fuselage camera) versions which had a cut-down top to the rear fuselage and a beautiful teardrop, or 'bubble', canopy giving un-

interrupted view to the rear. The Mk XIV was the most important Spitfire in the final year of World War II. It was joined by a few of the definitive Mk XVIII version, but the Mk VIII/IX saga was repeated and only a few XVIIIs were built. Last of the Spitfires with the original basic wing was the PR.XIX, the two-stage Griffon successor to the PR.XI and the type used on the RAF's last Spitfire sortie in Malaya in 1954. Post-war arabic numerals were used for the surviving aircraft such as the LF.16, FR.18 and PR.19.

After World War II three generally similar models of Spitfire entered service with a new airframe which took full advantage of the power of the two-stage Griffon and was markedly heavier. The wing, no longer of simple curving (so-called elliptical) shape, was even stronger than before and carried four cannon, extra fuel and stronger landing gear covered by wing doors when retracted. The large tail had metal-skinned rudder and elevators and the systems were totally re-engineered. The first of this new family was the F.21, in production from September 1944; some had the Griffon 85 with a six-blade contra-rotating propeller. The F.22 introduced a teardrop canopy and (like the last F.21s) 24-volt electrics; late F.22s had a long-span tailplane and the new vertical tail of the Spiteful, and a rear-fuselage fuel tank whose use was prohibited on grounds of directional instability. The last mark of all, the F.24, had a usable rear tank, and minor changes such as rocket launchers and electrical gun-firing. The last of 20,334 Spitfires, an F.24, was delivered in February 1948.

To meet an urgent Fleet Air Arm need for a modern carrier-based fighter in 1941, Air Service Training produced a navalised Spitfire VB called the Seafire IB. At this time the FAA also had many earlier Seafires, produced by converting Spitfires already built. The chief wartime Seafire, the Mk III, was a navalised Mk VC with a Merlin 32 or 55 giving high power at low level via a four-blade propeller, and with manually folded wings; Westland (which made many Spitfires) and Cunliffe-Owen shared production. The single-stage Griffon powered the Seafire XV, a much more deadly machine, and the trim Mk XVII with teardrop canopy. After the war the powerful Mks 45, 46 and 47 brought the Spitfire/Seafire family to a close with aircraft weighing 5783 kg (12,750 lb) yet capable of impressive all-round performance fully demonstrated in the Korean war. Seafire production amounted to 2,556 excluding conversions.

Henschel Hs 129

The Hs 129's unremarkable design and average performance did little to change the German opinion that aircraft were of little use to ground troops. When its time came, against the massed Russian armour on the Eastern Front, it proved its credentials to spectacular effect. As a tank destroyer and attack aircraft it was, and still is, almost unrivalled.

The Henschel Hs 129 was the only aircraft of World War II – and, apart from today's A-10 virtually the only aircraft in all history – to be designed explicitly for destroying hostile armour. Apart from the Soviet Stormovik, which was a more versatile armoured attacker, the Allies had no aircraft in this class. All the RAF had were a few Hurricanes fitted with 40-mm guns, which by comparison were totally inadequate. Yet Hitler's Germany completely failed to foresee how crucially important the Hs 129 would become, and there were nothing like sufficient numbers to make much impact on the tide of Soviet armour in 1944-45.

When the infant Luftwaffe was laying its plans for the future in 1935 it was generally believed that aircraft could do little to influence a land battle. Aircraft in close proximity to hostile armies were clearly highly vulnerable. If they were heavily armoured they would be slow and sluggish, and their weapon load would be severely restricted. The effect of a few bullets or bombs seemed likely to be minimal, but in the Spanish Civil War of 1936-39 aircraft were seen to be not only effective but sometimes decisive (though against troops in unprepared positions). In April 1937 the Technische Amt issued a specification for a close support aircraft, to carry at least two 20-mm cannon and to have two low-powered engines and the smallest possible size, with armour and 75-mm glazing around the crew.

The finalists in the competition were Henschel, which proposed a neat single-seater, and Focke-Wulf, which scored because it suggested using a modified version of the Fw 189, which was already being built. The Fw 189 version was very much a compromise, but so was the rival Hs 129, the first prototype of which was flown in February or March 1939. Comparative testing was hampered by the fact that both aircraft were disastrous. They were sluggish in the extreme, and the Hs 129 had such a cramped cockpit that the engine instruments had to be mounted on the inner sides of the engine nacelles, and the control column was so short that great force was needed for even modest manoeuvres.

In the end, what tipped the scales in favour of the Hs 129 was that it was smaller and cost only about two-thirds as much as the Focke-Wulf rival. The decision was taken to go ahead with eight pre-production Hs 129A-0 aircraft, and these were all delivered by the time the Blitzkrieg was unleashed in Western Europe on 10 May 1940. They were put through prolonged trials and evaluation programmes and some later equipped the Schlachtflieger training staffel at Paris–Orly.

Basically, the Hs 129 was a completely conventional aircraft with a simple stressed-skin structure. The wing, with all the taper on the trailing edge, carried hydraulically driven slotted flaps, and was built as a centre-section integral with the fuselage and two bolted outer panels. The 343.8-kW (465-hp) Argus As 410A-1 aircooled inverted V-12 engines driving Argus automatic controllable-pitch propellers were almost identical to the installations used in the Fw 189, which was already in production. Fuel was housed in a single cell in the

Ground crew re-arm and refuel an Hs 129B-2/R2 of IV(Pz)/SG 9 at Czernovitz in March 1944. On the Eastern Front in winter aircraft were often daubed with white distemper over their regular camouflage for operations. This was soluble and easily washed off.

Henschel Hs 129

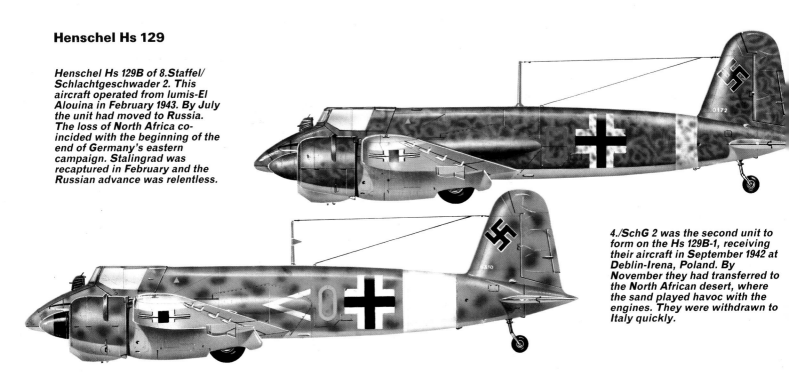

Henschel Hs 129B of 8.Staffel/Schlachtgeschwader 2. This aircraft operated from Iumis-El Alouina in February 1943. By July the unit had moved to Russia. The loss of North Africa coincided with the beginning of the end of Germany's eastern campaign. Stalingrad was recaptured in February and the Russian advance was relentless.

4./SchG 2 was the second unit to form on the Hs 129B-1, receiving their aircraft in September 1942 at Deblin-Irena, Poland. By November they had transferred to the North African desert, where the sand played havoc with the engines. They were withdrawn to Italy quickly.

fuselage and a tank in each wing inboard of the nacelles. The single-wheel main landing gears retracted backwards hydraulically, part of each wheel remaining exposed to avoid damage in a wheels-up landing.

Where the Hs 129 was unusual was that the fuselage was remarkably slim, with a triangular section (narrow at the top, broad at the bottom), with the front end in the form of a cramped cockpit surrounded by welded armour of 6-mm or 12-mm thickness, and with small panes of glass 75 mm thick. Total weight of the nose armour was 1080 kg (2,380 lb). As already noted, the great wish to minimise overall dimensions severely hampered the pilot's ability to fly a practical ground-attack mission, and for a large pilot made it almost impossible. On the other hand the aircraft did carry the required armament, there being one 20-mm MG FF cannon in each side of the fuselage (with a prominent blister fairing over the ammunition drum) superimposed over a 7.92-mm MG 17 machine-gun in the lower flank of each forward fuselage with the breech ahead of the wing spar.

It was obvious to Chief Engineer Dipl Ing Fr. Nicolaus that a much better aircraft could be built, using more powerful engines. His team accordingly prepared drawings for the P.76, a slightly larger aircraft

An Hs 129B-1/R2 being towed along a Libyan road near Tripoli in December 1942. 8./SchG 2 was the fifth staffel to get the Hs 129, formed from former JG 27 and JG 53 staff. Following a move to the Eastern Front, the unit was redesignated 13.(Pz)/SchG 9 in October 1943.

The Hs 129A-0 pre-production aircraft were powered by the Argus As 410-A-1 inline engine, which proved woefully underpowered. After disastrous service trials with 5./LG 2, the Hs 129As were relegated to a schlachtflieger training unit, 4./SG 101 at Paris-Orly.

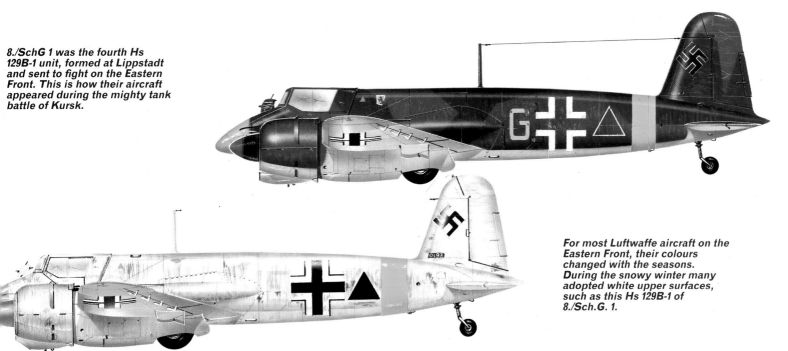

8./SchG 1 was the fourth Hs 129B-1 unit, formed at Lippstadt and sent to fight on the Eastern Front. This is how their aircraft appeared during the mighty tank battle of Kursk.

For most Luftwaffe aircraft on the Eastern Front, their colours changed with the seasons. During the snowy winter many adopted white upper surfaces, such as this Hs 129B-1 of 8./Sch.G. 1.

to be powered by two 522.0-kW (700-hp) Gnome-Rhône 14M radials, large numbers of which had become available following the defeat of France. It was decided, however, that too much time would be lost in tooling up for a bigger aircraft, and so the final compromise was merely to modify the existing Hs 129A to take the bigger and more powerful French radial engines. Remarkably few modifications were needed, but in one respect the resulting Hs 129B did incorporate a major improvement. The cockpit was modified with large slabs of armour glass to give much better vision, though possibly at the expense of slight increase in vulnerability. The French engines were installed very much in the way used in existing French aircraft, driving three-bladed Ratier electrically controlled constant-speed propellers.

Into the limelight

Overall, the Hs 129B was a great improvement, though it was still a poor performer. It was slower than the Ju 87D, had a much shorter range and was nothing like so agile or pleasant to fly, despite continual tinkering with the flight controls which resulted in the addition of fast-acting electric trim tabs.

After the invasion of the Soviet Union in June 1941 it rather suddenly became evident that the Hs 129 was in principle an aircraft of great importance. In Poland and France the little Hs 123, despite the fact that it was an obsolescent biplane of very limited capability, had

demonstrated what the General Staff had previously been reluctant to believe: that aircraft could play a valuable, and even crucial, role in land battles. So the Hs 129B was put into immediate production with high priority. A late change was to replace the MG FF cannon by the much harder-hitting MG 151, occasionally in the high-velocity 15-mm form but usually in 20-mm calibre, with 125 rounds each (the bulges on each side of the fuselage were retained). Provision was also made for the addition of various field modification kits to add specialised weapons or equipment, normally hung either beneath the fuselage or under each outer wing.

The first pre-production Hs 129B-0 was delivered at the end of 1941, but Henschel suffered many severe problems and delays which seriously held back the build-up of the planned Schlachtgeschwader force. Modifications were continually having to be introduced to rectify faults, equipment and parts were late on delivery, and the planned output of 40 per month was not attained until mid-1943. By far the biggest single problem was the engine, which showed itself to be severely intolerant of either dust on the Eastern Front or, worse, sand in North Africa. Its reliability was extremely poor, and despite the most urgent investigations it took six months to find any sort of

The trailing-edge taper of the Hs 129 was a characteristic feature. Rustsätz conversions for the B-1 included the R2 (one 30-mm MK 101 cannon in ventral pack), R3 (four uncowled 7.9-mm MG 17 machine-guns under fuselage), R4 (bomb racks) and R5 (internal reconnaissance camera).

This Hs 129B-1 is seen in RAF colours after capture. On either side of the nose were mounted MG 17 7-9-mm machine-gun (lower) and a MG 151 20-mm cannon (upper). The machine-gun had 500 rounds per gun in the fuselage, while the cannon had only 125.

real cure. The first staffel, 4/Sch.G.1, had a most depressing experience in the push for the Caucasus in mid-1942, while at the end of the year the next unit, 4/Sch.G.2, suffered a series of disasters in North Africa and was eventually evacuated with no aircraft.

During 1943 the tempo of Hs 129B effort increased greatly, but difficulties in production and high attrition made the actual build-up of Sch.G. units a frustrating process. On the other hand, the combat effectiveness of the aircraft increased considerably with the fitting of the modification kits, most notably the addition of a huge 30-mm MK 101 gun under the fuselage, with 30 shells. This had lethal effect against all armoured vehicles except main battle tanks, and even these were sometimes vulnerable when attacked from the rear. Other add-on loads included an internal camera, a battery of four MG 17 machine-guns or various loads of small bombs, especially boxes of 4-kg (8.8-lb) SD4 hollow-charge bomblets which had considerable armour-penetration capabilities.

Production gave way to the Hs 129B-2/Wa, the suffix (Waffenträger) meaning that the very powerful MK 103 gun was fitted not as a field modification but at the factory. The MK 103 had greater anti-

tank effectiveness. As an alternative some aircraft were fitted with a BK 3,7, as used on the very effective Ju 87G. This gun necessitated removal of the MG 17 machine-guns in order to accommodate its ammunition. (Of course, whereas the Ju 87G had carried two of the 37-mm guns, the Hs 129B-2 carried only one.)

The massive build-up in Soviet strength with thick-skinned tanks contrasted with the faltering strength of the Sch.G. units, which continued to be afflicted by poor engine reliability despite the addition of properly designed air filters. The over-riding need was for more powerful anti-armour weapons, and on 10 January 1944 a special unit, Erprobungskommando 26, was formed at Udetfeld out of previous Sch.G. units to centralise the desperate effort to devise new weapons and tactics. Its Hs 129s soon appeared with various new armament, some of which were patently too much for what was, after all, a small aircraft.

The outstanding example of the new weapons was the radically different Förstersonde SG 113A. This comprised a giant tube rather like a ship's funnel in the centre fuselage just behind the fuselage tank. Inside this were fitted six smooth-bore tubes, each 1.6 m (5 ft 3 in) long and of 77-mm calibre. The tubes were arranged to fire down and slightly to the rear, and were triggered as a single group by a photocell sensitive to the passage of a tank close beneath. Inside

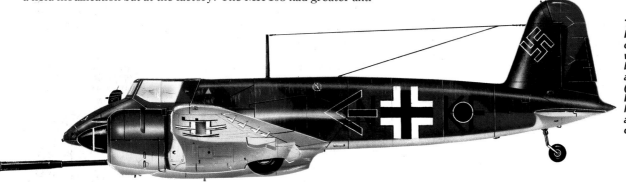

Two units received the Hs 129B-3/Wa for operational use in the winter of 1944/45, these being 10. (Pz)/SchG 9 and 14. (Pz)/SchG 9 (illustrated). With the PaK-40 fitted, the two MG 17s were removed and the trough faired over.

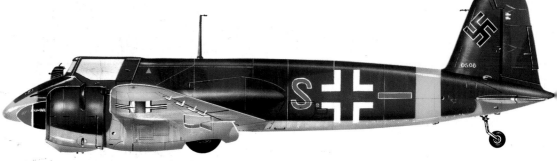

Standard colour scheme for the Eastern Front was a dark splinter camouflage on the upper surfaces and pale blue underneath. Yellow theatre markings were carried on the rear fuselage, wingtip and nose. The excrescence on the nose was the Revi C 12/C gunset, offset to starboard.

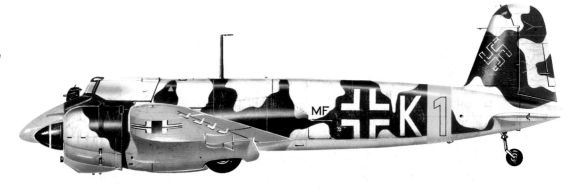

Hs 129B-2/R2 of IV (Pz)/SchG 9 in temporary winter markings. The B-2 incorporated various improvements over the B-1, mostly as a result of combat experience. As the Soviet tank armies grew larger, so the R2 30-mm cannon became standard factory fit.

each tube was a combined device consisting of a 45-mm armour-piercing shell (with a small high-explosive charge) pointing downwards and a heavy steel cylinder of full calibre pointing upwards. Between the two was the propellant charge, with a weak tie link down the centre to joint the parts together. When the SG 113A was fired, the shells were driven down by their driving sabots at high velocity, while the steel slugs were fired out of the top of each tube to cancel the recoil. Unfortunately, trials at Tarnewitz Waffenprüfplatz showed that the photocell system often failed to pick out correct targets.

Tank destroyer

Another impressive weapon was the huge PaK 40 anti-tank gun of 75-mm calibre. This gun weighed 1500 kg (3,306 lb) in its original ground-based form, and fired a 3.2-kg (7-lb) tungsten-carbide cored projectile at 933 m/sec (3,060 ft/sec). Even at 1000 m (3,280 ft) range the shell could penetrate 133 mm of armour if it hit square-on. Modified as the PaK 40L the gun had a much bigger muzzle brake to reduce recoil and electro-pneumatic operation to feed successive shells automatically. Installed in the Hs 129B-3/Wa the giant gun was provided with 26 rounds which could be fired at the cyclic rate of 40 rounds per minute, so that three or four could be fired on a single pass. Almost always, a single good hit would destroy a tank, even from head-on. The main problem was that the PaK 40L was too powerful a gun for the aircraft. Quite apart from the severe muzzle blast and recoil, the sheer weight of the gun made the Hs 129B-3/Wa almost unmanageable, and in emergency the pilot could sever the gun's attachments and let it drop.

In late September 1944 the entire manufacturing programme was abandoned, along with virtually all other German aircraft except for the 'emergency fighter programme'. Total production had amounted to only 870, including prototypes. Because of attrition and other problems the Hs 129 was never able to equip the giant anti-tank force that could be seen to be needed as early as winter 1941-42, and its overall effect on the war was not great. Towards the end, in autumn 1944, operations began to be further restricted by shortage of high-octane petrol, and by the final collapse only a handful of these aircraft remained.

In order to provide a hard-hitting weapon against Soviet tanks, the Hs 129B-3/Wa was evolved, with a 75-mm Panzerabwehrkanone-40 in a large ventral fairing. Performance and agility were drastically reduced, although one shot could knock out the biggest Soviet tank.

The Hs 129B equipped the three staffeln of the 8th Assault Wing of the Royal Romanian Air Corps. On 23 August 1944 there was a coup in Romania, as a result of which the country changed from being an ally of Germany to being an enemy. These Hs 129Bs accordingly were used against the German armies, finally being combined into a unit equipped with the Ju 87D.

There were plans for a supposedly improved Hs 129C, but this was never built. It would have been powered by 626.8-kW (840-hp) Isotta-Fraschini Delta IV inverted V-12 engines, giving improved performance, and would normally have carried twin Mk 103 guns mounted in a kind of turret beneath the fuselage with a small amount of traverse under pilot control. This version was abandoned because of non-availability of the Italian engines.

The angular yet sturdy lines of the Hs 129B are illustrated here by this aircraft captured in North Africa. It was shipped to the United States for evaluation, wearing the 'Foreign Equipment' registration 'FE-4600'. The white fuselage band denoted the Mediterranean theatre.

Henschel Hs 129

Specification
Henschel Hs 129B-2

Type: single-seat close support aircraft

Powerplant: two Gnome-Rhône 14M 4/5 radial engines developing 522 kW (700 hp) for take-off

Dimensions: wing span 14.2 m (46 ft 5 in); length 9.75 m (31 ft 9 in); height 3.25 m (10 ft 6 in); wing area 29 m² (312 sq ft)

Weights: empty 3810 kg (8,400 lb); maximum loaded 5250 kg (11,574 lb)

Performance: maximum speed 407 km/h (253 mph); range 688 km (427 miles); initial climb rate 486 m/min (1,600 ft/min); service ceiling 9000 m (29,530 ft)

Armament: two 7.9-mm MG 17 machine-guns and two 20-mm MG 151 cannon in nose; either one 30-mm MK 101 cannon in ventral pod, four MG 17 machine-guns, four 50-kg (110-lb) bombs, 92 2-kg (4.4-lb) anti-personnel bombs or one 250-kg bomb beneath fuselage; two 50-kg (110-lb) bombs or 48 2-kg (4.4-lb) anti-personnel bombs on wing racks

The Henschel Hs 129 is best remembered in its Hs 129B-3/Wa form, carrying the PaK-40 75-mm anti-tank cannon. However, most of its work was performed with weapons of a much smaller calibre. This is a typical Eastern Front aircraft, a B-2 with the centreline 30-mm MK 101 cannon fairing, in addition to the internal MG 17 machine-guns and MG 151 cannon. Small racks on the wings could carry small bombs for use against personnel or vehicles. After an inauspicious start to its life, dogged by reliability problems with the engines, the Hs 129 did achieve some success in the later months of the war.

Nakajima Ki-84 Hayate

Undoubtedly the best Japanese fighter to see large-scale service during the final year of the Pacific war, the Ki-84 Hayate was as feared by Allied aircrews as it was praised by Japanese pilots. Well protected, adequately armed, fast and manoeuvrable, this fighter gave a good account of itself in the desperate battles of 1944 and 1945.

Long after fighter pilots in Europe and America had recognised the importance of armour, fuel tank protection and heavy armament, their Japanese counterparts still insisted on extreme manoeuvrability at the expense of these items. The Koku Hombu (Air Headquarters) of the Imperial Japanese Army had, however, realised the need for those items considered unnecessary and too heavy by the aircrews. Accordingly, in 1940 it had initiated the development of a successor to the Nakajima Ki-43, a lightly armed and unprotected fighter about to be placed in production. The newer type was to be an adequately armed all-purpose fighter with limited armour and fuel tank protection, and was intended to be powered by the Kawasaki Ha-40 liquid-cooled engine, a licence-built version of the German-designed Daimler-Benz DB 601A. To fulfil this requirement, two competitive designs were undertaken by Kawasaki Kokuki Kogyo KK (Kawasaki Aircraft Engineering Co. Ltd) and Nakajima Hikoki KK (Nakajima Aeroplane Co. Ltd). As Kawasaki had greater experience with aircraft powered by liquid-cooled engines, and as Nakajima was already fully occupied with the production of its Ki-43 and Ki-44 fighters, it was the former's Ki-61 which was retained for further development and eventual production.

Even though its Ki-62 had lost the competition for Ha-40-powered fighters, the design team led by T. Koyama had gained valuable experience from the preliminary engineering of the Ki-62 and Ki-63, the latter being a proposed version to be powered by a 783-kW (1,050-hp) Mitsubishi Ha-102 radial. Koyama and his team were thus well prepared to submit a design in answer to a specification issued early in 1942 by the Koku Hombu. This specification called for an all-purpose, long-range fighter with a top speed of 640/680 km/h (398/423 mph) and capable of operating at combat rating for 1 hour 30 minutes at 400 km (250 miles) from base. A wing area of 19 to 21 m^2 (204.5 to 226 sq ft) and wing loading not exceeding 170 kg/m^2 (34.8 lb/sq ft) were recommended. Power was to be supplied by a

Nakajima Ha-45, a version of the NK9A Homare (honour) 18-cylinder radial being developed for the Imperial Japanese Navy, and the specified armament was to comprise two 12.7-mm (0.5-in) Type 1 (Ho-103) machine-guns and two 20-mm Ho-5 cannon. In a marked departure from prior requirements for army fighters, the aircraft was to incorporate provision for armour and self-sealing fuel tanks.

Drawing heavily on the preliminary design of the Ki-62 and Ki-63, the prototype of the new Ki-84 fighter was designed and built in 10 months, roll-out taking place at the end of March 1943. Of low-wing monoplane configuration, with conventional retractable landing gear and a three-piece canopy with rearward-sliding centre section, the Ki-84 flew for the first time from Ojima airfield in April 1943; two months later it was joined in the manufacturer's flight trial programme by a second prototype.

Powerplant improvements

Tests and preliminary service evaluation proceeded rapidly and smoothly, with few modifications required to prepare the aircraft for mass production. Several changes and improvements, as well as several versions of its powerplant (1342 kW/1,800 hp Ha-45-11, 1361 kW/1,825 hp Ha-45-12 and 1417 kW/1,900 hp Ha-45-21), were evaluated on Ki-84s from the large batch of service trials aircraft which were largely hand-built as Nakajima had not yet set up the required tooling. Few of these changes, however, were adopted for the production aircraft. The only significant ones to be incorporated on the assembly lines were the provision for two underwing drop tanks in place of the single ventral tank initially used, minor alterations of the shape and area of the vertical tail surfaces to improve

Nakajima Ki-84-Ias of the 101st Sentai prepare for take-off during the defence of Okinawa. Formed in the latter part of 1944 with the 102nd Sentai, the unit had particular success in attacks, both day and night, on American airfields in northern Okinawa.

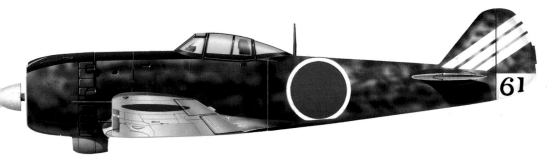

Formed in June 1944 alongside the 71st and 72nd Sentais, the 73rd Hiko Sentai was immediately assigned to defence duties in the Philippines, this theatre of operations receiving priority in Ki-84 distribution at the time. Illustrated is a Ki-84-Ia operated by the 73rd's 1st Chutai.

control on take-off as the aircraft suffered from propeller-induced torque, and the replacement of the two large exhaust collector pipes (one on each side of the cowling) by individual ejector exhaust stubs.

Service pilots, who by then had realised the need for armour, self-sealing tanks, and heavy armament, criticised only the heaviness of the elevators at high speeds and the mushiness of the rudder at low speeds. These, however, were minor complaints on an otherwise highly capable machine. Accordingly, as soon as Nakajima were able to make room in their Nos. 1 and 4 airframe plants at Ota and Utsono-miya respectively, the aircraft was placed in quantity production under the designation Army Type 4 Fighter Model 1A (Ki-84-Ia). In addition, Ki-84-Is were to be built by Mansyu Hikoki Seizo KK (Manchurian Aeroplane Manufacturing Co. Ltd) in Harbin, Manchu-kuo. It was named Hayate (hurricane).

Production under stress

Requiring 44 per cent less tooling than the lighter Ki-43 fighter, the Ki-84 was built in large numbers, with Nakajima delivering 3,288 production Ki-84s between April 1944 and mid-August 1945, and Mansyu adding 94 aircraft during 1945. These impressive production numbers do not reflect the great difficulties experienced by the Munitions Ministry and the contractors in implementing this ambitious programme: an insufficient number of skilled workers, aggravated by the drafting of civilian employees without regard to skills or to industry requirements, and the shortage of raw materials and poor standards of metallurgy, played havoc with the programme. Quality control, particularly in the manufacture of engines and specialised equipment (landing gear, radio, etc), resulted in poor serviceability and numerous accidents. Even when not involved in accidents, the performance and reliability of production Ki-84s seldom matched those of the hand-built service trials machines. Moreover, in service these problems were magnified by the paucity of trained maintenance personnel and by the need to service the aircraft under primitive and often dangerous conditions. For the Allies, however, this was a fortunate turn of events as, immediately upon entering service, the Hayate had proved to be a potent foe with performance closely matching that of the most advanced Allied aircraft (Chance Vought F4U, Lockheed P-38J/L, Republic P-47D, North American P-51D) and superior to such important types as the Grum-man F6F Hellcat then equipping most US Navy carrier-based fighter squadrons.

The large number of service trials and pre-production aircraft which had been ordered enabled manufacturers' and service tests to proceed rapidly, with Ki-84s becoming available to form a service evaluation *chutai* (squadron) in October 1943, a mere six months after the prototype's maiden flight. However, another six months were required to set up the assembly lines, and the first Ki-84-Ia built with production tooling was not completed by Nakajima until April 1944. From then on the production rate was stepped up, with monthly deliveries going from 54 Ki-84-Is in April 1944 to a peak of 373 in December of that year, and averaging 200 aircraft per month.

The availability in quantity of the superlative Hayate came none too soon for the hard-pressed fighter *sentais* (regiments or groups) of the Imperial Japanese Army as, except on the Chinese front, they had lost the initiative. Moreover, their Kawasaki Ki-61s, Nakajima Ki-43s and Nakajima Ki-44s were no longer superior to most types of fighter aircraft by then fielded by the Allies.

The Hayate made its operational debut in March 1944 when the 22nd Sentai, flying a mix of Ki-84-Ia and Nakajima Ki-44-II fighters from Hankow, supported a Japanese ground offensive. Opposed mainly by obsolescent Curtiss P-40s flown by American and Chinese pilots, the 22nd Sentai pilots did much to establish the Hayate as a formidable foe possessing most of the virtues and few of the vices of earlier Japanese fighters. However, within five weeks of their debut, the Ki-84s of the 22nd Sentai had to be transferred to the Philippines where the next Allied offensive was anticipated to take place.

The Philippines campaign

During the eight-month Philippines campaign, which began on 20 October 1944, with American landings at Tacloban and Dulag on Leyte, 11 *sentais* (the 1st, 11th, 22nd, 29th, 50th, 51st, 52nd, 71st, 72nd, 73rd and 200th) equipped with Ki-84s fought desperately in an effort to halt the Allied offensive. However, the Japanese forces were now on the defensive and their air units were operating under exacting conditions. Unfortunately for them, the outnumbered Hayates, which as a result of inferior workmanship often suffered from failures of fuel pressure and hydraulic systems, and from weak landing-gear struts, could not do enough to alter the course of events. The situation repeated itself when the 47th, 52nd, 101st and 102nd Sentais were thrown in to repulse the American assault on Okinawa in April 1945. Even on the Asian mainland, where the Ki-84 (known to the Allies by the codename 'Frank') had first operated with success, the 13th, 25th, 64th, 85th and 104th Sentais were ineffective as by then their Hayates were opposed by numerically superior Allied fighters such as P-38J/Ls, P-47Ds and P-51Ds. The same fate befell the 20th Sentai, which flew Ki-84s from Formosa.

In the Japanese home islands, Hayates fared well in combat against the long-range P-47Ns and P-51Ds operating from Iwo Jima, and against the carrier-based aircraft of the US and British fleets. Against the high-flying Boeing B-29s, however, they were far from effective as their Ha-45 engine did not endow them with the necessary high-altitude performance.

The need to produce the maximum number of aircraft, to re-equip as many *sentais* as possible and to make up operational and combat attrition in already established units, had meant that only limited priority was given by the Koku Hombu and the Ministry of Munitions to the development of more-advanced versions. Whatever efforts could be spared were directed towards three development objec-

One of the initial batch of 83 pre-production Ki-84 Hayates photographed in August 1943 at Tachikawa, where it was operated by the Army Air Arsenal as a service trials aircraft. Pilot reaction to the new type was, in general, extremely positive.

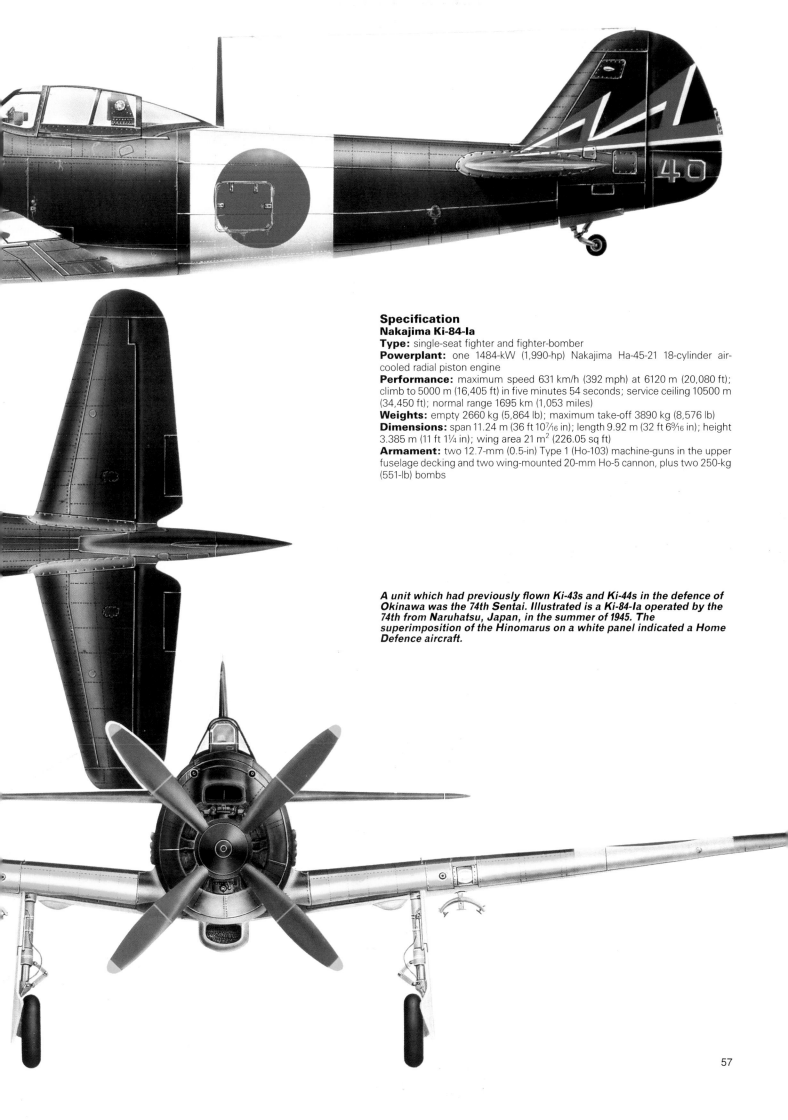

Specification
Nakajima Ki-84-Ia

Type: single-seat fighter and fighter-bomber

Powerplant: one 1484-kW (1,990-hp) Nakajima Ha-45-21 18-cylinder air-cooled radial piston engine

Performance: maximum speed 631 km/h (392 mph) at 6120 m (20,080 ft); climb to 5000 m (16,405 ft) in five minutes 54 seconds; service ceiling 10500 m (34,450 ft); normal range 1695 km (1,053 miles)

Weights: empty 2660 kg (5,864 lb); maximum take-off 3890 kg (8,576 lb)

Dimensions: span 11.24 m (36 ft 10$\frac{7}{16}$ in); length 9.92 m (32 ft 6$\frac{9}{16}$ in); height 3.385 m (11 ft 1$\frac{1}{4}$ in); wing area 21 m^2 (226.05 sq ft)

Armament: two 12.7-mm (0.5-in) Type 1 (Ho-103) machine-guns in the upper fuselage decking and two wing-mounted 20-mm Ho-5 cannon, plus two 250-kg (551-lb) bombs

A unit which had previously flown Ki-43s and Ki-44s in the defence of Okinawa was the 74th Sentai. Illustrated is a Ki-84-Ia operated by the 74th from Naruhatsu, Japan, in the summer of 1945. The superimposition of the Hinomarus on a white panel indicated a Home Defence aircraft.

Nakajima Ki-84 variants

Ki-84: two prototypes, 83 service trials aircraft and 42 pre-production aircraft; the two prototypes and the service trials aeroplanes were mostly hand-built and were used to test different features (e.g. longer wing span, various models of the Ha-45 engine, etc), whereas the pre-production aircraft were built with production tooling to common standards; 1342-kW (1,800-hp) Nakajima Ha-45-11 radial engine driving a four-bladed constant-speed propeller, but some aircraft were powered by a 1361-kW (1,825-hp) Ha-45-12 or 1484-kW (1,990-hp) Ha-45-21 engine; a ventral drop tank was initially used but gave place to two wing drop tanks; two fuselage-mounted 12.7-mm (0.5-in) Ho-103 machine-guns and two wing-mounted 20-mm Ho-5 cannon

Ki-84-Ia, Ki-84-Ib and Ki-84-Ic: all improvements progressively introduced on the service trials and pre-production aircraft were incorporated on this first production model built by Nakajima Hikoki KK at Ota and Utsunomiya and by Mansyu Hikoki KK at Harbin, Manchuria; the three Ha-45 models as fitted to the experimental aircraft were initially used for these production aircraft, the Ha-45-12, and later the Ha-45-21, being standardised during the course of production; a few aircraft were powered by the more reliable 1417-kW (1,900-hp) Ha-45-23 engine; the Ki-84-Ib differed from the Ki-84-Ia in being armed with four 20-mm cannon (with two Ho-5 cannon replacing the fuselage-mounted Ho-103 machine-guns), whereas the Ki-84-Ic, built as a bomber-destroyer, had two fuselage-mounted 20-mm Ho-5 cannon and two wing-mounted 30-mm Ho-105 cannon; some aircraft had their radio equipment removed and a jump seat installed aft of the pilot's seat to be used for familiarisation flights

Ki-84-II: built in relatively small numbers, this version differed from the Ki-84-Ia in being fitted with wooden rear fuselage and wingtips built in Nakajima's Tabuma shadow factory; powered by 1417-kW (1,900-hp) Ha-45-23 or 1491-kW (2,000-hp) Ha-45-25 engines

Ki-84-III: projected version to be powered by a Ha-45 Ru engine with a turbosupercharger mounted in the fuselage belly

Ki-84N, Ki-84P and Ki-84R: preliminary design designations given to projected developments of the Hayate; the first two were to have been powered by the 1864-kW (2,500-hp) Nakajima Ha-44-13 18-cylinder radial and were to have been fitted with enlarged wing with an area of 22.5 m² (242.2 sq ft) and 24.5 m² (263.7 sq ft) respectively; the Ki-84R, a prototype which was 80 per cent complete at war's end, retained the standard airframe but was powered by a 1491-kW (2,000-hp) Ha-45-44 with a mechanically-driven two-stage three-speed supercharger

Ki-106: version designed by Tachikawa Hikoki KK and featuring an all-wood airframe; three prototypes were built in 1945 but the planned production could not proceed before the surrender; armament was to have consisted of either two or four 20-mm cannon

Ki-113: designation given to a prototype partially built of steel, carbon steel for the cockpit section, ribs and bulkheads and steel sheet skinning; powered by an Ha-45-21; aircraft built by Nakajima in early 1945 but did not fly as it was decidedly overweight

Ki-116: one prototype built by Mansyu Hikoki Seizo KK; airframe similar to that of the Ki-84-Ia but powered by a 1119-kW (1,500-hp) Mitsubishi Ha-33-62 14-cylinder radial engine driving a three-bladed propeller

Ki-117: projected production version of the Ki-84N

With the aim and intention of replacing certain parts of the airframe with wooden components, the Ki-106 evolved into a complete wooden airframe project, but by the time the first prototype flew, interest in the project had waned.

Nakajima Ki-84-Ia Hayate cutaway drawing key

1 Starter dog
2 Spinner
3 Constant-speed electrically-operated Pe-32 propeller
4 Propeller reduction gear housing
5 Carburettor air intake
6 Starboard 20-mm Ho-5 cannon muzzle
7 Gun camera port
8 Starboard leading-edge fuel tank (14.7 Imp gal/67 litre capacity)
9 Mainspar
10 Starboard navigation light
11 Starboard wingtip
12 Fabric-covered aileron
13 Aileron control link fairing
14 Aileron trim tab
15 Flap track extension fairing
16 Starboard Fowler-type flap
17 Wing cannon ammunition box access
18 Wing cannon access covers
19 Carburettor intake trunking
20 Machine-gun blast tube
21 Machine-gun trough
22 Army Type 4 Model 21 (Nakajima Ha-45-21) 18-cylinder radial air-cooled engine
23 Cowling fasteners
24 Aluminium cylinder fans
25 Oil cooler intake
26 Starboard mainwheel
27 Oil cooler housing
28 Ejector exhaust stubs
29 Cowling gills
30 Engine bearers
31 Oil tank (11 Imp gal/50 litre capacity)

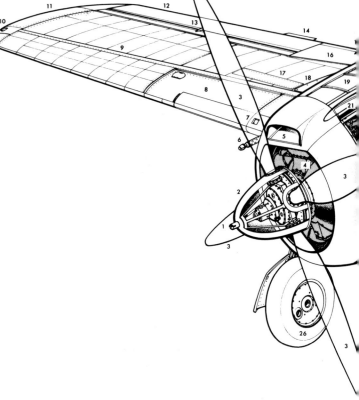

Originally operated by the 2nd Chutai of the 11th Sentai, this Ki-84-Ia was flight-tested by the US Technical Air Intelligence Command in the Philippines and later in the USA. Rebuilt in 1963, it returned to its homeland in 1973.

32 Vent
33 Gun cooling muffle
34 Firewall/bulkhead
35 Ho-103 machine-gun (two) of 13-mm calibre
36 Main fuel tank (47.7 Imp gal/217 litre capacity)
37 Port ammunition tank (350 rounds)
38 Fuel filler cap
39 Rudder pedals
40 Control column
41 Instrument panel
42 Fuselage flush-riveted stressed-skin panels
43 Reflector sight (offset to starboard)
44 Armourglass (65-mm) windscreen
45 Aft-sliding cockpit canopy
46 Canopy lock/release
47 Pilot's headrest
48 Pilot's head armour/turnover support
49 Canopy fixed aft glazing
50 Canopy track
51 Entry handgrip
52 Pilot's 13-mm back armour
53 Elevator trim handwheel
54 Pilot's seat (adjustable vertically)
55 Throttle quadrant
56 Flap setting lever
57 Undercarriage selector lever

58 Underfloor control runs
59 Flap-rod linkage
60 Water-methanol tank
61 Mid-fuselage construction break
62 Radio equipment tray
63 Type 4 Hi no.3 radio communications pack
64 Aerial lead-in
65 Aerial mast
66 Aerials
67 Light alloy semi-monocoque fuselage structure
68 Fuselage upper longeron
69 Oval section fuselage aft frames
70 Aft fuselage construction break
71 Starboard tailplane
72 Elevator balance
73 Starboard elevator (fabric covered)
74 Elevator trim tab
75 Tailfin leading edge

76 Tailfin structure
77 Rear navigation/formation light
78 Aerial stub attachment
79 Rudder upper hinge
80 Rudder frame (fabric covered)
81 Rudder trim tab
82 Rudder centre hinge
83 Rudder lower section
84 Elevator trim tab
85 Elevator frame (fabric covered)
86 Tailplane structure
87 Tailwheel doors
88 Solid rubber tyre
89 Aft-retracting tailwheel

90 Fuselage lower longeron
91 Tail surface control cables
92 Oxygen cylinders
93 Radio access
94 Retractable entry step
95 Wing root fairing
96 Fairing former
97 Port main wing tank (40 Imp gal/173 litre capacity)

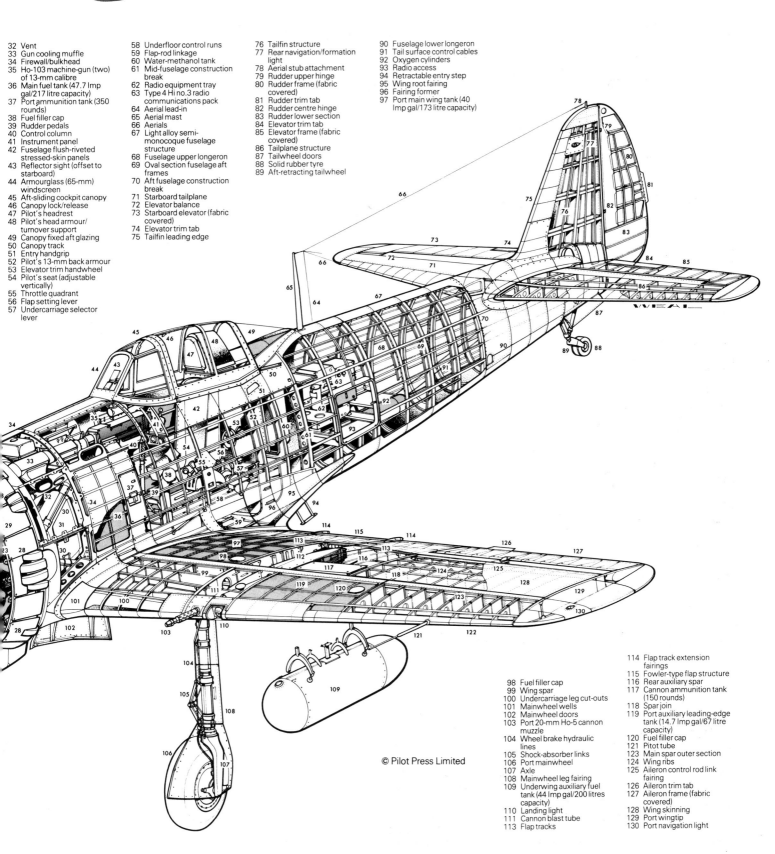

© Pilot Press Limited

98 Fuel filler cap
99 Wing spar
100 Undercarriage leg cut-outs
101 Mainwheel wells
102 Mainwheel doors
103 Port 20-mm Ho-5 cannon muzzle
104 Wheel brake hydraulic lines
105 Shock-absorber links
106 Port mainwheel
107 Axle
108 Mainwheel leg fairing
109 Underwing auxiliary fuel tank (44 Imp gal/200 litres capacity)
110 Landing light
111 Cannon blast tube
113 Flap tracks

114 Flap track extension fairings
115 Fowler-type flap structure
116 Rear auxiliary spar
117 Cannon ammunition tank (150 rounds)
118 Spar join
119 Port auxiliary leading-edge tank (14.7 Imp gal/67 litre capacity)
120 Fuel filler cap
121 Pitot tube
123 Main spar outer section
124 Wing ribs
125 Aileron control rod link fairing
126 Aileron trim tab
127 Aileron frame (fabric covered)
128 Wing skinning
129 Port wingtip
130 Port navigation light

Nakajima Ki-84 Hayate

A Ki-84-Ia in the markings of the 1st Chutai of the 102nd Hiko Sentai operating from Kyushu, Japan, in April 1945. Formed in late 1944 for the defence of Okinawa, the 102nd was kept extremely active by the air units supporting the American invasion.

With the majority of Ki-84s wearing variations on the mottled camouflage scheme, the natural metal finish on this Ki-84-Ia may appear conspicuous, but it was widely used in the final stages of the Pacific conflict. The 29th Sentai fin emblem was a stylised breaking wave, the cobalt blue colour indicating a Sentai Hombu aircraft.

tives. Firstly, there was a need to reduce the use of alloys which were available only in limited quantities. Accordingly, a few Ki-84-II Hayate Kai aircraft, embodying wooden rear fuselage, certain fittings and modified wingtips, were built by Nakajima; three prototypes of the Ki-106, an all-wood version of the Ki-84-Ia, were produced by Tachikawa Hikoki KK (Tachikawa Aeroplane Co. Ltd); and Nakajima completed, but did not fly, a Ki-113 prototype partially built of steel. Secondly, following heavy bombing of the Musashi plant in which Nakajima produced the Ha-45 engine, it became necessary to find a substitute powerplant for the Hayate. To that end, Mansyu lightened and modified its fourth Ki-84-Ia airframe to take a 1119-kW (1,500-hp) Mitsubishi Ha-33-62 engine; designated Ki-116, the modified aircraft was undergoing tests at the time of Japan's defeat.

The objective of the third line of Hayate developments was to obtain an aircraft with better high-altitude performance. The Ki-84-III was a straightforward adaptation of the basic airframe to take a turbosupercharged Ha-45 Ru engine; the Ki-84R was a similar development to be powered by an Ha-45-44 with a mechanically-driven two-stage three-speed supercharger; and the Ki-84N and Ki-84P versions were proposed with 1864-kW (2,500-hp) Mitsubishi Ha-44-13 and increased wing span and area.

During the last month of the war, while the Ki-84-I remained in full production along with a few Ki-84-IIs, plans were in hand for the production of the Ki-84-III, Ki-106, Ki-113, Ki-116 and Ki-117 (redesignated Ki-84N).

In 1945-46 a captured Ki-84-Ia from the 11th Sentai was extensively tested in the Philippines and the United States, this evaluation confirming the high opinion in which the Hayate was held by Allied aircrews. Since then, this aircraft was rebuilt twice before being returned to Japan in 1973 for permanent preservation, a fitting tribute for an outstanding warplane.

Total production amounted to 3,514 aircraft, including 3,416 aircraft built by Nakajima Hikoki KK (two Ki-84 prototypes, 83 Ki-84 service trials aircraft, 42 Ki-84 pre-production aircraft, 3,288 Ki-84-I and Ki-84-II production aircraft, and one Ki-113 prototype), 94 Ki-84-I production aircraft and one Ki-116 prototype built by Mansyu Hikoki Seizo KK, and three Ki-106 prototypes built by Tachikawa Hikoki KK.

Looking rather the worse for wear after capture by the Chinese forces, this Ki-84-Ia was previously operated by the 22nd Sentai, which clashed with the United States 14th Air Force for five weeks over China in March 1944.

Hawker Typhoon

The Typhoon was intended as a pure fighter, but it didn't make the grade. Instead, it brought a whole new concept to air warfare as the originator of what we would call today 'close air support'. Waiting, just behind the fighting, in 'cab ranks', the Typhoons of the 2nd Air Force were always on hand as Allied forces advanced towards Berlin.

In the second half of 1944 the Hawker Typhoon struck terror into the German army in Western Europe. With its pugnacious snub nose, four long-barrelled cannon and whining Sabre engine, its appearance meant imminent destruction to even crack armoured units under a hail of bombs and rockets. Yet a mere 18 months previously this potent warplane lay under the threat of cancellation. A product of the famed design team of Sydney Camm at Kingston, it suffered terribly from its ill-starred engine, proved to have a performance far inferior to what had been expected, and killed many pilots through a variety of causes including structural failure of the rear fuselage. It never did become the superior air-combat fighter it was intended to be, but made up for it by its toughness, its high speed at low level (which enabled it to catch Focke-Wulf Fw 190s on 'hit and run' bombing attacks on Britain's coastal towns) and above all its superb effectiveness in the ground-attack role.

The Typhoon was the chief result of Air Ministry specification F.18/37, the main provisions of which were settled by early 1938. Hawker Aircraft suggested an armament of 12 7.7-mm (0.303-in) Browning machine-guns, but at last the Air Ministry had come to appreciate the advantages of heavier-calibre cannon and F.18/37 stipulated, as prime armament, no fewer than four 20-mm Hispano guns, formidable for a single-engined fighter. Clearly an engine in the 1492-kW (2,000-hp) class was called for, and the UK, in company with a few other nations, was in the fortunate position of having a choice of possible power units. Hindsight was to show that the best would turn out to be the Bristol Centaurus sleeve-valve radial, but experience with the Schneider Trophy had blinded many officials and

designers to the fact that air-cooled radials could result in fast fighters, and the immense potential of the Centaurus was tragically almost ignored. Instead the new Camm design was planned in two versions, the N (Napier Sabre) and R (Rolls-Royce Vulture).

In early 1938 four prototypes were ordered, two of the R type (to be given the name Tornado) and two of the N type (named Typhoon). The Tornado's Vulture engine was basically comprised of two sets of V-12 Peregrine cylinder blocks arranged in X form round a common crankcase. The Sabre was even more unconventional: its 24 cylinders were fitted with sleeve valves and were arranged in the form of two horizontally-opposed 12-cylinder engines one above the other, the two crankshafts driving a common reduction gear at the front. Great things were expected of both engines, which had water/glycol liquid cooling and offered power in the region of 1492 kW (2,000 hp).

The basic aircraft, common to both engines, was almost overstrong in the Camm tradition; and, in the same tradition, the fuselage was based on a truss structured assembly by bolting or riveting steel tubes, with gusset plates to reinforce the joints, and with mountings at the front for the big engine. Though of aluminium alloy, the inner wing was also a strong truss structure, its strength being increased by remarkable thickness – even thicker than the wing of the Hawker

This aircraft of No. 175 Squadron, being bombed up for a 'Rhubarb' attack sortie with two short-tail 227-kg (500-lb) bombs, shows that even by the EJ/EK serial range the bubble canopy had not been introduced. This Typhoon IB does, however, have the smoothly faired cannon barrels which made a welcome improvement to maximum speed.

Hawker Typhoon

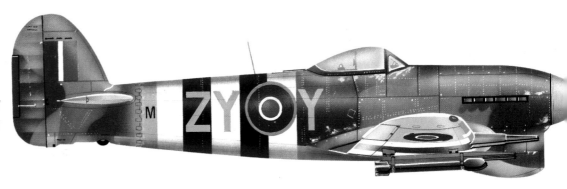

This weatherbeaten Typhoon with the new sliding canopy was MN363, aircraft Y of No. 247 Sqn (two years later the first unit equipped with the Vampire I). It is seen with Invasion Stripes and rockets, operating from an advanced base at Colombelles in June 1944. By this time many 'Tiffies' had the four-bladed de Havilland propeller.

Hurricane, then in full production at the main Kingston works and at the new plant at Langley near Slough. Unlike the Hurricane the new F.18/37 fighter did have a semi-monocoque stressed-skin rear fuselage and stressed-skin outer wings, and the ailerons and elevators (but not the rudder) moved on from fabric to metal skin. An unusual feature was that the horizontal tail was ahead of the rudder, so no cut-outs were needed in the trailing edge of the elevators. The main landing gears had very wide track and retracted inwards outboard of the fuselage, hydraulic actuation being used for these units and for the tailwheel and split flaps. The cockpit had a car-type door on each side.

The first Tornado (P5219) was built at Kingston and flown at Langley by P. G. Lucas on 6 October 1939. It had B-type (red and blue) roundels, and was distinguished by two sets of exhaust stubs on each side and a radiator under the belly giving a faint family likeness to the Hurricane. Soon afterwards Hawker Aircraft was given an order for 1,000 of the new fighters, 500 to be Tornados and 250 Typhoons, the other 250 to be decided when it was known which engine was superior. Early results with the Tornado showed bad airflow around the radiator at high speeds, and before the end of the year P5219 had been given a chin radiator like that already chosen for the Typhoon. The first Typhoon (P5212), flown by Lucas from Langley on 24 February 1940, was doped green above and silver below, with regular red, white and blue roundels, and was confidently predicted to reach 747 km/h (464 mph). Unfortunately the engine was unreliable, and in any case on 9 May 1940 the fuselage broke aft of the cockpit, Lucas pulling off a masterly forced landing.

Hawker Aircraft could not handle mass-production on top of that of the Hurricane, so the Tornado was assigned to Avro and the Typhoon to Gloster, both sister-firms in the Hawker-Siddeley Group. In 1941 both fighters appeared to be close to production after numerous changes, including fitting a larger fin and much larger rudder, wheel-well doors hinged first to the leg fairings and then to the wing roots, wings fitted for four cannon, extra windows aft of the

canopy and, in the case of the Tornado, a separate engine air inlet above the front of the cowling (on the Typhoon it was in the middle of the large chin radiator group which also included the oil cooler). The most worrying feature was the disastrous behaviour of both engines; eventually Hawker was allowed to fit a Tornado with a Centaurus and this aircraft (HG641) flew on 23 October 1941. But by this time the entire Vulture programme had collapsed, and with it the Tornado, just a single production machine (R7936) flying from Avro's aerodrome at Woodford in August 1941. The obvious thing to do would have been to continue with the Centaurus-powered Tornado, because HG641 not only flew better, more quietly and more reliably than any of the others, but also was clearly the fastest. Far from 747 km/h (464 mph), the Typhoon was only just capable of reaching 644 km/h (400 mph), whereas the Tornado with the Centaurus

Flight above the clouds was a relatively rare experience for a Typhoon, for its real aptitude lay in low-level work. However, this photograph of a late production Typhoon IB, uncluttered by external stores, shows the aircraft in the medium for which it was originally intended.

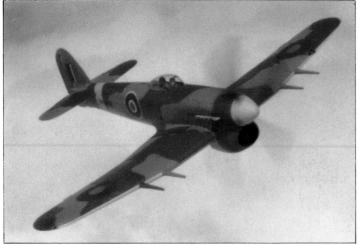

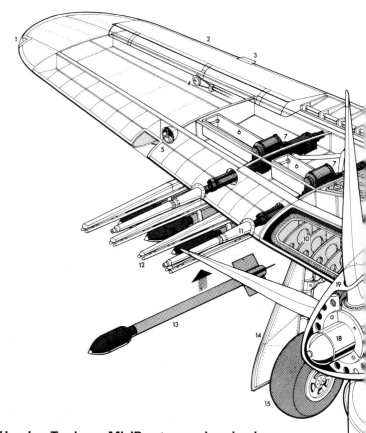

Hawker Typhoon Mk IB cutaway drawing key

1 Starboard navigation light	47 Forward fuselage steel	95 Ammunition boxes, 140
2 Starboard aileron	tube construction	rounds per gun
3 Fixed trim tab	48 Pilot's seat	96 Gun heater air ducts
4 Aileron hinge control	49 Safety harness	97 Port aileron
5 Landing lamp	50 Back and head armour plate	98 Fixed aileron tab
6 Ammunition boxes	51 Pneumatic system air	99 Wing tip construction
7 Starboard 20-mm Hispano	bottle	100 Port navigation light
Mk II cannon	52 Rearward sliding canopy	101 Wing rib construction
8 Split trailing edge flaps	cover	102 Wing stringers
9 Starboard main fuel tank,	53 Aft fuselage joint	103 Front spar
capacity 40 Imp gal (182	54 Canopy rails	104 Leading edge nose ribs
litres)	55 Radio transmitter/receiver	105 Gun camera
10 Self-sealing leading edge	56 Fuselage double frame	106 Camera port
fuel tank, capacity 35 Imp	57 Whip aerial	107 Landing lamp
gal (159 litres)	58 Fuselage skinning	108 1,000-lb (454-kg) bomb
11 Cannon barrel fairings	59 Starboard tailplane	109 Long range tank, capacity
12 Rocket launcher rails	60 Starboard elevator	90 Imp gal (409 litre)
13 60-lb (27-kg) ground attack	61 Elevator trim tab	110 Underwing stores pylon
rockets	62 Fin leading edge	111 Cannon barrel fairings

Few Typhoons had the luck of DN406, of No. 609 Sqn. Among its confirmed targets destroyed while on offensive sweeps over France were 18 locomotives, recorded on the fuselage. In addition, on 12 March 1943, while flown by Flying Officer L. W. F. Stark, it caught and destroyed an Fw 190 raiding London. Home base at this time was Manston.

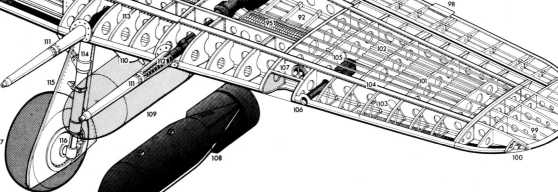

14 Main undercarriage leg fairing
15 Starboard mainwheel
16 De Havilland four-bladed propeller
17 Air intake
18 Propeller pitch change mechanism
19 Spinner
20 Armoured spinner backplate
21 Coolant tank, 7¼ Imp gal (33 litres) capacity
22 Supercharge ram air intake
23 Oil radiator

63 Fin construction
64 Rudder sternpost
65 Fabric covered rudder construction
66 Rudder trim tab
67 Tail navigation light
68 Elevator trim tab
69 Port tailplane construction
70 Tailplane spar attachments
71 Tailwheel hydraulic jack
72 Forward retracting tailwheel
73 Dowty oleo-pneumatic tailwheel strut
74 Tailplane spar fixing double bulkhead

112 Recoil spring
113 Leading edge construction
114 Main undercarriage leg
115 Undercarriage leg fairing door
116 Oleo-pneumatic shock absorber strut
117 Port mainwheel
118 Undercarriage locking mechanism
119 Mainwheel hydraulic jack
120 Wing spar inboard girder construction
121 Port leading edge fuel tank, capacity 35 Imp gal (159 litres)

24 Coolant radiator
25 Radiator shutter
26 Engine mounting block
27 Tubular steel engine support framework
28 Exhaust stubs
29 Napier Sabre II, 24-cylinder flat H engine
30 Engine cowlings
31 Cartridge starter
32 Engine compartment fireproof bulkhead
33 Oxygen bottle
34 Gun heating air duct
35 Hydraulic reservoir
36 Footguards
37 Rudder pedals
38 Oil tank, capacity 18 Imp gal (82 litres)
39 Oil tank filler cap
40 Instrument panel
41 Bullet-proof windscreen
42 Reflector sight
43 Control column handgrip
44 Engine throttle controls
45 Trim handwheels
46 Emergency hydraulic handpump

75 Tailplane attachment joint strap
76 External strengthening fishplates
77 Elevator mass balance
78 Elevator cross shaft
79 Cable guides
80 Tailplane control cables
81 Rear fuselage frame and stringer construction
82 Wing root fillet
83 Spar root pin joints
84 Undercarriage door hydraulic jack
85 Mainwheel door
86 Main undercarriage bay
87 Rear spar
88 Port main fuel tank, capacity 40 Imp gal (182 litres)
89 Flap shroud construction
90 Port split trailing edge flaps
91 Flap hydraulic jack
92 Port gun bays
93 20-mm Hispano Mk II cannon
94 Ammunition feed drum

This aircraft represents the ultimate standard of build of the **Typhoon IB**, which accounted for all but approximately 105 of the entire production run. The four-bladed propeller was introduced in 1943 but did not completely supplant the original unit. The aircraft shown flew with **No. 181 Sqn, 2nd Tactical Air Force**, serving in France in June 1944, and is armed with rockets.

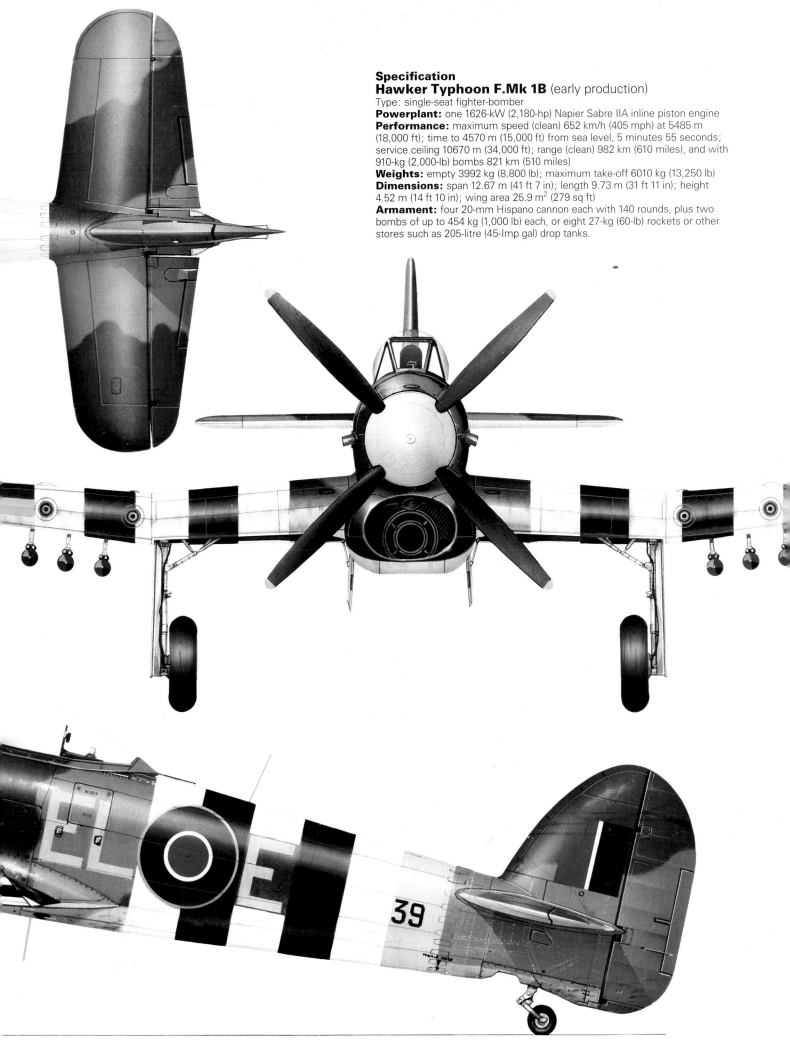

Specification
Hawker Typhoon F.Mk 1B (early production)
Type: single-seat fighter-bomber
Powerplant: one 1626-kW (2,180-hp) Napier Sabre IIA inline piston engine
Performance: maximum speed (clean) 652 km/h (405 mph) at 5485 m (18,000 ft); time to 4570 m (15,000 ft) from sea level, 5 minutes 55 seconds; service ceiling 10670 m (34,000 ft); range (clean) 982 km (610 miles), and with 910-kg (2,000-lb) bombs 821 km (510 miles)
Weights: empty 3992 kg (8,800 lb); maximum take-off 6010 kg (13,250 lb)
Dimensions: span 12.67 m (41 ft 7 in); length 9.73 m (31 ft 11 in); height 4.52 m (14 ft 10 in); wing area 25.9 m² (279 sq ft)
Armament: four 20-mm Hispano cannon each with 140 rounds, plus two bombs of up to 454 kg (1,000 lb) each, or eight 27-kg (60-lb) rockets or other stores such as 205-litre (45-Imp gal) drop tanks.

One of the less-fortunate Typhoons was this example serving with No. 3 Sqn based at West Malling, near Maidstone. One of the original type with unfaired cannon barrels, it is seen as it was on its last mission, on 18 May 1943. Flown by Pilot Officer Inwood, it was one of five shot down by the Bf 109s of I./JG 27 during an attack on Poix airfield.

This early Typhoon IB was the aircraft of the CO of the Duxford Wing (then comprising Nos 56, 266 and 609 Sqns) in June 1942. He was Wing Commander John Grandy, whose initials appeared on the fuselage in the usual way. Subsequently, in 1967-71, Grady was to be Chief of the Air Staff, retiring as a Marshal of the Royal Air Force.

quickly reached 677.5 km/h (421 mph), faster than any other fighter in the world at that time, and with proper development would have gone faster.

Cannon replace machine-guns

What killed the Centaurus-Tornado was the implacable opposition of Air Marshal Wilfrid Freeman, czar of procurement, who intensely disliked Bristol radial engines. (In July 1942 Camm at last managed to fit a Centaurus into the thin-wing Typhoon II, later called Tempest, but Freeman immediately ordered it taken out again; the Centaurus-Tempest was kept on the ground until August 1943, seriously delaying the one really successful fighter in the entire family, which led to the post-war Fury and Sea Fury.) Instead, Hawker had to soldier on with the almost hopelessly unreliable Sabre. Production Typhoons had very slowly begun to appear from 27 May 1941 when Gloster's Hucclecote works flew R7576. Hawker built just 15, the first (R8198) flying in November 1941. About 100 early examples were Typhoon 1As with 12 machine-guns, all the rest being Typhoon IBs with four 20-mm cannon with most of the barrel projecting ahead of the wing in an impressive manner. Studies were made of long-span and clipped Typhoons and various other additions including one or two turbo superchargers, but the only trial installations flown were AI Mk VA radar (drawings for the installation were done by John W. R. Taylor, former editor of *Jane's All the World Aircraft*) and the FR.IB with

various camera fits and only the outer cannon. Eventually about 60 of the FR version were delivered.

The Typhoon, known in the RAF as the 'Tiffy', reached No. 56 Sqn at Duxford in late September 1941. Though the engine ran like the proverbial sewing machine when it worked, it hardly ever worked; and in any case the overhaul period was a mere 25 hours. Handling the Tiffy was fine, but view was bad, performance – especially climb and at height – nothing like as good as that of the Spitfire IX, and the big fighter was rated inferior in a dogfight to an early Fw 190. Worse, many aircraft were lost, some fatally, by the tail coming off. It is a reflection on instrumentation techniques that the cause was not found until almost the end of the war, when it was discovered it could be cured merely by changing the elevator balance masses! As it was, elevator flutter continued to be a menace, and Typhoons grew a row of reinforcing plates around the rear fuselage to keep the tail on. Special credit is due to R. P. Beamont, a young pilot of No. 609 Sqn and later one of the world's most renowned test pilots, who not only flew some of the toughest flight tests but whose persuasive arguments in 1942-43 were crucial in making the Air Staff and Ministry of Aircraft Production change their minds; they had decided Typhoon should be cancelled, but instead Gloster were kept on building it.

Beamont argued by deeds as much as words, and personally made

The very first Hawker F.18/37 fighter was the first prototype Tornado (P5219). With one of the first Vulture engines, it was the only aircraft of the entire Tornado/Typhoon/Tempest/Fury series to have a cooling radiator under the wing, in the same position as on the earlier Hurricane.

The second prototype Tornado (P5224) had the radiator moved to the underside of the engine as in the Typhoon. It also introduced a modified tail with a larger rudder, additional rear-vision cockpit windows, aerial mast, wheel-well covers and various other modifications added to the first prototype Typhoon in autumn 1940.

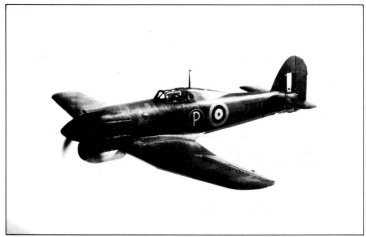

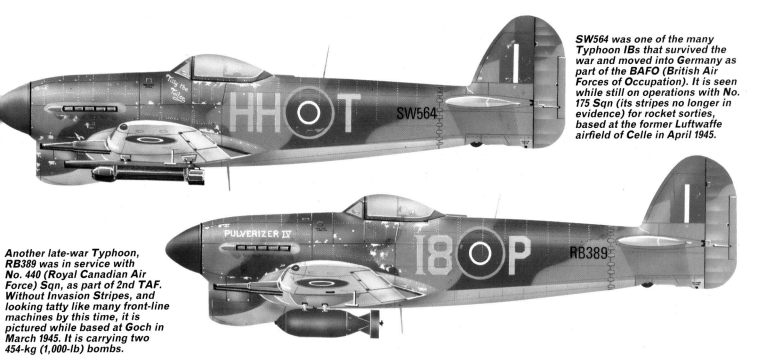

SW564 was one of the many Typhoon IBs that survived the war and moved into Germany as part of the BAFO (British Air Forces of Occupation). It is seen while still on operations with No. 175 Sqn (its stripes no longer in evidence) for rocket sorties, based at the former Luftwaffe airfield of Celle in April 1945.

Another late-war Typhoon, RB389 was in service with No. 440 (Royal Canadian Air Force) Sqn, as part of 2nd TAF. Without Invasion Stripes, and looking tatty like many front-line machines by this time, it is pictured while based at Goch in March 1945. It is carrying two 454-kg (1,000-lb) bombs.

56 offensive sorties over Europe, mostly by night. Though the Typhoon had much to commend it as a destroyer of low-level raiders, it was clear by late 1942 that the true *forte* of this powerful and robust machine was ground attack. Following very successful trials with drop tanks, 454-kg (1,000-lb) bombs and eight 27-kg (60-lb) rockets on underwing rails, the whole Typhoon force was assigned to the newly formed 2nd Tactical Air Force to hit European ground targets and German shipping. It is a comment on standards of aircraft recognition that, to prevent confusion with the Fw 190 (!), Typhoons were in 1943 painted with a bold pattern of black and white stripes under their wings. At the same time, and for the same reason, P-47 Thunderbolts in England were given white cowls and white tail bands. In 1944 similar stripes appeared on all Allied aircraft.

A new kind of firepower

Not very much more was done to the Typhoon during its brief service life. Pilot view was improved by fitting a clear blown hood at the rear, and then dramatically improved by throwing out all the clobber behind the pilot's head (except the armour) and fitting a neat sliding bubble hood of the type which later became common on almost all fighters. A sliding hood, of course, meant the doors could be deleted, and this was welcomed by pilots because the doors either

stuck or else came unlocked in combat; fixed cockpit walls could also be used for better location of trimmers and other controls. The de Havilland Hydromatic propeller was given four blades, able to make full use of the slowly increasing engine power, and the rigid radio mast was replaced by a low-drag whip aerial on the rear fuselage. The cannon were neatly faired into the wing, their vital feeds were made more reliable, and the sighting for bombs and rockets perfected.

By D-Day (6 June 1944), Gloster had built nearly 2,000 Typhoons and the 2nd TAF's 26 combat-ready squadrons were about to justify all the heartbreaking effort that had gone into making them work. From the start of the Allied invasion, the ground forces were able to call on a new kind of firepower: fighter-bombers on the so-called 'cab-rank' system. Via army radio, the ground units could call for devastating attacks by cannon, bombs and rockets on any strongpoint, or even on an individual tank, holding up their advance. The climax of the Typhoon's career came in the third week of August 1944 when the whole surviving German army (5th Panzer Army, 7th Army and Panzer Group 'Eberbach') in northern France, the rem-

Typhoon IBs of No. 56 Sqn take off from RAF Manston for an operational sortie across the Channel in 1943. At this time No. 56 Sqn was using the Typhoon for small-scale fighter or fighter-bomber attacks on ground targets of opportunity.

Hawker Typhoon

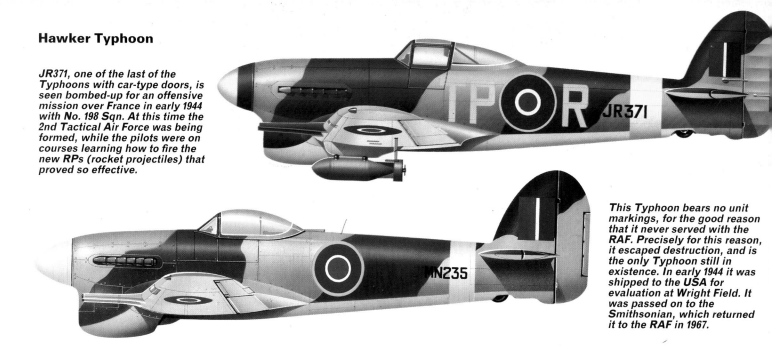

JR371, one of the last of the Typhoons with car-type doors, is seen bombed-up for an offensive mission over France in early 1944 with No. 198 Sqn. At this time the 2nd Tactical Air Force was being formed, while the pilots were on courses learning how to fire the new RPs (rocket projectiles) that proved so effective.

This Typhoon bears no unit markings, for the good reason that it never served with the RAF. Precisely for this reason, it escaped destruction, and is the only Typhoon still in existence. In early 1944 it was shipped to the USA for evaluation at Wright Field. It was passed on to the Smithsonian, which returned it to the RAF in 1967.

nants of 16 divisions including nine Panzer divisions, were caught in a trap near Falaise, Argentan and Chambois. Typhoons, mainly from Harry Broadhurst's No. 83 Group, simply poured rockets, 20-mm shells and bombs into them until hardly one German vehicle could move. This was the devastating end to Hitler's power west of the Rhine.

Execution to order

Most of the Typhoons responsible for this fantastic execution were based on hastily constructed strips near the north coast of France, where pierced-steel planks or Sommerfield matting (steel mesh) were laid directly on the ground. August was hot, and the swirling dust churned by the big propellers rapidly eroded the engines, especially their sleeve valves. In 1943 three desert-painted Typhoons had done tropical trials at Aboukir, but now something different was needed. To show what British industry can do when it has to, a dynamic ram-type impact filter dome that kept the dust and sand particles out of the intake duct to the injection-type carburettor of the late-model Sabre engines was designed in 12 hours, put into production on the following day and the first batch delivered by a Douglas Dakota to the air bases on the night of the third day; all 500 Typhoons on those airstrips had the filter in place on the fifth day.

There were in fact three marks of Sabre used in production Typhoons, all basically the same. The Sabre IIA was rated at 1626 kW (2,180 hp), the IIB at 1641 kW (2,200 hp) and the IIC at 1686 kW (2,260 hp); in 1944 the related Tempest was being fitted with the Sabre VII, in which water/methanol injection enabled over

2238 kW (3,000 hp) to be pulled for up to five minutes. All late production Sabres had a Hobson injection-type carburettor and were much more reliable than the pathetic Sabres of 1939-42 (much of the credit being due to the rival Bristol company, which managed to use sleeve valves designed for the Taurus as a basis for reliable Sabre valve gear that went into production with Bristol technicians in attendance to help overcome any residual snags). Not least of the unusual features of the Sabre was its Coffman starter, driven by a kind of gigantic shotgun cartridge the size of a large tin of fruit juice. When the pilot pressed the button there was a most impressive – if contained – detonation, and the giant four-bladed propeller got into action in no uncertain manner. To anyone used to other aircraft the Sabre was also remarkable in its speed of operation. On take-off most large engines could turn at 2,600 to 3,000 rpm, the Merlin just reaching the latter figure; but the Sabre wound up to 3,700 or even 3,850 rpm, with its 24 small cylinders putting out a whining song that nobody who heard will ever forget. Even flying overhead, the 'Tiffy' (and its later partner, the Tempest) was absolutely distinctive in its sound. It was a sound that meant death to Hitler's troops in 1944.

Once the European war was won, the Typhoon quickly disappeared from the scene, though the last (SW772) was not delivered from Gloucester until November 1945. Altogether Gloster Aircraft delivered 3,300, and Hawker built 15 plus two prototypes. A few were used as tugs for banner targets, or as squadron hacks, into 1946, but few survived into 1947. One Typhoon (R8694) was used by Napier at Luton for annular radiator trials. Distressingly, only one Typhoon survives to the present.

Hawker Typhoon variants

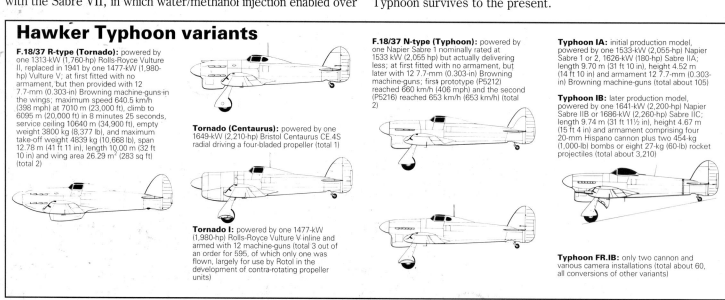

F.18/37 R-type (Tornado): powered by one 1313-kW (1,760-hp) Rolls-Royce Vulture II, replaced in 1941 by one 1477-kW (1,980-hp) Vulture V; at first fitted with no armament, but then provided with 12 7.7-mm (0.303-in) Browning machine-guns in the wings; maximum speed 640.5 km/h (398 mph) at 7010 m (23,000 ft), climb to 6095 m (20,000 ft) in 8 minutes 25 seconds, service ceiling 10640 m (34,900 ft), empty weight 3800 kg (8,377 lb), and maximum take-off weight 4839 kg (10,668 lb), span 12.78 m (41 ft 11 in), length 10.00 m (32 ft 10 in) and wing area 26.29 m² (283 sq ft) (total 2)

Tornado (Centaurus): powered by one 1649-kW (2,210-hp) Bristol Centaurus CE.4S radial driving a four-bladed propeller (total 1)

Tornado I: powered by one 1477-kW (1,980-hp) Rolls-Royce Vulture V inline and armed with 12 machine-guns (total 3 out of an order for 595, of which only one was flown, largely for use by Rotol in the development of contra-rotating propeller units)

F.18/37 N-type (Typhoon): powered by one Napier Sabre 1 nominally rated at 1533 kW (2,055 hp) but actually delivering less; at first fitted with no armament, but later with 12 7.7-mm (0.303-in) Browning machine-guns; first prototype (P5212) reached 660 km/h (406 mph) and the second (P5216) reached 653 km/h (653 km/h) (total 2)

Typhoon IA: initial production model, powered by one 1533-kW (2,055-hp) Napier Sabre 1 or 2, 1626-kW (180-hp) Sabre IIA; length 9.70 m (31 ft 10 in), height 4.52 m (14 ft 10 in) and armament 12 7.7-mm (0.303-in) Browning machine-guns (total about 105)

Typhoon IB: later production model, powered by one 1641-kW (2,200-hp) Napier Sabre IIB or 1686-kW (2,260-hp) Sabre IIC; length 9.74 m (31 ft 11½ in), height 4.67 m (15 ft 4 in) and armament comprising four 20-mm Hispano cannon plus two 454-kg (1,000-lb) bombs or eight 27-kg (60-lb) rocket projectiles (total about 3,210)

Typhoon FR.IB: only two cannon and various camera installations (total about 60, all conversions of other variants)

Dewoitine D.520

Roughly comparable with the RAF's Hurricane, the Dewoitine D.520 suffered the penalties of French indifference, irresolution and inertia so prevalent in the months before World War II. When it finally entered service it proved scarcely a match for the Bf 109, but its pilots fought with great skill and bravery to bring the type some respectability during the fall of France. It was later turned against the Allies by Vichy forces, and was used as a trainer by the Luftwaffe.

The Hawker Hurricane prototype had already been flying for a year when work started in earnest on the design of the Dewoitine D.520. As long before as July 1934 the French air ministry had issued a requirement for fighters to replace the contemporary generation of interceptors, of which the D.510 was Emile Dewoitine's latest member. To meet the new demands Dewoitine submitted his D.513 tender, but this possessed a performance inferior to that of the Morane-Saulnier M.S.405 and was rejected.

In June 1936 Dewoitine established an autonomous design bureau under Robert Castello, and gave instructions to start project studies for a new fighter design, employing a 671-kW (900-hp) Hispano-Suiza 12Y-21 engine and with a target performance of 500 km/h (311 mph). The design was again rejected by the French air force authorities as they had already set their sights on a speed of 520 km/h (323 mph). Castello's design, now termed the D.520, on account of the speed demanded, underwent modification by a reduction of the wing span and a change to the proposed new 895-kW (1,200-hp) engine being developed by Hispano-Suiza.

Despite further rejection of this design, this time on account of official preference for the MS.406, Dewoitine decided to persevere with detail design and building of two prototypes at private expense, an initiative that was not rewarded by a government contract until 3 April 1938, by which time the first aircraft, the D.520.01, was nearing completion.

The first prototype's maiden flight was made by Marcel Doret at Toulouse-Francazals on 2 October 1938 with an Hispano-Suiza 12Y-21 engine driving a wooden fixed-pitch two-bladed propeller; not surprisingly the prototype barely reached a speed of 483 km/h (300 mph), but after replacement of the twin underwing radiators by a single central radiator and substitution of the early engine by an HS 12Y-29 engine with three-bladed propeller, the D.520.01 achieved

its design speed of 520 km/h (311 mph). Indeed, on 7 February 1939 Léopold Galy dived the aircraft to a speed of 825 km/h (513 mph). The second prototype (D.520.02) with redesigned tail unit, cockpit canopy, strengthened landing gear and armament of hub-firing 20-mm cannon and a pair of underwing machine-guns, was first flown on 28 January 1939 and, flown on test at CEMA, Villacoublay, by Capitaine Rozanoff, returned a speed of 527 km/h (327 mph). Only one other example, the D.520.03 with Szydlowski supercharger in place of the Hispano-Suiza type previously fitted, had flown when war broke out in September 1939.

Contrasts in national inertia

At the end of 1938 France's single-engined fighter defence comprised 378 aircraft, of which 16 M.S.405s and M.S.406s were the only aircraft that could be regarded as modern. The situation in the RAF, let it be remarked, was not significantly different. Yet nine months later, when the war started, RAF Fighter Command possessed 19 squadrons of Hurricanes and nine of Supermarine Spitfires for a total of 486 eight-gun fighters; by contrast, the Armée de l'Air fielded a total of 271 M.S.406s in Metropolitan France, and these aircraft were painfully inferior in every respect to the standard Luftwaffe Messerschmitt Bf 109E fighter and scarcely able to catch any of the German bombers in service.

However, realisation of the parlous state of their fighter equipment had dawned on the French authorities early in 1939, and on 17 April an order for 200 D.520s had been placed, delivery being

D.520 no. 408 finally reached the Armée de l'Air on 24 June 1940, but France had collapsed two days previously. It fought against the Allies in the Vichy air force, but survived the war and in 1977-80 was beautifully restored. It is painted to represent the very successful no. 90, which served with GC II/3.

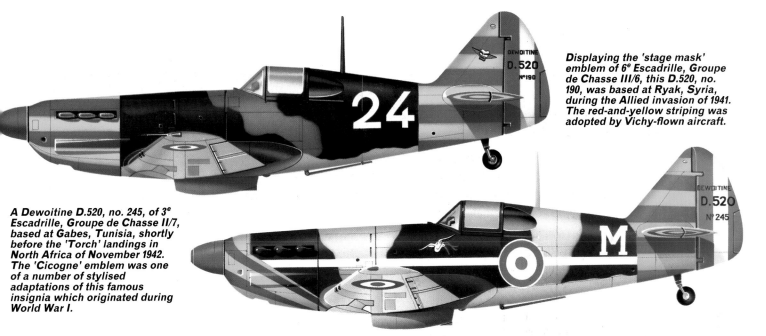

Displaying the 'stage mask' emblem of 6e Escadrille, Groupe de Chasse III/6, this D.520, no. 190, was based at Ryak, Syria, during the Allied invasion of 1941. The red-and-yellow striping was adopted by Vichy-flown aircraft.

A Dewoitine D.520, no. 245, of 3e Escadrille, Groupe de Chasse II/7, based at Gabes, Tunisia, shortly before the 'Torch' landings in North Africa of November 1942. The 'Cicogne' emblem was one of a number of stylised adaptations of this famous insignia which originated during World War I.

demanded by the end of the year; subsequent contracts in June 1939, September 1939, January 1940, April 1940 and May 1940 increased the total number on order to 2,200 D.520s (including 120 for the Aéronavale). Production rates were required to increase from 50 aircraft per month in September 1939 to 350 a month in November 1940.

In the event the first production D.520 was not flown until 2 November 1939; by 1 January only 13 aircraft had been completed, and these aircraft, lacking ejector exhaust stubs and with makeshift supercharger intakes, were capable of only 509 km/h (316 mph). Thereafter production slowly accelerated and by the date (10 May) on which the German attack in the West opened, 36 operationally-cleared D.520s had been issued to Groupe de Chasse I/3 at Cannes-Mandélieu. Non-operational aircraft had been delivered to GC II/3, GC II/7 and GC III/3 for use as conversion trainers.

Despite being scarcely ready for combat in its new fighters, GC I/3 was rushed to the combat zone and was in action for the first time on 13 May, shooting down three Henschel Hs 126s and a Heinkel He 111 without loss. The next day the groupe joined combat over Sedan, destroying four Messerschmitt Bf 110s, two Bf 109s, two Dornier Do 17s and two He 111s for the loss of two pilots killed. However, on 17 May the group's base at Wez-Thuizy was attacked by the Luftwaffe and seven D.520s were destroyed on the ground; after this GC I/3 was withdrawn to Meaux-Esbly.

Next in combat was GC II/3 on 21 May, based at Bouillancy and in the following three weeks this unit claimed the destruction of 31 German aircraft (including 12 Junkers Ju 87s) for the combat loss of 20 of its own aircraft, of which two were shot down by French ground fire.

June brought GC II/7 and GC III/3 into action, the former unit's pilots fetching their own aircraft direct from the factory at Toulouse in ones and twos. Based at Avelange in the Zone d'Operations Aériennes Est (Eastern Zone of Air Operations) as part of Groupement 22 commanded by Colonel Dumemes, GC II/7's task was to intercept German bombers returning home after raids; during their period in combat, GC II/7's pilots destroyed 12 enemy aircraft for the loss of 14 D.520s and three pilots killed. GC III/3 fared worse, claiming only eight aircraft for the loss of 17 D.520s.

In the south, Groupe de Chasse III/6 at Le Luc received its first D.520 on 10 June, the day on which Italy entered the war. Without the benefit of previous conversion training, this group first flew its new fighters against the Italians on 13 May, and two days later two pilots, Adjudant Pierre Le Gloan and Capitaine Assolant, fought a large formation of Fiat CR.42s. While Assolant destroyed one of the enemy fighters Le Gloan shot down three more, as well as a reconnaissance Fiat BR.20. This pilot, patrol leader of the 5e Escadrille, GC III/6, had previously destroyed four enemy aircraft while flying the M.S.406, and had shot down two BR.20s in his D.520 on 13 May; he went on to achieve a score of 22 combat victories in World War II.

After the Armistice

Shortly before the final collapse in France, two further Groupes de Chasse, GC II/6 and GC III/7, were converting from the M.S.406 to the D.520, but saw no combat. During the last fortnight 26 D.520s were delivered to the Aéronavale's Escadrilles AC1 and AC2, and on the eve of the Armistice AC3 and AC4 received 26 others, but again none was flown in combat.

With all the appearance of a racing aircraft rather than a fighter, the prototype D.520.01 differed considerably from the definitive production aircraft, notably in the very low aspect ratio fin and rudder, absence of spinner and open cockpit. This picture was taken during the second flight (on 8 October 1938) and shows Marcel Doret at the controls.

D.520s of the first production batch seen here during the autumn of 1939; they appear to have been fitted with their ejector exhaust stubs, shortage of which (among other components) seriously delayed deliveries of otherwise complete aircraft to the combat units of the Armée de l'Air.

Dewoitine D.520

One of the last remaining D.520s that survived seizure by the Germans, this aircraft eventually finished up with GCB I/18 Vendée in April 1945. Aircraft of this unit carried an individual numeral on their fin.

D.520s of JG 105 at Chartres in 1944. Choice of this aircraft to provide fighter training was an indication of the desperate situation facing the Luftwaffe in 1944, for the handling characteristics of the D.520 differed considerably from any German fighter and the accident rate was fairly high.

By 25 June a total of 437 D.520s had been completed at Toulouse, a remarkable figure and one that demonstrated the potential motivation that existed in France only after German forces set foot on French territory. Of these aircraft, 351 had been taken on charge by the Armée de l'Air and 52 by the Aéronavale; 106 had been lost either in combat or in accidents. Of the remainder, 153 were located in the unoccupied zone of France, 175 were flown to North Africa by surviving pilots of the French air forces and three were flown to England by escaping pilots of GC III/7 on 25 June, where they became part of the 1st Fighter Group of the 'Free French Air Force', formed at RAF Odiham on 29 August.

As the Germans initially forbade the deployment of any D.520 unit in the unoccupied zone of the French mainland, many of the surviving aircraft provided the equipment of GC I/3, GC II/3, GC III/6 and GC II/7 in North Africa; later Aéronavale Escadrilles 1AC and 2AC (previously AC1 and AC2) received D.520s. In April 1941 the German Armistice Commission in France approved plans for 1,074 aircraft to be produced by plants in the unoccupied zone, and in August that year the SNCASE organisation (which had absorbed the Toulouse factory) received a contract for 550 D.520s. A total of 349 of these had been completed by the end of 1942, including 197 aircraft powered by the 612-kW (820-hp) Hispano-Suiza 12Y-49 engine driving Chauvière propellers.

Meanwhile D.520s had taken part in operations against the Fleet Air Arm during the Syrian campaign of 1941, GC III/6, GC II/3, GC I/7 and Escadrille 1AC being credited with the destruction of 31 British aircraft for the loss of 32 of their own number. By far the most successful of the French pilots was Pierre Le Gloan, who was credited with the destruction of 11 British aircraft.

At the time of the Allied landings in North Africa in November 1942, Vichy forces included a total of 173 D.520s, of which 142 were combat-ready with GC II/3, GC III/3, GC III/6, GC II/7, GC II/5 and Escadrilles 1AC and 2AC. GC II/6 was based in Senegal with 30 D.520s. In the savage air fighting that took place between 8 and 10 November the Aéronavale lost 19 D.520s and seven Martin 167 bombers, while the Armée de l'Air de l'Armistice lost 56 aircraft, including 13 D.520s. Among the 44 Allied aircraft destroyed by the French was an entire formation of nine Fairey Albacores from HMS *Furious*, shot down by GC III/3. Shortly after this the majority of the French pilots opted to join the Allies (but Pierre Le Gloan was tragically killed in a flying accident in a Bell Airacobra on 11 September 1943).

Vichy aircraft seized

The outcome of the Allied landings in North Africa was the German seizure of unoccupied France, and on 27 November 1942 the Vichy air force was demobilised. Of the 1,876 aircraft sequestrated by the Germans were 246 D.520s, of which 13 were awaiting repair and four subsequently written-off as beyond repair; 169 other D.520s, of which 19 were in flying condition, were seized at the Tou-

Dewoitine D.520 cutaway drawing key

1 Cannon port
2 Spinner
3 Three-blade Ratier Electric propeller
4 Cannon barrel blast tube
5 Coolant water tank
6 Safety vent
7 Cowling forward frame
8 Auxiliary intake
9 Chin intake
10 Coolant piping
11 Oil cooler intake
12 Intake duct
13 Oil radiator
14 Engine bearer frames
15 Engine accessories
16 Exhaust stubs
17 Hispano-Suiza 12Y45 engine
18 Cowling rear frame
19 Cannon ammunition drum (60 rounds)
20 Oil tank
21 Starboard wing fuel tank
22 Wing skinning
23 Starboard navigation light
24 Starboard aileron
25 Aileron hinge
26 Emergency ring and bead gunsight
27 Fuselage main fuel tank
28 Fuselage main frame upper member
29 Engine bearer upper attachment
30 Bulkhead
31 20-mm HS 404 cannon breech
32 Compressor outlet
33 Extinguisher
34 Szydlowski compressor
35 Engine bearer support frame
36 Wing root fairing
37 Starboard mainwheel
38 Port mainwheel well
39 Ventral radiator bath intake
40 Undercarriage retraction mechanism
41 Mainwheel leg pivot
42 Wing machine-gun blast tubes

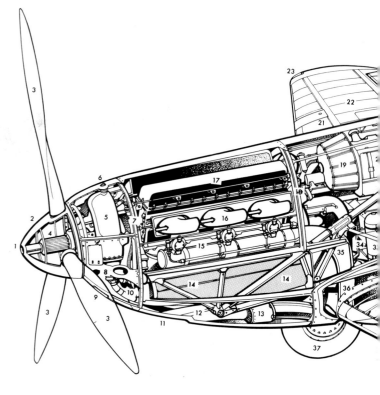

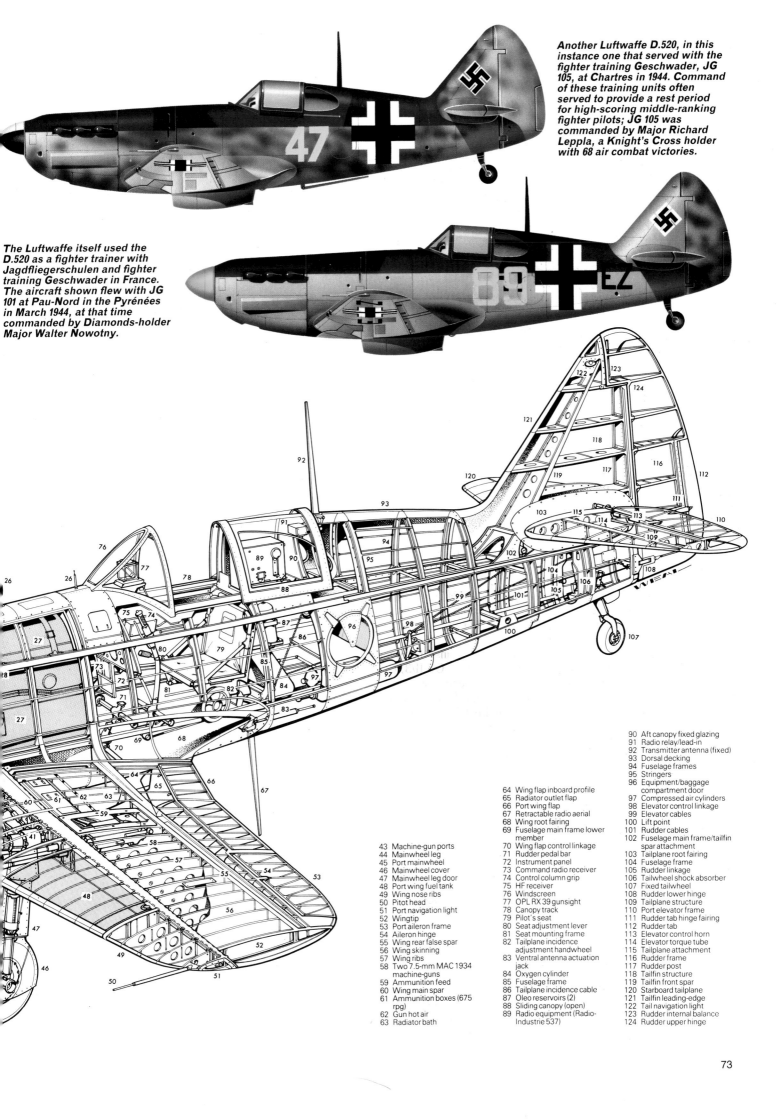

Another Luftwaffe D.520, in this instance one that served with the fighter training Geschwader, JG 105, at Chartres in 1944. Command of these training units often served to provide a rest period for high-scoring middle-ranking fighter pilots; JG 105 was commanded by Major Richard Leppla, a Knight's Cross holder with 68 air combat victories.

The Luftwaffe itself used the D.520 as a fighter trainer with Jagdfliegerschulen and fighter training Geschwader in France. The aircraft shown flew with JG 101 at Pau-Nord in the Pyrénées in March 1944, at that time commanded by Diamonds-holder Major Walter Nowotny.

43 Machine-gun ports
44 Mainwheel leg
45 Port mainwheel
46 Mainwheel cover
47 Mainwheel leg door
48 Port wing fuel tank
49 Wing nose ribs
50 Pitot head
51 Port navigation light
52 Wingtip
53 Port aileron frame
54 Aileron hinge
55 Wing rear false spar
56 Wing skinning
57 Wing ribs
58 Two 7.5-mm MAC 1934 machine-guns
59 Ammunition feed
60 Wing main spar
61 Ammunition boxes (675 rpg)
62 Gun hot air
63 Radiator bath
64 Wing flap inboard profile
65 Radiator outlet flap
66 Port wing flap
67 Retractable radio aerial
68 Wing root fairing
69 Fuselage main frame lower member
70 Wing flap control linkage
71 Rudder pedal bar
72 Instrument panel
73 Command radio receiver
74 Control column grip
75 HF receiver
76 Windscreen
77 OPL RX 39 gunsight
78 Canopy track
79 Pilot's seat
80 Seat adjustment lever
81 Seat mounting frame
82 Tailplane incidence adjustment handwheel
83 Ventral antenna actuation jack
84 Oxygen cylinder
85 Fuselage frame
86 Tailplane incidence cable
87 Oleo reservoirs (2)
88 Sliding canopy (open)
89 Radio equipment (Radio-Industrie 537)
90 Aft canopy fixed glazing
91 Radio relay/lead-in
92 Transmitter antenna (fixed)
93 Dorsal decking
94 Fuselage frames
95 Stringers
96 Equipment/baggage compartment door
97 Compressed air cylinders
98 Elevator control linkage
99 Elevator cables
100 Lift point
101 Rudder cables
102 Fuselage main frame/tailfin spar attachment
103 Tailplane root fairing
104 Fuselage frame
105 Rudder linkage
106 Tailwheel shock absorber
107 Fixed tailwheel
108 Rudder lower hinge
109 Tailplane structure
110 Port elevator frame
111 Rudder tab hinge fairing
112 Rudder tab
113 Elevator control horn
114 Elevator torque tube
115 Tailplane attachment
116 Rudder frame
117 Rudder post
118 Tailfin structure
119 Tailfin front spar
120 Starboard tailplane
121 Tailfin leading-edge
122 Tail navigation light
123 Rudder internal balance
124 Rudder upper hinge

Dewoitine D.520

Factory-fresh production D.520, no. 494, in March 1942 at Toulouse, displaying the mandatory red-and-yellow stripes worn by Vichy aircraft. The photo well illustrates the aft location of the cockpit, providing an excellent downward field of view behind the wing, but demanding considerable weaving during taxiing.

Dewoitine D.520 variants

D.520.01: first prototype; Hispano-Suiza 12Y-21 engine; no armament
D.520.02: second prototype; HS 12Y-29 engine; one cannon and two machine-guns
D.520.03: third prototype; HS 12Y-31 engine and Szydlowski supercharger
D.520: total of 905 production aircraft of which 437 were completed before the fall of France in June 1940, and 468 were produced from August 1941 onwards; the former aircraft had HS 12Y-45 engines driving Ratier propellers and 197 of the latter had HS 12Y-49 engines driving Chauvière propellers; many served with the Luftwaffe, 60 with the Regia Aeronautica, 120 with the Bulgarian air force and some with the Romanian air force
D.520Z: single aircraft (the 465th production D.520) test flown with alternative engine cooling system and Messier landing gear
SE.520Z: projected development of D.520Z with Hispano-Suiza 12Z engine and increased armament; one prototype only
D.521.01: single aircraft (the 41st production D.520) test flown with Rolls-Royce Merlin III engine
D.523: single aircraft (the 45th production D.520) test flown with Hispano-Suiza 12Y-51 engine
D.524: the D.521.01 (see above) re-engined with Hispano-Suiza 12Z-89ter, but reverted to standard D.520
D.550: racing aircraft produced in 1939 with Hispano-Suiza 12Ycrs (later 12Y-51) engine
D.551: military version of the D.550; total of 18 aircraft produced but never flown; HS 12Y-51 engine
HD.780: floatplane version produced experimentally as a D.520 conversion

Specification
Dewoitine D.520
Type: single-seat interceptor fighter
Powerplant: one 634-kW (850-hp) Hispano-Suiza 12Y-45 12-cylinder Vee liquid-cooled piston engine
Performance: maximum speed 535 km/h (332 mph) at 5500 m (18,045 ft); climb to 4000 m (13,125 ft) in 5 minutes 48 seconds; service ceiling 10250 m (33,630 ft); normal range 890 km (553 miles); maximum range 1540 km (957 miles)
Weights: empty 2125 kg (4,685 lb); maximum take-off 2790 kg (6,151 lb)
Dimensions: span 10.2 m (33 ft 5½ in); length 8.76 m (28 ft 8¾ in); height 2.57 m (8 ft 5¼ in); wing area 15.95 m² (171.69 sq ft)
Armament: one hub-firing 20-mm Hispano-Suiza HS404 cannon with 60 rounds and four 7.5-mm (0.295-in) MAC 1934 M39 guns in wings with 675 rounds per gun

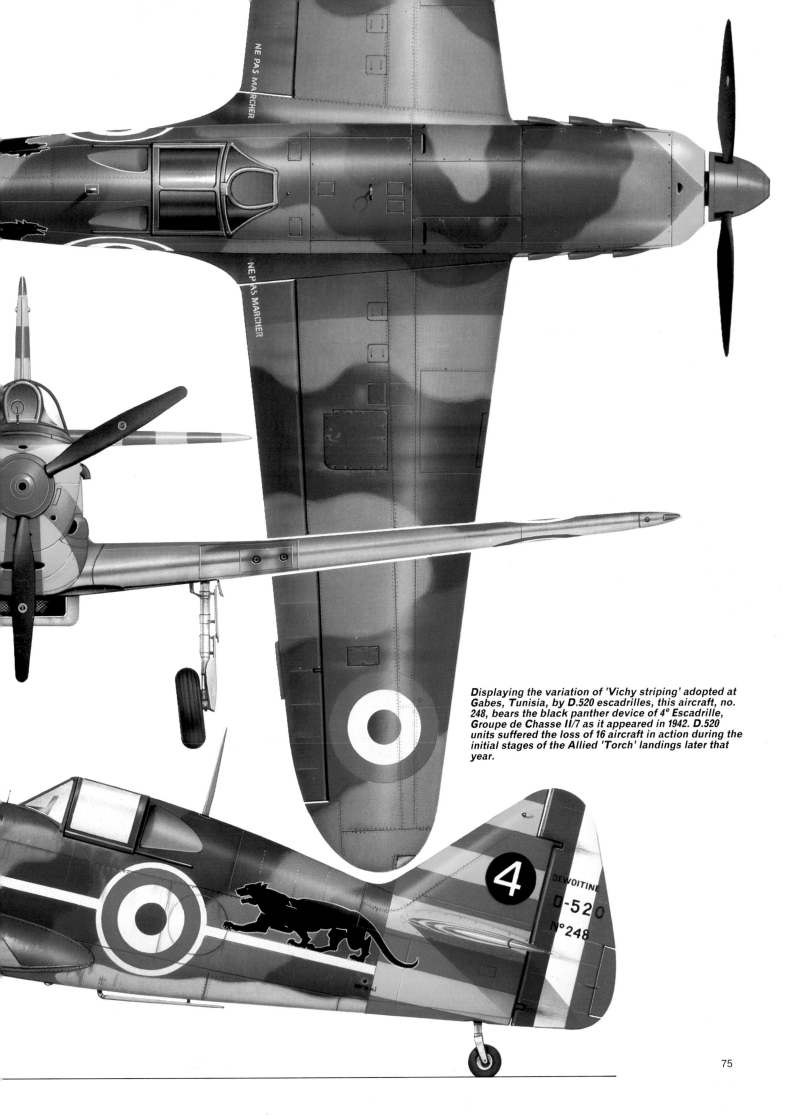

Displaying the variation of 'Vichy striping' adopted at Gabes, Tunisia, by D.520 escadrilles, this aircraft, no. 248, bears the black panther device of 4^e Escadrille, Groupe de Chasse II/7 as it appeared in 1942. D.520 units suffered the loss of 16 aircraft in action during the initial stages of the Allied 'Torch' landings later that year.

Dewoitine D.520

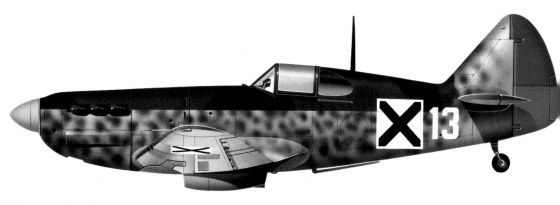

Distribution of Dewoitine D.520s after German occupation of Vichy-governed France included deliveries to the Bulgarian air force; the D.520 served with the 3rd Fighter Squadron, III(Bulg)/JG 6 alongside Luftwaffe units at Bojourishté in February 1944.

louse plant. In March 1943 SNCASE was ordered to complete the 150 unfinished aircraft; in little over a year this was accomplished, bringing the total to 905 D.520s built.

From this time onwards the D.520 saw fairly widespread service with the Axis air forces, being used initially as a fighter trainer, but also to a limited extent operationally by Jagdgeschwader of the Luftwaffe on the Eastern Front. Other training Jagdgeschwader included JG 105 which, based at Chartres and elsewhere, was wholly equipped with D.520s in 1943, JG 103 at Zeltweg, Austria, and JG 101 at Pau-Nord, commanded by the famous Luftwaffe fighter pilot, Walter Nowotny, early in 1944.

Sixty D.520s were delivered to the Regia Aeronautica in 1942-43 and served with a single squadriglia of each of the 13°, 22°, 24° and 167° Gruppi based on the Italian mainland for local defence. A small number of D.520s was allotted to the Romanian air force, ostensibly for the defence of the vital oilfields, but they proved inadequate to counter Allied bombing raids and were eventually sent to join Romanian elements on the Russian front. One hundred and twenty Dewoitine D.520s were supplied by Germany to the Bulgarian air force in 1943 and these equipped at least two squadrons of the 6th Air Force defending Sofia at the time of the Allied air attacks on the country; most were destroyed by Lockheed P-38 Lightnings of the US 9th Air Force, however.

French air force reconstituted

Following the liberation of southern France by the Allies in mid-1944 a French fighter group was formed in the Forces Françaises de l'Intérieur, equipped with D.520s. Named Groupe Doret after its commander Marcel Doret (the former test pilot), it comprised two escadrilles based at Tarbes-Ossun and Toulouse and participated in attacks on the pockets of Wehrmacht forces at Pointe de Grave and Royan.

When the French air force was formally reconstituted on 1 December 1944 Groupe Doret was redesignated GC II/18 'Saintonge' and equipped with 15 D.520s. Three months later GC II/18 re-equipped with Spitfire Mk VBs and the D.520s were passed on to GCB I/18 'Vendée' and to a training unit at Toulouse. Some 50 D.520s were recovered from the Germans during the final months of the war, and to these were added about 20 aircraft brought back to France when the Centre d'Instruction de Chasse at Meknès in North Africa was disbanded.

After the war in Europe ended, an instructors' school base, No. 704, was opened at Tours with a number of aircraft that included 17 D.520s, and on the initiative of its commanding officer one of these was converted to a two-seat trainer; it was approved by the service authorities and about a dozen further aircraft were converted and termed D.520DC (Double Commande). By the time school base No. 704 was disbanded on 31 August 1947 it possessed 29 D.520s.

Last unit to fly the D.520 was the Escadrille de Présentation de l'Armée de l'Air (EPAA) 58. Having flown a number of Yakovlev Yak-3s (brought back from the Russian front by the 'Normandie-Niémen' Regiment) which were grounded through lack of spares in 1948, the escadrille was given seven D.520s (of which three were DC two-seaters); the last flight by one of these aircraft, a single-seater, was made on 3 September 1953.

Displaying the famous 'African mask' device on its fin, this D.520 of 5ᵉ Escadrille, Groupe de Chasse III/6, was flown by Sergeant Hardouin at Casablanca, Morocco, in November 1940.

Macchi MC.200, 202 and 205

Handicapped by a lack of standardisation brought about by professional and industrial jealousies, Italian wartime fighters were, in general, no more than mediocre. However, the MC.200, 202 and 205 were roughly comparable with the Hurricane Mk 1, Spitfire Mk V and Mk IX, respectively, although always deficient in gun armament.

During the spring of 1935, at a time when work was already well advanced on the Messerschmitt Bf 109 and the Hawker Hurricane, the chief designer of the Italian Macchi company, Ing. Mario Castoldi, undertook feasibility studies of a monoplane fighter project with retractable landing gear. The project was a private venture. When, the following year, an official requirement for a metropolitan defence fighter was promulgated, Castoldi's design was tendered as the Macchi MC.200 and construction of a prototype was launched. The single 12.7-mm (0.5-in) gun originally specified was increased to two such guns, but the legacy of this puny armament concept was to dog Italian fighter design for eight years, and represented the single most serious deficiency.

By and large, however, the Macchi design was sturdy, compact and imaginative, though seriously compromised by the lack of a suitably powerful (895-kW/1,200-hp plus) engine. Instead it employed the Fiat A.74 14-cylinder two-row air-cooled radial which delivered no more than 649 kW (870 hp) for take-off. Careful attention to design detail nevertheless allowed a top speed of 504 km/h (313 mph) at 4520 m (14,830 ft), only slightly less than the Hurricane with 768-kW (1,030-hp) Merlin. But the weight of fire was no more than one-third of that of the British battery of eight Brownings.

The prototype MC.200 was flown by the company's chief test pilot, Guiseppe Burei, on 24 September 1937 (at exactly the time the first RAF Hurricanes were reaching squadron service), and in due course this aircraft was flown in competition with the Caproni-Vizzola F.5, Reggiane Re.2000, AUT.18 and Meridionali Ro.51 fighters, ostensibly to find a winner.

At the time of these competitive trials the Italian Air Ministry was battling to expand aircraft production and to increase the strength of the air force ('Programme R') and, partly as a result of attrition in the Spanish Civil War, this expansion was running considerably behind schedule, a situation quickly exploited by each manufacturer who, pointing to the volume of spare production capacity in his works,

advocated building not one fighter but all under consideration. Thus the ridiculous situation existed whereby the Macchi MC.200, Fiat CR.42 and G.50, and Reggiane Re.2000 came to be built simultaneously. None was outstanding, and had efforts been made to concentrate development on either the MC.200 or the G.50 a truly impressive design might well have materialised.

As it was, the MC.200 gave place eventually to the MC.202 and then to the MC.205; the Re. 2000 was followed by the Re.2001 and later the Re.2005; and the G.50 was succeeded by the G.55. At no stage during this cycle was any of these aircraft able to compete on equal terms with the latest German, British or American fighters, although when well flown they frequently achieved notable successes against obsolescent opponents.

Briefly, the MC.200 Saetta (Lightning) was a low-wing all-metal semi-monocoque structure with the pilot's cockpit set high in the fuselage over the wing trailing edge, thereby providing an excellent field of view. The landing gear retracted inwards hydraulically, allowing good strength and wide track, and a pair of synchronised 12.7-mm (0.5-in) SAFAT machine-guns was located in the fuselage nose decking to fire between the characteristic engine rocker-box fairings on the cowling. Later in service a field modification allowed carriage of up to 295 kg (650 lb) of bombs externally. All control surfaces were fabric-covered and the tailplane was of variable incidence. The prototypes and early production aircraft had a retractable tailwheel, but this was later fixed.

'Programme R' called for the MC.200 to enter service with three fighter *stormi* by the end of 1940. First of these was 4° Stormo 'Cavallino Rampante', but its pilots expressed a preference for

*Line-up of MC.200 Saettas of the 90ª Squadriglia CT (Caccia Terrestre), 10° Gruppo CT, 4° Stormo CT, in Sicily in 1941. On the fuselage band can be seen the 4° Stormo's famous **Cavallino Rampante** badge, while the 90ª Squadriglia's red elephant is displayed on a white disc below the cockpit.*

Macchi MC.200, 202 and 205

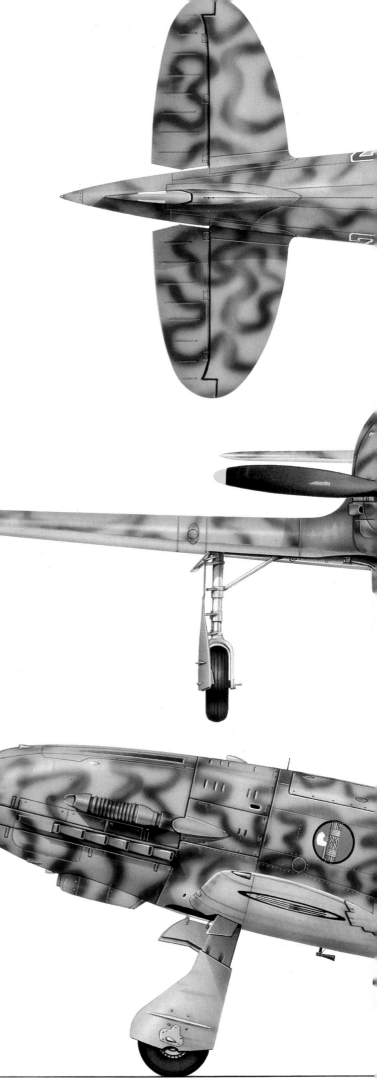

Specification
Macchi MC.202 Series VIII Folgore
Type: single-seat fighter
Powerplant: one 802-kW (1,075-hp) Alfa Romeo R.A.1000 RC.41-1 Monsoni (Monsoon) inverted V-12
Performance: maximum speed 600 km/h (373 mph) at 5600 m (18,375 ft); climb to 5000 m (16,405 ft) in 4 minutes 40 seconds; service ceiling 11500 m (37,730 ft); range at maximum take-off weight 765 km (475 miles)
Weights: empty 2490 kg (5,489 lb); maximum take-off 3010 kg (6,636 lb)
Dimensions: span 10.58 m (34 ft 8⅔ in); length 8.85 m (29 ft 0½ in); height 3.50 m (11 ft 5¾ in); wing area 16.82 m² (180.83 sq ft)
Armament: two 12.7-mm (0.5-in) Breda-SAFAT machine-guns in nose, each with 360 rounds, and two 7.7-mm (0.303-in) Breda-SAFAT guns in wings, each with 500 rounds

Identified as an aircraft of the 22° Gruppo by the Spauracchio (scarecrow) device on the fuselage band, and by the numerals as belonging to the 369ª Squadriglia, this mid-series MC.202 was based at Capodichino, Naples as part of the 53° Stormo CT at the time of the invasion of Sicily in July 1943. Although its maximum speed of 600 km/h (373 mph) was adequate to match Allied fighters of the Spitfire Mk V's generation, the purpose of deploying aircraft such as the MC.202 to defend Italian cities from attacks by Allied bombers was questionable, as their light armament was quite inadequate for the role of bomber-destroyer.

biplanes and were allowed to exchange their MC.200s for the Fiat CR.42 biplanes of the 1° Stormo. By the time Italy entered World War II in June 1940, Saettas equipped the 152° Gruppo at Airasca and the 153° Gruppo at Vergiate (both belonging to the 54° Stormo) and the 6° Gruppo of the 1° Stormo at Palermo. They did not take part in the brief campaign against France in June 1940 (having been temporarily grounded following two unexplained crashes), and received their baptism of fire when 6° Gruppo started operating against Malta in September of that year.

In the Greek campaign the CR.42 was said to be holding its own so long as nothing better than the Gloster Gladiator opposed it, but when the Hurricane gave the RAF a clear superiority (until the arrival of the Luftwaffe), 22° Gruppo with 36 Saettas was sent to Tirana, while the 7°, 10°, 16° and 153° Gruppi with 134 aircraft (of which about half were serviceable) took part in the campaign against Yugoslavia. It was largely the high attrition occasioned by these campaigns that prompted the Germans to deploy X. Fliegerkorps in the Mediterranean at that time.

It was, of course, in North Africa that the Saetta saw most action, this being made possible by the addition of dust filter equipment to the engine intake (changing the designation to MC.200AS, for Africa Settentrionale or North Africa). The first unit to arrive was the 374ª Squadriglia in April 1941, followed by the 153° and 157° Gruppi in July.

By the end of that year, the Hurricane Mk II and the Curtiss P-40 had gained the upper hand over the older Italian fighters in North Africa, and it was during the Axis offensive of 1942 that the Saetta was first used with some success as a fighter-bomber under the protection of more modern fighters.

In August 1941 the Saettas of the 22° Gruppo had been moved to the Eastern Front as the first component of the ĊSIR (Italian Expeditionary Corps in Russia), followed by the 21° Gruppo after eight months, these two units flying a total of 6,361 combat sorties and claiming the destruction of 85 Soviet aircraft for the loss of 15 of their own number.

By the date of the Allied invasion of Sicily in July 1943 the Saetta was wholly outdated, although some 42 serviceable aircraft remained on the front-line order of battle; of these, 23 were eventually flown to the Allied lines at the time of the armistice in September 1943.

As noted above, the failure to use an Italian high-power engine suitable for military use had stultified fighter design in that country before World War II, despite Castoldi's considerable success with very powerful racers (of which the MC.72 had gained the world speed record at 709.21 km/h/440.68 mph in 1934).

When in 1940 Macchi imported from Germany a Daimler-Benz DB 601 and plans were put in hand for its licence-production by Alfa Romeo, Mario Castoldi undertook a development of the MC.200

Last but four of the seventh series of MC.200s (MM7705) built by Macchi was modified to become the prototype Macchi MC.201, but this was not proceeded with. Obvious differences include the bulged fairings over the nose guns.

Macchi MC.200 (Series XIX) Saetta cutaway drawing key

1 Propeller hub
2 Variable-pitch propeller
3 Hub plate
4 Casing
5 Pitch control mechanism
6 Oil radiator
7 Cowling ring
8 Fiat A.74 R.C.38 14-cylinder radial air-cooled engine
9 Cowling rocker arm fairings
10 Carburettor intake
11 Intake housing
12 Starboard mainwheel
13 Intake filter
14 Exhaust outlet
15 Engine mounting ring
16 Exhaust collector ring
17 Adjustable cowling gills
18 Zenith compressor
19 Engine ring bearer frames
20 Oil filler access
21 Undercarriage retraction jack attachment
22 Firewall bulkhead
23 Cooling louvres
24 Oil tank (9.2 Imp gal/42 litre capacity)
25 Machine gun muzzle ports

© Pilot Press Limited

Late production MC.200s of the 81ª Squadriglia, 6° Gruppo, 1° Stormo, based at Catania, Sicily, late in 1940; this unit participated in many sorties over Malta at that time.

Macchi MC.200 of the 86ª Squadriglia, 7° Gruppo, 54° Stormo CT, based at Crotone in Sicily, early in 1942. The tiger's head emblem denoted the 54° Stormo CT whose aircraft operated over Malta as escorts on bombing attacks. Note the absence of cockpit canopy.

26 F.M. 62 gun camera (mounted mid-chord starboard wing join)
27 Starboard mainplane
28 Starboard pitot tube (heated)
29 Starboard navigation light
30 Aerial attachment
31 Starboard aileron
32 Cowling access panels
33 Fuel filler cap
34 Allocchio Bacchini B.30 R/T set

35 Battery
36 Twin 12.7-mm Breda-SAFAT machine guns
37 Gun synchronization mechanism
38 Link and case ejector chute
39 Gun mounting arm
40 Ammunition feed chute
41 Fuselage forward frame (Frame 0)
42 Supplementary magazine

43 Ammunition magazine
44 Link/spent case collector
45 Main fuel tank (52.3 Imp gal/238 litre capacity)
46 Centre-section rear spar carry-through
47 Fuselage frame (Frame 4)
48 Rudder pedal/heel rest assembly
49 Control column
50 Aerial attachment

51 Instrument panel
52 San Giorgio reflector gunsight
53 Windscreen
54 Canopy side-panel lock/release
55 Cutaway canopy side-panels
56 Cutaway canopy side-panels
57 Turnover pylon structure

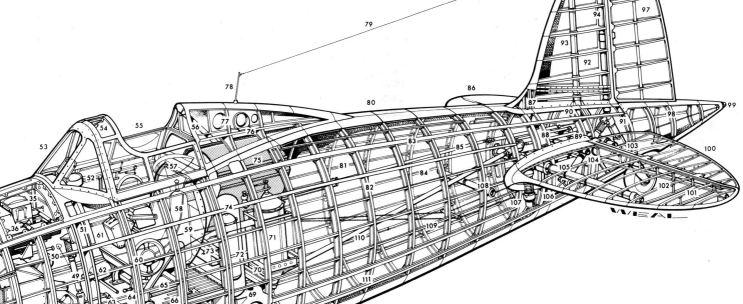

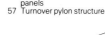

58 SILMA CO_2 fire-extinguisher bottle (fuselage starboard wall)
59 Pilot's seat
60 Adjustable tailplane trim wheel
61 Throttle quadrant
62 Pilot's oxygen cylinder (to right of seat)
63 Control linkage
64 Seat adjustment handle
65 Seat maining frame
66 Cockpit floor
67 Underfloor fuel tank (16.5 Imp gal/75 litre capacity)
68 Lower longeron
69 Entry foothold
70 Cylinder support frame

71 Compressed air cylinder (2.2 Imp gal/10 litre capacity)
72 Hydraulic reservoir (flap actuation)
73 Garelli compressor (fuselage starboard wall)
74 Hydraulic reservoir (undercarriage actuation)
75 Auxiliary fuel tank (18.26 Imp gal/83 litre capacity)
76 Fuel filler access cut-out
77 Fairing formers
78 Stub aerial mast
79 Aerial
80 Fuselage skin
81 Fuselage structure
82 Frame
83 Upper longeron
84 Stringer
85 Rudder control rod
86 Starboard horizontal tail surfaces
87 Tailfin front attachment
88 Fuselage frame (Frame 16)
89 Elevator control horns
90 Tailplane attachment (Frame 17)
91 Fuselage aft frame (Frame 18)
92 Tailfin structure
93 Support tube
94 Rudder post
95 Aerial attachment
96 Rudder balance
97 Rudder frame
98 Tail cone
99 Tail navigation light
100 Port elevator
101 Port tailplane structure
102 Non-retractable tailwheel
103 Tailwheel shock strut
104 Tailplane incidence torque tube (+1°45'' to −5°30'')
105 Tailplane support tube
106 Tailwheel strut attachment
107 Tailplane incidence screw
108 Lifting tube
109 Tailplane incidence control cables

110 Elevator control rod
111 Lower longeron
112 Wingroot fillet
113 Flap profile
114 Flap-operating rod
115 Flap structure
116 Wing rear spar
117 Port aileron structure
118 Wing outer section ribs
119 Port wingtip structure
120 Port navigation light
121 Port pitot tube (unheated)
122 Wing front spar
123 Leading-edge rib sections
124 Wing skin
125 Aerial
126 Undercarriage/rear spar attachment
127 Wing outer/inner section rear spar join
128 Wing root fairing former
129 Undercarriage rotation spindle
130 Centre-section outer rib
131 Wing outer/inner section front spar join
132 Frame O carry-through
133 Undercarriage retraction strut
134 Port mainwheel well
135 Mainwheel door inner section
136 Auxiliary jettisonable fuel tank (33 Imp gal/150 litre capacity)
137 Attachment lugs
138 Fuel connections
139 Mainwheel leg well
140 Undercarriage pivot
141 Mainwheel leg
142 Retraction strut attachment
143 Leg doors (hinged)
144 Torque links
145 Shock strut
146 Port mainwheel
147 Mainwheel door outer section
148 Axle fork
149 Underwing stores pylon
150 Bomb

Early series MC.200 Saetta of the 371° Squadriglia (note the Cucaracha device on the rear fuselage), 52° Stormo CT, based at Ciampino at the time of Italy's entry into the war. At that time the underwing fasces markings had a white background.

Macchi MC.200 of the 373ª Squadriglia, 153° Gruppo Autonomo, based in Cyrenaica during 1942 and flown by F. Raffaelli, commander of Eastern Sector Forces. The star on the blue panel was the pennant of a Generale di Brigata (brigadier general). The Assi di Bastoni (ace of spades) badge distinguished the 153° Gruppo Automomo, and aircraft of this unit frequently displayed the large characters CLIII in red forward of the fuselage band.

with this much larger engine, the prototype being first flown by Carestiato on 10 August that year. Within 12 months production aircraft, designated C.202 Folgore (Thunderbolt), were being completed by Macchi as a parallel production line was being assembled at Breda's Milan plant, while a widespread subcontract network was undertaking component manufacture.

The superior MC.202

The MC.202 was an excellent design, incorporating all the best features of the Saetta (thereby accelerating much of the component manufacture), combined with a sleek nose profile enclosing the new German engine. The canopy fairing was lengthened and blended into the upper line of the fuselage, and a radiator was located under the fuselage in line with the wing trailing edge. The twin 12.7-mm (0.5-in) SAFAT gun armament in the nose was retained, but from the MC.202 Series VI this was increased by the addition of two 7.7-mm (0.303-in) guns in the wings; at least some degree of weapon respectability had been achieved.

The Folgore eventually achieved a maximum speed of 600 km/h (373 mph) at 5600 m (18,375 ft), roughly the same as the Supermarine Spitfire Mk V and somewhat better than the P-40 Tomahawk

which still served with the RAF in North Africa in 1941, when the Folgore joined the Regia Aeronautica.

First to receive the MC.202 was the 1° Stormo at Udine in the summer of 1941, but this unit's 6° and 17° Gruppi were not ready to move to North Africa until November that year, and it was said in many quarters that the late arrival at the front of this excellent fighter was a major factor that allowed the RAF to maintain air superiority during the Allied offensive in Cyrenaica.

It was during the subsequent Axis offensive, which eventually ran out of steam at El Alamein during 1942, that the Folgore fought its most successful campaign. At the beginning of the year the 6° Gruppo was based at Ara Fileni and the 17° Gruppo at Tamet. In April the 4° Stormo was deployed in Sicily for the spring assault on Malta, but two months later this unit too was sent to Libya. In May Folgores and Bf 109s gained ascendency over the Hurricanes and P-40s of the Desert Air Force, and for a short period the Regia Aeronautica and Luftwaffe enjoyed air superiority in the skies over the advancing Allied forces, except when confronted by the growing number of RAF Spitfire Mk Vs.

On the eve of the Battle of El Alamein the Folgore equipped the 4° Stormo at Fuka and the 3° Stormo at Benghazi and Abug Aggag, the

Late picture of the first Macchi MC.200 prototype, MM336. First flown on 24 December 1937 by Guiseppi Burei, the aircraft originally featured an unsupported rear canopy section but vibration prompted the addition of longitudinal and transverse frames.

The Cucaracha (cockroach) device on the rear fuselage identifies these early MC.200s as belonging to the 22° Gruppo (in fact its 371ª Squadriglia), of the 52° Stormo, deployed at Ciampino in 1940 for the defence of Rome.

First four-gun installation in a Macchi MC.202 Series III (MM7731); the nose guns remained 12.7-mm (0.5-in) Breda-SAFAT weapons, and the wing guns were 7.7-mm (0.303-in) calibre. The yellow nose and spinner of this aircraft probably denoted its experimental status.

Macchi MC.200, MC.202 and MC.205 variants

MC.200: two prototypes (MM336 and 337); first flown 24 December 1937 and powered by the Fiat A.74 RC 38
MC.200 Saetta: seven series, total of 345 built by Macchi; first 144 with retractable tailwheel and fully enclosed cockpit, both features dropped in later aircraft
MC.200 Saetta: six series, total of 436 built by Breda, all with fixed tailwheel
MC.200 Saetta: six series, total of 124 built by SAI Ambrosini
MC.200 Saetta: Series XX, XXIII and XXIV; unknown total buit by SAI Ambrosini
MC.200 Saetta: Series XXI and XXV; unknown total built by Breda
MC.200 Saetta: Series XXII; 50 aircraft built by Macchi in 1941
MC.200 Saetta: MM8191 experimentally fitted with Piaggio P.XIX radial engine by Breda

MC.202: prototype (MM445); first flown 10 August 1940 and powered by the DB 601A-1
MC.202 Folgore: five series, total of 392 built by Macchi; final series introduced underwing provision for stores, and ram-air intake to supercharger
MC.202 Folgore: six series, total of about 1,100 aircraft built by Breda; Series VI introduced pair of wing machine-guns
MC.202 Folgore: MM7768 development prototype with radiator moved to 'chin' position
MC.202 Folgore: MM91974 development prototype with two underwing MG 151 guns
MC.202V Veltro: Daimler-Benz DB 605 engine; production total 262
MC.205N-1 Orione: DB 605A (Fiat R.A.1050 Tifone), four 12.7-mm and one 20-mm MG 151 guns
MC.205N-2: three 20-mm MG 151 and two 12.7-mm guns

1° Stormo having returned to Italy. In the subsequent fighting RAF numerical strength overwhelmed the Axis air forces, operating as they were with overstretched supply routes. As spares, fuel and ammunition stocks dwindled, the two MC 202 *stormi* contracted to one, and this was eventually withdrawn to Tunisia. At the same time, Sicily-based Folgores were being engaged in furious air battles over the convoys being sailed to relieve Malta as they strove to protect the Junkers Ju 87s and Savoia-Marchetti S.M.79s attacking the ships.

After the collapse of the Axis forces in North Africa and on the eve of the invasion of Sicily, the total strength of Folgores in the Mediterranean theatre amounted to 186 aircraft, of which just 100 were serviceable; these served with the 2° Stormo (Lonate Pozzolo), 3° Stormo (Cerveteri), 4° Stormo (Catania), 21° Gruppo (Firenze and Chinisia), 22° Gruppo (Capodichino), 24° Gruppo (Venafiorita), 155° Gruppo (Monserrato), 153° Gruppo (Palermo), 154° Gruppo (Rhodes) and 161° Gruppo (Reggio di Calabria).

As the Allied pressure in the Mediterranean grew inexorably, nothing that either the Luftwaffe or the Regia Aeronautica could do could blunt the offensive against their airfields, and the majority of losses suffered were the result of bombing attacks against their bases. Thirty-three Allied aircraft are reckoned to have fallen to the guns of the Folgores, but by the time of the Italian armistice only 53 of them remained airworthy.

Like the Saetta, the Folgore also served on the Russian front, although the demands being made in the Mediterranean theatre imposed severe limitations on its deployment. Indeed, only 12 of the new fighters were sent to the Eastern Front in September 1942, being used to supplement the aircraft being used by the 21° Gruppo. They took part in the offensive by the 8th Army towards the Don, and were based successively at Voroshilovgrad, Millerovo and Kan-

temirovka, being acknowledged by the Germans as among the best aircraft available.

During the late summer of 1943 the Folgore was recognised on all fronts as being outdated, for not only was it outclassed in performance and manoeuvrability by such aircraft as the Spitfire Mk IX, P-40 Warhawk and Lockheed P-38 Lightning, it also lacked the ability to destroy enemy bombers with its very feeble gun armament. A number of aircraft underwent experiments to improve performance and armament (one with undernose radiator, and another with a pair of underwing 20-mm Mauser MG 151 guns), but all these schemes were discarded.

Given that Italy had become firmly identified with the Axis cause in the years immediately before World War II, it was extraordinary that greater efforts were not made to rectify the lack of a powerful engine suitable for fighter application. Had the DB 601 been supplied as early as 1938 (and manufacture of the engine was well under way by then), the MC.202, which was arguably Italy's best fighter of World War II, could well have imposed a decisive presence in the Mediterranean and North Africa as soon as Italy entered the war. However, to have done so would also have demanded total alteration of aircraft design policy with regard to fighter armament. It is probably true to say that Italian fighter design pandered to the excellence of flying skills of the nation's pilots rather than their recognised prowess in air-to-air combat.

The greatly improved MC.205V Veltro with uprated Daimler-Benz engine started appearing in small numbers in 1943, but were too few and too late to seriously contest Allied air superiority in the Mediterranean. It led to the MC.205N Orione, the N-1 shown here having four 12.7-mm (0.5-in) guns in the nose plus a 20-mm MG 151 firing through the propeller hub.

Bristol's Whispering Death

Dubbed 'Whispering Death' by the Japanese when it arrived in the Far East during World War II, the RAF's heavily-armed Beaufighter did more than most aircraft to drive the Japanese back across South East Asia. Of equal importance, it did more than any to defeat the Luftwaffe's night bombing offensive over the British Isles, while later in the war it became the scourge of Axis coastal shipping, carrying rockets and torpedoes.

As one of a number of high-speed heavily-armed fighter projects being pursued by the Bristol Aeroplane Co. Ltd in the period immediately before World War II, Leslie Frise's two-seat Type 156 was to be powered by a pair of Bristol Hercules sleeve-valve radial engines and armed with four 20-mm cannon grouped in the nose. Key to the Air Ministry's acceptance of this design was its proposed use of existing Beaufort outer wings, tail unit and landing gear, enabling production to be switched from one aircraft to the other with minimum disruption to the factory layout. Immediately after the Beaufort's first flight on 15 October 1938 orders were placed for four Type 156 prototypes, to be named Beaufighter; the first being flown on 17 July 1939 – just 45 days before the outbreak of war. At the same time Bristol received a production contract for 300 aircraft.

Although Hercules III engines were specified, Bristol was instructed to examine the alternative use of Rolls-Royce Merlin and Griffon engines, but the Battle of Britain and its heavy drain on Merlin resources delayed this work and the first production aircraft were flown with the Hercules during the summer of 1940, undergoing trials at Boscombe Down. A handful of early aircraft saw operational service with the Fighter Interception Unit (FIU) during the Battle of Britain, and early in September single aircraft were delivered to night-fighter squadrons. The Beaufighter's first operational sortie was flown by the FIU early in September, and the first aircraft was lost on operations on 13 September. Maximum speed of these early aircraft was 497 km/h (309 mph), compared with an anticipated 539 km/h (335 mph).

At the end of the Battle of Britain, Beaufighter Mk IFs (the F denoting Fighter Command) were being delivered fitted with oper-

Although many early crews were apprehensive of the Beaufighter, partly on account of its tricky low-speed handling qualities and high critical speed, confidence in the heavily-armed fighter was quickly established and the aircraft gave magnificent service in many war theatres, particularly in the Mediterranean and Far East whose hot and dusty environment was more suited to its robust airframe and radial engines than the Mosquito.

This Beaufighter Mk IF was one of the first 'Beaus' to enter service. It flew with No. 25 Squadron at North Weald in the late summer of 1940.

This Beaufighter TF.Mk X flew with No. 455 Squadron, RAAF, from Dallachy in the United Kingdom in late 1944. As part of Coastal Command, the squadron flew anti-shipping strikes along the Norwegian coast.

ationally-cleared airborne radar (AI Mk IV) and as RAF operators gained proficiency with this equipment so the first successful night engagements were achieved. By the end of the German night Blitz in May 1941 five home-based night-fighter squadrons (Nos 25, 29, 219, 600 and 604) had re-equipped, and between them had claimed some 60 victories using AI. The first 50 aircraft produced at Filton were armed only with the four nose-mounted 20-mm cannon, but thereafter the Beaufighter (including the 1,000 aircraft produced at the 'shadow' factories) carried the full complement of four cannon and six wing-mounted Browning machine-guns, two in the port and four in the starboard outer wing. By 1941 Beaufighters were being built at Filton, Stockport, Weston-super-Mare and Blythe Bridge in Staffordshire.

Meanwhile a Merlin-powered Beaufighter Mk II prototype had flown on 26 July 1940 and the first production deliveries were made to No. 600 Squadron in April 1941, followed by the Canadian No. 406 Squadron in June and No. 255 in July. A modification originally introduced in the Merlin Beaufighter was a 12° dihedral tailplane (found necessary to counter take-off swing) included in all subsequent versions.

Range of projects

By the end of May 1941 207 Beaufighter Mk IFs and Mk IIFs had been taken on charge by the RAF, this figure also including the first Mk IC (the C denoting Coastal Command) aircraft delivered to No. 272 Squadron (flying from Malta) in April; the Mk IC differed from

Fighter Command's aircraft by the addition of specialised navigation and radio equipment. Production of both versions totalled 910, in addition to 450 Beaufighter Mk IIFs.

A number of Beaufighter projects and experiments are worth mentioning here. A single Rolls-Royce Griffon-powered aircraft was produced as a trial installation for the projected Beaufighter Mk IV but was abandoned, as was an aircraft with twin fins and rudders produced in an attempt to overcome directional stability problems. A four-gun power-operated dorsal turret was fitted immediately behind the cockpit on two aircraft termed Mk Vs, and comparative trials with Vickers and Rolls-Royce 40-mm anti-tank guns were conducted in 1941 with one of each type fitted under the nose of a Beaufighter prototype. (Some years after the war a Beaufighter was similarly fitted with a 30-mm Aden gun for assessment trials.) The proposed Hercules VI-powered Beaufighter Mk III was not built.

However, the 1194-kW (1,600-hp) Hercules VI (and XVI) engine was used in the next major production variant, the Mk VI of which both 'F' and 'C' versions were produced – the latter introducing a Vickers K gas-operated machine-gun in the observer's rear station. The 'F' served with 16 home-based night-fighter squadrons, while the 'C' joined 10 squadrons of Coastal Command flying patrols over

Typical of many Coastal Command Beaufighters is this Mk X of No. 236 Squadron, headquartered at North Coates from 1942 until 1945 but with many detachments around the coast. Underneath the wing are the rockets that made the type such a devastating weapon against light craft.

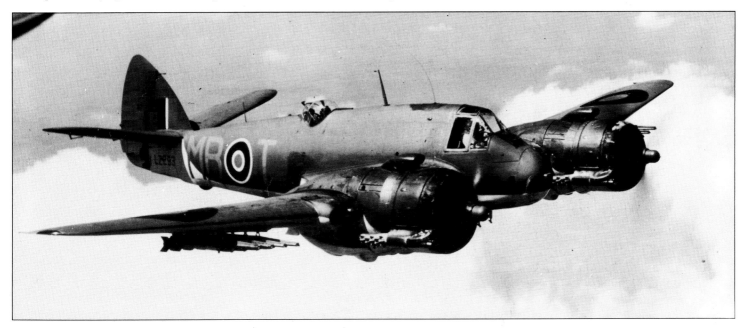

Specification
Bristol Beaufighter TF.Mk X
Type: two-seat anti-shipping strike fighter
Powerplant: two 1294-kW (1,735-hp) Bristol Hercules XVII
sleeve-valve radial engines
Performance: maximum speed 488 km/h (303 mph) at 400 m
(1,300 ft); climb to 1525 m (5,000 ft) in 3 minutes 30 seconds;
service ceiling 4575 m (15,000 ft); normal range 2367 km (1,470
miles)
Weights: empty 7082 kg (15,600 lb); maximum take-off 11441 kg
(25,200 lb)
Dimensions: span 17.64 m (57 ft 10 in); length 12.71 m (41 ft 8 in);
height 4.83 m (15 ft 10 in); wing area 47.13 m^2 (503 sq ft)
Armament: four nose-mounted 20-mm cannon and one rear
7.7-mm (0.303-in) machine-gun, plus one 750-kg (1,650-lb) or
966-kg (2,127-lb) torpedo, or eight 27-kg (60-lb) rockets and two
113-kg (250-lb) bombs under the wings

*T4638 was the 16th Bristol
Beaufighter Mk IF night-fighter
built by the Fairey Aviation
Company; equipped with AI Mk
IV, characterised by the broad
arrow nose aerial and outer wing
arrays, and carrying an armament
of four 20-mm and six 7.7-mm
(0.303-in) guns, T4638 joined No.
604 (County of Middlesex)
Squadron at Middle Wallop in
1941. At this time the squadron,
commanded by Wing
Commander John Cunningham,
was the top-scoring night-fighter
unit in the RAF, and had been
one of the first to receive the
Beaufighter at the height of the
Battle of Britain in September
1940. Although crews had been
slow to master the use of AI
radar, by the end of the German
night blitz of 1940-1 the
Beaufighter had become the
world's most effective night-
fighter.*

the Bay of Biscay against German long-range maritime aircraft as well as against enemy submarines and blockade runners. In July 1942 No. 272 Squadron, Coastal Command, deployed with Beaufighters on Malta to provide long-range cover over Allied convoys passing through the Sicilian straits. They destroyed 49 enemy maritime aircraft and damaged many more. In northern Europe the aircraft embarked on night intruder operations over enemy-occupied territory, attacking German bombers over their bases and causing widespread damage to enemy road and rail targets. One of the most famous adventures involved a No. 236 Squadron Beaufighter Mk VIC flown by Flight Lieutenant Ken Gatward, who in broad daylight dropped a *tricolore* from low level over the Champs-Elysées in Paris before attacking the nearby Gestapo headquarters with cannon fire.

Beaufighter Mk IFs and Mk VIFs were first sent to the Far East in January 1943 with No. 176 Squadron, newly-formed from No. 89 Squadron, operating from Calcutta against the Japanese. One of the pilots, Sergeant Pring, was ordered off on the first night and destroyed three enemy bombers. Between then and the end of the war eight RAF squadrons, based in the Far East, were equipped with the Beaufighter, joining 54 Mk ICs produced by Fairey in the UK for the Royal Australian Air Force.

Following the success of the aircraft in Europe it was decided to open up a new production line in Australia and, as the Beaufighter Mk XXI, the first aircraft to be completed at Fishermen's Bend, Victoria, was flown on 26 May 1944. A total of 364 Australian-built Beaufighters was completed by the end of 1945. One of the Fairey-built Mk ICs for Australia was modified with Wright Double Cyclone GR 2600-A5B engines as a prototype for a proposed Australian Mk VIII and Mk IX, but in the event these versions did not materialise.

Burma bomber

It was largely the Beaufighters of Nos 176 and 217 Squadrons, operating over Burma, that were responsible for the Japanese Army's respect for the aircraft after a devastating low-level strike against a military ceremonial parade at Myitkyina, to celebrate the emperor's birthday. With bombs, rockets and guns the Beaufighter wrought widespread havoc among river and jungle targets throughout the Burma campaign that lasted until the final liberation of Rangoon.

Despite the arrival of the Mosquito which gradually superseded the Beaufighter, the tactics of Fighter Command's Beaufighter Mk VIFs were never better demonstrated than by Wing Commander J.R.D. Braham, commanding No. 219 Squadron and the RAF's highest-scoring night-fighter pilot. He would infiltrate groups of enemy night-fighters as they approached British streams and, by use of his forward and rearward scanning radar, would entice the German fighters to approach from the rear before pulling a snap turn that would bring him into a firing position on the enemy's tail. Such tactics were emulated by the Mosquito bomber support group, but the

Conditions in the Far East theatre were often primitive, the 'Beaus' using makeshift landing strips. The type's metal structure coped with the hot and humid conditions far better than that of the wooden Mosquito, which was intended to replace it on fighter-bomber duties.

Beaufighter Mk VIF intruder continued in service until the end of 1944.

Several Beaufighter night-fighter squadrons, including Nos 255 and 600, were moved to North Africa in 1943 in time to join the massacre of German transport aircraft during the attempted evacuation of Tunisia – as exemplified by Flight Sergeant Downing of No. 600 Squadron, who destroyed five Junkers Ju 52/3ms in 10 minutes off Setif on 30 April. AI Mk IV radar-equipped Beaufighter Mk VIFs were also supplied from field stocks to the I Tactical Air Command of the USAAF in North Africa, whose night-fighter squadrons were awaiting delivery of the Northrop P-61 Black Widow (which did not in the event arrive in Europe until 1944).

It was the suggestion of the C-in-C, Coastal Command, Air Chief Marshal Sir Philip Joubert de la Ferté, that the Beaufighter be adapted to carry a torpedo, and that composite anti-shipping strike wings be formed using Beaufighters as fighters, fighter-bombers and torpedo strike aircraft, that led to an entirely new chapter in the aircraft's career. The first such wing was formed at North Coates in Lincolnshire in November 1942 with No. 143 Squadron flying fighters, No. 236 flying fighter-bombers carrying two 113-kg (250-lb) bombs under the wings, and No. 254 Squadron with torpedo Beaufighters. The aircraft had undergone development to carry either the British 45.7-cm (18-in) or American 53.3-cm (21-in) naval torpedo, with the first aircraft commencing trials in May 1942. Sixty further interim torpedo fighters termed Mk VI(ITF) were converted and had joined No. 254 Squadron before the end of the year.

A very early Beaufighter Mk IF (R2153) of No. 219 (Fighter) Squadron at Tangmere early in 1941. At that time night-fighting was in its infancy and night camouflage had yet to be adopted. No. 219 Squadron was then commanded by Wing Commander Tom Pike, later to become Commander-in-Chief of Fighter Command.

One of many experimental Beaufighters, X7579 was a Mk IF equipped with AI Mark VIII in a 'thimble' nose; this provided a radar display for the pilot, as evidenced by the raised decking forward of the windscreen. It proved unpopular with service crews and was soon abandoned.

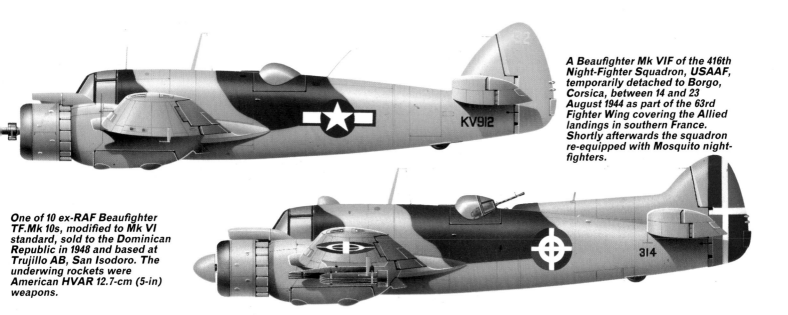

A Beaufighter Mk VIF of the 416th Night-Fighter Squadron, USAAF, temporarily detached to Borgo, Corsica, between 14 and 23 August 1944 as part of the 63rd Fighter Wing covering the Allied landings in southern France. Shortly afterwards the squadron re-equipped with Mosquito night-fighters.

One of 10 ex-RAF Beaufighter TF.Mk 10s, modified to Mk VI standard, sold to the Dominican Republic in 1948 and based at Trujillo AB, San Isodoro. The underwing rockets were American HVAR 12.7-cm (5-in) weapons.

North Sea strike force

The strike wings would be sent against enemy convoys in the North Sea, now heavily protected by fighters and Flak ships, and, while the fighter Beaufighters engaged the Luftwaffe overhead, the bomb-carrying aircraft would cover the attacks by the torpedo Beaufighters. After a premature start to such attacks, which were abortive because of inadequate training and bad weather, the North Coates Wing began successful operations on 18 April 1943, and the following month was joined by Beaufighter Mk VICs modified to carry up to eight 27-kg (60-lb) rocket projectiles under the wings (in place of the wing machine-guns). These aircraft were occasionally referred to as 'Flakbeaus'. Two other such strike wings were soon formed with Nos 144, 235, 404 (RCAF), 455 (RAAF) and 489 (RNZAF) Squadrons.

Stemming directly from the Mk VIC, the Beaufighter Mk X was the major production version, and was flown almost exclusively by Coastal Command, apart from some fighter squadrons in the Middle East and Far East. It was powered by two 1294-kW (1,735-hp) Bristol Hercules XVII engines and featured the torpedo-carrying equipment of the Mk VI(ITF). The AI Mk VIII, adapted for ASV purposes, was nose-mounted in a thimble-shaped radome. Also introduced was a Browning machine-gun (occasionally a twin-gun installation) in place of the old Vickers gas-operated gun in the rear hatch.

The increased weight of these and other modifications had, however, been found to impair the aircraft's directional and longitudinal stability beyond the remedial effect of the dihedral tailplane, with the result that the Mk X featured a long dorsal fin extension and elevators of increased area. A total of 2,205 of this version was produced at the 'shadow' factory at Weston-super-Mare and by Rootes at Blythe Bridge. Final production variant was Coastal Command's

Beaufighter Mk XIC, of which 165 were produced and which was simply a Mark X without torpedo-carrying gear.

As Coastal Beaufighters continued to fly patrols against enemy blockade runners in the Bay of Biscay, the Beaufighter Mk Xs of the strike wings moved north to Scotland early in 1944 to begin 'Rover' patrols against German shipping carrying supplies to the *Tirpitz*, which was sheltering in a Norwegian fjord, and returning with iron ore from Narvik. Then, as the forthcoming Normandy landings approached, the wings were brought south again to bases in East Anglia and Kent to watch for enemy activity nearer the invasion coast. To participate in support operations over the landings it had been hoped to introduce a new Beaufighter (the Mk XII) with streng-

R2274 was the experimental Beaufighter Mk V. Originally one of the first production batch of Merlin-powered Mk II night-fighters, this aircraft was modified to feature a power-operated four-gun turret immediately aft of the pilot's cockpit while still retaining the AI radar.

A Beaufighter Mk X (NE798) of No. 445 Squadron, Royal Australian Air Force, based in East Anglia in mid-1944 for anti-shipping strike duties. Note the 'invasion stripes' and the pair of 227-kg (500-lb) bombs under the fuselage; the aircraft also carries underwing racks for 113-kg (250-lb) bombs.

Bristol's Whispering Death

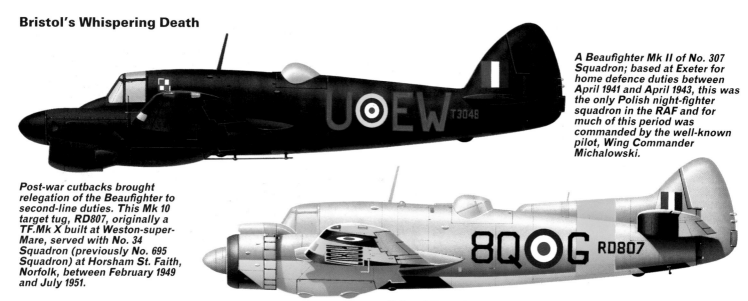

A Beaufighter Mk II of No. 307 Squadron; based at Exeter for home defence duties between April 1941 and April 1943, this was the only Polish night-fighter squadron in the RAF and for much of this period was commanded by the well-known pilot, Wing Commander Michalowski.

Post-war cutbacks brought relegation of the Beaufighter to second-line duties. This Mk 10 target tug, RD807, originally a TF.Mk X built at Weston-super-Mare, served with No. 34 Squadron (previously No. 695 Squadron) at Horsham St. Faith, Norfolk, between February 1949 and July 1951.

thened airframe to carry two 454-kg (1,000-lb) bombs under the wings, but components for the proposed Hercules 27 engines were not ready in time, and this version was abandoned. Instead the Mk X was modified to carry two 227-kg (500-lb) bombs under the fuselage in addition to the smaller wing bombs. These aircraft were flown to good effect against German E- and R-boats attempting to attack the Allies' artificial harbours off Normandy.

In the Mediterranean, rocket-firing Beaufighters sank the 55,000-ton Italian liner *Rex* near Trieste after scoring 55 hits below the waterline. Elsewhere in southern Europe Beaufighters of RAF and SAAF squadrons co-operated with the Balkan air forces supporting operations with Yugoslav partisans under Marshal Tito.

In the Far East Australian-built Beaufighters were employed to give long-range bomber escort during the Tarakan landings on 2 May 1945, and played a prominent part in the campaign to deny the Japanese use of coastal waters off Burma. By February 1945 the Beaufighters of No. 224 Group (in particular No. 211 Squadron) had sunk about 700 small vessels.

After the war most surviving Beaufighter squadrons in the RAF were either disbanded or re-equipped by 1946, although No. 84 Squadron continued to fly its Mk Xs until 1949 and No. 45 retained its aircraft until 1950; both were eventually based at Kuala Lumpur, flying rocket attacks against the Malayan terrorists.

At home 35 Beaufighter Mk Xs were converted to target tugs with a standard windmill-driven winch on the starboard side of the fuselage just aft of the wing (a conversion that had been suggested in 1942 when it seemed that Beaufighters would be wholly replaced by the Mosquito); 35 Beaufighter TT.Mk 10s were delivered to RAF units between 1948 and 1950, serving in Ceylon, Cyprus, Gibraltar, Malaya and Malta – the last of these being scrapped at Singapore in May 1960. Other war-surplus Beaufighters were exported to Turkey, Dominica and elsewhere. Total Beaufighter production was 5,564 in the UK and 364 in Australia.

The first prototype Bristol Type 156 Beaufighter (R2052) at Filton in July 1939. Powered by Hercules I engine and lacking armament, this aircraft featured the landing gear, outer wings and tailplane of the Beaufort, but these were extensively changed in production examples.

Bristol Beaufighter I cutaway drawing key

1 Starboard navigation light (fore) and formation-keeping light (aft)
2 Wing structure
3 Aileron adjustable tab
4 Starboard aileron
5 Four Browning 0.303-in (7.7-mm) machine guns
6 Machine gun ports
7 Starboard outer wing fuel tank, capacity 87 Imp gal (395 litres)
8 Split trailing-edge flaps, hydraulically actuated
9 Starboard flap
10 Flap operating jack
11 Starboard nacelle tail fairing
12 Oil tank, capacity 17 Imp gal (77 litres)

28 Control column
29 Cannon ports
30 Seat adjusting lever
31 Pilot's seat
32 Instrument panel
33 Clear-vision panel
34 Flat bullet proof windscreen
35 Fixed canopy (sideways-hinged on later aircraft)
36 Spar carry-through step
37 Nose centre section attachment point
38 Fuselage/centre section attachment point
39 Pilot's entry/emergency escape hatchway
40 Underfloor cannon blast tubes

51 Starboard cannon (two 20-mm)
52 Floor level
53 Steps
54 Observer's swivel seat (normally forward-facing)
55 Radio controls and intercom
56 Observer's cupola
57 Hinged panel
58 Aerial
59 Oxygen bottles
60 Vertical control cable shaft
61 Sheet metal bulkhead
62 Control cables
63 Tailplane structure
64 Elevator
65 Elevator balance tab
66 Fin structure

13 Starboard inner wing fuel tank, capacity 188 Imp gal (855 litres)
14 Cabin air duct
15 Hinged leading-edge sections
16 Engine bulkhead
17 Engine bearers
18 Auxiliary intake
19 Supercharger air intake
20 Engine cooling flaps
21 1,650 hp Bristol Hercules III radial engine
22 De Havilland Hydromatic airscrew
23 Airscrew spinner
24 Lockheed oleo-pneumatic shock-absorber
25 Starboard mainwheel, with Dunlop brakes
26 Forward identification lamp in nose cap
27 Rudder pedals

41 Fuselage/centre section attachment points
42 Centre section attachment longeron reinforcement
43 Cabin air duct
44 Cannon heating duct
45 Rear spar carry-through
46 Bulkhead cut-out (observer access to front hatch)
47 Bulkhead
48 Hydraulic header tank
49 Aerial mast
50 Monocoque fuselage construction

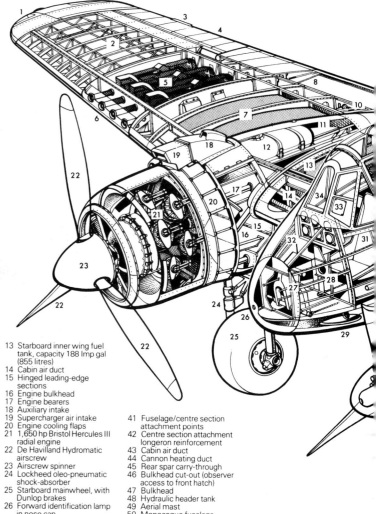

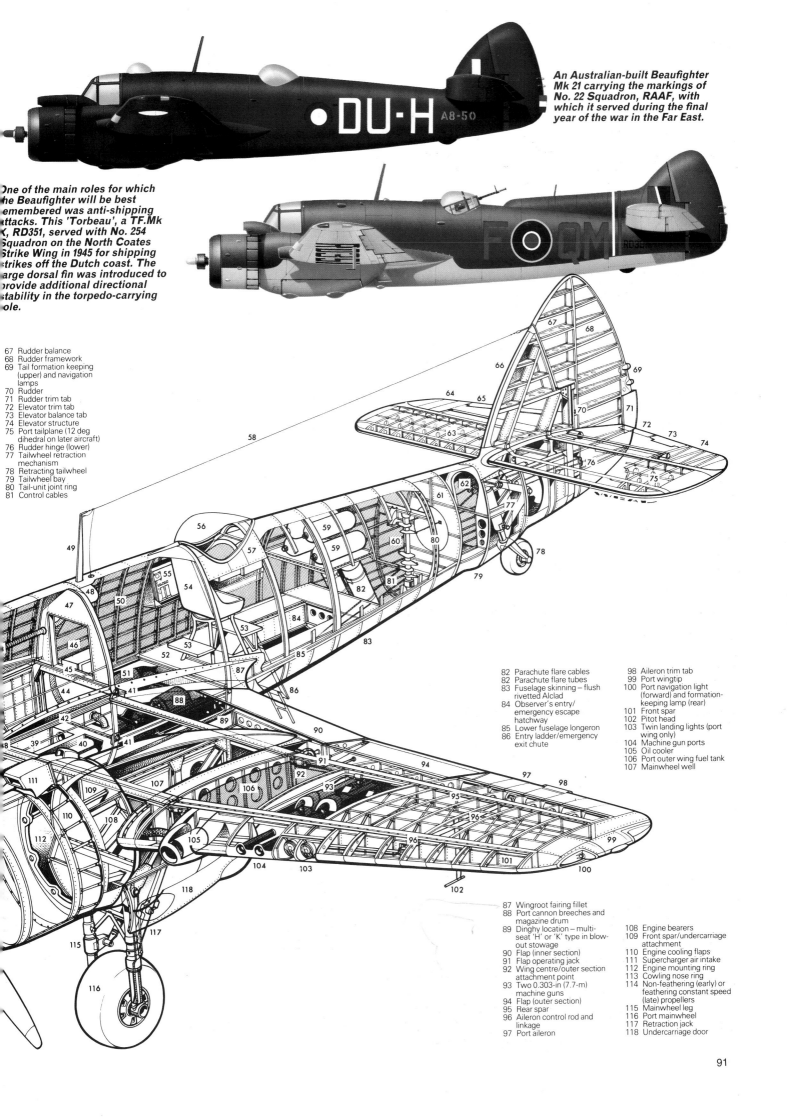

An Australian-built Beaufighter Mk 21 carrying the markings of No. 22 Squadron, RAAF, with which it served during the final year of the war in the Far East.

One of the main roles for which the Beaufighter will be best remembered was anti-shipping attacks. This 'Torbeau', a TF.Mk X, RD351, served with No. 254 Squadron on the North Coates Strike Wing in 1945 for shipping strikes off the Dutch coast. The large dorsal fin was introduced to provide additional directional stability in the torpedo-carrying role.

67 Rudder balance
68 Rudder framework
69 Tail formation keeping (upper) and navigation lamps
70 Rudder
71 Rudder trim tab
72 Elevator trim tab
73 Elevator balance tab
74 Elevator structure
75 Port tailplane (12 deg dihedral on later aircraft)
76 Rudder hinge (lower)
77 Tailwheel retraction mechanism
78 Retracting tailwheel
79 Tailwheel bay
80 Tail-unit joint ring
81 Control cables

82 Parachute flare cables
82 Parachute flare tubes
83 Fuselage skinning – flush rivetted Alclad
84 Observer's entry/ emergency escape hatchway
85 Lower fuselage longeron
86 Entry ladder/emergency exit chute

98 Aileron trim tab
99 Port wingtip
100 Port navigation light (forward) and formation-keeping lamp (rear)
101 Front spar
102 Pitot head
103 Twin landing lights (port wing only)
104 Machine gun ports
105 Oil cooler
106 Port outer wing fuel tank
107 Mainwheel well

87 Wingroot fairing fillet
88 Port cannon breeches and magazine drum
89 Dinghy location – multi-seat 'H' or 'K' type in blow-out stowage
90 Flap (inner section)
91 Flap operating jack
92 Wing centre/outer section attachment point
93 Two 0.303-in (7.7-m) machine guns
94 Flap (outer section)
95 Rear spar
96 Aileron control rod and linkage
97 Port aileron

108 Engine bearers
109 Front spar/undercarriage attachment
110 Engine cooling flaps
111 Supercharger air intake
112 Engine mounting ring
113 Cowling nose ring
114 Non-feathering (early) or feathering constant speed (late) propellers
115 Mainwheel leg
116 Port mainwheel
117 Retraction jack
118 Undercarriage door

Mitsubishi A6M 'Zero'

During the early months of 1942, as the victorious Japanese swept through South East Asia and the Pacific at breakneck speed, the name 'Zero' sent shivers down the spines of Allied airmen. However, this much-vaunted and much-used fighter proved in the end to be just another good design, and not the miracle once thought.

When the Japanese Navy struck at Pearl Harbor on Sunday, 7 December 1941, the Americans already possessed files on the A6M in the form of detailed combat reports from Colonel Claire Chennault in far-off Chungking, China. Nobody had bothered to disseminate the information, and for a second time this agile and well-armed fighter caused a great shock and made mincemeat of the motley collection of aircraft that opposed it. In six months the Sentais (fighter groups) equipped with the A6M had so dominated the sky that the Imperial forces had conquered over 37.3 million km^2 (12 million square miles), a far greater area than had ever previously been overrun by one nation. The A6M kept appearing in places where Japanese fighters had been judged 'impossible', sometimes almost 1610 km (1,000 miles) from the nearest advanced Japanese airbase or carrier. In combat it could outmanoeuvre practically every Allied fighter, and its firepower was also superior.

The A6M came to symbolise the previously unappreciated fact that Japanese weapons were not made of bamboo and rice-paper, nor were they inferior copies of Occidental ones. In its own homeland it was the focal point of a part-religious belief in Nipponese invincibility. The name of Jiro Horikoshi was better-known in Japan even than that of Reginald Mitchell in the UK, because he was the genius who had created the miraculous fighter that decimated its enemies.

Of course the A6M was not really miraculous. Back in 1937 the British Gloster company had flown a prototype fighter that almost precisely paralleled the A6M in size, shape, weight, power and performance – and it was not even accepted for the RAF. At that time Horikoshi was making the first drawings of his new fighter to try to meet a newly issued Imperial Navy specification that called for a shipboard fighter with the manoeuvrability of his earlier A5M (one of the most agile aircraft ever built) despite the burden of two 20-mm cannon as well as the two machine-guns carried by the A5M, two 60-kg (132-lb) bombs, full radio, an engine to give a speed of 500 km/h (311 mph) and an endurance of eight hours with a drop tank. (It should be noted that the Imperial Navy measured speeds in knots, so that required of the new fighter was 270 knots.)

The result was wholly conventional, with stressed-skin structure, split flaps, wide-track inward-retracting landing gear and a radial engine driving a variable-pitch propeller. After some argument a sliding canopy was added over the cockpit, and the newly demanded cannon (Type 99 Model 1, derived from the Oerlikon) were fitted in the wings, outboard of the propeller disc. Its designation was naturally A6M, A for carrier-based fighter and 6M for the sixth such type by Mitsubishi. Its popular name was Reisen (Rei-sen, zero fighter), from the Japanese year 2600 (1940 A.D.). The first A6M1, with a 582-kW (780-hp) Mitsubishi Zuisei 13 engine, flew at Kagamigahara on 1 April 1939, and showed outstanding qualities except in its speed of 489 km/h (304 mph), which just missed the target. A constant-speed propeller gave an increase in all-round performance, but more power was needed and on 28 December 1939 the third prototype, designated A6M2, flew with the 690-kW (925-hp) Nakajima Sakae 12. This prototype exceeded all expectations, and by July 1940 the A6M2 had been cleared for production. It was decided to send 15 to China to test them in action with the 12th Rengo Kokutai. They got their first victim on 13 September 1940, and though two A6M2s were shot down by ground fire their air combat record was a remarkable 99 victories for no losses before they were redeployed for the war in the Pacific.

From the 22nd A6M2 the rear spar was strengthened, and from the 65th the outermost 50.8 cm (20 in) of the wings was hinged to fold upwards manually. In June 1941 the A6M3 had these tips omit-

This frame from a Japanese ciné film shows an A6M2 (foreground) and B5N2 torpedo bombers ranged on the deck of a 1st Koku Kantai carrier early on Sunday 7 December 1941: destination, Pearl Harbor. The US Navy caption gives the carrier as the Hiryu but the insignia are not those of the 2nd Sentai.

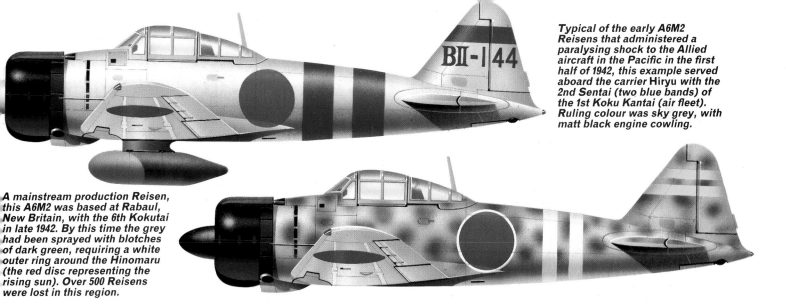

Typical of the early A6M2 Reisens that administered a paralysing shock to the Allied aircraft in the Pacific in the first half of 1942, this example served aboard the carrier Hiryu with the 2nd Sentai (two blue bands) of the 1st Koku Kantai (air fleet). Ruling colour was sky grey, with matt black engine cowling.

A mainstream production Reisen, this A6M2 was based at Rabaul, New Britain, with the 6th Kokutai in late 1942. By this time the grey had been sprayed with blotches of dark green, requiring a white outer ring around the Hinomaru (the red disc representing the rising sun). Over 500 Reisens were lost in this region.

ted, and with the 843-kW (1,130-hp) Sakae 21 engine offered higher speed and more rapid roll, though turn radius was slightly worsened. At Pearl Harbor the Imperial Navy had 328 A6Ms embarked aboard carriers, and from the start they achieved complete mastery over the Curtiss P-40, Curtiss-Wright CW-21A, Brewster Buffalo, Hawker Hurricane I and other opponents. For example the hapless Buffaloes of the RAF, RAAF, RNZAF and Dutch East Indies were so outflown their 12.7-mm (0.5-in) guns were replaced by 7.62-mm (0.303-in) weapons, ammunition was cut by half and fuel by more than one-third, and still they could not bring their guns to bear over the more agile and much harder-hitting A6M.

Not knowing what the fighter was called, the Allies named it 'Ben' then 'Ray' and finally 'Zeke'. The clipped-wing model was called 'Hap', until someone recalled that that was the nickname of the USAAF Chief of Staff, General H. H. Arnold, when it became 'Hamp'. When the type was recognized as merely another version of the 'Zeke' it was called 'Zeke 32'. But desperate attempts to gather even pieces of the almost supernatural fighter proved elusive, until suddenly US troops found a perfect A6M2 in the Aleutians. Petty Officer Koga had taken off from the carrier *Ryujo* on 3 June to attack Dutch Harbor, but two bullets had severed the fuel supply pipe and he had glided in to the uninhabited island of Akutan. Landing on marshy ground, the A6M had somersaulted and Koga had broken his neck. The valuable prize was soon on test at NAS North Island, San Diego, where the myths were blown away and the A6M's numerous shortcomings revealed.

For one thing, it is possible to do only so much on 843kW (1,130hp). The A6M airframe was lightly built, and the vital parts were by Western standards deficient in armour. Tactics were worked out to gain superiority in combat, but at least as important was the first flight, on the other side of the United States, of the first Grumman F6F Hellcat in June 1942. Larger and heavier than the A6M, this US Navy fighter had a 1492-kW (2,000-hp) engine: this enabled it to be stronger, tougher and better protected and yet out-

fight the A6M in a dogfight. Another US Navy and Marines fighter, the bent-wing Vought F4U Corsair, was even more formidable, and the US Army's P-38 was not only much faster but could stay with an A6M at all heights above 3050m (10,000ft) despite being much larger. And all these Allied fighters had firepower that could actually cause an A6M to break up into pieces.

Seaplane variant

In autumn 1940 an Imperial Navy specification called for a fighter seaplane to operate over isolated beachheads and beyond the range even of the A6M, and, while the powerful Kawanishi N1K1 (which in turn was eventually to lead to a formidable land-based fighter) was developed, the Nakajima company was instructed to build a seaplane A6M. The resulting A6M2-N flew on the day of Pearl Harbor and was soon in action. Though as neat a conversion as could be imagined, it was inevitably inferior to Allied fighters and though 327 were delivered, the last in September 1943, they did not achieve very much. Another off-mainstream variant was the tandem dual-control A6M2-K advanced trainer, which was the responsibility of the 21st Naval Air Arsenal, at Sasebo. Not even started until 1943, the first two-seater flew in November that year, and eventually 515 were built in two versions, with cannon and landing-gear doors removed to save weight. At Mitsubishi, Horikoshi had from 1940 pressed for a successor to the A6M, with his company's 1641-kW (2,200-hp) MK9 engine, but this was repeatedly delayed, and the old A6M had to be kept in production, both at the parent firm and (in even greater numbers) by Nakajima.

A 1943 attempt to improve performance at medium and high altitudes came to nothing: the 1st Air Technical Arsenal at Yokosuka fitted two A6M2s with turbocharged Sakae engines, but these were gravely unreliable. Nothing could be done but hastily to contrive an interim improved version, the A6M5; and, like so many hasty interim fighters, such as the Spitfire Mk IX, it was made in greater numbers than all the others. The chief modification was a new wing, with fixed rounded tips of 11.00m (36ft 1in) span and thicker skins to enable the new version to dive at much higher speeds; previously limitations in diving speed had made the Zero easy to catch. This added 189kg (416lb) to the weight, and did nothing for manoeuvrability, but a slight improvement in performance resulted from fitting individual or paired exhaust pipes to the 14 cylinders with nozzles arranged to give forward thrust at full power. Together with a careful detail refinement all this added up to a significantly better fighter, and when it reached combat units in numbers in the autumn of 1943, the A6M5 did something to redress the balance which had rather quickly tilted towards the US Navy with the entry to combat duty of the F6F Hellcat.

If any one aircraft can be said to have destroyed the myth of Japanese invincibility in the air, that aircraft was the F6F. In fact, in a pure test of turn radius, the F6F would be hard-pressed to hold any A6M that was skilfully flown, but that was not the end of the story.

Few air-to-air photographs survive from Japanese air operations in World War II. This picture was taken a year before Pearl Harbor as pre-series A6M2 fighters were blooded in combat over China with the 12th Rengo Kokutai. Nobody today knows what happened to the reports of the new fighter that were sent to Washington.

Off Okinawa in April 1945 hundreds of aircraft of the Imperial Navy were lost trying to stem the Allied advance. About half were suicide (so-called Kamikaze) attacks by various fighter and attack aircraft carrying bombs. Here an A6M5 just fails to reach the deck of the USS Missouri on 28 April 1945, glancing off the side.

Sheer lack of power in the Japanese fighter meant that it was far behind its opponent in armour and firepower, and in its ability to withstand battle damage. Lack of power was also the reason for the rate of climb falling off, compared with the lighter earlier versions, to levels below that of the heavyweight F6F. Even with thicker wing skins the A6M could not escape by diving away; in fact faced with an F6F, F4U or Spitfire Mk VIII there was no way an A6M pilot could survive except by exceptional flying, amazing luck or shooting down his opponent. And, as 1943 proceeded, this became more and more difficult.

Fortune turns

For one thing, the Allied fighters were not only getting dramatically superior but they were arriving in floods that completely overwhelmed the Japanese. Even in 1941-2 the Zeros had been outnumbered, but they had been deployed in concentrated groups that gained total local control and inflicted catastrophic losses, whilst the motley collections of Allied machines were scattered and often under no central direction. By 1943 the US Navy, US Marines, US Army Air Force and British Commonwealth forces were all co-ordinated and enjoyed numerical superiority everywhere. Not least of the Imperial Navy's problems was its rapid attrition in aircraft-carriers. Even as early as the Battle of Midway in June 1942 – often regarded as the start of the turnaround in fortunes in the Pacific war – the great carriers *Akagi, Hiryu, Kaga* and *Soryu* were all sunk; the light carrier *Shoho* had been sunk a month earlier, and *Ryujo* went to the bottom in August 1942. These crippling losses in seagoing air power gravely restricted the Imperial Navy's ability ever again to achieve command of the sky, at any place or at any time.

There was yet a further serious problem which had as much effect as all other factors combined. In air combat the man is every bit as

These A6M2-N fighter seaplanes appear to be on the catapult of a surface warship, but this is a false impression. They are on the slipway of a surface base, perhaps at Tulagi, heavily lashed down and with control locks in place. Fighter seaplanes were generally outclassed and had little impact on operations in World War II

Mitsubishi A6M2 'Zero' cutaway drawing key

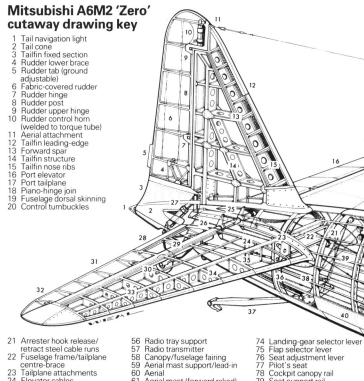

1 Tail navigation light
2 Tail cone
3 Tailfin fixed section
4 Rudder lower brace
5 Rudder tab (ground adjustable)
6 Fabric-covered rudder
7 Rudder hinge
8 Rudder post
9 Rudder upper hinge
10 Rudder control horn (welded to torque tube)
11 Aerial attachment
12 Tailfin leading-edge
13 Forward spar
14 Tailfin structure
15 Tailfin nose ribs
16 Port elevator
17 Port tailplane
18 Piano-hinge join
19 Fuselage dorsal skinning
20 Control turnbuckles

21 Arrester hook release/ retract steel cable runs
22 Fuselage frame/tailplane centre-brace
23 Tailplane attachments
24 Elevator cables
25 Elevator control horns/ torque tube
26 Rudder control horns
27 Tailwheel combined retraction/shock strut
28 Elevator trim tab
29 Tailwheel leg fairing
30 Castored tailwheel
31 Elevator frame (fabric-covered)
32 Elevator outer hinge
33 Tailplane structure
34 Forward spar
35 Elevator trim tab control rod (chain-driven)
36 Fuselage flotation bag rear wall
37 Arrester hook (extended)
38 Arrester hook pivot mounting
39 Elevator trim tab cable guide
40 Fuselage skinning
41 Fuselage frame stations
42 Arrester hook position indicator cable (duralumin tube)
43 Elevator cables
44 Rudder cables
45 Trim tab cable runs
46 Arrester hook pulley guide
47 Fuselage stringers
48 Fuselage flotation bag front wall
49 Fuselage construction join
50 Wingroot fillet formers
51 Compressed air cylinder (wing gun charging)
52 Transformer
53 'Ku'-type radio receiver
54 Oxygen cylinder (starboard); COf fire-extinguisher cylinder (port)
55 Battery

56 Radio tray support
57 Radio transmitter
58 Canopy/fuselage fairing
59 Aerial mast support/lead-in
60 Aerial
61 Aerial mast (forward raked)
62 Canopy aft fixed section
63 Aluminium and plywood canopy frame
64 Crash bulkhead/headrest support
65 'Ku'-type D/F frame antenna mounting (late models)
66 Canopy track
67 Turnover truss
68 Pilot's seat support frame
69 Starboard elevator control bell-crank
70 Aileron control push-pull rod
71 Wing rear spar/fuselage attachment
72 Fuselage aft main double frame
73 Aileron linkage

74 Landing-gear selector lever
75 Flap selector lever
76 Seat adjustment lever
77 Pilot's seat
78 Cockpit canopy rail
79 Seat support rail
80 Elevator tab trim handwheel
81 Fuel gauge controls
82 Throttle quadrant
83 Reflector gunsight mounting (offset to starboard)
84 Sliding canopy
85 Plexiglass panels
86 Canopy lock/release
87 Windscreen
88 Fuselage starboard 0.303-in (7.7-mm) machine gun
89 Control column
90 Radio control box
91 Radio tuner

© Pilot Press Limited

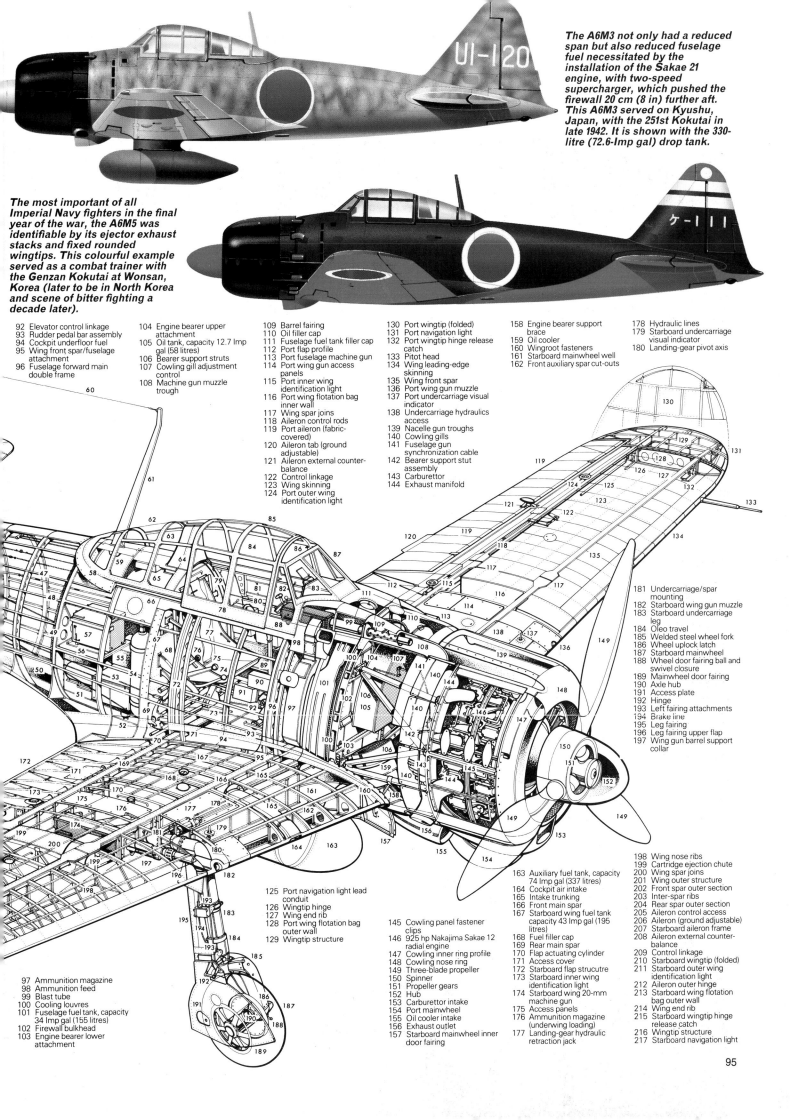

The A6M3 not only had a reduced span but also reduced fuselage fuel necessitated by the installation of the Sakae 21 engine, with two-speed supercharger, which pushed the firewall 20 cm (8 in) further aft. This A6M3 served on Kyushu, Japan, with the 251st Kokutai in late 1942. It is shown with the 330-litre (72.6-Imp gal) drop tank.

The most important of all Imperial Navy fighters in the final year of the war, the A6M5 was identifiable by its ejector exhaust stacks and fixed rounded wingtips. This colourful example served as a combat trainer with the Genzan Kokutai at Wonsan, Korea (later to be in North Korea and scene of bitter fighting a decade later).

92 Elevator control linkage
93 Rudder pedal bar assembly
94 Cockpit underfloor fuel
95 Wing front spar/fuselage attachment
96 Fuselage forward main double frame
97 Ammunition magazine
98 Ammunition feed
99 Blast tube
100 Cooling louvres
101 Fuselage fuel tank, capacity 34 Imp gal (155 litres)
102 Firewall bulkhead
103 Engine bearer lower attachment
104 Engine bearer upper attachment
105 Oil tank, capacity 12.7 Imp gal (58 litres)
106 Bearer support struts
107 Cowling gill adjustment control
108 Machine gun muzzle trough
109 Barrel fairing
110 Oil filler cap
111 Fuselage fuel tank filler cap
112 Port flap profile
113 Port fuselage machine gun
114 Port wing gun access panels
115 Port inner wing identification light
116 Port wing flotation bag inner wall
117 Wing spar joins
118 Aileron control rods
119 Port aileron (fabric-covered)
120 Aileron tab (ground adjustable)
121 Aileron external counter-balance
122 Control linkage
123 Wing skinning
124 Port outer wing identification light
125 Port navigation light lead conduit
126 Wingtip hinge
127 Wing end rib
128 Port wing flotation bag outer wall
129 Wingtip structure
130 Port wingtip (folded)
131 Port navigation light
132 Port wingtip hinge release catch
133 Pitot head
134 Wing leading-edge skinning
135 Wing front spar
136 Port wing gun muzzle
137 Port undercarriage visual indicator
138 Undercarriage hydraulics access
139 Nacelle gun troughs
140 Cowling gills
141 Fuselage gun synchronization cable
142 Bearer support stut assembly
143 Carburettor
144 Exhaust manifold
145 Cowling panel fastener clips
146 925 hp Nakajima Sakae 12 radial engine
147 Cowling inner ring profile
148 Cowling nose ring
149 Three-blade propeller
150 Spinner
151 Propeller gears
152 Hub
153 Carburettor intake
154 Port mainwheel
155 Oil cooler intake
156 Exhaust outlet
157 Starboard mainwheel inner door fairing
158 Engine bearer support brace
159 Oil cooler
160 Wingroot fasteners
161 Starboard mainwheel well
162 Front auxiliary spar cut-outs
163 Auxiliary fuel tank, capacity 74 Imp gal (337 litres)
164 Cockpit air intake
165 Intake trunking
166 Front main spar
167 Starboard wing fuel tank capacity 43 Imp gal (195 litres)
168 Fuel filler cap
169 Rear main spar
170 Flap actuating cylinder
171 Access cover
172 Starboard flap strucute
173 Starboard inner wing identification light
174 Starboard wing 20-mm machine gun
175 Access panels
176 Ammunition magazine (underwing loading)
177 Landing-gear hydraulic retraction jack
178 Hydraulic lines
179 Starboard undercarriage visual indicator
180 Landing-gear pivot axis
181 Undercarriage/spar mounting
182 Starboard wing gun muzzle
183 Starboard undercarriage leg
184 Oleo travel
185 Welded steel wheel fork
186 Wheel uplock latch
187 Starboard mainwheel
188 Wheel door fairing ball and swivel closure
189 Mainwheel door fairing
190 Axle hub
191 Access plate
192 Hinge
193 Left fairing attachments
194 Brake line
195 Leg fairing
196 Leg fairing upper flap
197 Wing gun barrel support collar
198 Wing nose ribs
199 Cartridge ejection chute
200 Wing spar joins
201 Wing outer structure
202 Front spar outer section
203 Inter-spar ribs
204 Rear spar outer section
205 Aileron control access
206 Aileron (ground adjustable)
207 Starboard aileron frame
208 Aileron external counter-balance
209 Control linkage
210 Starboard wingtip (folded)
211 Starboard outer wing identification light
212 Aileron outer hinge
213 Starboard wing flotation bag outer wall
214 Wing end rib
215 Starboard wingtip hinge release catch
216 Wingtip structure
217 Starboard navigation light

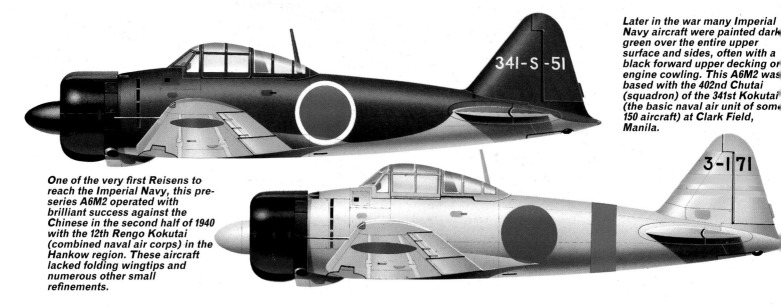

Later in the war many Imperial Navy aircraft were painted dark green over the entire upper surface and sides, often with a black forward upper decking or engine cowling. This A6M2 was based with the 402nd Chutai (squadron) of the 341st Kokutai (the basic naval air unit of some 150 aircraft) at Clark Field, Manila.

3-1 71

One of the very first Reisens to reach the Imperial Navy, this pre-series A6M2 operated with brilliant success against the Chinese in the second half of 1940 with the 12th Rengo Kokutai (combined naval air corps) in the Hankow region. These aircraft lacked folding wingtips and numerous other small refinements.

important as the machine. Even flying an inferior aircraft, in the rather primitive days of World War II, a brilliant and courageous pilot could often run up strings of victories over opponents flying faster or better-armed aircraft. In 1941 the Imperial Navy pilots had been well trained, and were aggressive and in most cases experienced. Many had seen a year or more of actual fighting in China or against the USSR, and in their hands a Zero was deadly. By 1943 hardly any of these pilots were still alive, and their replacements were by comparison ineffectual. The home-based training programme was wholly inadequate, and by autumn 1944 the once-dominant Sentais were being reorganised into kamikaze (suicide) squads in a desperate attempt to stem the tide of Allied advance.

Improved armament

Throughout the war the need for long range had been manifest, but whereas at the start the A6M had been supreme in this regard, especially after its experienced pilots had learned correct long-range cruise techniques at high boost pressure but low crankshaft revolutions, by 1943 the Sakae 21 had resulted in smaller fuselage tankage (in part rectified by adding two small 45-litre/9.9-Imp gal tanks in the outer wings) and appreciably higher fuel consumption. Crucial need to keep weight down precluded heavier armament, though the Type 99 cannon was improved through several versions with a longer barrel and higher muzzle velocity, rate of fire increased from 490 to an eventual 750 rounds per minute, and a 125-round belt in place of the original 100-round drum. The greater muzzle velocity had the possibly important effect of extending the effective range (typically from 800 m/2,624 ft to 1000 m/3,281 ft), this was one factor where the A6M could have scored over the US fighters that relied on the 12.7-mm (0.5-in) Browning. In practice, Japanese pilots lacked the shooting skill to open fire accurately at long ranges, and at normal air-combat distances the much more rapid rate of strikes from the

typical US armament of six 12.7-mm (0.5-in) guns proved decisive.

When fitted with the long-barrel belt-fed cannon the A6M5 became the A6M5a, available from production in the spring of 1944. Within weeks the A6M5b, was coming off the line, and this partly rectified one of the type's gravest shortcomings, lack of protection. The A6M5b had improved armour, automatic fire-extinguishers in the main fuel tanks and a slab of bullet-proof glass behind the windscreen. A small increase in firepower resulted from substituting the 13.2-mm (0.52-in) Type 3 heavy machine-gun for one of the rifle-calibre weapons ahead of the windscreen. Hundreds of A6M5a and A6M5b fighters took part in the great battles around the Marianas and Philippines in the summer of 1944, but the first major engagement of the A6M5b was such a slaughter at the hands of F6Fs that US pilots called it 'The Marianas Turkey Shoot'. To a considerable degree this was because of the superior skill of the American pilots.

Desperate measures

This debacle spurred the Imperial Navy into a further desperate attempt to improve the A6M, a requirement being issued for racks for underwing rockets, extra 13.2-mm (0.52-in) guns outboard of the cannon, a large additional fuel tank behind the cockpit and a fully armoured pilot seat. If the A6M had needed extra power beforehand, it doubly needed it now, but permission to fit a larger engine was not granted. After building 93 with the improvements demanded Mitsubishi did receive some Sakae 31 engines, with extra power gained by injecting water/methanol to prevent detonation at full throttle, but most of these engines were retained by the maker, Nakajima, which went into production with the resulting A6M6c at the end of 1944. This was the final model of Reisen to see action, and

Off Okinawa in April 1945 hundreds of aircraft of the Imperial Navy were lost trying to stem the Allied advance. About half were suicide (so-called Kamikaze) attacks by various fighter and attack aircraft carrying bombs. Here an A6M5 just fails to reach the deck of the USS Missouri on 28 April 1945, glancing off the side.

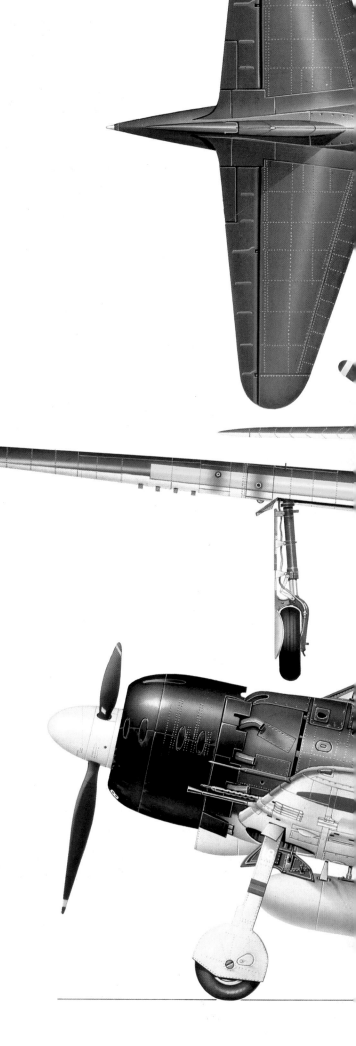

it could not do more than earlier models to hold back the overwhelming advance of the Allied land, sea and air forces towards Japan.

The A6M7 was equipped to carry a 250-kg (551-lb) bomb as well as outer-wing drop tanks. The A6M8 at last had a more powerful engine, the 1164-kW (1,560-hp) Mitsubishi Kinsei 62, resulting in a slightly larger cowling and removal of the machine-guns previously fitted above it. This did not fly until May 1945 and no production aircraft could be completed. There were many experimental forms of armament and special equipment fits, but by far the most important were the kamikaze lash-ups with, usually, a 250-kg (551-lb) bomb hung on the rack normally used for the centreline drop tank.

Total production of the A6M was 10,449 (3,879 by Mitsubishi and 6,570 by Nakajima), and these were complemented by 327 Nakajima-built A6M2-Ns, and 515 A6M2-Ks and A6M5-Ks (236 by Dai-Nijuichi Kaigun Kokusho and 279 by Hitachi Kokuki KK).

Specification
Mitsubishi A6M5c Reisen
Type: carrier-based fighter-bomber
Powerplant: one 843-kW (1,130-hp) Nakajima NK1F Sakae 21 radial piston engine
Performance: maximum speed 565 km/h (351 mph); cruising speed 370 km/h (230 mph); climb to 6000 m (19,685 ft) in 7 minutes; service ceiling 11740 m (38,520 ft); maximum range 1922 km (1,194 miles)

Weights: empty 1876 kg (4,136 lb); maximum take-off 2733 kg (6,025 lb)
Dimensions: span 11.00 m (36 ft 1 in); length 9.12 m (29 ft 11.25 in); height 3.50 m (11 ft 6 in); wing area 21.3 m² (229.27 sq ft)
Armament: one 13.2-mm (0.52-in) Type 3 heavy machine-gun in the fuselage decking (breech in the cockpit), two 20-mm Type 99 cannon in the wings and two 13.2-mm (0.52-in) Type 3 guns in the wings outboard of the cannon, plus two 60-kg (132-lb) bombs under the wings (suicide mission, one 250-kg/551-lb bomb)

Mitsubishi A6M Reisen variants

Mitsubishi A6M1: first two prototypes, powered by the 582-kW (780-hp) Zuisei 13 engine
Mitsubishi A6M2: initial production version, powered by the 701-kW (940-hp) Sakae 12 engine, with an armament of two 20-mm and two 7.7-mm (0.303-in) guns, span 12.00 m (39 ft 4.5 in) and normal take-off weight 2410 kg (5,313 lb); initial aircraft of the batch, up to c/n 21, had an unreinforced rear spar, aircraft from c/n 22 onwards had the reinforced rear spar (both sub-types being designated **Model 11**), and from c/n 65 the wingtips were capable of manual folding (the sub-type being designated **Model 21**)
Mitsubishi A6M3 Model 32: improved production model powered by the 843-kW (1,130-hp) Sakae 21; from the fourth aircraft 20-mm cannon ammunition was increased, and later aircraft had square-tipped wings of 11.00 m (36 ft 1 in) span compared with the **A6M3 Model 22**'s rounded tips of 12.00 m (39 ft 4.5 in); normal take-off weight 2544 kg (5,609 lb)
Mitsubishi A6M4: unsuccessful experimental variant with turbocharged Sakae engine
Mitsubishi A6M5 Model 52: improved A6M3 with thicker skins, rounded wingtips and thrust-augmenting exhaust stacks; normal take-off weight 2733 kg (6,025 lb)
Mitsubishi A6M5a Model 52A: derivative of the A6M5 with thicker skins and improved Type 99 Model 2 Mark 3 cannon
Mitsubishi A6M5 Model 52B: improved A6M5a with extra protection, fire extinguishing system for the fuel tanks, and one 7.7-mm (0.303-in) machine-gun replaced by a 13.2-mm (0.52-in) Type 3 weapon
Mitsubishi A6M5c Model 52C: yet further improved model, with two 13.2-mm (0.52-in) Type 3 machine-guns added outboard of the cannon, armour behind the pilot, extra fuel capacity, and racks for eight 10-kg (22-lb) unguided air-to-air rockets
Mitsubishi A6M6c Model 53C: improved A6M5c with 903-kW (1,210-hp) Sakae 31 plus methanol/water boost, and self-sealing wing tanks
Mitsubishi A6M7 Model 63: dive-bomber version of the A6M6c intended for use from small carriers; centreline provision for one 250-kg (551-lb) bomb and underwing points for two 350-litre (77-Imp gal) drop tanks
Mitsubishi A6M8 Model 64: uprated model with 1164-kW (1,560-hp) Kinsei 62 engine, no fuselage guns, better protection, and normal take-off weight 3150 kg (6,945 lb)
Mitsubishi A6M2-K: dual-control trainer version of the A6M2
Mitsubishi A6M5-K: dual-control version of the A6M5
Nakajima A6M2-N: floatplane version of the A6M2 with single main float and two underwing stabilising floats; normal take-off weight 2460 kg (5,423 lb)

The subject of this illustration was one of the rare late-war stop-gap variants which tried to stem the tide of Allied air power until the A7M Reppu could be cleared for production. An A6M5c of the 210th Kokutai, it combined the non-folding rounded wingtips and thick wing skins, separate exhaust stacks and other improvements of the basic A6M5 (Model 52) with heavier firepower from two 13.2-mm (0.52-in) guns added in the wings outboard of the cannon. Most had better protection, with rear armour and self-sealing wing tanks, but the crucial fault of inadequate power was not rectified and only 93 of this model were built. Note the absence of a white border to the Hinomaru insigne.

Focke-Wulf Fw 190 'Butcher Bird'

When the Fw 190 appeared in the skies over France in September 1941, RAF Intelligence simply could not credit that this squat, angular fighter really had the measure of the sleek, slender Spitfire Mk V. Yet Kurt Tank's 'Butcher Bird' not only came to dominate the skies for eight months but remained one of the finest fighters in Europe until the end of Hitler's war.

Conceived in 1937 as a contemporary of the Hawker Typhoon and for the same reason – to replace the first generation of monoplane interceptors (the Hawker Hurricane and the Messerschmitt Bf 109) – the design of the Focke-Wulf Fw 190 was tendered with two alternative engines, the Daimler-Benz DB601 inline and the BMW 139 radial, the latter being selected to power the prototype on account of its assumed higher power development potential. Detail design commenced under the leadership of Oberingenieur Blaser and the first prototype was flown by test pilot Hans Sander at Bremen on 1 June 1939.

The first two aircraft featured large, low-drag ducted spinners but these were soon discarded as they were thought to cause engine overheating, and after the BMW 139 had been abandoned the Fw 190A entered production with the BMW 801 14-cylinder radial with fan-assisted cooling. The first nine pre-production Fw 190A-0s featured small wings of 15.00 m² (161.46 sq ft) area, but the definitive version had larger wings of 18.30 m² (196.99 sq ft) area.

Service trials at Rechlin went ahead in 1940 without undue problems, although Luftwaffe pilots suggested that the proposed armament of the Fw 190A-1 (four synchronised 7.92-mm/0.31-in MG 17 machine-guns) would meet with spirited criticism in combat service. Production of the 100 Fw 190A-1s at Hamburg and Bremen was completed by the end of May 1941, and these were powered by 1194-kW (1,600-hp) BMW 801C engines which bestowed a top speed of

624 km/h (388 mph). The aircraft were flown by Erprobungsstelle Rechlin and 6./JG 26, the latter based at Le Bourget in August. The following month the first combats were reported with RAF Supermarine Spitfire Vs, showing the German fighters to be markedly superior, albeit lacking in weapon punch.

New armament

Already, however, the early gun criticisms had led to the Fw 190A-2 version with two wing root-mounted synchronised 20-mm MG FF cannon and two MG 17 guns; with a speed of 614 km/h (382 mph), this up-gunned version still had the edge over the Spitfire V. By the end of March 1942, JG 26, commanded by Adolf Galland, was fully equipped with Fw 190A-2s. Thirty Fw 190As had accompanied the escort forces during the famous Channel break-out by the battle-cruisers *Scharnhorst* and *Gneisenau* in February, Fw 190A-2s of III/JG 26 being involved in the one-sided action against Lieutenant Commander Eugene Esmonde's Fairey Swordfish torpedo strike.

As the RAF desperately sought to introduce an answer to the Fw 190, production of the German fighter was stepped up as Focke-Wulf factories at Cottbus, Marienburg, Neubrandenburg, Schwerin, Sorau and Tutow joined the programme, as well as the Ago and Fie-

Although not showing the grace and elegance of the Spitfire, few fighters have looked more purposeful than the Fw 190. This aircraft, devoid of weapons, is an Fw 190 captured by the Americans.

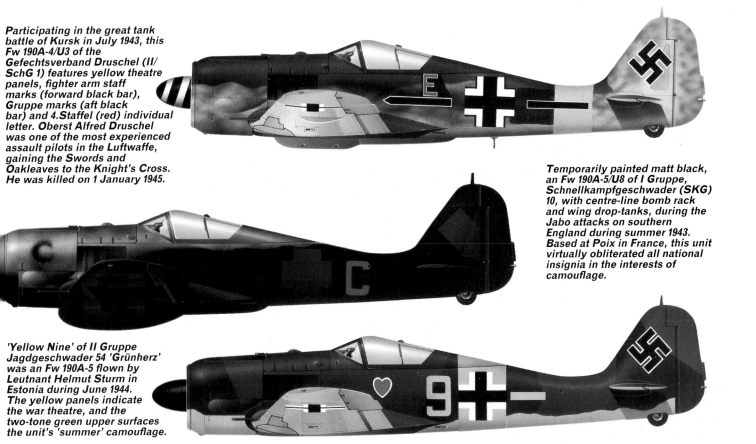

Participating in the great tank battle of Kursk in July 1943, this Fw 190A-4/U3 of the Gefechtsverband Druschel (II/SchG 1) features yellow theatre panels, fighter arm staff marks (forward black bar), Gruppe marks (aft black bar) and 4.Staffel (red) individual letter. Oberst Alfred Druschel was one of the most experienced assault pilots in the Luftwaffe, gaining the Swords and Oakleaves to the Knight's Cross. He was killed on 1 January 1945.

Temporarily painted matt black, an Fw 190A-5/U8 of I Gruppe, Schnellkampfgeschwader (SKG) 10, with centre-line bomb rack and wing drop-tanks, during the Jabo attacks on southern England during summer 1943. Based at Poix in France, this unit virtually obliterated all national insignia in the interests of camouflage.

'Yellow Nine' of II Gruppe Jagdgeschwader 54 'Grünherz' was an Fw 190A-5 flown by Leutnant Helmut Sturm in Estonia during June 1944. The yellow panels indicate the war theatre, and the two-tone green upper surfaces the unit's 'summer' camouflage.

seler plants. The Fw 190A-3, with 1268-kW (1,700-hp) BMW 801DG, four 20-mm (0.79-in) and two 7.92-mm (0.31-in) guns, joined II/JG 26 in March 1942 and shortly afterwards the only other Luftwaffe fighter Geschwader in the West, JG 2.

Thus, by the time the RAF was ready to introduce its new Spitfire IX and Typhoon fighters to combat over the Dieppe landings in August 1942, the Luftwaffe could field some 200 Fw 190As in opposition. Unfortunately not only had the RAF underestimated the number of these fighters available but they were unaware that a new version, the Fw 190A-4, had appeared with a water-injected 1567-kW (2,100-hp) BMW 801D-2 engine and a top speed of 670 km/h (416 mph), and that a bomb-carrying variant, the Fw 190A-3/U1, was in service. (The suffix 'U' indicated *Unrüst-Bausatz*, or factory conversion set.) The result was a stinging defeat for the RAF, which lost a total of 106 aircraft, including 97 to Fw 190s. As a result largely of mismanagement, neither the Spitfire IX nor the Typhoon had been able to redress the balance.

It would have been of little comfort had the RAF known that the Germans had for many months devoted all the Fw 190 resources to the Channel front, such was the esteem held for the Spitfire V. Indeed, despite the ferocious tempo of battle on the Eastern Front, which had opened in June 1941, no Fw 190A fighters fought on that front until well into 1942 when I/JG 51 received Fw 190A-4s. Fw 190A-3s and A-4s were also issued to IV/JG 5 and to JG 1 for home defence and protection of German fleet units in Norway. A reconnaissance version of the Fw 190A-3 was first flown by 9.(H)/LG 2 in March 1942 on the Russian Front. The Fw 190A-4/U4 reconnaissance fighter joined NAufklGr 13 in France, and Fw 190A-4/Trop ground-attack fighter-bombers appeared in North Africa with I/SG 2 during 1942. Before the end of that year Fw 190A-3/U1s and A-4/U8s of SKG 10, each able to carry a 500-kg (1,100-lb) bomb, had embarked on a series of daylight low-level 'tip and run' attacks against cities and ports in southern England, forcing Fighter Command to deploy disproportionately heavy fighter defences to counter the threat. Some measure of the dependence now placed on the Fw 190 may be judged from the fact that more than 1,900 Fw 190A-3s and A-4s had reached the Luftwaffe in 1942 (compared with some 500 Typhoons and Spitfire IXs for the RAF).

The unarmed Focke-Wulf Fw 190V1 (first prototype, D-OPZE) with fan-cooled BMW 139 and ducted spinner, at the time of its first flight on 1 June 1939. Numerous other differences from subsequent production versions are evident, including small tail-wheel, absence of fuselage wheel doors, and the hinged door covers on the wheel leg.

Early Focke-Wulf Fw 190A-1s undergoing final assembly at Bremen in 1941. Particularly evident in this picture is the exceptionally wide-track main landing gear and the large number of hinged panels providing access to the compact BMW 801 radial engine. Just visible are the pair of nose-mounted MG 17 machine-guns.

Pale grey Fw 190A-6/R11 of 1./NJG 10 flown by Oberleutnant Hans Krause from Werneuchen in August 1944. The pilot's insignia consisted of his nickname 'Illo' beneath the Wilde Sau emblem. Note Neptun radar arrays and two-shade grey on upper wing surface. Krause was later awarded the Knight's Cross and gained 28 night victories.

'Defence of the Reich' Fw 190A-8 (note red fuselage band) of I Gruppe, Jagdgeschwader 1, based at Twenthe in the Netherlands in December 1944. An aircraft with 'double chevrons' was being flown by Major Hans Ehlers, the Gruppenkommandeur, when he was shot down and killed on 27 December 1944.

Rocket-launchers

Early in 1943 there appeared the Fw 190A-5 with slightly lengthened engine mountings, and with it a much increased range of *Rüstsätze* (field conversion kits), including the R6 that enabled the Fw 190A-5 (in modified form Fw 190A-5/R6) to carry two underwing WG21 21-cm (8.27-in) rocket-launchers for use against the growing Boeing B-17 and Consolidated B-24 bomber fleets operated by the USAAF. The Fw 190A-5/U2 night bomber could carry a 500-kg (1,100-lb) bomb and two 300-litre (66-Imp gal) drop-tanks; the Fw 190A-5/U3 carried up to 1000 kg (2,205 lb) of bombs; the Fw 190A-5/U12 was a heavily-armed fighter with six 20-mm MG 151/20 cannon and two MG 17s; while the Fw 190A-5/U15, of which three examples were built in November 1943, was equipped to carry a 950-kg (2,094-lb) LT950 torpedo. A torpedo-carrying Fw 190A-5/U14, a lighter version of the U15 torpedo-fighter, is said to have been flown in action by Hauptmann Helmut Viedebannt of SKG 10.

The Fw 190A-6, in its standard form with reduced wing structure weight, was armed with four fast-firing 20-mm guns inside the wings (in addition to the two MG 17s in the nose); the Fw 190A-6/R1 carried six 20-mm guns in underwing packs; and the Fw 190A-6/R6 mounted four 30-mm MK 108 cannon in these packs, making it the most heavily-armed single-seater of the war. The Fw 190A-6/R4, with turbocharged BMW 801TS, had a top speed of 683 km/h (424 mph) at 10500 m (34,450 ft). Fighter-bomber versions of the Fw 190A-6 were able to carry a 1000-kg (2,205-lb) bomb under the fuselage.

The greatest single victory by Fw 190A-6s of JG 1, JG 5, JG 26, JG 51 and JG 54 was gained on 14 October 1943, when they decimated the US 8th Air Force's daylight bombers attacking Regensburg and Schweinfurt, destroying 79 and damaging 121 out of the force of 228. Had it not been for the introduction of superlative American close-

First of the 190 series to be powered by the 1238-kW (1,660-hp) BMW 801C-0 engine were the Fw 190 V5k and V5g, the former with small wing (15.0 m²/161.46 sq ft area), illustrated here, and the latter with enlarged wing (18.3 m²/196.98 sq ft area). The latter was chosen for production on account of superior manoeuvrability.

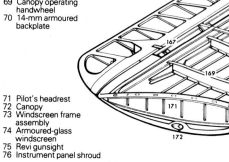

Focke-Wulf Fw 190A-3 cutaway drawing key

1 Rudder fixed tab
2 Tail navigation light
3 Leads
4 Rudder hinge/attachment
5 Tailwheel extension spring
6 Tailwheel shock-absorber leg retraction guide
7 Tailfin spar
8 Rudder post assembly
9 Rudder frame
10 Rudder upper hinge
11 Aerial attachment
12 Tailfin structure
13 Canted rib progression
14 Port elevator fixed tab
15 Port elevator
16 Mass balance
17 Port tailplane
18 Tailplane incidence motor unit
19 Tailwheel retraction pulley cables
20 Tailplane attachment
21 Starboard tailplane structure
22 Elevator fixed tab
23 Starboard elevator frame
24 Mass balance
25 Tailplane front spar
26 Semi-retracting tailwheel
27 Drag yoke
28 Tailwheel recess
29 Tailwheel locking linkage
30 Access panel
31 Actuating link
32 Push-pull rod
33 Rudder cables
34 Rudder control differential linkage
35 Fuselage/tail unit join
36 Elevator control differential
37 Fuselage lift tube
38 Elevator control cables
39 Bulkhead (No. 12) fabric panel (rear fuselage equipment dust protection)
40 Leather grommets
41 Rudder push-pull rods
42 Fuselage frame
43 Master compass
44 Flat-bottomed (equipment bay floor support) frame
45 First-aid kit

46 Optional camera (2 x Rb 12) installation (A-3/U4)
47 Control runs
48 Access hatch (port side)
49 Electrical leads
50 Distribution panel
51 Canopy channel slide cut-outs
52 Canopy solid aft fairing
53 Aerial
54 Head armour support bracket
55 Aerial attachment/take-up pulley
56 Equipment/effects stowage
57 FuG 7a/FuG 25a radio equipment bay
58 Battery
59 Cockpit aft bulkhead
60 Control runs
61 Cockpit floor/centre-section main structure
62 Wingroot fillet
63 Underfloor aft fuel tank (64 Imp gals/291 litres)
64 Underfloor forward fuel tank (51 Imp gal/232 litres)
65 Cockpit sidewall control runs
66 Seat support brackets
67 Armoured bulkhead
68 Pilot's seat
69 Canopy operating handwheel
70 14-mm armoured backplate

71 Pilot's headrest
72 Canopy
73 Windscreen frame assembly
74 Armoured-glass windscreen
75 Revi gunsight
76 Instrument panel shroud

77 Throttle
78 Port control console (trim switches/buttons)
79 Control column
80 Seat pan
81 Starboard control console (circuit breakers)
82 Underfloor linkage
83 Electrical junction box
84 Rudder pedal assembly
85 Instrument panel sections
86 Screen support frame
87 Two 7.9 mm MG 17 machine guns
88 Ammunition feed chute
89 Panel release catches
90 Fuselage armament ammunition boxes
91 Forward bulkhead
92 Inboard wing cannon ammunition boxes
93 Engine mounting lower attachment point
94 Cooling air exit louvres
95 Engine mounting upper attachment point
96 Oil pump assembly
97 Engine mounting ring

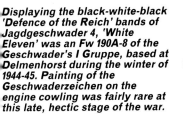

Displaying the black-white-black 'Defence of the Reich' bands of Jagdgeschwader 4, 'White Eleven' was an Fw 190A-8 of the Geschwader's I Gruppe, based at Delmenhorst during the winter of 1944-45. Painting of the Geschwaderzeichen on the engine cowling was fairly rare at this late, hectic stage of the war.

'Blue Eight' of Schlachtgeschwader 4 during Unternehmen 'Bodenplatte' of 1 January 1945. This Fw 190F-8 with Spiralschnauze (spiral nose) markings was based at Köln-Wahn and featured the blue Staffel colour characteristic of bomber units.

98 Fuselage MG 17 ammunition cooling pipes
99 Machine gun front mounting brackets
100 Machine gun breech blister fairings
101 Port split flap section
102 Flap actuating electric motor
103 Port outer 20-mm MG FF cannon
104 Aileron control linkage
105 Aileron fixed tab

114 Aileron link assembly
115 Fuselage MG 17 muzzles
116 Muzzle troughs
117 Upper cowling panel
118 Fuselage MG 17 electrical synchronizing unit
119 Exhaust pipes
120 Cowling panel ring
121 BMW 801D-2 radial engine
122 Former ring
123 Upper panel release catches
124 Forward cowling support ring
125 Oil tank armour
126 Oil tank (10 Imp gal/ 45.5 litres)
127 Annular oil cooler assembly
128 Cooler armoured ring
129 Engine twelve-blade cooling fan

130 Three-blade propeller
131 Propeller boss
132 Oil cooler airflow track
133 Airflow duct fairing (to rear cylinders)
134 Lower panel release catches
135 Cowling lower panel section
136 Wingroot fairing
137 Centre-section wheel covers
138 Inboard 20-mm cannon muzzle
139 Wheel cover operating cable
140 Starboard wheel well
141 Mainwheel leg rib cut-out
142 Undercarriage retraction jack
143 Locking unit assembly
144 Inboard 20-mm cannon spent cartridge chute

145 Front spar inboard assembly
146 Ammunition feed chute
147 Fuselage/front spar attachment
148 Ammunition box bay
149 Starboard inboard 20-mm MG 151 cannon
150 Breech blister fairing
151 Fuselage/rear spar attachment
152 Rear spar
153 Starboard flap assembly
154 Inboard solid ribs
155 Rotating drive undercarriage retraction unit
156 Radius rod hinge
157 Outboard 20-mm cannon muzzle

158 Mainwheel leg strut mounting assembly
159 Undercarriage actuation drive motor
160 Starboard outboard 20-mm MG FF cannon
161 Front spar assembly
162 Ammunition drum
163 Rib cut-out
164 Aileron control linkage

165 Aileron fixed tab
166 Starboard aileron frame
167 Aileron hinge points
168 Rear spar
169 Wing lower shell outer 'floating ribs'
170 Wing undersurface inner skinning
171 Starboard detachable wingtip

106 Port aileron
107 Aileron hinge points
108 Port detachable wingtip
109 Port navigation light
110 Front spar
111 Wing lower shell
112 MG FF muzzle
113 Port mainwheel leg fairing

172 Starboard navigation light
173 Leading-edge assembly
174 Nose rib attachment lips
175 Mainwheel leg fairing
176 Mainwheel leg
177 Brake lines
178 Fairing
179 Torque links
180 Axle hub assembly
181 Mainwheel fairing
182 Starboard mainwheel
183 Pitot head
184 Ventral bomb-rack aluminium aft fairing
185 Ventral bomb-rack carrier unit
186 ETC 500 ventral bomb-rack (A-3/U1)
187 SC 500 optional bomb load

'Black Twelve', an Fw 190D-9 (with early-style cockpit canopy) of 10.Staffel, Jagdgeschwader 54 'Grünherz'. Participating in Unternehmen 'Bodenplatte' on New Year's Day, 1945, the aircraft crashed at Wemmel, Belgium. The yellow panels possibly indicate an aircraft withdrawn from the Eastern Front for the occasion.

Displaying pale blue-grey finish with dark grey dappling, this Fw 190D-9 of III/JG 2 'Richthofen' was based at Altenstadt in December 1944. Note the absence of white on fuselage and fin markings.

escort fighters, particularly the North American P-51 Mustang, the Fw 190-equipped Jagdflieger would have decisively suppressed American daylight bombing attempts early in 1944.

Nothwithstanding these successes, the changing fortunes of war forced the Luftwaffe to adopt a wholly defensive stance, of an increasingly desperate nature. As the RAF night bomber offensive increased in weight the Luftwaffe employed Fw 190As (in particular Fw 190A-5/U2s) in the night-fighting role on moonlit nights, and the 'Wild Boar' tactics of Hajo Hermann's 30. Jagddivision, with three Geschwäder, are reckoned to have accounted for some 200 RAF heavy bombers during the latter half of 1943.

While Fw 190A fighter-bombers were in action in the Mediterranean theatre, there appeared the Fw 190A-7 with a pair of 20-mm cannon in the nose decking (in addition to the various wing gun combinations), and the Fw 190A-8 with GM-1 nitrous-oxide power-boosting and all the adaptability afforded by earlier Rüstsätz additions. The Fw 190A-8/U1 was a two-seat version, of which three examples were produced to assist the conversion training of Junkers Ju 87 pilots to the Fw 190 for the ground-attack squadrons on the Eastern Front. The Fw 190A-8/U3 was the upper component of the Mistel (Mistletoe) composite weapon, riding the back of explosive-packed, unmanned Junkers Ju 88 aircraft. The Fw 190A-8/U11 anti-shipping strike aircraft, with a BT700 700-kg (1,543-lb) torpedo-bomb, was flown in attacks against the Russian Black Sea Fleet in February 1944. The Fw 190A-9, with armoured wing leading edge, was powered by a 1490-kW (2,000-hp) BMW 801F (although the Fw 190A-9/R11 had a turbocharged BMW 801TS). The Fw 190A-10, of which only prototypes were completed, featured provision for an increased range of bombs. Among the purely experimental versions of the Fw 190A were the Fw 190V74 with a seven-barrelled 30-mm SG117 Rohrblock cannon aimed by a Revi 242 gunsight, and the extraordinary Fw 190V75 with seven 45-cm (17.72-in) downward-firing mortars intended for low-level anti-tank use from a height of

about 10 m (33 ft). Another interesting experiment was the use of large Doppelreiter overwing fuel tanks on the Fw 190A-8, evaluated by Erprobungskommando 25 under Major Georg Christl in July 1944.

New power

The arrival of the Spitfire IX in Fighter Command and its threat to combat domination by the Fw 190A led to the development of the Fw 190B series with GM-1 power-boosted BMW 801D-2 engine and pressure cabin, but trouble with the latter led to the abandonment of this version after only a few prototypes had been produced. The Fw 190C series, of which five prototypes were completed with DB603 inline engines, annular radiators, Hirth 9-2281 superchargers and four-bladed propellers, was also abandoned early in 1944.

The Fw 190D, with 1320-kW (1,770-hp) Junkers Jumo 213A-1 engine and annular radiator in a much-lengthened nose (necessitating increased fin and rudder area), proved very successful after it had first flown at Langenhagen in May 1944. The first production Fw 190D-9s (so termed because they followed the Fw 190A-8s at the factories, and widely known as 'Dora-Nines' in the Luftwaffe) joined III/JG 54 in September 1944 to defend the jet base of Kommando Nowotny. Among the sub-variants of the Fw 190D series was the Fw 190D-10 with a single 30-mm MK 108 cannon located between the engine cylinder banks and firing through the propeller hub. The Fw 190D-12/R21, a ground-attack version of the hub-gunned Fw 190D-10 and power-boosted with MW50 water-methanol injection, was almost certainly the fastest of all Fw 190s with a top speed of 730 km/h (453 mph) at 11000 m (36,090 ft). Dora-Nines equipped most of the Luftwaffe's fighter units during the last fateful months of the Third Reich, but in combat with the Allies – particularly their P-51s and Spitfire XIVs – they were frequently overwhelmed. The Luftwaffe's problems centred on a shortage of fuel, which allowed only small formations of fighters, and of battle-hardened veteran

First of several torpedo-carrying versions of the Fw 190 was the A-5/U14 (c/n 871), shown here carrying an LT F5b torpedo. The rack fairing of this version was deeper than that on the U15 which carried an LT 950 (950-kg/2,090-lb) weapon. Note the considerably lengthened tailwheel assembly.

Second unarmed prototype for the proposed high-altitude Fw 190C-series was the V18, shown here in its U1 guise with DB 603A engine (which replaced the earlier DB 603G), four-bladed propeller and Hirth 9-2281 turbocharger. Inclusion of a pressure cabin is evidenced by strengthening members on the canopy.

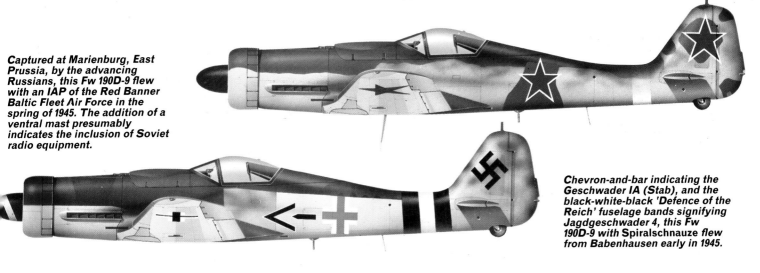

Captured at Marienburg, East Prussia, by the advancing Russians, this Fw 190D-9 flew with an IAP of the Red Banner Baltic Fleet Air Force in the spring of 1945. The addition of a ventral mast presumably indicates the inclusion of Soviet radio equipment.

Chevron-and-bar indicating the Geschwader IA (Stab), and the black-white-black 'Defence of the Reich' fuselage bands signifying Jagdgeschwader 4, this Fw 190D-9 with Spiralschnauze flew from Babenhausen early in 1945.

pilots. For instance, when JG 6 (commanded by Major Gerhard Barkhorn, the German pilot who had a combat record of 301 air victories) in April 1945 took delivery of 150 brand-new Dora-Nines, it could only fly patrols by four aircraft at a time against massed wings of Allied fighters.

The Fw 190F and Fw 190G series were essentially ground-attack versions, the Fw 190F ('Panzer-Blitz') armoured assault aircraft appearing in the spring of 1944. Externally similar to the Fw 190A series, but with a bulged hood, this version featured gun armament reduced to two MG 17s and two 20-mm cannon, but had the ability to carry the 1000-kg (2,205-lb) bomb plus two 50-kg (110-lb) fragmentation bombs. Most important sub-variant was the Fw 190F-8, which could carry 14 21-cm (8.27-in) rocket bombs, six 28-cm (11.02-in) rocket-launchers or 24 R4M unguided rockets; Fw 190F-8s first joined III(Pz)/KG 200 in the autumn of 1944.

The Fw 190G series actually entered operational service long before the Fw 190F, the first aircraft being sent to North Africa, joining SG 2 at Zarzoun, Tunisia, following the 'Torch' landings in November 1942. The majority, however, went to the Eastern Front where they played an active part in the great tank battle of Kursk in early July 1943. The Fw 190G-1 version, with greatly strengthened undercarriage, could lift a 1800-kg (3,968-lb) bomb.

Long-nose derivative

Mention must also be made of a development of the Fw 190, the Ta 152 (its designation finally reflecting Kurt Tank's overall design responsibility). This 'long-nose' derivative of the Fw 190D series retained the hub-firing 30-mm gun but introduced increased electrical systems. Various prototypes of the Ta 152A, B and C variants were produced, but it was the Ta 152H-1 version with one 30-mm and two 20-mm guns and a maximum speed of 760 km/h (472 mph) at 12500 m (41,010 ft) that was selected for operational service; only about a dozen aircraft of this type had been completed and delivered to JG 301 when the war ended. A total of 26 Ta 152 prototypes and 67 pre-production and production aircraft was completed.

Having regard to the nature of the Luftwaffe's defensive operations during the last 30 months of the war, it is scarcely surprising that production assumed impressive proportions, no fewer than 20,087 Fw 190s (including 86 prototypes) being produced during the 1939-45 period, the peak daily production rate of 22 aircraft being reached early in 1944.

By the same token many Luftwaffe pilots achieved remarkable combat feats at the controls of Fw 190s (not forgetting that of Josef Würmheller who shot down seven Spitfire Vs in one day over the Dieppe beaches – despite concussion and a broken leg suffered in a recent accident). Pride of place must go to Oberleutnant Otto Kittel, the Luftwaffe's fourth highest scoring pilot, of whose 267 air victories some 220 were gained in Fw 190A-4s and -5s. Other very high scorers in the Fw 190s included Walter Nowotny, Heinz Bär, Hermann Graf and Kurt Bühligen, all of whose scores included more than 100 victories gained with the guns of the aptly-named 'Butcher Bird'.

Focke-Wulf Fw 190 and Ta 152 variants

Fw 190V1 to V80 (plus six others): prototypes and progressive development aircraft, 1939-44; served as prototypes for Fw 190A to G series and some Ta 152s
Fw 190A-0: nine aircraft with small wings, remaining 11 with large wings; BMW 801C-1; four 7.92-mm (0.31-in) guns
Fw 190A-1: four 7.92-mm (0.31-in) guns
Fw 190A-2: two 20-mm and two 7.92-mm (0.31-in) guns; BMW 801C-2
Fw 190A-3: four 20-mm and two 7.92-mm (0.31-in) guns; BMW 801D-2; also U1 fighter-bomber, U3 ground-attack fighter, U4 reconnaissance fighter and U7 fighter-bomber; 'Trop' sub-variants
Fw 190A-4: FuG16Z radio; BMW 801D-2 with MW50 injection; U1 and U8 fighter-bombers, U4 ground-attack fighter, R6 bomber-destroyer; 'Trop' sub-variants; introduced first Rüstsätz
Fw 190A-5: slightly lengthened mounting for BMW 801D-2; U2 night ground-attack aircraft, U3 similar with increased bomb load, U4 reconnaissance aircraft, U6 and U8 fighter-bombers, U11 bomber-destroyer, U13 ground-attack fighter, U14 and U15 torpedo-fighters, U16 bomber-destroyer, U17 was prototype for Fw 190F-3; 'Trop' sub variants
Fw 190A-6: FuG16Ze and FuG25 radio; lighter wing structure; R1 to R4 bomber-destroyer, R4 with BMW 801TS; R6 bomber-destroyer with underwing rockets; 'Trop' sub-variants
Fw 190A-7: two 20-mm and two 13-mm (0.51-in) guns; Rüstsätz conversions as for Fw 190A-6
Fw 190A-8: FuG16ZY radio; GM-1 powerboosting; Rüstsätz conversions R1 to R6 as for Fw 190A-6; R7 had armoured cockpit; R11 all-weather fighter had PKS12 and FuG125 radio similar but with two 30-mm guns; U1 two-seat trainer, U3 upper component of Mistel weapon; U11 fighter/torpedo bomber
Fw 190A-9: BMW 801F; Rüstsätz conversions similar to Fw 190A-6, but R11 had BMW 801TS, and R12 similar but two 30-mm guns
Fw 190A-10: numerous prototypes only; BMW 801TS/TH; three bomb or drop tank stations; four 20-mm and two 13-mm (0.51-in) guns
Fw 190B-0: three prototypes modified from Fw 190A-1s; various wing planforms; failure of pressure cabin caused discontinuation; one Fw 190B-1 not completed
Fw 190C-0: six prototypes, including one modified Fw 190A-0; various engines with Hirth supercharger; development abandoned
Fw 190D-0: 10 aircraft converted from Fw 190A-7s; Junkers Jumo 213A engines with annular radiators; first 'long-nose' Fw 190s
Fw 190D-9: Jumo 213A; two 20-mm and two 13-mm (0.51-in) guns; most aircraft had bulged hoods; R11 all-weather fighter with FuG125 radio
Fw 190D-10: two prototypes converted from Fw 190D-0s; single 30-mm hub gun replaced guns in nose decking
Fw 190D-11: seven prototypes only; two 20-mm and two 30-mm guns; R20 with PKS12 radio; R21 with FuG125 radio
Fw 190D-12: one 30-mm and two 20-mm guns; armoured Jumo 213F; R5 ground-attack fighter; R11 all-weather fighter; R21 with MW50 injection; R25 with Jumo 213EB
Fw 190D-13: Jumo 213EB; three 20-mm guns; R5, R11, R21 and R25 as for Fw 190D-12
Fw 190D-14: DB603A; two prototypes converted from Fw 190D-9 and Fw 190D-12
Fw 190D-15: DB603EB; not built; intended as conversions from Fw 190A-8s and Fw 190F-8s

Fw 190E: reconnaissance fighter project; not built
Fw 190F-1: armoured fighter bomber; one ETC501 and two ETC50 bomb racks; bulged canopy
Fw 190F-2: similar to Fw 190F-1 but additional ER4 adaptor bomb rack
Fw 190F-3: provision for underwing drop-tanks; R3 with two underwing 30-mm guns
Fw 190F-8: provision for variety of rockets and anti-personnel weapons; U1 was proposed two-seat trainer; U2 and U3 had provision to carry various torpedo-bombs and U14 was torpedo-fighter; R1, R2, R3, R5, R8, R11, R14, R15 and R16 all provided for various armament combinations
Fw 190F-9: armoured version of Fw 190A-9 and production in parallel; BMW 801TS
Fw 190F-10 to F-14: unbuilt projects
Fw 190F-15: one prototype; Fw 190A-8 wing; BMW 801TS/TH
Fw 190F-16: one prototype; increased armour; BMW 801TS/TH
Fw 190G-0: two 20-mm guns; maximum bomb load 1000 kg (2,205 lb)
Fw 190G-1: strengthened undercarriage; one 1800-kg (3,968-lb) bomb; Junkers bomb rack
Fw 190G-2: as above but Messerschmitt bomb rack
Fw 190G-3: as above but Focke-Wulf bomb rack; R5 could carry four fragmentation bombs under the wings
Fw 190G-4: three ETC503 bombracks
Fw 190G-7: was intended to carry single 900-litre (198-Imp gal) drop-tank
Fw 190G-8: BMW 801D-2, otherwise similar to Fw 190A-8; R4 had GM1 power boost
Fw 190H-1: proposed high-altitude fighter with DB603G, but not built
Ta 152A-1: unbuilt project similar to Fw 190D-9 with FuG24 radio
Ta 152A-2: unbuilt project as above but with four 20-mm guns
Ta 152B-1: unbuilt project with hub-firing 30-mm gun
Ta 152B-2: unbuilt project with GM1 power boost
Ta 152B-3: armoured ground-attack fighter project
Ta 152B-4: heavy fighter project; R1 with two 13-mm and two 20-mm guns; R2 with three 30-mm and two 20-mm guns
Ta 152B-5: one prototype built (Fw 190V53); three 20-mm guns; R11, three prototypes built (Ta 152V19, V20 and V21)
Ta 152C: three prototypes built; DB603L; all-weather fighter
Ta 152C-0 and C-1: three prototpyes completed; DB603L; many gun combinations proposed
Ta 152E-1: photo-reconnaissance aircraft; two prototypes completed
Ta 152E-2: high-altitude version of Ta 152E-1; one prototype (Ta 152V26) completed
Ta 152H: high-altitude fighter; Jumo 213E; three modified Fw 190 prototypes (Fw 190V29, V30 and V32) completed
Ta 152H-0: 20 pre-production aircraft built at Cottbus in 1944; Jumo 213EB; R11, R21 and R31 variants with engine boost and radio variations
Ta 152H-1: one prototype (Ta 152V26) modified from Ta 152E-2 and about a dozen production examples completed; Ta 152H-10 was fighter reconnaissance version not completed at the end of the war
Ta 153: one prototype (Fw 190V32) modified from Ta 152H prototype to include very high aspect ratio wing

Focke-Wulf Fw 190 'Butcher Bird'

Specification
Focke-Wulf Fw 190A-8
Type: single-seat fighter and fighter-bomber
Powerplant: one 1567-kW (2,100-hp) BMW 801D-2
Performance: maximum speed (clean) 654 km/h (408 mph); initial climb 720 m (2,363 ft)/min; normal range 805 km (500 miles); service ceiling 11400 m (37,400 ft)
Weights: empty 3170 kg (7,000 lb); maximum loaded 4900 kg (10,800 lb)
Dimensions: span 10.5 m (34 ft 5½ in); length 8.84 m (29 ft 0 in); height 3.96 m (13 ft 0 in); wing area 18.3 m² (196.98 sq ft)
Armament: (A-8/R2) two 7.9-mm MG17 machine-guns, four 20-mm MG151/20 cannon, one 500-kg (1,100-lb) and two 250-kg (550-lb) bombs, or one 300-litre (66-Imp gal) drop-tank

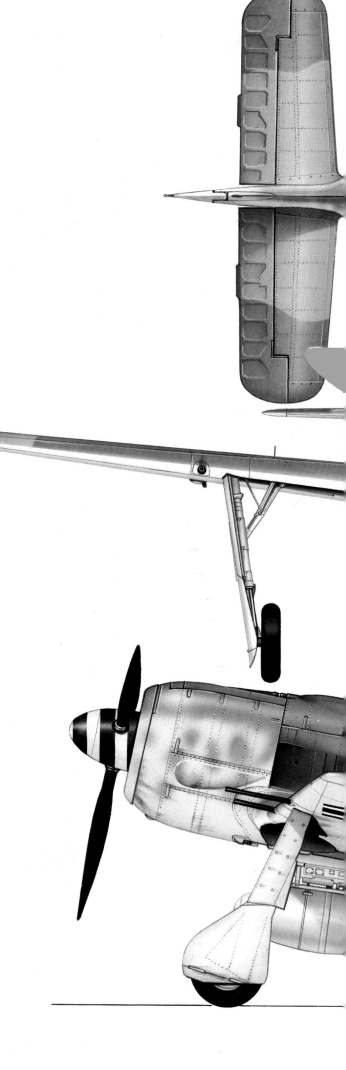

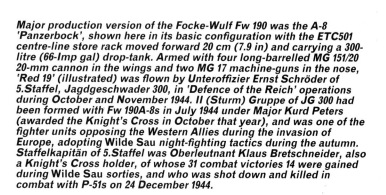

Major production version of the Focke-Wulf Fw 190 was the A-8 'Panzerbock', shown here in its basic configuration with the ETC501 centre-line store rack moved forward 20 cm (7.9 in) and carrying a 300-litre (66-Imp gal) drop-tank. Armed with four long-barrelled MG 151/20 20-mm cannon in the wings and two MG 17 machine-guns in the nose, 'Red 19' (illustrated) was flown by Unteroffizier Ernst Schröder of 5.Staffel, Jagdgeschwader 300, in 'Defence of the Reich' operations during October and November 1944. II (Sturm) Gruppe of JG 300 had been formed with Fw 190A-8s in July 1944 under Major Kurd Peters (awarded the Knight's Cross in October that year), and was one of the fighter units opposing the Western Allies during the invasion of Europe, adopting Wilde Sau night-fighting tactics during the autumn. Staffelkapitän of 5.Staffel was Oberleutnant Klaus Bretschneider, also a Knight's Cross holder, of whose 31 combat victories 14 were gained during Wilde Sau sorties, and who was shot down and killed in combat with P-51s on 24 December 1944.

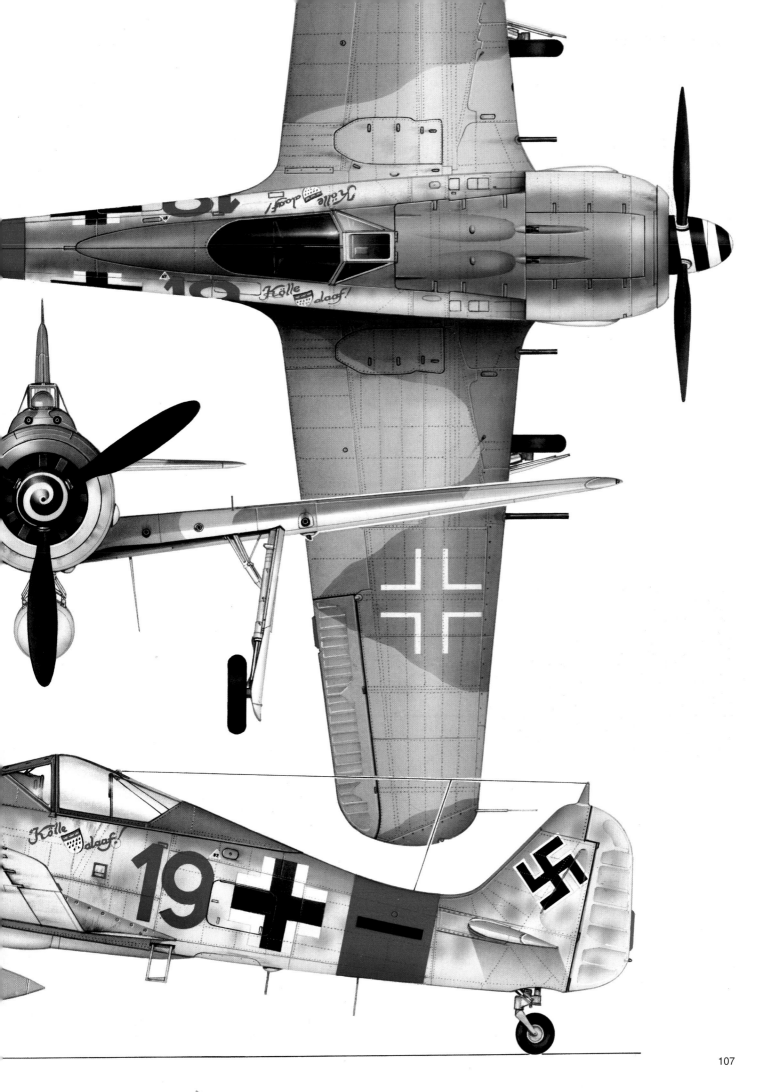

Nakajima Ki-43

Lightly armed and powered, the Nakajima Ki-43-I was obsolescent at the time of its service debut over Malaya in December 1941, yet this aircraft obtained a decisive advantage over Allied types during the first year of the war, and remained in production until the Japanese surrender, long after it had become totally outdated.

In the last days of peace in the Malay peninsula, the Commonwealth pilots assigned to Nos 21 and 453 Squadrons of the RAAF, Nos 67 and 243 Squadrons of the RAF, and No. 488 Squadron of the RNZAF exuded confidence. True, they were fully aware that their Brewster Buffaloes had been found hopelessly obsolete in the UK and had been rejected for first-line European operational service. Nonetheless they had been lured into complacency by the ill-founded belief that their Japanese opponents were flying even more obsolete aircraft. Tragically, a great number of these pilots soon paid the ultimate price, or ended the war in POW camps, as their Buffaloes were easily outmanoeuvred and outperformed by the Nakajima Ki-43-I Hayabusas of the Imperial Japanese Army.

At the onset of its offensive against Malaya, the Imperial Japanese Army assigned 173 fighters to its 3rd Hiko-Shidan (air division) operating from bases in Indo-China; 59 of these aircraft were the service's most modern fighters, the Ki-43-Is of the 59th and 64th Sentais (regiments or groups). Initially flying convoy escort sorties and airfield strafing attacks, the Ki-43s quickly established their ascendancy over the Buffaloes and, together with older Nakajima Ki-27s from three other *sentais*, soon eliminated the ineffective threat posed by the forces under the command of Air Chief Marshal Sir Robert Brooke-Popham. Even after Hawker Hurricane Mk IIs joined the fray, the Ki-43s retained air superiority as the Allied pilots had not yet developed the necessary tactics to fight the extremely nimble Japanese fighters.

First flown at the Ojima airfield in January 1939, the prototype of this effective fighter had a difficult gestation period and was saved from oblivion only after a major redesign had corrected initial deficiencies. Preliminary design work was begun in December 1937 when the Koku Hombu (Air Headquarters), giving up its longstanding policy of awarding competitive design contracts, instructed Nakajima Hikoki KK (Nakajima Aeroplane Co. Ltd) to design a single-seat fighter intended as a replacement for the Nakajima Ki-27 then just entering service. The specification for the new aircraft emphasised manoeuvrability, which was to be at least equal to the remarkable standard set by the Ki-27, and called for a top speed of 500 km/h (311 mph), a climb rate of 5 minutes to 5000 m (16,405 ft), a range of 800 km (497 miles) and an armament of two 7.7-mm (0.303-in) machine-guns. With the exception of manoeuvrability, these requirements were rather uninspired as by then faster and more heavily armed fighters were already flying in Europe.

The design team, led by Hideo Itokawa, elected to retain the wing planform and aerofoil of the Ki-27 for the new fighter, but adopted a longer rear fuselage to balance the heavier weight of the 690-kW (925-hp) Nakajima Ha-25 double-row radial driving a two-bladed fixed-pitch wooden propeller. Despite the provision of retractable main landing gear and a 30 per cent increase in take-off horsepower,

Bearing Chinese markings, this Ki-43-I-Hei (Ic) – the first flyable 'Oscar' to fall into Allied hands – was tested by US personnel. American pilots were impressed with its manoeuvrability, but commented adversely on its lack of protection and light armament. Note the great similarity to the Japanese navy's A6M Zero.

A Ki-43-I-Hei flown by the 64th Sentai during initial Japanese attempts to cut off China from Allied forces in India and Burma. The colour of the tail markings identified the Chutais within the Sentai, with blue being normally used for the Headquarters Chutai, white for the 1st, red for the 2nd, and yellow for the 3rd. The application of brown mottle over the usual dark green camouflage was fairly common on the China-Siam-Burma front.

the three Ki-43 prototypes proved barely faster than production Ki-27-Otsus (27b). Even more serious was the failure of the new fighter to equal, as required by the Koku Hombu, the manoeuvrability of the Ki-27. So, as most Imperial Japanese Army pilots considered the retractable landing gear to be a purely technical luxury and believed that air combats would continue to be fought as classic dogfights, the Ki-43 prototypes were found unsatisfactory by the army test organisation at Tachikawa.

At that point, the Koku Hombu seriously considered suspending further development of the type in favour of accelerated production of the Ki-27. In the event, prudence prevailed and the design team was instructed to proceed with a major redesign and the construction of 10 service trials aircraft. Consideration was then given to reverting to a fixed spatted landing gear but, as this solution would have resulted in insufficient performance, the service trials aircraft retained the more modern gear. The first of these aircraft was completed in November 1939 and introduced a refined and lightened fuselage, new vertical tail surfaces, a revised canopy improving vision to the rear, and a more powerful version of the Ha-25 engine. The results of these changes proved quite satisfactory, and performance met the revised and more demanding requirements set for these service trials machines.

An 821-kW (1,100-hp) Nakajima Ha-105 engine, with a two-speed supercharger instead of the single-speed supercharger of the Ha-25, was tested on the second and tenth pre-production machines, while the seventh and tenth mounted an armament of two 12.7-mm (0.5-in) Type 1 (Ho-103) machine-guns. The Ha-105 engine was not retained for production aircraft, but the heavier armament was adopted for late production versions. Also retained for incorporation in production aircraft was the provision for carrying two 200-litre (44-Imp gal) drop tanks beneath the wings. It was, however, the installation of 'butterfly' combat flaps (tested earlier by Nakajima on

the P.E. prototype of its Ki-27 and fitted in 1940 to the eighth Ki-43 service trials aircraft) which ensured the final acceptance as a service type of the Ki-43 as, with these flaps, the aircraft demonstrated truly exceptional manoeuvrability. Consequently, Nakajima was authorised in September 1940 to start production of the Ki-43-I as the Army Type 1 Fighter Model 1, three sub-versions being planned depending upon the availability of 12.7-mm (0.5-in) machine-guns; the Ki-43-I-Ko (Ia) had two 7.7-mm/0.303-in guns, the Ki-43-I-Otsu had one 7.7-mm (0.303-in and one 12.7-mm/0.5-in gun, and the Ki-43-I-Hei (Ic) two 12.7-mm/0.5-in machine-guns.

The falcon spreads its wings

Named Hayabusa (peregrine falcon), the new type entered service in June 1941, when the 59th Sentai began its conversion from Ki-27s, and soon after, before the Japanese entry into the war, re-equipped the 64th Sentai. The Ki-43s were soon blooded, besting the Buffaloes and more than holding their own against the Hurricanes. In fact, most losses incurred by the 59th and 64th Sentais during the first two months in combat were the result of operational causes, including fuel starvation and structural failures. The former problem was easily remedied when a sufficient number of drop tanks was delivered to these units, but the latter, which occurred even after initial production aircraft had undergone emergency strengthening at the Tachikawa Arsenal, required a major redesign of the wing structure.

Within months of the type's entry into service, both the manufacturer and the army recognised that the Ki-43-I's performance was inadequate and that, with the exception of its superb manoeuvrability, the type would soon find itself at considerable disadvantage when opposed by more modern Allied fighters. Unfortunately, as the original army requirement had unrealistically emphasised manoeuvrability over performance, little could be done to increase

The tenth pre-production Ki-43, construction no. 4313, was one of two aircraft experimentally powered by an 820-kW (1,100-hp) Nakajima Ha-105 radial, featuring adjustable cowling gills. This aircraft was armed with a pair of 12.7-mm (0.5-in) Ho-103 machine-guns, the armament later adopted for most production aircraft.

After participating in the Philippines campaign with the Nakajima Ki-27-Otsu, the 50th Sentai returned to Japan for its conversion to Ki-43-Is and its subsequent operations in Burma. Photographed at Tokorozawa in June 1942, these Ki-43-I-Hei belonged either to the unit's 1st Chutai (with white lightning markings) or 3rd Chutai (yellow lightning).

Nakajima Ki-43 variants

Ki-43: three prototypes and 10 service trials aircraft for the Imperial Japanese Army; the service trials aircraft feature major airframe revisions as described in the main text; powered by a 690-kW (925-hp) or 738-kW (990-hp) Nakajima Ha-25 radial engine (with the exception of the second and tenth service trials machines which were powered by a 821-kW/1,100-hp Nakajima Ha-105 radial) driving a two-bladed propeller; standard armament of two 7.7-mm (0.303-in) Type 89 machine-guns in forward fuselage, these guns being replaced by 12.7-mm (0.5-in) Type 1 machine-guns on the seventh and tenth service trials aircraft; 'butterfly' combat flaps first tested on the eighth service trials machine

Ki-43-I-Ko: all improvements progressively introduced on the service trials aircraft were incorporated on this first production model with Ha-25 engine, two-bladed propeller, and armament of two 7.7-mm (0.303-in) Type 89 machine-guns

Ki-43-I-Otsu and **Ki-43-I-Hei:** similar to the preceding model but armed with one 7.7-mm (0.303-in) machine-gun and one 12.7-mm (0.5-in) Type 1 machine-gun (Ki-43-I-Otsu), or two Type 1 guns (Ki-43-I-Hei)

Ki-43-II: five prototypes with reinforced wing of reduced span (10.84 m compared with 11.44 m/35 ft 6¾ in compared with 37 ft 6⅜ in) and area (21.4 m²/230.4 sq ft compared with 22m²/236.8 sq ft) and 858-kW (1,150-hp) Nakajima Ha-115 radial engine driving a three-bladed propeller; externally-carried weapon load increased from two 15-kg (33-lb) to two 30-kg or 250-kg (66-lb or 551-lb) bombs; addition of rudimentary protection for the pilot and fuel tanks

Ki-43-II-Ko: initial production version of the Ki-43-II built by Nakajima and the Tachikawa Dai-Ichi Rikugun Kokusho; inbuilt armament of two 12.7-mm (0.5-in) Type 1 machine-guns

Ki-43-II-Otsu: improved model which incorporated minor equipment changes and a revised powerplant installation; produced by Nakajima and Tachikawa Hikoki KK

Ki-43-II-KAI: three prototypes, built by Nakajima and fitted with individual exhaust stacks offering some thrust augmentation and replacing the exhaust collector ring of earlier versions, were followed by large scale manufacturing by Nakajima (until September 1944) and Tachikawa (until war's end)

Ki-43-III-Ko: 10 prototypes, built by Nakajima and powered by 888-kW (1,190-hp) Nakajima Ha-115-II radial engine; limited production by Tachikawa

Ki-43-III-Otsu: two prototypes produced by Tachikawa in the spring of 1945; powered by a 970-kW (1,300-hp) Mitsubishi Ha-112 radial engine driving a three-bladed propeller; two 20-mm Ho-5 cannon in upper fuselage decking

speed or armament dramatically. Nevertheless, by substituting a 858-kW (1,150-hp) Nakajima Ha-115 engine, which was a development of the earlier Ha-25 with a two-speed supercharger and driving a constant-speed three-bladed propeller in place of the two-pitch two-bladed pattern, Nakajima was able to increase maximum speed from 492 km/h (306 mph) at 5000 m (16,405 ft) for the Ki-43-I-Hei to 558 km/h (347 mph) at 5830 m (19,125 ft) for the Ki-43-II prototypes. However, this improvement was of short duration as, with the addition of 13-mm (0.51-in) head and back armour plating and a rudimentary form of self-sealing fuel tanks, the production versions of the Ha-115-powered Hayabusa could not do better than 530 km/h (329 mph) at 4000 m (13,125 ft).

In common with the Ki-43-II prototypes, the Ki-43-II-Ko, Ki-43-II-Otsu and Ki-43-II-KAI versions had wings of slightly reduced span and area with stronger spars. In addition, the underwing shackles, which during the course of the Ki-43-II-Otsu production were moved from aft of the main landing gear units to a position further outboard, were strengthened to carry bombs of up to 250 kg (551 lb). Other changes introduced on the assembly lines affected the powerplant installation: the oil cooler, which up to and including the Ki-43-II-Ko had been mounted in a ring within the cowling, was incorporated in the deepened carburettor intake of early production Ki-43-II-Otsu aircraft; later on, the oil cooler was removed from the carburettor intake and relocated separately beneath the centre fuselage. Finally, the Ki-43-II-KAIs were fitted with individual exhaust stacks offering some thrust augmentation and replacing the exhaust collector ring of earlier versions.

At the outset, Hayabusa production was undertaken exclusively in the main Nakajima plant at Otsa, in Gumma Prefecture, some 80 km (50 miles) north of Tokyo. Deliveries were slow, with the manufacturer completing only 157 Ki-43-Is (compared with 433 Ki-27s) during 1941. To speed production of the new fighter, the Otsa plant then began the phasing down of Ki-27 production. This new ordering of priorities was reflected in the production totals for 1942, 616 Ki-43s being built (compared with 289 Ki-27s), the last of the older type being delivered by Nakajima in November.

Broad front

With the Imperial Japanese Army now fighting over a broad front from the Chinese mainland to the jungle of New Guinea, this increased production rate was still insufficient to make up for combat losses in Ki-43 units (which at the end of 1942 included the 1st, 11th, 21st, 24th, 25th, 26th, 33rd, 50th, 59th, 64th, 203rd, and 248th Sentais) and to convert or re-equip additional Sentais. Accordingly, the Koku Hombu instructed both its Tachikawa Dai-Ichi Rikugun Kukusho (1st Army Air Arsenal at Tachikawa) and the Tachikawa Hikoki KK (Tachikawa Aeroplane Co. Ltd) to begin preparation for the manufacturing of the Hayabusa. The Arsenal failed to make a significant contribution to the war's effort, producing only 49 Ki-43-II-Ko fighters between October 1942 and November 1943. On the other hand, after a slow start (its first Ki-43-II-Otsu being delivered in May 1943, some seven months behind schedule) Tachikawa became the prime manufacturer of Hayabusas. The last Nakajima-built Ki-43 was delivered in September 1944, whereas Tachikawa was still manufacturing the type at war's end and, in spite of damage incurred during bombing raids by the US 20th Air Force, managed to deliver a final batch of 35 Ki-43s during the first half of August 1945.

Following the conquest of Malaya and the fall of Singapore on 15

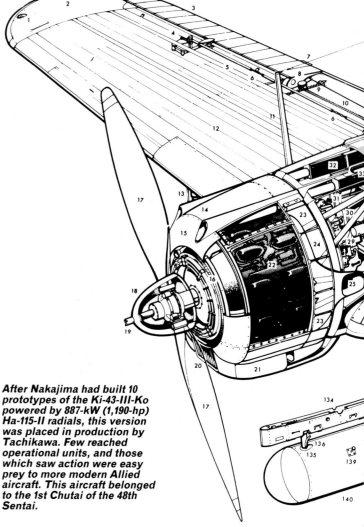

After Nakajima had built 10 prototypes of the Ki-43-III-Ko powered by 887-kW (1,190-hp) Ha-115-II radials, this version was placed in production by Tachikawa. Few reached operational units, and those which saw action were easy prey to more modern Allied aircraft. This aircraft belonged to the 1st Chutai of the 48th Sentai.

Nakajima Ki-43-I-Ko Hayabusa cutaway drawing key

1 Starboard navigation light
2 Wingtip
3 Starboard fabric-covered aileron
4 Aileron actuating linkage
5 Aileron control rod
6 Control rod connecting fittings
7 Aileron tab
8 Flap outer cable drum
9 Flap travel
10 Flap control cables
11 Radio mast
12 Light alloy wing skinning
13 Starboard undercarriage fairing
14 Gun port fairings
15 Nose ring
16 Annular oil cooler
17 Two-blade two-pitch metal propeller
18 Spinner
19 Starter dog
20 Supercharger air intake
21 Intake fairing
22 Nakajima Ha-25 (Type 99) 14-cylinder two-row radial engine
23 Cowling gills
24 Exhaust collector ring
25 Exhaust outlet

26 Engine lower bearers
27 Oil regulator valve
28 Oil pressure tank
29 Engine accessories
30 Engine upper bearers
31 Cowling gill controls
32 Two 0.5-in (12.7-mm) Type 89 machine-guns
33 Gun gas outlet
34 Cartridge link ejection chute
35 Fireproof (No.1) bulkhead
36 Ammunition magazine (500 rpg)
37 Cartridge ejection chute
38 Gun breech fairing
39 Telescopic gun sight
40 One-piece curved windscreen
41 Radio aerial
42 Aft-sliding cockpit canopy
43 Turnover structure
44 Seat back
45 Seat adjustment rails
46 Seat pan

47 Throttle quadrant
48 Instrument panel
49 Control column
50 Rudder pedals
51 Underfloor control linkage
52 Seat support frame
53 Control cable and rod bearings
54 Oxygen cylinders
55 Rudder cable pulleys
56 Transceiver
57 Type 96 Hi-3 radio installation
58 Receiver unit
59 Transmitter unit
60 Anti-vibration mounting slings
61 Fuselage construction break

62 Inspection/access panel
63 Fuselage stringers
64 Fuselage structure
65 Frame
66 Fuselage upper longeron
67 Elevator control cables
68 Fuselage skinning
69 Tailwheel shock strut
70 Tail unit attachment
71 Tailfin root fairing
72 Starboard tailplane
73 Elevator balance

93 Rudder cables
94 Tailfin skinning
95 Wing fillet
96 Flap inboard profiles
97 Flap actuating cylinder
98 Rear spar/fuselage attachment

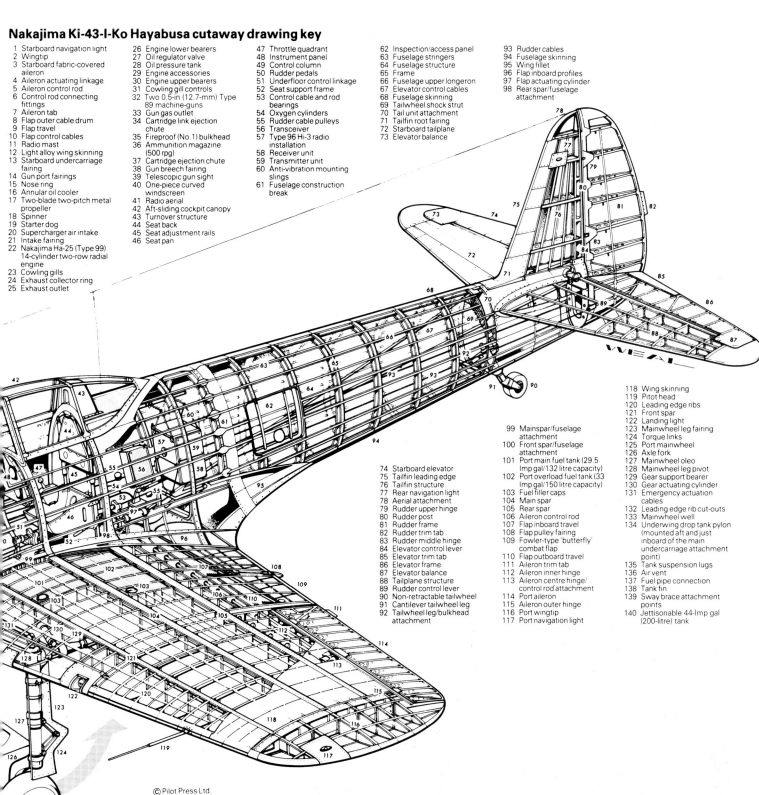

74 Starboard elevator
75 Tailfin leading edge
76 Tailfin structure
77 Rear navigation light
78 Aerial attachment
79 Rudder upper hinge
80 Rudder post
81 Rudder frame
82 Rudder trim tab
83 Rudder middle hinge
84 Elevator control lever
85 Elevator trim tab
86 Elevator frame
87 Elevator balance
88 Tailplane structure
89 Rudder control lever
90 Non-retractable tailwheel
91 Cantilever tailwheel leg
92 Tailwheel leg/bulkhead attachment

99 Mainspar/fuselage attachment
100 Front spar/fuselage attachment
101 Port main fuel tank (29.5 Imp gal/132 litre capacity)
102 Port overload fuel tank (33 Imp gal/150 litre capacity)
103 Fuel filler caps
104 Main spar
105 Rear spar
106 Aileron control rod
107 Flap inboard travel
108 Flap pulley fairing
109 Fowler-type 'butterfly' combat flap
110 Flap outboard travel
111 Aileron trim tab
112 Aileron inner hinge
113 Aileron centre hinge/ control rod attachment
114 Port aileron
115 Aileron outer hinge
116 Port wingtip
117 Port navigation light

118 Wing skinning
119 Pitot head
120 Leading edge ribs
121 Front spar
122 Landing light
123 Mainwheel leg fairing
124 Torque links
125 Port mainwheel
126 Axle fork
127 Mainwheel oleo
128 Mainwheel leg pivot
129 Gear support bearer
130 Gear actuating cylinder
131 Emergency actuation cables
132 Leading edge rib cut-outs
133 Mainwheel well
134 Underwing drop tank pylon (mounted aft and just inboard of the main undercarriage attachment point)
135 Tank suspension lugs
136 Air vent
137 Fuel pipe connection
138 Tank fin
139 Sway brace attachment points
140 Jettisonable 44-Imp gal (200-litre) tank

© Pilot Press Ltd.

Nakajima Ki-43

Specification
Nakajima Ki-43-II-Otsu
Type: single-seat fighter and fighter-bomber
Powerplant: one 858-kW (1,150-hp) Nakajima Ha-115 14-cylinder air-cooled radial piston engine
Performance: maximum speed 530 km/h (329 mph) at 4000 m (13,125 ft); climb to 5000 m (16,405 ft) in 5 minutes 49 seconds; service ceiling 11200 m (36,750 ft); normal range 1760 km (1,095 miles)
Weights: empty 1910 kg (4,211 lb); maximum take-off 2925 kg (6,450 lb)
Dimensions: span 10.84 m (35 ft 6¾ in); length 8.92 m (29 ft 3⁵⁄₁₆ in); height 3.27 m (10 ft 8¾ in); wing area 21.4 m² (230.4 sq ft)
Armament: two 12.7-mm (0.5-in) Type 1 (Ho-103) machine-guns in the upper fuselage decking, plus two 30-kg (66-lb) or 250-kg (551-lb) bombs

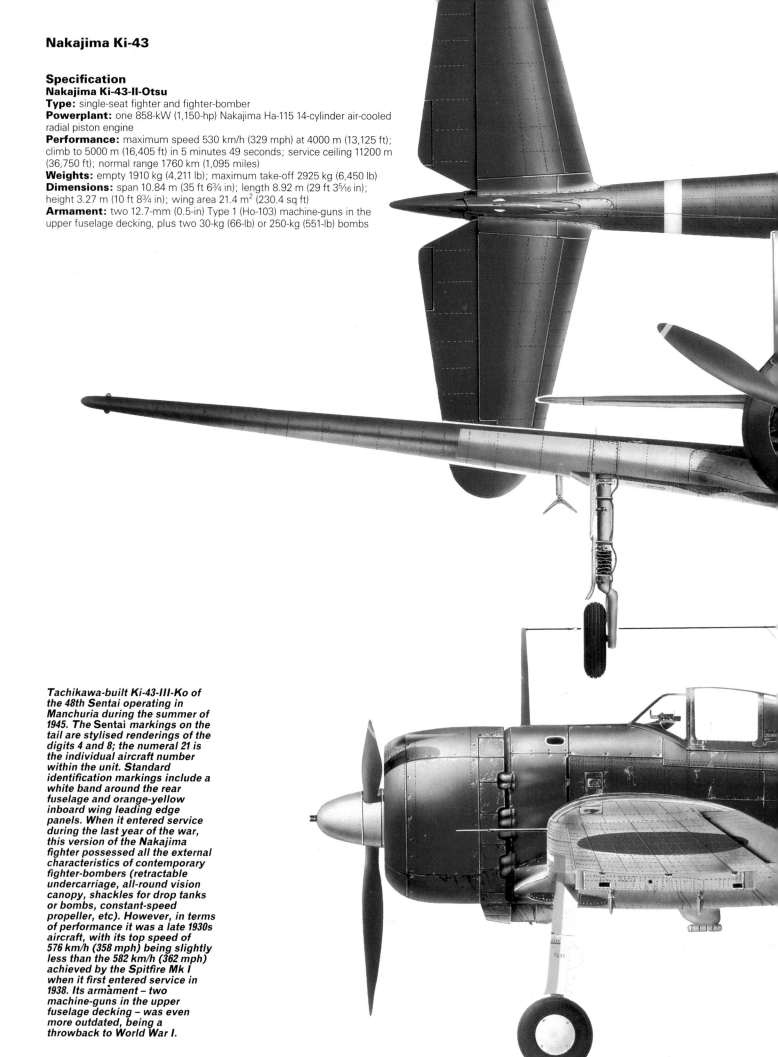

Tachikawa-built Ki-43-III-Ko of the 48th Sentai operating in Manchuria during the summer of 1945. The Sentai markings on the tail are stylised renderings of the digits 4 and 8; the numeral 21 is the individual aircraft number within the unit. Standard identification markings include a white band around the rear fuselage and orange-yellow inboard wing leading edge panels. When it entered service during the last year of the war, this version of the Nakajima fighter possessed all the external characteristics of contemporary fighter-bombers (retractable undercarriage, all-round vision canopy, shackles for drop tanks or bombs, constant-speed propeller, etc). However, in terms of performance it was a late 1930s aircraft, with its top speed of 576 km/h (358 mph) being slightly less than the 582 km/h (362 mph) achieved by the Spitfire Mk I when it first entered service in 1938. Its armament – two machine-guns in the upper fuselage decking – was even more outdated, being a throwback to World War I.

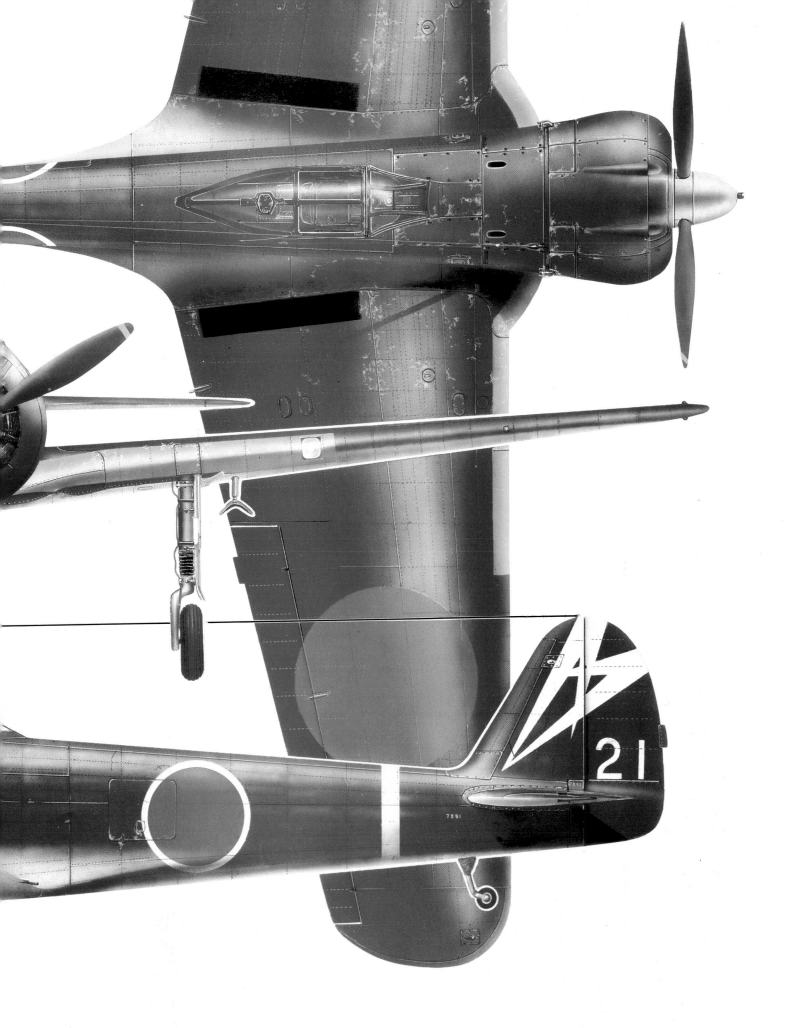

Nakajima Ki-43

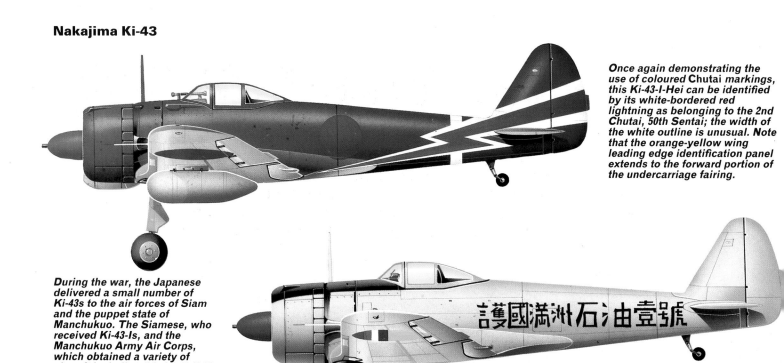

Once again demonstrating the use of coloured Chutai markings, this Ki-43-I-Hei can be identified by its white-bordered red lightning as belonging to the 2nd Chutai, 50th Sentai; the width of the white outline is unusual. Note that the orange-yellow wing leading edge identification panel extends to the forward portion of the undercarriage fairing.

During the war, the Japanese delivered a small number of Ki-43s to the air forces of Siam and the puppet state of Manchukuo. The Siamese, who received Ki-43-Is, and the Manchukuo Army Air Corps, which obtained a variety of aircraft including this Ki-43-II-Ko, made limited use of their fighters.

護國滿洲石油壹號

February 1942, the Imperial Japanese Army turned its attention to finishing off American defences in the Philippines and to advancing on new fronts. During the very swift conquest of the Dutch East Indies, the Ki-43-Is went on from success to success, with pilots racking up impressive scores: for example, on 19 February 1942 the 64th Sentai claimed 14 'kills' and five 'probables' for the loss of only one Ki-43. On the Burma front, however, things soon became less easy for the Hayabusa pilots as they faced the experienced pilots of the American Volunteer Group, the famous 'Flying Tigers' of General Chennault. From then on the Ki-43, which was known to Allied personnel by the codename 'Oscar', found itself on the defensive; the Allies were fielding increasing numbers of more modern fighters and had devised better tactics to counter the Hayabusas and other manoeuvrable Japanese fighters. Supplemented by Ki-44s from early 1942, by Ki-61s from the autumn of 1942, by Ki-84s from the summer of 1944, and by Ki-100s from early 1945, Ki-43s nevertheless still bore a heavy burden in the defensive campaign fought by the Imperial Japanese Army during the last two years of the war. At last, how-

ever, it was clear to all that even with its latest developments, the Ki-43-III-Ko and Ki-43-III-Otsu, the Hayabusa could no longer be considered an effective warplane.

More than any other type, the Ki-43 Hayabusa epitomised both the qualities and deficiencies of Japanese fighters of World War II. In a dogfight, it had no peer. However, from 1943 onward speed, heavy armament, and good protection were qualities of greater importance than manoeuvrability to success in air combat. Thus it is indeed quite remarkable that the Ki-43 became the only Japanese fighter aircraft to be used after the end of the war, when a small number of captured Hayabusas were operated in 1945-6 by the Indonesian People's Security Forces against the Dutch and by the French Groupes de Chasse I/7 and II/7 against Communist insurgents in Indo-China.

Total production of all Ki-43 variants amounted to 5,919, including 3,239 by Nakajima and 2,631 by Tachikawa.

Shining under the Chinese sun, this Ki-43-II-Otsu of the 2nd Chutai (red diagonal tailstripe), 25th Sentai, proves that the application of green mottle over the aircraft's natural metal skin was not a very effective form of camouflage.

Yakovlev Yak-1/3/7/9

Excluding the many research and experimental prototypes, 36,737 of these Yakovlev piston-engined fighters were built during (and for a few days after) World War II. No other family of fighters can equal this total, nor claim to have played such a part in winning the war during the last years in Europe.

Hitler struck at the Soviet Union on 22 June 1941, just at the time the V-VS (Red Air Force) was least able to win. Almost all the main front-line types were obsolescent. Among new fighter prototypes the best was probably the Yak, but even this fell into the same trap as the other Soviet fighters in having too big an engine in too small an aircraft, with too few guns, and proving desperately difficult to fly by ill-trained pilots asked to operate such a 'hot-ship' from rough airstrips of grass, mud or wooden planks. Despite this, the Yaks played a gigantic role in helping defeat the Luftwaffe.

Aleksandr S. Yakovlev had always wanted to design a fighter. His chance came in November 1938 when, the effort on the Ya-22 fast bomber trailing off, his bureau received permission to work on a 'frontal fighter', and this was initiated as the Ya-26, the official NKAP designation being I-26 (I for *istrebitel*, or fighter). Yakovlev had studied the Messerschmitt Bf 109 and Supermarine Spitfire at first hand, but had never used stressed-skin all-metal structure and decided to stick to traditional construction with a wooden wing, welded steel fuselage with mixed aluminium panels and fabric covering, and fabric-covered dural control surfaces. He was already friendly with V. Ya. Klimov and agreed to use the latter's M-106-I engine (distantly derived from the Hispano-Suiza 12Y) of 1,350 hp (1007 kW). By this time retractable landing gears were becoming less clumsy, and a good wide-track gear was designed, folding straight in ahead of the front spar. Pneumatic actuation was adopted, as it was for the duralumin split flaps. For minimum drag the combined glycol radiator and oil cooler were located in a duct under the trailing edge of the wing, whilst the carburettor air intakes were at the wing roots. Armament comprised one 20-mm ShVAK firing through the hub of the VISh-61 hydraulic propeller and two of the fast-firing ShKAS 7.62-mm (0.3-in) machine-guns above the engine, which had to be the 783-kW (1,050-hp) M-105.

When the first Ya-26 was almost complete the erection-shop workers called it *Krasavits* (beauty). It was then finished in the Yak OKB colour of bright red, with the rudder striped red and white. Chief pilot Yu. I. Piontkovskii made a successful first flight, without guns or radio, on 13 January 1940 (the early history has been very

One of the best of all Soviet wartime flying pictures, this shows a loose group of Yak-9s over the Crimea in 1944. The emblems on the nose are the insignia of the Guards and the Order of the Red Banner. Note the open tailwheel doors on two aircraft.

confused in Western reports), and the wheeled gear worked well from snow and ice. Sadly the aircraft crashed fatally on 27 April, but the cause was traced to a defect in manufacture. By this time the future was assured, and with V-VS designation Yak-1 the new fighter was to go into production at two factories, one being GAZ-115 adjoining the OKB on Leningradskii Prospekt in Moscow. At about the time of the crash the second prototype had been about to fly, and this incorporated most of the numerous changes demanded for the Yak-1, including relocation of the oil cooler under the nose, dividing the carburettor air duct to inlets in the wing roots, making the fuselage wider behind the canopy, increasing the fin chord and making the tailwheel non-retractable.

The second aircraft flew in the May Day parade and was put through NII official testing by P. M. Stefanovskii from 10 June 1940. By this time there was no question of rejection, but the Yak-1 was still immature. The most annoying fault was frequent fatigue failure of the aluminium fuel piping, which caused a few inflight fires. The pneumatic system was unreliable, guns frequently failed to fire and the hood often jammed. The Kremlin also wanted higher flight performance, but what mattered above all else was sheer numbers, and 64 were delivered in the final weeks of 1940. By this time Yakovlev's greatly expanded OKB was busy with improvements and derived versions, and in autumn 1941 production had to be evacuated to GAZ-286 at Kamensk-Uralsk and, in late 1942, to GAZ-153 (previously a LaGG-3 factory) at Novosibirsk. Each plant introduced its own local changes; despite the need for standardisation and high output, a contemporary observer considered there were hardly any two consecutive aircraft that were identical! Among major changes, from mid-1941 some aircraft had the two ShKAS replaced by a 12.7-mm (0.5-in) UBS (usually on the left), while a few had the weak armament of two UBS guns, one of them in place of the ShVAK. Simpler leg fairings were introduced, along with improved wing-root inlets, retractable skis and ply decking behind the canopy with side windows instead of a large curved sheet of Plexiglas.

Even with the original transparencies the rear view had been poor, and while part of the trouble was the rigid harness which prevented body rotation it was clear that the canopy could be improved. The best answer was found by a front-line unit which boldly cut down the light secondary structure above the rear fuselage and fitted a transparent fairing behind the sliding hood. Pilot view was often poor in any direction because of the lack of uniformity in Plexiglas mouldings available, but the new arrangement was adopted for production

with designation Yak-1B. Until this time many pilots had left the canopy open.

Performance improvements

A much more difficult modification was the Yak-1M programme launched under Sinelshchikov in October 1940 to reduce weight, and also to improve performance by introducing the VK-105PF engine (which Yakovlev pushed in the face of opposition from Klimov). The work took two years and more than 450 significant design changes, but reduced loaded weight from 2850 to about 2655 kg (6,283 to about 5,853 lb) despite a slight increase in fuel capacity, the heavier PF engine and type 105SV constant-speed propeller. All-round performance was improved significantly, and about half the 8,721 series Yak-1s delivered by summer 1943 were Yak-1Ms. This total does not include the numerous prototypes and experimental versions, such as the I-28, I-30 and I-33. These had various changes in airframe, engine/radiator installation and armament, one series having three 20-mm ShVAK and two machine-guns, a sharp contrast with most front-line Yaks.

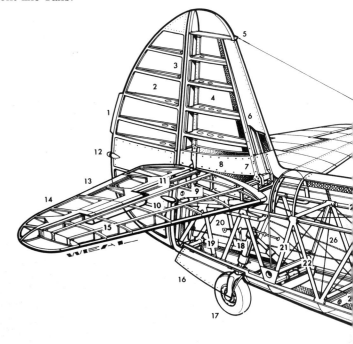

Yak variants

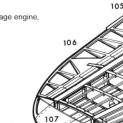

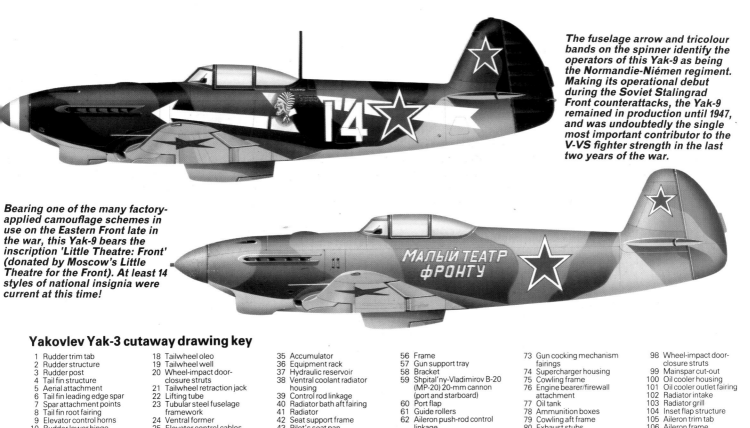

The fuselage arrow and tricolour bands on the spinner identify the operators of this Yak-9 as being the Normandie-Niémen regiment. Making its operational debut during the Soviet Stalingrad Front counterattacks, the Yak-9 remained in production until 1947, and was undoubtedly the single most important contributor to the V-VS fighter strength in the last two years of the war.

Bearing one of the many factory-applied camouflage schemes in use on the Eastern Front late in the war, this Yak-9 bears the inscription 'Little Theatre: Front' (donated by Moscow's Little Theatre for the Front). At least 14 styles of national insignia were current at this time!

Yakovlev Yak-3 cutaway drawing key

1 Rudder trim tab
2 Rudder structure
3 Rudder post
4 Tail fin structure
5 Aerial attachment
6 Tail fin leading edge spar
7 Spar attachment points
8 Tail fin root fairing
9 Elevator control horns
10 Rudder lower hinge
11 Elevator torque tube
12 Rear navigation light
13 Elevator trim tab
14 Elevator structure
15 Tailplane construction
16 Tailwheel doors
17 Retractable tailwheel
18 Tailwheel oleo
19 Tailwheel well
20 Wheel-impact door-closure struts
21 Tailwheel retraction jack
22 Lifting tube
23 Tubular steel fuselage framework
24 Ventral former
25 Elevator control cables
26 Diagonal brace wires
27 Dorsal former
28 Decking
29 Aerial
30 Aerial attachment/lead-in
31 Canopy fixed aft glazing
32 Armourglass screen
33 Canopy track
34 HF (RSI-6M) radio equipment
35 Accumulator
36 Equipment rack
37 Hydraulic reservoir
38 Ventral coolant radiator housing
39 Control rod linkage
40 Radiator bath aft fairing
41 Radiator
42 Seat support frame
43 Pilot's seat pan
44 Trim tab control console (port)
45 Padded (armoured) seat back
46 Switchbox
47 Aft-sliding cockpit canopy
48 Reflector sight
49 One-piece moulded armourglass windscreen
50 Instrument panel coaming
51 Control column
52 Instrument panel starboard console
53 Control linkage
54 Rudder pedal bar
55 Bulkhead
56 Frame
57 Gun support tray
58 Bracket
59 Shpital'ny-Vladimirov B-20 (MP-20) 20-mm cannon (port and starboard)
60 Port flap
61 Guide rollers
62 Aileron push-rod control linkage
63 Aileron trim tab
64 Port aileron
65 Port wingtip
66 Port navigation light
67 Pitot tube
68 Forward spar
69 Port outboard fuel tank
70 Fuel filler cap
71 Supercharger intake scoop
72 Intake ducting
73 Gun cocking mechanism fairings
74 Supercharger housing
75 Cowling frame
76 Engine bearer/firewall attachment
77 Oil tank
78 Ammunition boxes
79 Cowling aft frame
80 Exhaust stubs
81 Blast tubes
82 Gun muzzle troughs
83 Filler cap
84 Coolant header tank
85 Propeller pitch mechanism
86 VISh-107 variable-pitch metal propeller
87 Propeller spinner
88 Propeller hub
89 Auxiliary intake
90 Cowling attachment frames
91 Klimov M-107A (VK-107A) 12-cylinder liquid-cooled Vee engine
92 Coolant ducting
93 Port mainwheel
94 Engine bearer
95 Oil cooler intake
96 Ducting
97 Mainwheel well door inboard section
98 Wheel-impact door-closure struts
99 Mainspar cut-out
100 Oil cooler housing
101 Oil cooler outlet fairing
102 Radiator intake
103 Radiator grill
104 Inset flap structure
105 Aileron trim tab
106 Aileron frame
107 Starboard wingtip
108 Starboard navigation light
109 Outboard wing ribs
110 Rear spar
111 Stringers
112 Starboard outboard fuel tank
113 Front spar
114 Undercarriage/spar attachment plate
115 Undercarriage retraction cylinder
116 Mainwheel leg well
117 Undercarriage downlock strut
118 Brake lines
119 Torque links
120 Mainwheel oleo leg
121 Mainwheel leg fairing plate
122 Mainwheel fairing plate
123 Axle fork
124 Starboard mainwheel

© Pilot Press Limited

Yakovlev Yak-1/3/7/9

A Yak-1 of No. 183 IAP (fighter aviation regiment) in the summer of 1942. Flown by Senior Lieutenant M. D. Baranov, who even at this time had 27 kill stars, it was one of the many Yak-1s finished in tractor-paint because of a shortage of specification dope. The inscription says 'Death to Fascists'.

This Yak-1M was the personal aircraft of one of the greatest Soviet aces, Hero of the Soviet Union Sergei Lugansky; the dedication states that it was presented by the Young Communists of Alma-Ata, and the number in the laurel wreath shows Lugansky's current score at this time in early 1943.

In early 1940 the Ya-27 tandem trainer version had begun flight testing, and this quickly became a major programme. Though put into production initially as the UTI-26 trainer and two-seat liaison machine, it was recognised as being in many respects better than the Yak-1 fighter. The structure was simplified, the number of parts being reduced and the manufacturing effort greatly simplified. A visible example of this was seen in the landing gears. To maintain centre of gravity with removed armament and the extra cockpit, the radiator was moved forward under the wing. Small-scale production of the UTI-26 began in spring 1941, but the all-round ease of handling and simplicity of manufacture led to the idea of building a fighter version. In July 1941 this became the Yak-7B, the two-seater becoming the Yak-7V. GAZ-292 at Saratov tooled up and got into production so fast that it won an Order of Lenin in July 1942. Two-seaters usually had a long-span wing with pointed tips, and many had simple fixed main gears for wheels with outsize tyres or skis for use in front-line areas. By March 1943 about 5,000 Yak-7B fighters had been delivered out of 6,399 Yak-7s of all models, the fighters mostly having one ShVAK and two UBS weapons. There were dozens of experimental versions, including examples with the M-82 (ASh-82) engine, underwing ramjets, heavy anti-tank cannon, VIP cockpits and pressure cabins.

One group had wings with spars having aluminium-alloy webs and steel booms, while at least one machine had an all-metal wing. The change of material left more room for fuel, and pre-production examples were tested in action with designation Yak-7D and Yak-7DI (*dalnii istribitel*, or long-range fighter), most having the Yak-1B rear-view canopy. These had a range exceeding 1000 km (621 miles), and by mid-1942 they had led to full production of a refined development, the Yak-9. This had improved radiator and oil-cooler ducts, revised rudder, redesigned metal-spar wings with improved ailerons and flaps and doped fabric over the ply skin, simple tabs bent by pliers on all control surfaces, improved gun installations, retractable tailwheel, new exhaust stacks (first used on late Yak-7Bs) and minor changes. Usual armament comprised a ShVAK or MP-20 and one or two UBS, and there was provision for two FAB-100 bombs or six RS-82 rockets under the wings.

By May 1943 all the Yak factories had switched to Yak-9 versions, the variants being listed separately. Notable variants included anti-tank models with centreline guns of up to 57-mm calibre (this and the 45-mm were too big for the small aircraft) and the Yak-9B bomber with fuselage racks for four FAB-100 bombs carried 80° nose-up, or alternatively up to 128 PTAB 1,5 or 2,5 anti-personnel bombs. From mid-1943 the Yak OKB worked on the Yak-9U (*uluchshyennyi*, or improved) variants with numerous improvements to the airframe, fuel system and many other parts, including large oval engine air inlets projecting ahead of the leading-edge roots. Again there were many experimental models, including Yak-9P (*pushechnyi*, or cannon) versions with different arrangements including synchronised cannon in place of the machine-guns. This designation was often applied in Western accounts to the ordinary Yak-9U. Total output of series models totalled 16,769, with completion in late August 1945, of which over 3,900 were of the final Yak-9U models.

Back in late 1941 the Yak-1M search for a lightened Yak had led to a parallel development for the ultimate dogfighter for low/medium altitudes, and this was given the service number Yak-3 (already used for the Yakovlev OKB's own I-30 prototype). The urgent need for output, and delay with the chosen VK-107 engine, resulted in this being abandoned, but in August 1943 Oleg K. Antonov (detached from his own OKB to help the vital Yakovlev team) picked it up again and

The second Ya-26 (or I-26) prototype, which first flew in the hands of P. Ya. Fedrovi in April 1940. Painted like No. 1 in the Yakovlev red/white house livery, it had the oil cooler relocated under the engine and the carburettor air inlets moved to the wing roots, while other changes included a fixed tailwheel.

An important photograph showing a (possibly the) Yak-1M used as the development aircraft for the Yak-3 by O. K. Antonov in autumn 1943. Later the oil cooler below the spinner was moved to the wing roots and there were many other changes, but the engine had to remain the same old VK-105PF-2.

The inscription on this winter-painted Yak-1M reads: 'To the pilot of the Stalingrad Front Guards Major Comrade B. N. Yeremen (often misread in the West as "Yevemen"), from the collective farm workers, "Stakhanov", Comrade Golovatov'. The winter paint appears to have been factory-applied, with a high finish.

A Yakovlev Yak-1 flown by Lieutenant-Colonel A. E. Golubov of 18 IAP from Ichationki in the spring of 1943. Hardly the most trustworthy aircraft from the pilot's point of view, this immature design suffered from poor serviceability, the result of a truncated test and evaluation programme.

pressed it forward. At least two Yak-1Ms were used to fly new Yak-3 features, one having the small 9.2-m (30.2-ft) wing and another having the revised fuselage with a fully retractable tailwheel, long and shallow radiator duct, streamlined oil cooler installation with inlet just below the spinner, new main gears with the leg fork on the inner side of the wheel (as in the original Yak-1) and low-drag frameless windscreen. Later changes relocated the oil cooler to two ducts in the wing roots, fed by big root inlets as in the Yak-9, the engine being the PF-2 version as used in most Yaks after 1943. The first Yak-3 was sent for NII testing on 3 March 1944 (long after some Western accounts claimed the aircraft was in service!) and clearance for production was received in June. By this time GAZ-115 and GAZ-286 were tooled up to make the Yak-3 as well as the Yak-9, and GAZ-124 had reopened in Moscow, so that when production stopped in May 1945 a total of 4,848 Yak-3s had been delivered.

Dogfighter supreme

Though it is believed no front-line Yak-3 had the intended VK-107 engine (though many experimental Yak-3s did) the basic aircraft soon established a tremendous reputation as the best dogfighter on the Eastern Front, on either side. There is a famous Luftwaffe signal telling pilots to 'avoid combat with any Yak fighter lacking an oil cooler under the nose', and when in August 1944 the French Normandie-Niémen Regiment was given the choice of any type of Allied fighter it unanimously picked the Yak-3, and never had any cause to regret it. In 1945 this famed unit took its 42 surviving Yak-3s back to France.

Again, in the Yak-3 programme there were numerous experimental aircraft, not included in the production total. Fastest were the Yak-3B/108 with the VK-108 engine, which at full load reached

745 km/h (463 mph) and the Yak-3RD with a Glushko RD-1 booster rocket in the tail which reached 801 km/h (498 mph) whilst in a gentle climb. The best comment on one aircraft, the Yak-3T/57 with a 57-mm gun for tank-busting, is that it only flew once! It is worth mentioning that one variant, the tandem-seat Yak-3UTI trainer, went into production with the 522-kW (700-hP) ASh-21 radial engine and designation Yak-11. Moreover, the first Soviet jet fighter (though for political reasons kept on the ground until the rival MiG-9 was ready) was the Yak-15, which was almost a Yak-3 powered by an RD-10, the Soviet copy of the Jumo 004B, slung under the forward fuselage. This was finally allowed to fly on the same day as the first MiG-9, on 24 April 1946.

It is not easy for Western writers to assess the Yak fighters objectively. Certainly the VK series of V-12 engines, all originally derived from the Hispano-Suiza 12Y of 1934, fell well short of the British Merlin in specific power, and in particular in power at high altitude. Thus the fighters these engines powered were inevitably at a disadvantage at heights much above 6095 m (20,000 ft), and at all heights they were burdened by physically large engines in relatively small airframes. All the mass-produced Soviet fighters (the Yaks, the LaGGs and Las, and the MiGs) had wings with an area of some 17 m^2 (184 sq ft), compared with 22.5 m^2 (242 sq ft) for a Spitfire, 28.1 m^2 (302 sq ft) for a Hawker Tempest and 28.6 m^2 (308 sq ft) for a Republic P-47; thus they were cripplingly limited in the weight they could support whilst still having good power to manoeuvre.

But even this is only a small part of the story. The operating conditions on the Eastern Front were so appallingly harsh that only the toughest and simplest fighters could stay airworthy. Overall, the Yak family did more than any other group of aircraft to defeat the Luftwaffe.

A regular production Yak-3, in this case belonging to the Free French Normandie-Niémen regiment. Note the short span, redesigned fuselage and radiator installation and main landing gears almost the same as those of the Yak-1. This Yak-3 is lucky to have a paved apron, but refuelling must take a long time.

One of the 1,400-odd very simple and popular Yak-7V tandem two-seaters. Some of these had dual controls while others were plain liaison machines. There were very many variations, this example having fixed skis while many others had fixed wheels with outsize tyres for use on snow or ice.

119

Yakovlev Yak-1/3/7/9

This Yak-9 was one of those equipping the Free French Normandie-Niémen regiment in 1944. It can be seen to be normal in all visible features, with armament of one ShVAK and one BS and with the blunt wingtips introduced early in production at the same time that the wing ribs were changed to aluminium. Many colour schemes were used by VVS front-line regiments, and in winter it was usual to add a rough coat of white on the upper surfaces.

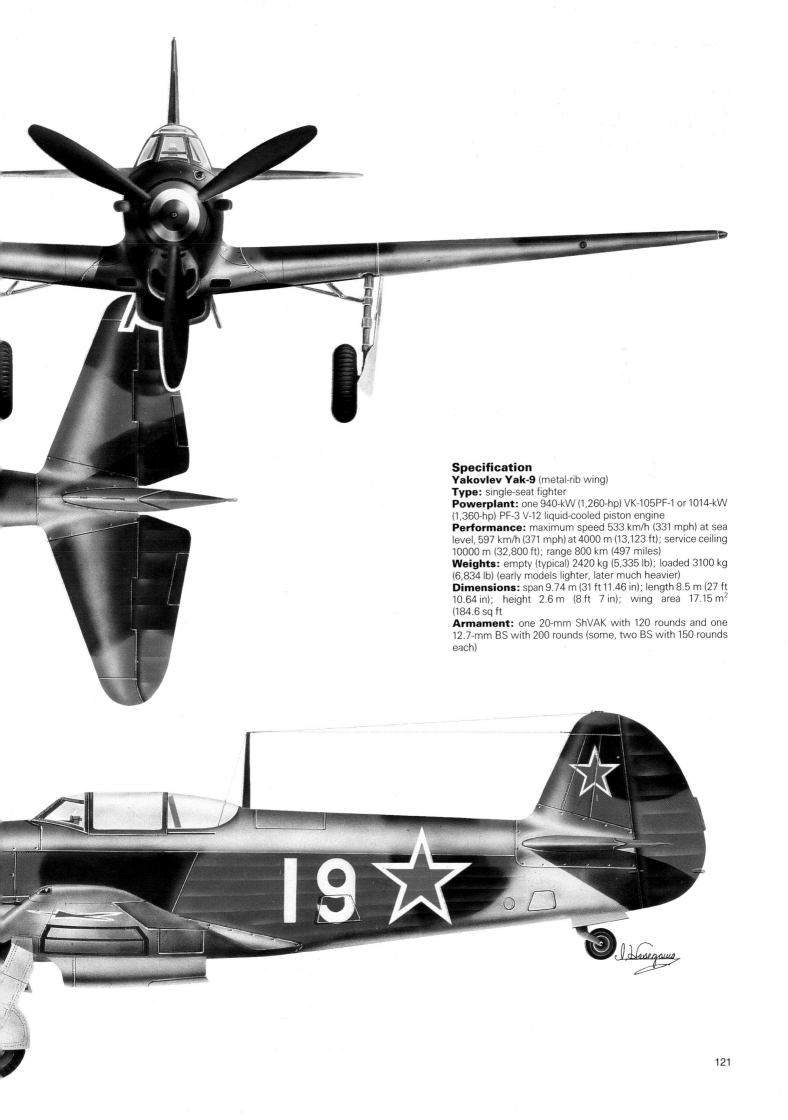

Specification
Yakovlev Yak-9 (metal-rib wing)
Type: single-seat fighter
Powerplant: one 940-kW (1,260-hp) VK-105PF-1 or 1014-kW (1,360-hp) PF-3 V-12 liquid-cooled piston engine
Performance: maximum speed 533 km/h (331 mph) at sea level, 597 km/h (371 mph) at 4000 m (13,123 ft); service ceiling 10000 m (32,800 ft); range 800 km (497 miles)
Weights: empty (typical) 2420 kg (5,335 lb); loaded 3100 kg (6,834 lb) (early models lighter, later much heavier)
Dimensions: span 9.74 m (31 ft 11.46 in); length 8.5 m (27 ft 10.64 in); height 2.6 m (8 ft 7 in); wing area 17.15 m² (184.6 sq ft
Armament: one 20-mm ShVAK with 120 rounds and one 12.7-mm BS with 200 rounds (some, two BS with 150 rounds each)

Hawker
Tempest and Sea Fury

*Another product of the prestigious drawing board of Sir Sidney Camm,
the Tempest was built to remedy the problems of the earlier Typhoon.
Much improved as a ground attack and fighter aircraft, it was followed
by the sleek Tempest II and Sea Fury which held the line in post-war
Germany and fought with distinction in Korea.*

Under their great teacher Sydney (later Sir Sydney) Camm, the Hawker design staff at Kingston toiled in 1937, before their Hurricane had entered service, to create a totally new fighter to specification F.18/37. It was to have a 1491-kW (2,000-hp) engine, either a Rolls-Royce Vulture or a Napier Sabre. The Vulture-engined Tornado was a flop, but the Sabre-engined Typhoon eventually, after narrowly escaping cancellation, matured as a great low-level fighter-bomber and rocket carrier.

The Typhoon was poor at high altitudes, its engine being perpetually unreliable and its thick wing prone to shock-stall and flow breakaway at modest diving speeds. A complete solution to the engine problem already existed in the superb Bristol Centaurus, the big 18-cylinder sleeve-valve engine originally intended for bombers but already flown on 23 October 1941 in an extra Tornado prototype, HG641. What has never been explained was why, in view of the outstanding performance and good handling achieved by this lone aircraft, the Tornado airframe was summarily cancelled. In its place came the Typhoon, but the Centaurus could not be fitted in this airframe. Bristol engine designer Sir Roy Fedden said Air Marshal Sir Wilfrid Freeman had a vendetta against him (and it is certainly true that he forced Camm to remove a Centaurus already fitted into a

later airframe) but the truth was probably the need to concentrate on just a few engine/airframe combinations. At the same time, in July 1941, the Ministry of Aircraft Production cancelled the planned prototypes with a Wright R-3350 Cyclone 18 and the Fairey Monarch.

While the engine scene in 1941 was dismal, work was in progress on another front. In March 1940 Camm had sanctioned study of a new wing with reduced thickness/chord ratio and a later aerofoil profile of the so-called 'laminar' type, with maximum thickness much farther aft than before. Only two draughtsmen could be spared for this, but by the spring of 1941 the Hawker P.1012 was taking shape with a wing 14.5 per cent thick at the root and 10 per cent thick at the tip, compared with the Typhoon's 18 per cent. Instead of 12 machine-guns it had to house four 20-mm cannon, and as these were installed farther back than in the Typhoon Mk IB, with the breeches and magazines well outboard behind the rear spar, large chord was necessary at this point. Thus an elliptical planform emerged. Camm

One of the first units to receive the Tempest was RAF No. 501 (RAuxAF) Sqn, three of whose Mk V Series 2 aircraft are pictured. The squadron was in action against flying bombs three days after converting to the Tempest in August 1944 and specialised in night interceptions; the CO alone got 6 V-1s.

Hawker Tempest and Fury Variants

Centaurus-Tornado: one aircraft (HG641) flown 1941
Typhoon Mk II: one aircraft (LA594); prototype incomplete
Tempest Mk I: one aircraft (HM599) with Sabre IV, wing radiators
Tempest Mk II: production fighter; prototypes LA602 and LA607; production by Bristol (Weston) from MW374, then by Hawker; total 36 Bristol plus 100 Hawker
Tempest FB.Mk II: multi-role fighter-bomber; total 14 Bristol plus 300 Hawker; post-war sales to India (89) and Pakistan (24), all from unused RAF stocks
Tempest Mks III and IV: prototypes with Griffon IIB (LA610) and Griffon 61 (LA614); LA610 completed as Fury, and LA614 cancelled

Tempest Mk V: temporary lash-up of new wing on Typhoon, prototype HM595 (previously called Typhoon Mk II); subsequently put into production; **Tempest Mk V Series 1** 100 aircraft with Mk II guns, from JN729; **Tempest Mk V Series 2** 705 aircraft with Mk V guns, from EJ518
Tempest Mk VI: uprated aircraft with Sabre V, tested on rebuild HM595; 142 production aircraft from NV997
Fury: four F.2/43 prototypes; NX798 Centaurus XII, NX802 same, LA610 (ex-Tempest Mk III) Griffon 85, and VP207 Sabre VII, assembled from available components extra to contract; LA610 later rebuilt with Sabre VII, fastest piston fighter at 781 km/h (485 mph)

Fury: exports of basic F.2/43 standard to Iraq (30) and Pakistan (93 **Fury Mk 60** including five converted ex-RN Sea Fury FB.Mk 11s)
Fury Trainer: special export tandem two-seater with separate cockpit canopies for Iraq (2) and Pakistan (5 **Fury T.Mk 61**)
Sea Fury: three prototypes to N.7/43: SR661, SR666 (fully navalised) and VB857 (Boulton Paul)
Sea Fury Mk X: production fighter; total 50 from TF895
Sea Fury FB.Mk 11: production fighter-bomber; total 615 from TF956, some supplied to Australia and Canada
Sea Fury T.Mk 20: naval tandem dual trainer with canopies connected by Perspex 'tunnel', and periscope for instructor; prototype VX818, production total 60 from VX280
Sea Fury Mk 50: fighter for Netherlands; total 10

Sea Fury Mk 51: fighter-bomber for Netherlands; total 12 by Hawker plus 210 licence-built by Fokker
Sea Fury: further exports were 12 new to Sea Fury FB.Mk 11 standard for Egypt, 18 secondhand Sea Fury FB.Mk 11 for Burma, three unused Sea Fury T.Mk 20 for Burma, 15 new single-seat and two two-seat for Cuba, 10 former Sea Fury T.Mk 20 rebuilt for target-towing for West Germany

later said, "The Air Staff wouldn't buy anything that didn't look like a Spitfire," but this may have been his dry humour. At first of 13.1 m (43 ft) span, the wing then had the tips squared off to give a span of 12.5 m (41 ft), slightly less than that of the Typhoon but, thanks to the elliptical shape, with area increased from 25.92 to 28.06 m² (279 to 302 sq ft).

A key feature of this wing was the use of integral radiators in the leading edge for the Sabre engine. These promised low drag, but they occupied space where the Typhoon had leading-edge fuel tanks. Combined with the thinner wing this seriously reduced fuel capacity, but it was found possible to lengthen the fuselage by 0.53 m (21 in) ahead of the cockpit. This did not greatly affect pilot view and made room for a much larger tank, but it did call for a larger vertical tail. The design was virtually complete by October 1941, specification F.10/41 was written around it, and on 18 November a contract was received for two prototypes, HM595 and HM599. Previously known at Kingston (or rather at Claremont House, Esher, to where the design office had been evacuated) as the Typhoon Mk II, the new fighter was officially named Tempest in January 1942. Five more prototypes were ordered at this time, making the programme: LA594 the cancelled Typhoon Mk II (Centaurus); HM595 Tempest Mk V (Sabre in Typhoon type installation); HM599 Tempest Mk I (Sabre IV and wing radiators); LA602 and 607 Tempest Mk II (Centaurus); and LA610 and 614 Tempest Mk III or IV (respectively Griffon IIB or 61 engines). In the event, LA594 was never built and LA610 and 614 were diverted to the later F.2/43 programme, as explained presently. HM599 ought to have been first, but because of the effort needed to refine the totally new engine/radiator installation Camm decided to rush ahead with HM595, leaving it virtually as a standard Typhoon with the new wing. It even had the old 'car door' cockpit, and in this form flew on 2 September 1942.

A month earlier, in August 1942, Hawker received a contract for 400 Tempest Mk Is. All the Hawker test pilots sampled HM595 and found it a great improvement on the Typhoon, though as soon as possible the cockpit was modified with sliding bubble canopy, tailplane chord was increased and a dorsal fin was added. Eagerly everyone awaited the completion of the 'real' Tempest Mk I, HM599, but engine unavailability held up first flight until 24 February

One of the most garish colour schemes applied to the Sea Fury was for the target-towing two-seat TT.Mk 20s in Germany. This machine returned to the UK but has since been sold in the United States.

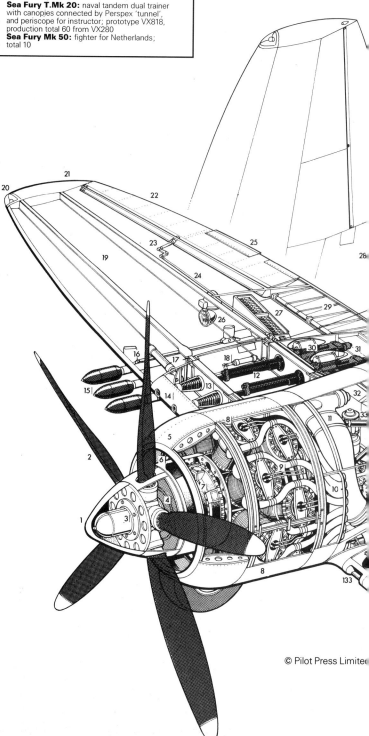

© Pilot Press Limited

Hawker Sea Fury FB.Mk 11 cutaway drawing key

1 Spinner
2 Rotol five-bladed constant-speed propeller of 12 ft 9 in (3.89 m) diameter
3 Propeller hub pitch change mechanism
4 Spinner backplate
5 Engine cowling ring
6 Cooling air intake
7 Propeller reduction gear casing
8 Detachable engine cowlings
9 Bristol Centaurus Mk 18 18-cylinder two-row radial sleeve valve engine
10 Exhaust stubs
11 Carburettor intake ducting
12 Starboard British Hispano Mk 5 20-mm cannon
13 Recoil springs
14 Cannon muzzles
15 60-lb (27.22 kg) ground attack rocket projectiles
16 Zero-length rocket launcher rails
17 Wing folding jack

Other than Britain's Fleet Air Arm, the sole European force to operate the Sea Fury was the Royal Netherlands navy, with 12 Mk 50s and 10 Mk 51s delivered from the UK in the late 1940s. These were followed by 210 FB.Mk 51s, licence-built by Fokker. The type saw service with two operational squadrons.

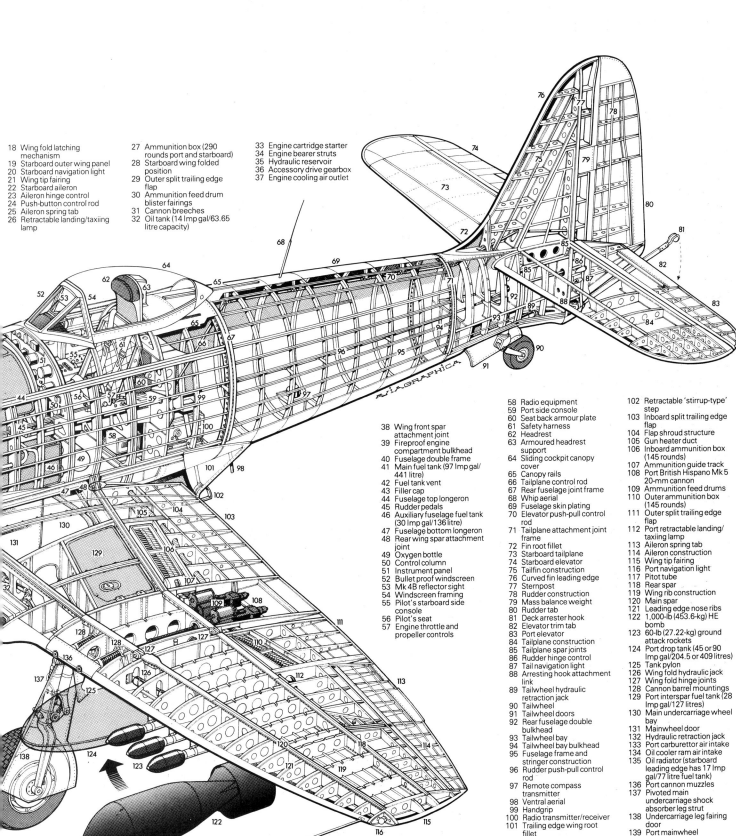

18 Wing fold latching mechanism
19 Starboard outer wing panel
20 Starboard navigation light
21 Wing tip fairing
22 Starboard aileron
23 Aileron hinge control
24 Push-button control rod
25 Aileron spring tab
26 Retractable landing/taxiing lamp

27 Ammunition box (290 rounds port and starboard)
28 Starboard wing folded position
29 Outer split trailing edge flap
30 Ammunition feed drum blister fairings
31 Cannon breeches
32 Oil tank (14 Imp gal/63.65 litre capacity)

33 Engine cartridge starter
34 Engine bearer struts
35 Hydraulic reservoir
36 Accessory drive gearbox
37 Engine cooling air outlet

38 Wing front spar attachment joint
39 Fireproof engine compartment bulkhead
40 Fuselage double frame
41 Main fuel tank (97 Imp gal/441 litre)
42 Fuel tank vent
43 Filler cap
44 Fuselage top longeron
45 Rudder pedals
46 Auxiliary fuselage fuel tank (30 Imp gal/136 litre)
47 Fuselage bottom longeron
48 Rear wing spar attachment joint
49 Oxygen bottle
50 Control column
51 Instrument panel
52 Bullet proof windscreen
53 Mk 4B reflector sight
54 Windscreen framing
55 Pilot's starboard side console
56 Pilot's seat
57 Engine throttle and propeller controls

58 Radio equipment
59 Port side console
60 Seat back armour plate
61 Safety harness
62 Headrest
63 Armoured headrest support
64 Sliding cockpit canopy cover
65 Canopy rails
66 Tailplane control rod
67 Rear fuselage joint frame
68 Whip aerial
69 Fuselage skin plating
70 Elevator push-pull control rod
71 Tailplane attachment joint frame
72 Fin root fillet
73 Starboard tailplane
74 Starboard elevator
75 Tailfin construction
76 Curved fin leading edge
77 Sternpost
78 Rudder construction
79 Mass balance weight
80 Rudder tab
81 Deck arrester hook
82 Elevator trim tab
83 Port elevator
84 Tailplane construction
85 Tailplane spar joints
86 Rudder hinge control
87 Tail navigation light
88 Arresting hook attachment link
89 Tailwheel hydraulic retraction jack
90 Tailwheel
91 Tailwheel doors
92 Rear fuselage double bulkhead
93 Tailwheel bay
94 Tailwheel bay bulkhead
95 Fuselage frame and stringer construction
96 Rudder push-pull control rod
97 Remote compass transmitter
98 Ventral aerial
99 Handgrip
100 Radio transmitter/receiver
101 Trailing edge wing root fillet

102 Retractable 'stirrup-type' step
103 Inboard split trailing edge flap
104 Flap shroud structure
105 Gun heater duct
106 Inboard ammunition box (145 rounds)
107 Ammunition guide track
108 Port British Hispano Mk 5 20-mm cannon
109 Ammunition feed drums
110 Outer ammunition box (145 rounds)
111 Outer split trailing edge flap
112 Port retractable landing/taxiing lamp
113 Aileron spring tab
114 Aileron construction
115 Wing tip fairing
116 Port navigation light
117 Pitot tube
118 Rear spar
119 Wing rib construction
120 Main spar
121 Leading edge nose ribs
122 1,000-lb (453.6-kg) HE bomb
123 60-lb (27.22-kg) ground attack rockets
124 Port drop tank (45 or 90 Imp gal/204.5 or 409 litres)
125 Tank pylon
126 Wing fold hydraulic jack
127 Wing fold hinge joints
128 Cannon barrel mountings
129 Port interspar fuel tank (28 Imp gal/127 litres)
130 Main undercarriage wheel bay
131 Mainwheel door
132 Hydraulic retraction jack
133 Port carburettor air intake
134 Oil cooler ram air intake
135 Oil radiator (starboard leading edge has 17 Imp gal/77 litre fuel tank)
136 Port cannon muzzles
137 Pivoted main undercarriage shock absorber leg strut
138 Undercarriage leg fairing door
139 Port mainwheel

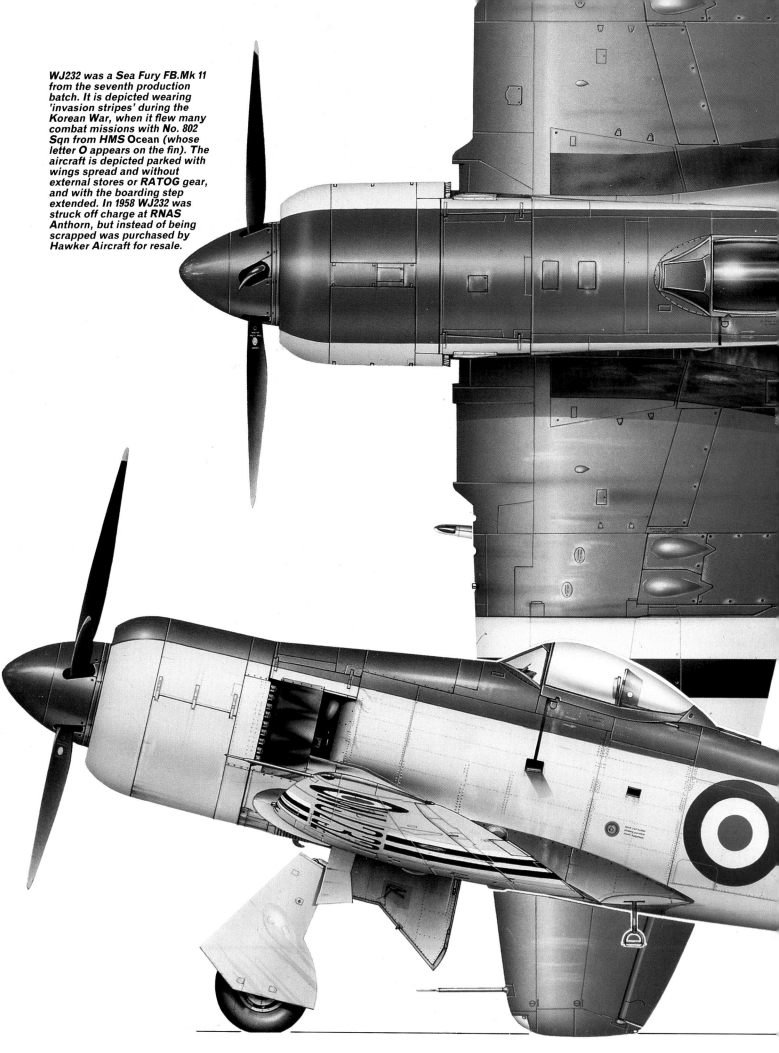

WJ232 was a Sea Fury FB.Mk 11 from the seventh production batch. It is depicted wearing 'invasion stripes' during the Korean War, when it flew many combat missions with No. 802 Sqn from HMS Ocean (whose letter O appears on the fin). The aircraft is depicted parked with wings spread and without external stores or RATOG gear, and with the boarding step extended. In 1958 WJ232 was struck off charge at RNAS Anthorn, but instead of being scrapped was purchased by Hawker Aircraft for resale.

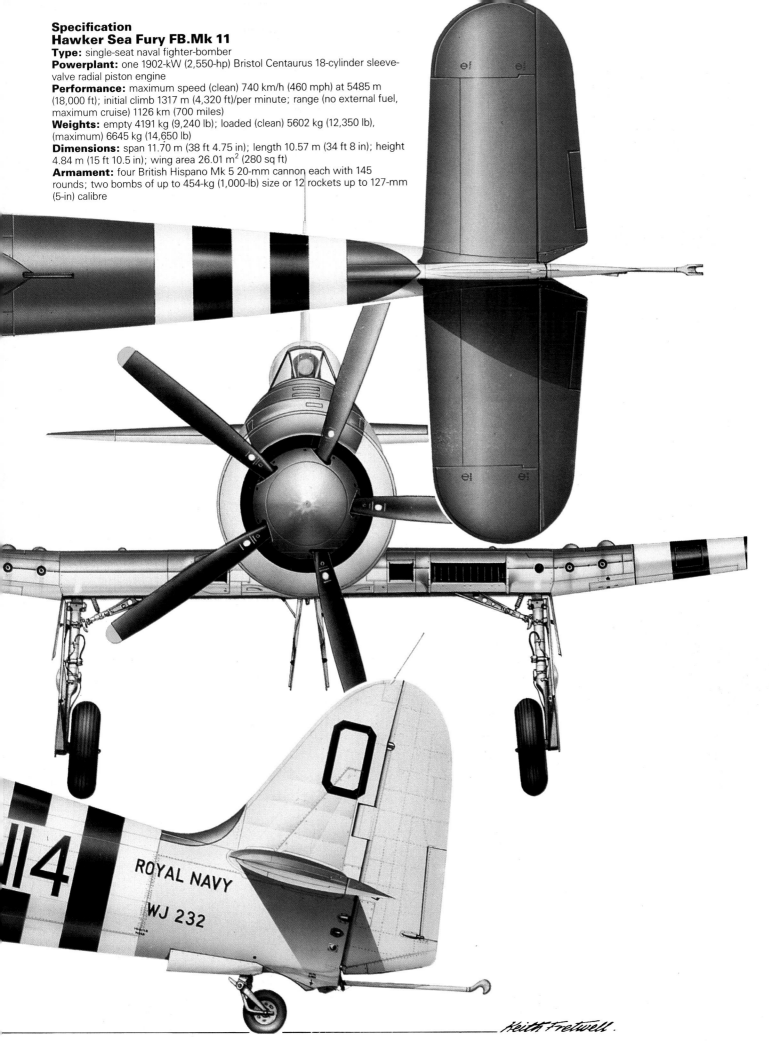

Specification
Hawker Sea Fury FB.Mk 11
Type: single-seat naval fighter-bomber
Powerplant: one 1902-kW (2,550-hp) Bristol Centaurus 18-cylinder sleeve-valve radial piston engine
Performance: maximum speed (clean) 740 km/h (460 mph) at 5485 m (18,000 ft); initial climb 1317 m (4,320 ft)/per minute; range (no external fuel, maximum cruise) 1126 km (700 miles)
Weights: empty 4191 kg (9,240 lb); loaded (clean) 5602 kg (12,350 lb), (maximum) 6645 kg (14,650 lb)
Dimensions: span 11.70 m (38 ft 4.75 in); length 10.57 m (34 ft 8 in); height 4.84 m (15 ft 10.5 in); wing area 26.01 m² (280 sq ft)
Armament: four British Hispano Mk 5 20-mm cannon each with 145 rounds; two bombs of up to 454-kg (1,000-lb) size or 12 rockets up to 127-mm (5-in) calibre

ROYAL NAVY

WJ 232

Keith Fretwell.

EJ783 was one of the second batch of Tempest Mk V Series 2s, and it was allocated to RAF No. 274 Sqn in late 1944. It was one of many Allied aircraft to have 'invasion stripes' on the underside of the fuselage only. Later in the year No. 274 was renumbered 174 and EJ783, like other Tempest Mk Vs, was scrapped.

1943. This too had the original Typhoon cockpit and tail, but was a fine performer, and fastest of all Hawker fighters to date at 750 km/h (466 mph). Camm hustled through the production tooling for the new wing at Langley (the Typhoon production having been farmed out to Gloster), but Sabre IVs continued to be unavailable. As a last resort Camm quickly schemed a 'productionised' Tempest V, based on HM595 but with a properly engineered tail, and the contract was transferred to this stop-gap version. Thus the RAF got a bit of a lash-up, just as in the Spitfire programme where the Mk IX (a Merlin 61 in a Spitfire Mk V) flooded off the lines instead of the definitive Mk VIII.

Production Tempest Mk Vs came off the line from 21 June 1943. As the radiator was under the engine, fuel could be put in the inboard leading edge, but in practice a tank was put in the left wing only. The first 100 aircraft had the usual Hispano Mk II cannon, and were called Tempest Mk V Series 1; subsequent machines introduced the short-barrel Mk V cannon with the muzzles inside the leading edge. More important to the pilot was the addition of spring tabs to the ailerons, for the first time on an RAF aircraft, giving all the roll power the pilot needed. Altogether 800 Mk V Tempests were delivered, entering service in numbers initially at the Newchurch Wing (Nos 3, 486 and later 56 Sqns) led by Wing Commander R.P. Beamont, who had previously played a central role in getting the Typhoon accepted by the RAF. This wing, later joined by No. 501 and then Nos 80 and 274 Sqns, proved the most successful of all units operating against V-1 flying bombs, destroying 638 of the RAF's total of 1,771. Tempests also performed most satisfactorily against ground targets and the increasingly rare Luftwaffe.

Powerplant delays

All this occurred while the much better Centaurus-Tempest had been delayed by one thing after another. Freeman curtly stopped the construction of the Centaurus-Typhoon Mk II LA594, but the prototype Tempest Mk IIs LA602 and 607 did go ahead. So great was the potential indicated by the old Centaurus-Tornado, HG641, that in September 1942 a contract was placed for 500 Tempest Mk IIs. They were to be built by Gloster, but that company was overloaded with Typhoons and the Meteor and hardly made a start with tooling.

At last LA602, with Typhoon tail but the new bubble canopy, made its first flight on 28 June 1943. The main problem was vibration, and eventually the big 18-cylinder sleeve-valve engine was mounted on six Silentbloc rubber shock-absorbers. For the first time in the UK (and unquestionably assisted by looking at the captured Fw 190A-3) a really efficient radial installation was achieved, with minimum drag, good cooling and ejector exhausts. Unfortunately, shortage of Centaurus testbeds resulted in LA602 being used to develop many marks of Centaurus not even planned for fighters, while production was further delayed by switching the whole programme to Bristol. The first 30 production Mk IIs did fly from Bristol (Weston-super-Mare factory), starting on 4 October 1944, but by this time it had all been handed back to Hawker at Kingston, which assembled 20 sets of parts from Weston and then delivered a further 402, mostly post-war.

Compared with the Typhoon and Sabre-Tempest, the Tempest Mk II was dramatically quieter in the cockpit, and all-round performance was slightly higher. This mark was, with various Spitfires and a handful of de Havilland Hornets, the chief piston-engined fighter in the post-war RAF, and 24 were sold to Pakistan and 89 to India. Most had bomb/rocket racks, Centaurus V engines and neat wing-root inlets to the injection carburettor and, slightly farther outboard on the right, the oil cooler. Precisely this arrangement was repeated on the last Sabre-engined Tempest version, the Mk VI, which had the uprated Sabre V which needed the whole duct area under the engine for its own coolant radiator. Hawker delivered 142 Tempest Mk VIs, hundreds being cancelled, and the last RAF Hawker piston-engined fighter was a Tempest Mk VI used for target-towing at Sylt in late 1953.

Back in September 1942 Camm had sketched a Tempest Light Fighter, basically a Tempest without the wing centre-section. Camm actually raised three project numbers, P.1018 (Sabre IV), 1019 (Griffon 61) and 1020 (Centaurus IV), and a new wing was designed with a horizontal centre-section but reduced span overall. The structure was refined (the massive Hawker mid-fuselage truss becoming modern stressed-skin semi-monocoque), the fuselage profile was altered to place the cockpit higher for improved view, and the vertical tail was redesigned. In all respects the 'TLF' was modern, whereas the Tempest retained many vestiges dating from

The combination of an improved wing design and the 1864-kW (2,500-hp) Sabre IV powerplant in the new streamlined housing offered a great increase in performance on the Hawker Tempest Mk 1, seen here with the single-piece canopy. Note the radiators along the inboard leading edges.

The only major modification to the Tempest during the war was carried out by the Napier company, which installed an annular radiator and, in this second test aircraft, a ducted spinner bringing the air intake ahead of the propeller blades. Test flying by Napier was carried out at Luton.

NX245 was one of the handful of Tempest Mk VI (post-war Tempest F.Mk 6) to see long service. Delivered to RAF No. 109 MU (Maintenance Unit), Shubra, it went from there to No. 213 Sqn at Shallufa, near the Suez Canal, where it carried the squadron hornet emblem on the fin. Later, until 1951, it operated from Nicosia.

Making its RAF operational service debut in late 1945, the Bristol Centaurus-powered Tempest Mk II missed out on combat in World War II but went on to see wide use both in Germany and the Far East in the post-war years. Two RAF squadrons, Nos 54 and 247 Sqns, saw service with the type solely in the UK, an aircraft of the former being shown here.

the early 1930s. Specification F.2/43 was written around it, but in April 1943 Camm persuaded the Admiralty the same basic aircraft could meet naval Specification N.7/43 and this was accepted, the naval version being entrusted to Boulton Paul at Wolverhampton.

From Tempest to Sea Fury

Hawker went ahead with two prototypes with the Centaurus XXII, one with Centaurus XII and two with the Griffon 85. First to fly, on 1 September 1944, was NX798, with a rigidly installed Centaurus XII with four-bladed propeller. Next came the ex-Tempest Mk III LA610, with contraprops driven by a Griffon 85. In late 1944 the type was named Fury, the naval model becoming the Sea Fury Mk X. Two of the Kingston prototypes were completed as Sea Furies, SR661 and SR666. The former had a Centaurus XII, four-blade propeller and short arrester hook, while SR666 had a shock-absorbed Centaurus XV, five-bladed propeller and not only a hook but also hydraulically folding wings. NX802, the second Fury (as distinct from Sea Fury) flew on 25 July 1945, but the RAF terminated its interest. Last of the prototypes was VB857, built at Wolverhampton but delivered for erection at Kingston and flown in January 1946. Boulton Paul's contract was cancelled, and further work concentrated on the Sea Fury Mk X for post-war Fleet Air Arm use.

Production Sea Fury Mk Xs emerged from 7 September 1946 after swift and successful development which was greatly helped by fitting the five-bladed propeller, a longer hook and redesigned rudder. Sea Fury Mk Xs replaced Supermarine Seafires in FAA No. 870 Sqn at Eglinton in August 1947, and 50 were built, but meanwhile

trials with external stores and RATOG (rocket-assisted take-off gear) had led to the Sea Fury Mk XI, known in post-war designation as the Sea Fury FB.Mk 11. This aircraft, the pinnacle of not just Camm's but the UK's piston-engined fighter development, proved extremely successful and popular, and no fewer than nine production batches were delivered, totalling 615 aircraft, plus four batches of tandem-seat dual Sea Fury T.Mk 20 trainers and large numbers of exports (see variants list). Bearing in mind that it emerged into a world of jets, the success of the Sea Fury was exceptional; far more were built than of any previous Hawker fighter in peacetime.

Sea Fury FB.Mk 11s were among the very few types of British aircraft to see action during the Korean War. Operating from HMS Theseus, HMS Ocean, HMS Glory and HMAS Sydney, Sea Furies were used mainly in the interdiction role, using not only all the available ground-attack weapons but also sea mines which were placed outside Communist harbours. The accuracy of weapon delivery was, on average, among the best ever achieved in the old 'manual' era; famed test pilot Lieutenant Commander 'Winkle' Brown, when with No. 802 Sqn, recorded mean errors of 12-13.7 m (13-15 yd) for bombing and 4.6-5.5 m (5-6 yd) for rocketing at dive angles up to 30°. Moreover, though Communist aircraft were scarce, Sea Furies downed more than any other non-US aircraft, including at least two Mikoyan-Gurevich MiG-15s!

Exports are shown in the variants list. Many still exist, some in flying condition and including several racers in North America, the most remarkable being the winner of the 1983 Reno meet, Dreadnought, NX20SF, completely rebuilt with R-4360 engine and tall fin.

A fine echelon of Tempests from CFE, the busy RAF Central Fighter Establishment at West Raynham, in 1945, where most of the RAF's trials and evaluations on fighter-type aircraft were conducted. All are Mk V Series 2: SN328, SN108 and EJ884. SN328 has eight of the lengthened rocket rails fitted.

With the reduced wing span and higher-placed cockpit, this ex-Tempest Mk III was powered by a Griffon 85 driving contraprops, with a semi-annular radiator and oil cooler, both beneath the engine. The aircraft was named Fury in late 1944 and was a forerunner of the production Sea Fury.

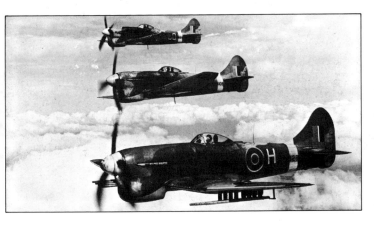

Polikarpov I-16

While others were building fixed-gear biplanes, Polikarpov's diminutive I-16 was a pointer to future fighter designs. Its lead was soon overtaken, however, and it was easy prey for the invading Luftwaffe.

By 1930 the Soviet Union was finding its feet in military aviation. The protracted civil war and almost complete extermination of all the various dissident elements had been completed, and the aircraft industry was beginning to flex its muscles. The NII V-VS, the air force scientific research institute, was engaged in a growing number of investigations including new forms of armament (such as rockets and large recoilless guns), and how best to use combat aircraft. One of its findings was that agile biplanes could out-manoeuvre monoplanes, but the monoplanes could probably be made faster. Almost all the world's fighters were biplanes, but with the TB-1 and TB-3 the Tupolev bureau had shown that, where heavy bombers were concerned, the monoplane appeared to be potentially superior. To try to get the best of both worlds the NII decided to recommend a mix of agile biplanes and fast monoplane fighters, used in large combined formations.

At the time the two Soviet fighters, both powered by the Bristol Jupiter or its licensed M-22 version, were the Tupolev I-4 and the Polikarpov I-5. The former was a sesquiplane, but with a bottom wing so small that the aircraft was almost a parasol monoplane (in one version the lower wing was omitted). The Polikarpov machine was a conventional biplane. There was little to choose between them, and in fact the biplane was the faster.

The decision was taken at the very end of 1931 to order new monoplane fighters faster and of more advanced design than any others.

All-metal construction, unbraced cantilever structure and retractable landing gear were favoured. The task was assigned to the most experienced monoplane OKB (experimental aircraft bureau), that of A. N. Tupolev. He put P. O. Sukhoi in charge of the I-14 project, and on 7 May 1933 the prototype, also known as the ANT-31, made its maiden flight. It was by far the most modern fighter in the world, with all the new features plus a sliding canopy over the cockpit and a long-chord low-drag engine cowl.

A race against time

This was bad news for Nikolai Nikolayevich Polikarpov, who had designed almost all the Soviet Union's smaller military aircraft up to that time. Worse, he was in prison, along with his design team, but the success of his I-5 won his freedom on January 1933. He was full of ideas for improving the I-5, and these led to the I-15 and its successors which were destined to form the 'agile biplane' part of the future fighter mix. His immediate priority, however, was to find out about the I-14 and get permission to design a rival. He went ahead at once, and from March 1933 his team designed a totally new monoplane

A Polikarpov I-16 Type 24 undergoes bore sighting tests in 1942. Several alternative gun arrangements were applicable, as were alternative underwing stores, including two 110-kg (220-lb) bombs or six RS-82 rockets. Visible in front of the pilot is the standard PBP-1A reflector gunsight.

fighter, with the central construction bureau number TsKB-12. The team applied itself to the task 18 hours a day, just as it had done under the eyes of the OGPU guards. The work naturally went very quickly, and in December the red-painted prototype was rolled out into the snow. Famed pilot V. P. Chkalov flew it on the last day of 1933.

The prototype had plenty of character, but in many respects it was seemingly inferior to the I-14. Its structure was extremely mixed, the fuselage being a wooden semi-monocoque skinned with layers of *shpon* (birch veneers moulded to shape before being glued into multi-layer ply). The wings were of metal, with chrome-steel spars built up from tubular booms and sheet webs, with duralumin built-up lattice ribs. The skin was dural back to the front spar and fabric to the rear. The tail, and the almost full-span ailerons, were of duralumin with fabric covering, and because of the very 'hot' nature of this dangerous-looking machine the ailerons were arranged to droop 15° when the landing gears were lowered to serve as flaps, thus limiting landing speed in early versions to 100 km/h (62 mph), still considered very fast. The main gear had oleo shock struts, and could be retracted with great effort by turning a cockpit handwheel.

Stubby and unstable

The overwhelming impression created by the TsKB-12 was that the designer appeared deliberately to have made the aircraft as short as possible; the length of under 6 m (20 ft) was shorter even than most biplane fighters. Observers ever since have wondered if Polikarpov was influenced by the Gee Bee racer that gained a world speed record in September 1932. The Gee Bees were tricky to the point of being dangerous, and so was the TsKB-12. Like a fighter for the 1990s it was almost unstable about all three axes, and had to be flown with ceaseless attention. The slightest pilot control input caused an almost violent reaction, so much so that airsickness became a problem. The good result was that rolls and loops were so fast as to be quite startling, but trying to bring guns to bear on another aircraft needed great skill and concentration. With the engine throttled back the nose had to be kept far below the horizon to avoid a stall. The rate of descent was excessive, and it was impossible to make a power-off landing. Trying to haul back on the stick during landing caused a wing to drop, invariably resulting in a fatal accident. Any prolonged air combat, or tight turns, needed great skill and experience if the aircraft was not to flick and spin.

Moreover, Polikarpov had been unable to obtain the engine he wanted, a Wright Cyclone of over 522 kW (700 hp). Negotiations for building the Cyclone under licence as the M-25 took more than two years, and the TsKB-12 had to fly with an old M-22 (Jupiter) of 358 kW (480 hp). The wish for agility, which was behind the ultra-short length, resulted in the engine being mounted on a firewall in line with the front spar, so that the front face of the engine was almost in line with the leading edge of the wing! A close-fitting cowl reduced drag, with a fairing dish over the crankcase. Despite the many problems the TsKB-12 was judged potentially superior to the I-14, even though the prototype of the latter had a Bristol Mercury engine. Accordingly an imported Cyclone R-1820-F3 was fitted to

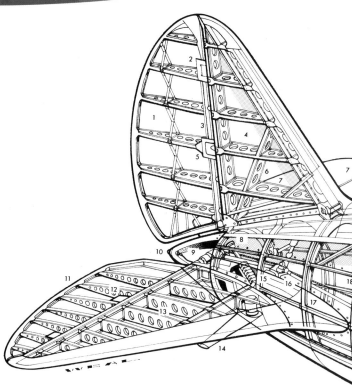

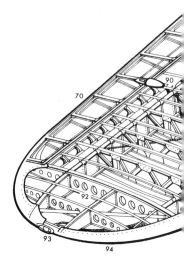

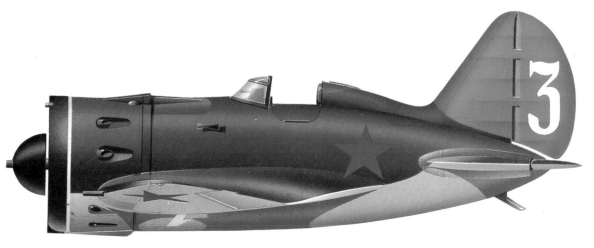

The red vertical tail on this I-16 Type 24 identifies it as an eskadril leader of an IAP in defence of Odessa in September 1941. Although outclassed by Luftwaffe opposition, the I-16 could, in the hands of a good pilot, avoid destruction through superior manoeuvrability. The I-16 was also the first aircraft to be used on a large scale in aerial taran (ram) attacks, the first such strike accounting for the loss of a Messerschmitt Bf 110 on 22 June 1941.

Polikarpov I-16 Type 10 cutaway drawing key

1 Rudder construction
2 Rudder upper hinge
3 Rudder post
4 Fin construction
5 Rudder lower hinge
6 Fin auxiliary spar
7 Port tailplane
8 Rudder actuating mechanism
9 Tail cone
10 Rear navigation light
11 Elevator construction
12 Elevator hinge
13 Tailplane construction
14 Tailskid
15 Tailskid damper
16 Control linkage (elevator and rudder)
17 Tailplane fillet
18 Fuselage half frames
19 Fin root fairing
20 Dorsal decking
21 Fuselage monocoque construction
22 Main upper longeron
23 Rudder control cable
24 Elevator control rigid rod
25 Main lower longeron
26 Control linkage crank
27 Seat support frame
28 Pilot's seat
29 Headrest
30 Cockpit entry flap (port)
31 Open cockpit
32 Rear-view mirror (optional)
33 Curved one-piece windshield
34 Tubular gunsight (PBP-1 reflector sight optional)
35 Instrument panel
36 Undercarriage retraction headcrank
37 Control column
38 Rudder pedal
39 Fuselage fuel tank, capacity 56 Imp gal (255 litres)
40 Fuel filler caps
41 Ammunition magazines
42 Machine-gun fairing
43 Split-type aileron (landing flap)
44 Aileron hinge fairing
45 Fabric wing covering
46 Port navigation light
47 Aluminium alloy leading-edge skin
48 Two-blade propeller
49 Conical spinner
50 Hucks-type starter dog
51 Hinged main wheel cover
52 Port main wheel
53 Lip intake
54 Adjustable (shuttered) cooling apertures
55 Propeller shaft support frame
56 Machine-gun muzzles
57 750-hp (559-kW) M-25V radial engine
58 Oil tank
59 Starboard synchronized 7.62-mm ShKAS machine-gun
60 Exhaust exit ports
61 Engine bearers
62 Firewall/bulkhead
63 Centre-section trussed-type spar carry-through
64 Wheel well
65 Fuselage/front spar attachment point

66 Retraction linkage
67 Fuselage/rear spar attachment point
68 Wingroot frames
69 Wingroot fillet
70 Aileron construction
71 Ammunition access panel
72 Starboard wing 7.62-mm ShKAS machine-gun
73 Undercarriage pivot point
74 Machine-gun muzzle
75 Centre/outer wing section break-point
76 Mainwheel leg
77 Leg cover
78 Starboard mainwheel
79 Mainwheel cover
80 Axle
81 Hinged cover flap
82 Actuating rod cover
83 Retraction actuating rod
84 Cover flap
85 Pitot head
86 Leading-edge construction
87 KhMA chrome-molybdenum steel alloy front spar
88 Alternate dural ribs/frames
89 KhMA chrome-molybdenum steel alloy rear spar
90 Aileron hinge fairing
91 Wire cross-bracing
92 Wingtip construction
93 Starboard navigation light
94 Wingtip edging

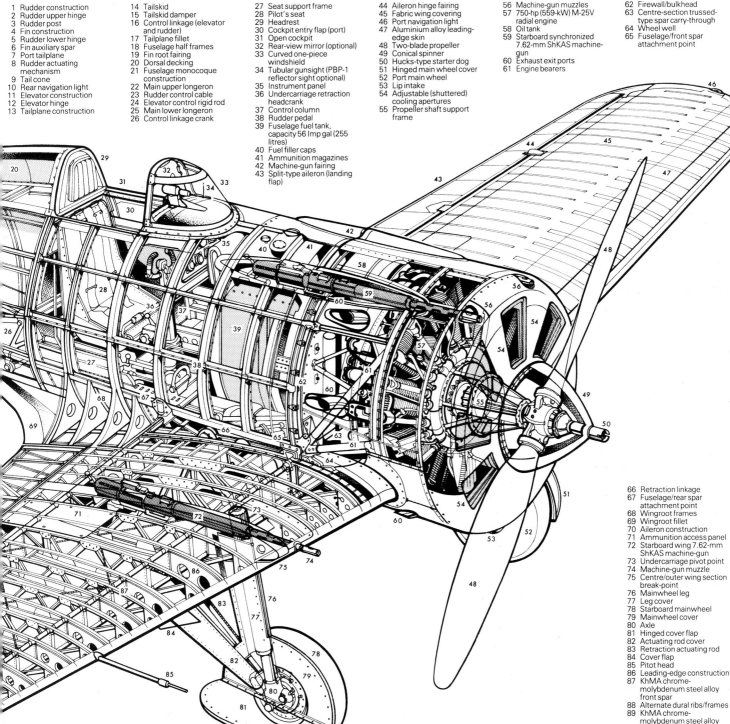

Specification
Polikarpov I-16 Type 24
Type: single-seat monoplane fighter
Powerplant: one Shvetsov M-62 nine-cylinder radial air-cooled engine rated at 746 kW (1,000 hp) at 2,000 rpm for take-off and 597 kW (800 hp) at 2,100 rpm at 4200 m (13,780 ft) driving an AV-2 two-bladed two-pitch propeller
Performance: maximum speed 440 km/h (273 mph) at sea level; 489 km/h (304 mph) at 3000 m (9,840 ft); range (clean) 600 km (373 miles), 1,100 km (600 miles) with external fuel tanks; climb rate to 5000 m (16,405 ft) of 5.8 minutes; maximum ceiling 9470 m (31,070 ft)
Weights: empty equipped 1475 kg (3,252 lb); normal loaded 1,912 kg (4,215 lb); maximum take-off 2,060 kg (4,541 lb)
Dimensions: span 8.88 m (29 ft 1⅗ in); length 6.04 m (19 ft 8⅛ in); height 2.41 m (7 ft 9¾ in); wing area 14.87 m² (160.06 sq ft)
Armament: four 7.62-mm Shpital 'ny-komaritsky ShKAS machine-guns (two synchronised in fuselage and two unsynchronised in wings) with 650 rpg, or two fuselage-mounted ShKAS and two wing-mounted 20-mm Shpital 'ny-Vladimirov ShVAk cannon with 180 rpg; a single 12.7-mm Berezin UB machine-gun with 300 rounds could be added to the fuselage-mounted armament and with which the wing-mounted armament was usually deleted

Obsolescent and outclassed by the opposition's fighters during World War II, the diminutive Polikarpov I-16 was destined to serve with front-line units into late 1943. It was the mount of 1 IAP, the first fighter aviation regiment to receive the coveted 'Guards' title in December 1941. Sadly, the Soviets failed to capitalise on the lead offered in fighter design by the I-16 in the late 1930s, a fact which saw the I-16 committed to scenarios during the German assault in which it was at a natural disadvantage. Nevertheless, the valuable contribution of Polikarpov's 'Fly' in the Russian defence cannot be underestimated.

The first prototype of the I-16 was the TsKB-12 (Tsentralnoye Konstruktorskoye Byuro, or Central Design Bureau). The first flight on 31 December 1933 was just nine months after design was initiated on the drawing boards.

A Polikarpov I-16 Type 18 wearing the markings of its Finnish air force captors. Of note is the local modification to the undercarriage whereby skis have been substituted to facilitate operations from snow-covered airfields.

the second TsKB-12, driving a two-position bracket-type Hamilton propeller, and with this fitted there was no doubt. The stubby fighter was accepted for service as the I-16, and Polikarpov's position remained secure.

Such was the importance of the I-16 that in about May 1934 production was organised at two factories, GAZ-1 at Moscow-Khodinka and GAZ-21 at Gorkii. In the absence of the definitive engine the M-22 had to be used, and the I-16 Type 1 began to come off the line in late 1934, the armament being two of the new rapid-firing 7.62-mm (0.3-in) ShKAS machine-guns in the wings, each with 900 rounds. The narrow cockpit had a hinged drop-down door on the left, and on top was fitted a sliding canopy of metal and glass with the vee wind-

I-16s abandoned in the face of Operation Barbarossa. In the early days of the German invasion, Lieutenant Ivanov deliberately rammed a Luftwaffe Bf 110 with his I-16, as did eight other Soviet pilots.

shield built in as one unit. The whole canopy could be cranked forwards in flight, assisted by bungee cords which helped to overcome air resistance and kept the canopy open on the ground. Many pilots disliked being enclosed, but in the Soviet Union there was little provision for feedback of opinion and the NII had accepted it.

By 1935 a large consignment of Wright-built Cyclones had arrived, and almost all of these went to power I-16 Type 4 fighters which also introduced a new long-chord cowl with a flat front with nine adjustable cooling-air inlets and an optimum cooling-air slit at the rear. Doors to cover the retracted wheels were also added. Subsequently there were many variants, far more than in any other fighter of the mid-1930s, these being listed separately. In 1935 production began of the first UTI (fighter trainer) version with a pair of tandem cockpits, neither in exactly the original position, and almost the same size of fuselage fuel tank. These machines had the M-22 Jupiter engine at

The 'Double Six' emblem on the fin identifies this Spanish I-16 as a Super Mosca operated by the 3ᵃ Escuadrilla de Mosca based at Albacete during 1937. The I-16 was to play a significant part in early air operations during the Spanish Civil War, with Republican aircraft such as this helping to claw back much air superiority.

This I-16UTI, alias UTI-4, was captured by the Finns in September 1941 and pressed into service as a trainer. The new forward cockpit was for the pupil, although in blind flying training he occupied the rear covered cockpit.

A trio of 4th Guards IAP-16 Type 24s, the definitive production version, with the nearest aircraft sporting underwing launch rails for six RS-82 rockets, unfaired undercarriage and the novel addition of a quilted engine cover. Note the 'Guards' emblem under the cockpit.

first, but later used the M-25 when these were plentiful. Later production usually had simple fixed landing gear. The slogan in the training schools was 'If you can fly an I-16, you can fly anything.'

Towards the end of Type 4 production in the spring of 1935 the seat was provided with 8-mm/0.315-in (often 9-mm/0.35-in) back armour, and this was standard on the Type 5 which was the first with the licensed engine and AV-1 propeller. Racks were added for two wing bombs of 100-kg (220-lb) size and the engine installation was revised with prominent exhaust pipes from each cylinder in single or paired ejectors all round the cowling. The Type 6 (see variants) was the last to have an enclosed cockpit, the preference of the pilots at last making itself felt in an open cockpit with a deep front windshield through which projected the tubular gunsight derived from the British Aldis.

The outbreak of civil war in Spain led to urgent pleas for help by the Spanish government, who became known as the Republicans. Stalin was doubtless on their side, because they were essentially Communist, but solidarity became very commercial and the Soviet Union demanded payment in gold for all assistance. This was eventually agreed, and in September 1936 the *Rostok* docked at Cartagena and unloaded a big batch of Type 6 fighters along with pilots and ground staff. Over 100 were in action by November, when battle was joined with the opposing Fascist machines, and the I-16 mastered most with ease, though a well-flown Fiat C.R.32 was roughly equal in manoeuvrability. Repair shops were set up near Alicante, and eventually I-16s are said to have been built there, using imported Cyclones, though details and numbers built are lacking. Combat reports from Spain assisted in defining future improvements, as outlined in the variants list. Many survived in Spain until almost 1950.

In 1937 more than 250 I-16s of various types, including two-seat UTIs, were supplied to China together with increasing numbers of 'volunteer' pilots and ground staff, this time apparently with no payment in gold. Chinese I-16s fought over China until at least 1943, finding the Mitsubishi A5M of the Imperial Japanese Navy a roughly

equal opponent (all other Japanese types were easy meat). In 1940, however, the Mitsubishi A6M proved better in virtually all respects, as one would expect.

Further large-scale action took place in the fighting between the Soviet Union and Japan between 11 May and 16 September 1939 over the Khalkin Gol and Nomonhan plateau on the borders of Mongolia. The I-16 was the chief Soviet fighter, pitted against many Japanese types of which the Army Type 97 (Nakajima Ki-27) was by far the most formidable. At least as agile as the A5M, this very light fighter

Polikarpov I-16 variants

TsKB-12: first prototype, M-22 engine
TsKB-12bis: second prototype, flown 18 February 1934 with Cyclone engine and Hamilton propeller
I-16 Type 1: initial production with 358-kW (480-hp) engine; small number only
UTI-2: initial tandem trainer, rebuilt from Type 1
UTI-3: new-build trainer with long-chord cowl, fixed landing gears and (from 1936) blind-flying hood and gyro instruments
I-16 Type 4: first major production fighter, imported engine and propeller, long-chord cowl faired into fuselage, doors over main gear
I-16 Type 5: 522-kW (700-hp) M-25 engine and AV-1 propeller, improved drooping ailerons and shrouds, wing bomb racks and seat armour
UTI-4: generalised designation for subsequent trainers, variously with M-22 or M-25 but always in long-chord cowl, often with retractable gear, usually no armament and always with separate open cockpits
I-16Sh: prototype, also designated TsKB-18, of proposed *shturmovik* armoured attack version with four PV-1 or ShKAS guns and bombs
I-16P: prototype with two 20-mm ShVAK cannon at outer ends of centre section firing outside propeller disc, plus two ShKAS above engine, plus wing racks for six Der-31 cluster bomb units; modified from Type 5
I-16 Type 6: basic 1936 production with 544-kW (730-hp) M-25A and locally strengthened structure
SPB: also called **TsKB-29** as prototype, designation SPB from fast dive-bomber; modified Type 5 with pneumatically actuated gears and added dive breaks on strengthened wings; tested with two 100-kg (220-lb)

FAB-100 bombs in May 1936 and later with 250-kg (551-lb) FB-250 bombs and often with wing cannon; many converted in field in 1941-42 for combat missions
I-16 Type 10: built in largest numbers (2,600-plus), 559-kW (750-hp) M-25V, open cockpit, four ShKAS (two above engine, two in wings), reflector sight (later of standard PBP-1 type), first model whose winter skis could be retracted, using standard legs and fairings
TsKB-12P: revised cannon installation with guns in stiffened leading edge ahead of spar with all barrels projecting, with 150-round box inboard, accepted for future production
I-16 Type 17: basic 1938 production, two ShVAK (wings) plus two ShKAS (above engine), stronger spars, from 1939 with six (rarely eight) RS-82 rockets on wing rails, improved longer-stroke main gears and often fitted with tailwheel instead of skid
I-16TK: designation covered several (possibly many) I-16s, mostly Type 10, with two turbochargers and usually improved propeller for high-altitude performance
I-16 Type 18: basic 1939 model with 686-kW (920-hp) M-62, often VISh-6A propeller, modified exhaust system, smaller fuselage tank but two drop tanks as on I-153 in place of bombs or rockets
I-16 Type 24: late 1939, 820-kW (1,100-hp) M-63, stiffened wing, great variety of weapons, improved equipment, better radio and oxygen and larger drop tanks; inboard part of ailerons replaced by dive brakes on SPB were usually omitted on subsequent fighters, and absent on all Type 24
I-16 Types 28 and 30: final models from reopened production line at GAZ-21 in 1941 with direct-drive M-63

Polikarpov I-16

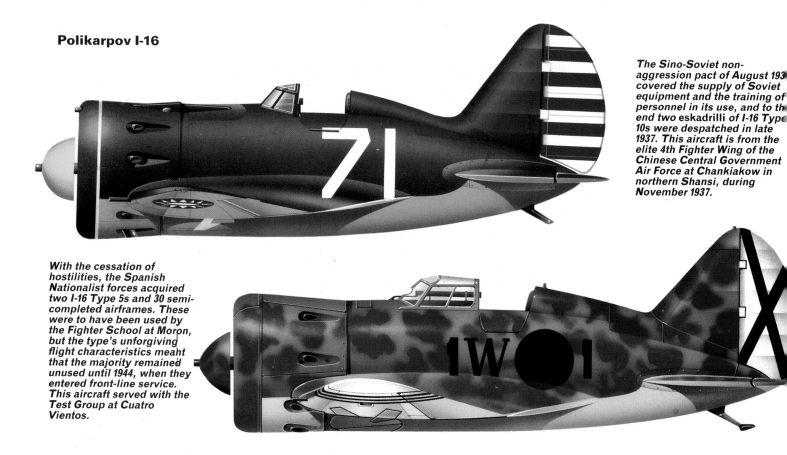

The Sino-Soviet non-aggression pact of August 193[] covered the supply of Soviet equipment and the training of personnel in its use, and to th[] end two *eskadrilli* of I-16 Type 10s were despatched in late 1937. This aircraft is from the elite 4th Fighter Wing of the Chinese Central Government Air Force at Chankiakow in northern Shansi, during November 1937.

With the cessation of hostilities, the Spanish Nationalist forces acquired two I-16 Type 5s and 30 semi-completed airframes. These were to have been used by the Fighter School at Moron, but the type's unforgiving flight characteristics meant that the majority remained unused until 1944, when they entered front-line service. This aircraft served with the Test Group at Cuatro Vientos.

could out-turn the I-16, and the V-VS (Soviet air force) therefore tended not to engage in dogfights but to make slashing sweeps, flying at full throttle through Japanese formations picking off targets as they went. At the end of this major war the V-VS had claimed 645 Japanese aircraft destroyed in the air and on the ground, the true figure being 162 plus 220 severely damaged; the Japanese claimed 1,260 victories against the actual V-VS losses of 145 (air) plus 62 (ground).

The I-16 had pretty well held its own up to this point, and also coped reasonably well in the Winter War against Finland in 1939-40, by which time the chief variant was the Type 24. Production terminated in the spring of 1940, but on 22 June 1941 the I-16 was still by far the most numerous V-VS fighter. Hundreds were destroyed in the Luftwaffe's initial attacks on airfields, where many were arranged in neat lines, and from the start of the 'Great Patriotic War' it was obvious the I-16 was no match for the Messerschmitt Bf 109F and Bf 109G or Focke-Wulf Fw 190. Despite this, the need for fighters was so desperate the tooling was again put into use and a further 450 of Types 28 and 30 quickly delivered. This brought the total to 7,005, not including 1,639 UTI two-seaters.

Most of the 1941 survivors were quickly shot down, destroyed on the ground or bravely used for ramming attacks on Luftwaffe bombers. A few were modified as SPB fast bombers which were carried under the wings of TB-3 heavy bombers just as I-16 fighters had been during earlier Vakhmistrov 'Zvyeno' (link) experiments. On 25 August 1941 six TB-3s carrying 12 SPBs flew to the vital Chernovod rail bridge over the Danube in Romania. All 12 SPBs attacked, with two 250-kg (551-lb) bombs each, bringing down this difficult and distant target.

In 1938 Polikarpov produced the I-16 Type 17 which was fitted with a tailwheel instead of a simple skid. This feature was retained on subsequent versions until production halted in 1940.

GRIFFON SPITFIRES

Sentiment associates the Spitfire with the Merlin engine, but by the end of World War II development had long been concentrated entirely on variants powered by the bigger Griffon engine. These were in many ways quite different aircraft, but they put new life into the great story of one of the world's most famous warplanes.

The Supermarine Type 300, the Spitfire prototype, first flew on 5 March 1936. From the very beginning its flight development was conducted under pressure, and the pressure increased as the years went by. Ten years later well over 20,000 Spitfires (and over 2,000 Seafires) had been delivered to many customers. Only then was it possible to take a breather and discover that the aircraft at the end of the line were twice as heavy, more than twice as powerful and far more capable than the little Model 300, which seemed like a sprightly elf by comparison. Jeffrey Quill, chief test pilot over almost the entire period of Spitfire development, pointed out that, in terms of gross weight, a Seafire Mk 47 was equal to a Spitfire Mk I plus 32 standard airline passengers each with 18 kg (40 lb) of baggage.

Quill also surprised some by commenting that in his opinion the nicest Spitfire to fly was DP845. This was unexpected because, of all the much-rebuilt hack development Spitfires, DP845 beat the lot. Among many other claims to fame it was the very first Spitfire to be powered by a Griffon engine; an odder claim is that the same serial number was carried by a Miles Whitney Straight (G-AEVG in its original civil guise).

Supermarine and Rolls-Royce had discussed the possibility of mating the big Griffon to the little Spitfire as early as August 1939. With a capacity of 36.7 litres (2,239 cu in) compared with the Merlin's 27 litres (1,648 cu in), the Griffon was being developed for the naval Fairey Barracuda and Fairey Firefly. Its potential for fighters was enhanced when Rolls-Royce carefully revised the design to bring down the frontal area to almost the same as that of the Merlin, though it was clear the tops of the cylinder blocks would project slightly above the existing Spitfire cowl line. Pilot view dead ahead, however, could actually be slightly improved. No more could be done at the time, but discussions were not terminated and in 1940 the Air Ministry issued Specification F.4/40 for a single-seat high-altitude fighter. Supermarine managed to get a contract for two special Spitfires to this specification, strengthened to accept 'various engines including the Griffon'.

These two aircraft (DP845 and DP851) had the Supermarine designation Type 337 and much in common with the Spitfire Mk III, though the mark number assigned was IV. By early 1941, however, the same number had been assigned to the Spitfire PR.Mk IV photo-reconnaissance production version, so DP845, the only one to fly at that time, was restyled Spitfire Mk XX. It flew in 1941, with a Griffon IIB and four-bladed propeller. The planned armament was six His-

At the end of World War II, the latest Spitfire in service was the F.Mk 21. This was developed immediately into the F.Mk 22 and later into the F.Mk 24; small numbers of each variant were used after the end of hostilities. Here two F.Mk 22s and an F.Mk 21 are seen flying from the Supermarine test airfield at High Post.

pano cannon, and this armament was mocked-up on DP845. It was hoped to go into production with Griffon Spitfires at once, all with mark numbers of XX or higher, and 750 Spitfire Mk XXs were ordered from the Castle Bromwich factory on 23 August 1941, but somebody in the Ministry of Aircraft Production changed the mark number to the regular Merlin-engined Spitfire Mks VB and VC for these aircraft, whose serials were in the range ER206-ES369.

Thus in 1941-42 there were just two Griffon-engined Spitfires, flying mainly from Rolls-Royce's Hucknall airfield until the new engine could be considered reasonably mature. The engine was variously a Mk IIB or Mk III, with a variety of four-bladed propellers and asymmetric radiators of Morris QCY type, larger than that of the Spitfire Mk V aircraft but looking similar from a distance. The big change from the pilot's viewpoint was that the propeller rotation was reversed. On take-off other Spitfires tended to swing to the left, but with the Griffon there was a much more powerful swing in the opposite direction. The drill was to wind the rudder trim full left before opening the throttle. In a powered landing, varying engine power caused reactions on the rudder pedals. General handling was much like that of other Spitfires, though the extra power was useful at low level in faster and steeper climbs, and to some extent in pulling even tighter turns without any fear of flicking into a high-speed stall. The only real fault of all Spitfires in 1941 was that at high speeds the ailerons froze almost solid, and only a very strong pilot could generate enough stick movement for a fast roll.

By the summer of 1942, while longer-term development of the Griffon-engined Spitfire was in full swing, Focke-Wulf Fw 190As were making hit-and-run raids with single heavy bombs against south coast towns and causing an increasing nuisance. The new Hawker Typhoon was good as a low-level interceptor, but it was obvious that a Griffon-engined Spitfire might be even better. DP845 was modified in a matter of days as the prototype Supermarine Type 366, or Spitfire Mk XII, with two cannon and four machine-guns (standard 'B' armament) plus a broad fin and pointed rudder. Various batches of aircraft already in production were earmarked for completion as Spitfire Mk XIIs. All 100 had been ordered as Spitfire Mk VC aircraft, but they were completed to two slightly differing standards. Basically the Spitfire Mk XII was a Mk VC with a strengthened airframe, and a special attachment at Frame 5 for the completely different semi-cantilever beam on which was placed the 1294-kW (1,735-hp) Griffon III or IV, driving a Rotol propeller with four blades of duralumin or Jablo densified wood. The deep asymmetric radiator and broad pointed rudder were retained, and LF clipped wings were fitted. These wings were of Universal type, but the B-type armament was fitted to all 100 aircraft. The slight difference was that the first 45 (EN221/238 and EN601/627) had fuselages of Mk IX type, with fixed tailwheel, while 55 (MB794/805, 829/863, 875/882) had Mk VIII-type fully retractable tailwheels. Not least of the remarkable features of the Spitfire Mk XII was that empty and normal loaded weight was in each case lighter than that of a Spitfire Mk IX!

Striving for the ultimate Spitfire

Back in 1941, two years before delivery of the Spitfire Mk XIIs, Joe Smith and Alan Clifton had been working on the Type 356 as the ultimate Spitfire. Its mark number was to be 21, but by 1942 the differences were so fundamental that it had become a new fighter altogether, and for a time it was planned to name it the Victor. To assist development of the powerful machine, Rolls-Royce was assigned six Spitfire airframes, JF316/321, originally ordered as Spitfire Mk VIIIs with retracting tailwheels and normal-span Universal wings. They were trucked to Hucknall where the first four were fitted with the Griffon 61, first of the new two-stage Griffons with an intercooler, driving a new Rotol propeller with five broad blades, and with deep symmetrical radiators. The last two aircraft were fitted with the Griffon 85 driving a six-bladed contraprop, usually also of Rotol

make. Because of its naval ancestry the Griffon had a cartridge starter with a five-round breech, making the aircraft independent of ground electrical power. The much longer nose of these aircraft necessitated an even larger vertical tail, the first type being an unlovely pointed type with a straight leading edge which gave way to a very broad assembly with a graceful rounded outline.

JF317 was the first of this group to fly, and intensive and often hairraising development flying took place in the hands of Rolls-Royce and Supermarine test pilots. From the start it was clear that the twostage Griffon made the Spitfire a real he-man's aeroplane, and what happened next was predictable: there was a crash programme for a

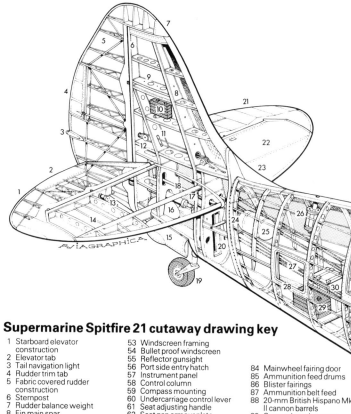

Supermarine Spitfire 21 cutaway drawing key

1. Starboard elevator construction
2. Elevator tab
3. Tail navigation light
4. Rudder trim tab
5. Fabric covered rudder construction
6. Sternpost
7. Rudder balance weight
8. Fin main spar
9. Tailfin construction
10. Tail ballast weights
11. Fin secondary spar
12. Rudder trim jack
13. Tailplane trim jack
14. Tailplane construction
15. Tailwheel doors
16. Mudguard
17. Tailwheel retraction jack
18. Elevator control rods
19. Tailwheel
20. Fuselage double bulkhead
21. Port elevator
22. Port tailplane
23. Fin root fillet fairing
24. Tail assembly joint frame
25. Oxygen cylinder
26. Six-cartridge signal flare launcher
27. Tailplane control cables
28. Access door
29. Fuselage ballast weights
30. Battery
31. R.3067 radio receiver
32. Radio access door
33. Whip aerial
34. Harness release
35. TR.1143 radio transmitter
36. Radio track
37. Fuselage frame and stringer construction
38. Wing root trailing edge fillet
39. Control cable runs
40. Fuselage main longeron
41. Port side access panel
42. Canopy aft glazing
43. Sliding canopy rail
44. Voltage regulator
45. Fuselage double frame
46. Seat support framework
47. Back armour
48. Pilot's seat
49. Sutton harness
50. Head armour
51. Sliding cockpit canopy cover
52. Rear-view mirror
53. Windscreen framing
54. Bullet proof windscreen
55. Reflector gunsight
56. Port side entry hatch
57. Instrument panel
58. Control column
59. Compass mounting
60. Undercarriage control lever
61. Seat adjusting handle
62. Seat pan armour plate
63. Wing root armour
64. Radiator shutter jack
65. Coolant radiator, oil cooler on port side
66. Gun heating duct
67. Wing rear spar
68. Flap hydraulic jack
69. Flap shroud ribs
70. Tubular flap spar
71. Starboard split trailing edge flap
72. Aileron control bellcrank
73. Aileron hinge
74. Aileron tab
75. Aluminium skinned aileron construction
76. Wing tip fairing
77. Starboard navigation light
78. Wing tip construction
79. Aileron outer hinge rib
80. Wing rib construction
81. Main spar
82. Leading edge nose ribs
83. Ammunition boxes, 150 rounds per gun
84. Mainwheel fairing door
85. Ammunition feed drums
86. Blister fairings
87. Ammunition belt feed
88. 20-mm British Hispano Mk II cannon barrels
89. Cannon barrel support fairing
90. Recoil springs
91. Fuel filler cap
92. Leading edge fuel tank, capacity 17 Imp gal (77 litres)
93. Main undercarriage wheel well
94. Mainwheel blister fairing
95. Undercarriage retraction link
96. Undercarriage leg pivot
97. Shock absorber leg strut
98. Hydraulic brake pipe

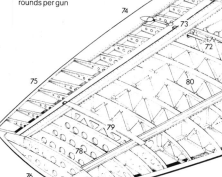

99 Starboard mainwheel
100 Mainwheel leg fairing door
101 Undercarriage torque scissors
102 Fuel pipe runs
103 Main spar stub attachment
104 Lower main fuel tank, capacity 48 Imp gal (218 litres)
105 Upper main fuel tank, capacity 36 Imp gal (164 litres)
106 Fuel filler cap
107 Oil tank vent
108 Oil tank, capacity 9 Imp gal (41 litres)
109 Oil tank access door
110 Engine compartment fireproof bulkhead
111 Port split trailing edge flap
112 Flap hydraulic jack
113 Flap synchronizing jack
114 Port twin 20-mm Hispano cannon
115 Spent cartridge case ejector chute
116 Ammunition feed drums
117 Ammunition belt feeds
118 Ammunition boxes, 150 rounds per gun
119 Aileron control bellcrank
120 Aileron tab

121 Port aileron
122 Wing tip fairing
123 Port navigation light
124 Pitot tube
125 Cannon barrel fairings
126 Cannon barrels
127 Port leading edge fuel tank, capacity 17 Imp gal (77 litres)
128 Upper engine cowling
129 Hydraulic fluid tank
130 Intercooler
131 Compressor intake
132 Generator
133 Heywood compressor
134 Engine bearer attachment
135 Hydraulic pump
136 Coolant pipes
137 Gun camera
138 Camera port
139 Engine air intake duct
140 Port mainwheel
141 Engine bearer
142 Cartridge starter
143 Exhaust stubs

144 2,035 hp (1517-kW) Rolls-Royce Griffon 61 engine
145 Engine magnetoes
146 Coolant header tank
147 Front engine mounting

Supermarine Griffon Spitfire and Seafire variants

Spitfire Mk IV: two aircraft (DP845 and 851), latter reserved for Mk 21; first with larger engine, later Mk XX

Spitfire Mk XII: interim low-level fighter based on existing Mk V or Mk VIII; B armament in Universal clipped wing; Griffon III or IV and four-bladed propeller; total 100

Spitfire Mk XIV: interim fighter with two-stage high-altitude Griffon (in production Mk 65 or 67 with five-bladed propeller); strengthened Mk VIII airframe, enlarged tail; Universal wing (often clipped by local action), **Spitfire XIVE** with two 20-mm and two 12.7-mm (0.5-in) guns, later batches with bubble hood, and **Spitfire FR.Mk XIV** versions with cameras and rear-fuselage tank; total 957

Spitfire Mk XVIII (post-war **Spitfire F.Mk 18** and **Spitfire FR.Mk 18**): definitive variant with improved wing with tanks, FR with rear-fuselage fuel and cameras; extruded spar booms used on this mark only (abandoned on Mk 21); total 100 F plus 200 FR

Spitfire Mk XIX (post-war **Spitfire PR.Mk 19**): unarmed photo version with Mk VC wing of 'bowser' type as on Mk XI; first 20 Griffon 65 and unpressurised, followed by 205 Griffon 66 and pressurised

Spitfire Mk XX: further stage in life of Mk IV DP845

Spitfire Mk 21: redesigned aircraft with completely new wing; total 120

Spitfire Mk 22: bubble hood and cut-down rear fuselage; often Mk 85 engine and contraprop; later with Spiteful tail; total 278

Spitfire Mk 23: unbuilt Mk 22 with different wing profile

Spitfire Mk 24: zero-length rocket launchers, two 150-litre (33-Imp gal) rear-fuselage tanks, Mk 5 guns fired electrically; total 54 plus 27 Mk 22 with rear tanks not included under Mk 22

Seafire Mk XV: basic Griffon variant derived from Spitfire Mk XII; total six prototypes plus 250 from Westland and 134 from Cunliffe-Owen

Seafire Mk XVII: (decision to avoid duplicating mark numbers left Mk XVI to Spitfire) as Mk XV with bubble hood, new windscreen, rear-fuselage tank except in **Seafire FR.Mk XVII** (post-war **Seafire FR.Mk 17** to complement **Seafire F.Mk 17**) sub-type; total 212 from Westland and 20 from Cunliffe-Owen

Seafire Mk 45: interim model based on Spitfire Mk 21; total 50

Seafire Mk 46: interim model based on Spitfire Mk 22; total 24

Seafire Mk 47: definitive model with many improvements, Mk 87 or 88 engine driving contraprop, folding wings, extra fuel/weapons; total 90

© Pilot Press Limited

148 Lower engine cowling
149 Spinner backplate
150 Propeller hub pitch change mechanism
151 Spinner
152 Rotol five-bladed constant speed propeller

141

Griffon Spitfires

Stemming from the original Griffon Seafire, the Seafire Mk XV, the Mk XVII featured several improvements such as tear-drop canopy with steeply raked windscreen, strengthened undercarriage and a rear fuselage tank. These were popular machines and served with the RNVR squadrons until 1954. This example served with No. 778 Sqn at Lee-on-Solent.

lash-up interim fighter to go into the earliest possible production. The load on the designers was immense, for in addition to over a dozen current marks there was the Type 356 and a totally new next-generation fighter with a small laminar wing, for which airframe NN660 had been reserved and which became the Spiteful. To meet the urgent new need the team under Smith hastily contrived the Type 379 as the optimum short-term marriage of the big two-stage engine and the strengthened Spitfire Mk VIII airframe. It was given the mark number XIV.

The first jet kill

Several of the surviving six prototypes were brought up to Spitfire Mk XIV standard, with the Griffon 65 or 67, five-bladed propeller, definitive fin/rudder and new extended horn-balanced elevators (all control surfaces being structurally redesigned). The first 50 were ordered on 14 August 1943 from the Supermarine works, and again there was a compromised serial, the first Spitfire Mk XIV being RB140, which was the serial borne by the last of a batch of Slingsby Cadet gliders for the ATC! The Mk XIV was the dominant Spitfire in the 2nd TAF from mid-1944 over France and Belgium, 957 in all being delivered of which 430 were Spitfire FR.Mk XIVs with a rear-fuselage tank and oblique reconnaissance camera. Those with suffix E had two 20-mm and two 12.7-mm (0.5-in) guns, and other variations, without a separate mark, were a bubble hood and cut-down rear fuselage and clipped wings carried out at unit level for extra speed low down, especially on 'Diver' patrols to shoot down flying bombs. On 5 October 1944 a Spitfire Mk XIV scored the first victory over a Messerschmitt Me 262 twin-jet fighter.

History repeated itself precisely in that, just as the properly designed Merlin-engined Spitfire Mk VIII was continually deferred

while lash-up Spitfire Mk IXs poured from the lines, so did the Spitfire Mk XIV join the RAF in hundreds while the planned 'Super Spitfire' version, the Spitfire Mk XVIII, was delayed and never saw action (not until troubles in Israel, that is). It had a stronger airframe, extra wing fuel and the bubble hood, and the Spitfire FR.Mk XVIII (post-war Spitfire FR.Mk 18) added vertical and/or oblique cameras. Last of the regular wartime models was the definitive unarmed photo-reconnaissance version, the Spitfire PR.Mk 19, which was odd in many respects such as having a pressurised cockpit without the familiar hinge-down access door on the left. At 740 km/h (460 mph) it was the fastest Spitfire in service.

High-speed handling difficulties

The type number for the Spitfire Mk 18 was 394, whereas the final sub-family, the Mks 21 to 24, were all based on the Type 356 of 1942 design. Chief test pilot Jeffrey Quill had not appreciated how dreadful was the aileron problem at high speeds until he fought with No. 65 Squadron in the Battle of Britain. No real cure was found until, in the Type 356, the entire wing was redesigned. Instead of having the torsion box comprising the front spar and the skin over the leading edge, the new wing was based on six very strong torque boxes aft of the front spar, and it was calculated that control reversal would not occur until a speed of 1328 km/h (825 mph) was reached! The metal-skinned ailerons were totally new, and had geared tabs. The plan shape was visibly different, and the only armament provided was four 20-mm cannon, in a new installation tested on a Spitfire Mk XIV, JF319. There were many other changes, including new and very strong landing gear, but not all were built into the first interim Spitfire Mk 21, which was none other than DP851, the 'missing' Mk XX. One of its non-standard features was the long-span pointed wing of

DP845, considered by Jeffrey Quill the most enjoyable of all the 20,000-plus Spitfires, was also the most frequently rebuilt. It is shown after becoming the first Griffon-Spitfire, with a Mk IIB engine. The rudder, tailwheel and windscreen/canopy are non-standard, but the dummy six cannon are absent.

First of the Griffon-engined Spitfires to enter service, the Mk XII was also the only species to have the low-blown single-stage engine (Mk III or IV, with different propeller drive ratios), asymmetric radiators and four-bladed propeller. This Mk XII, seen before delivery, had the Mk VIII airframe.

In 1948, No. 80 Sqn replaced its Tempest Mk Vs with the ultimate land-based Spitfire, the F.Mk 24, becoming the only squadron to operate this mark. For the first year the squadron was in Germany but soon moved to Kai Tak, Hong Kong, where this example is pictured wearing Korean stripes (even though the aircraft did not see active service in that campaign).

The ultimate Spitfire – the Seafire FR.Mk 47 served with several Fleet Air Arm squadrons and saw combat in the Korean war, for the most part on ground-attack sorties armed with unguided rockets. This example flew with No. 800 Sqn from the deck of HMS Triumph during this period.

the HF.Mk VII, and a similar wing was fitted to the first production Spitfire F.Mk 21 (LA187), which had PRU livery with B-type markings. In between came PP139, yet another compromised serial, the first specially built Spitfire Mk 21. Vast orders were placed with both Supermarine and Castle Bromwich, but the war's ending caused slashing cuts and only 122 were built, variously with 12- or 24-volt electrics and all with the original canopy.

Spitfire F.Mk 21s joined No. 91 Squadron in March 1945, and in the same month the first Spitfire F.Mk 22 (PK312) was delivered from Castle Bromwich, and was distinguishable by its bubble hood. The cut-down rear fuselage caused stability problems of the kind now deliberately designed into 1990s fighters, and the rear-fuselage tank had to be sealed off until, during the run of 278 of this mark, the much bigger Spiteful-type tail was fitted. Last of all, bringing the Spitfire total up to 20,351, was the Spitfire F.Mk 24, with operative rear tank, short Mk 5 guns, rocket launchers and various other detail modifications. VN496, the 81st Spitfire F.Mk 24, emerged from the South Marston works on 20 February 1948.

As the Griffon was intended for the Fleet Air Arm it naturally was considered for the Seafire. Following discussions in 1942, Specification N.4/43 was raised to cover a naval edition of the Spitfire Mk XII. The Type 377 emerged with a manually folding wing with extra wing tankage, Griffon VI driving a four-bladed Rotol and (though not a two-stage engine) with symmetric radiators, and an A-frame hook and catapult spools. Six prototypes were built, starting with NS487, and by late 1944 Westland were beginning a run of 250 and Cunliffe-Owen its batch of 134. From no. 51 the hook was of the sting type, and the final two batches (from SW876) had the bubble hood. The

latter was standard with the Seafire Mk XVII, the prototype of which was the modified third Seafire Mk XV (NS493), and other features included a steeply raked windscreen with extra framing, long-stroke strengthened main legs, rocket-assisted take-off attachments as standard and, except in the FR version, a rear-fuselage tank.

From land bases to carrier decks

The Seafire Mk XVII was a popular machine which served postwar in the RNVR as the Seafire F.Mk 17 and Seafire FR.Mk 17 until the end of 1954. This was two years after the withdrawal of the later Seafire Mks 45, 46 and 47, which were based on the Type 356 (Spitfire Mk 21). Castle Bromwich built 50 Seafire Mk 45s, to Specification N.7/44, as an interim navalised Spitfire Mk 21 with a hook and tailwheel cable deflector. Cunliffe-Owen developed the Seafire Mk 46, with bubble hood and later with the Spiteful tail, the small production batch coming from South Marston. The ultimate variant was the Seafire Mk 47, a naval Spitfire Mk 24, the first two off the South Marston line (PS944/945) serving as prototypes. The installation of the Griffon 85 and contraprops used on many Seafire Mk 45s and Mk 46s was made standard, though on production it became the Mk 87 or Mk 88 engine with Stromberg or Rolls-Royce injection carburettor and the carburettor air inlet extended right to the front of the cowling. Early in production a folding wing was introduced, without the extra folding tips of earlier Seafires, and later still the fold was made hydraulic. Almost all were Seafire FR.Mk 47s with oblique cameras and 105-litre (23-Imp gal) blister tanks under the outer wings. The last of 90, VR972, was delivered in March 1949, and these fine machines served with No. 800 Squadron in Malaya and Korea.

Almost all surviving Spitfires are Merlin-engined. An exception is N20E, registered in the USA, seen here when it was flying in Canada. Before that it had come third in the Tinnerman Trophy at Cleveland, Ohio, in 1949. Earlier still it had been FR.Mk XIV TZ138 on winterisation tests in Canada.

Among the last Spitfires to continue serving in the RAF in the fighter role, these FR.Mk 18s (post-war designation) are seen parked on pierced-steel planks at Butterworth in 1950. No. 60 Sqn flew the very last Spitfire strike against bandit camps on 1 January 1951. The PR.Mk 19 went on until 1 April 1954 in the reconnaissance role.

Griffon Spitfires

MV349 was a Spitfire F.Mk XIVE built by Supermarine and delivered in late 1944. As the markings show it immediately went out to the Far East Air Force, being shipped to Bombay and flown to Burma, where it operated with RAF No. 28 Sqn on the Malayan front until the end of the war. The actual end of fighting came just as No. 28 Sqn, with the other squadrons, was being readied to go aboard carriers from where they were to fly off to Malayan airfields during the final assault in that theatre. As can be seen, MV349 was fitted with a low-level oblique camera aft of the cockpit, as in the FR.Mk XIVE, but did not have the latter's clipped wings. Standard E armament was fitted: two 20-mm Hispano Mk II cannon and two 12.7-mm (0.5-in) Browning machine-guns. The vertical tail had had to be increased in area to counter the longer nose, and the rear-view hood and cut-down rear fuselage ideally needed even greater fin area in compensation.

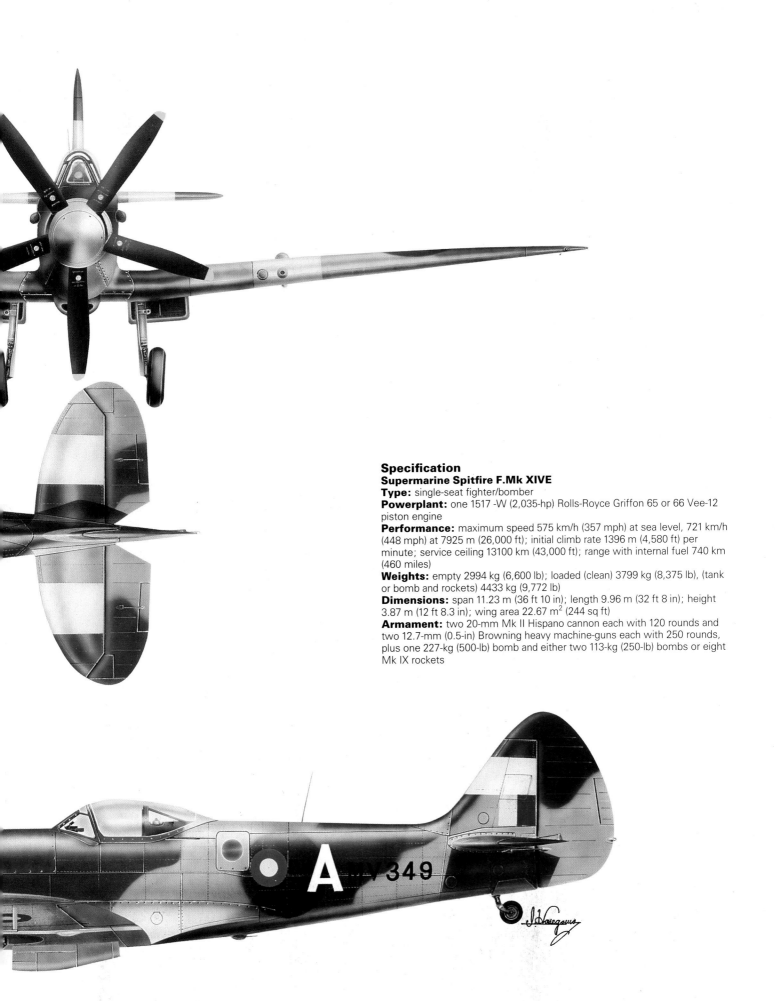

Specification
Supermarine Spitfire F.Mk XIVE
Type: single-seat fighter/bomber
Powerplant: one 1517 -W (2,035-hp) Rolls-Royce Griffon 65 or 66 Vee-12 piston engine
Performance: maximum speed 575 km/h (357 mph) at sea level, 721 km/h (448 mph) at 7925 m (26,000 ft); initial climb rate 1396 m (4,580 ft) per minute; service ceiling 13100 km (43,000 ft); range with internal fuel 740 km (460 miles)
Weights: empty 2994 kg (6,600 lb); loaded (clean) 3799 kg (8,375 lb), (tank or bomb and rockets) 4433 kg (9,772 lb)
Dimensions: span 11.23 m (36 ft 10 in); length 9.96 m (32 ft 8 in); height 3.87 m (12 ft 8.3 in); wing area 22.67 m^2 (244 sq ft)
Armament: two 20-mm Mk II Hispano cannon each with 120 rounds and two 12.7-mm (0.5-in) Browning heavy machine-guns each with 250 rounds, plus one 227-kg (500-lb) bomb and either two 113-kg (250-lb) bombs or eight Mk IX rockets

Messerschmitt Bf 110

The Bf 110 was the result of a concept unique to the Luftwaffe planners of the 1930s. It was an assault fighter, a Zerstörer , designed to be a persistent, heavily-armed fighter, capable of wreaking havoc among enemy bombers. The concept proved to be fatally flawed once confronted with the nimble single-seat fighters of the RAF, but the Bf 110 gained an undeserved reputation for vulnerability. The strengths of the design were underlined by its career as Germany's premier night-fighter.

Speed, acceleration and tight manoeuvrability in the cut and thrust of a dogfight were the objectives laid before the fighter designers of all nations following the end of the war in Europe in 1918, and accordingly it was the single-seat biplane, of high power:weight ratio and relatively low wing-loading, that held the position of pre-eminence in the world's air forces. Then came the monoplane revolution of the 1930s, with monocoque fuselages, retractable landing gear, cantilever tail units, and stressed single or double-spar wings; the configuration of the fighter remained essentially the same, with armament and fuel tankage carefully restricted so as not to detract from speed and manoeuvrability. However, combat operations over the Western Front during 1917-18 had accentuated the need for fighters with extended range and endurance, and in particular for those with a combat radius of action that could enable them to accompany bombers on missions deep into enemy airspace, either as escort fighters or in order to gain local air supremacy in an appointed area. To design such an aircraft was considered to be well nigh impossible but, in 1934, the idea was resurrected. Whether the long-range strategic fighter concept was to be committed to offensive or defensive tasks is still a matter for argument. For the Luftwaffe at least the requirement for this type, termed the *Zerstörer* (destroyer), was the pursuit and destruction of enemy bombers operating over the Reich and the additional ability to harass over a lengthy period on the withdrawal.

While waiting for the supply of new engines to become less erratic, Messerschmitt redesigned the aircraft and produced the higher-performance Bf 110C, the main protagonist in the Battle of Britain.

Attending to the RLM specifications for the development of a heavy strategic fighter, the team at the Bayerische Flugzeugwerke AG (later Messerschmitt AG) started work on the project in the summer of 1935 with their wayward brilliance, ignoring much of the specification data and concentrating their efforts on the design of a lean, all-metal, twin-engine monoplane. The prototype, the Messerschmitt Bf 110 V1, first flew from Augsburg-Haunstetten on 12 May 1936, with Rudolf Opitz at the controls. Powered by two Daimler-Benz DB 600A engines, the Bf 110 V1 achieved maximum speed of 505 km/h (314 mph) at 3175 m (10,415 ft), considerably in excess of that reached by the single-engine Messerschmitt Bf 109B-2 fighter. Of course acceleration and manoeuvrability, as noted by the test pilots and later by those at the *Erprobungsstelle* (service trials detachment) on this and subsequent prototypes, in no way compared with those of lighter fighters. But Hermann Goering ignored the misgivings of the Luftwaffe as to the Messerschmitt Bf 110's potentialities, and ordered that production should proceed. The first pre-production model, the Bf 110B-01 powered by two Junkers Jumo 210Ga engines, first flew on 19 April 1938 in the wake of a major reorganisation of the Luftwaffe's units.

The shortage of Daimler-Benz powerplants and the retention of the Jumo 210Ga engines conferred only a mediocre capability on the Bf 110B-1 series that emanated from the Augsburg production lines in the summer. Armed with two 20-mm Oerlikon MG-FF cannon and four 7.92-mm (0.31-in) MG 17 machine-guns, the Bf 110B-1 had a maximum speed of 455 km/h (283 mph) at its rated altitude of 4000 m (13,125 ft); the service ceiling was 8000 m (26,245 ft). This

A Messerschmitt Bf 110C-4 operated by Zerstörergeschwader 52 flies over the French coastline in late 1940. Such units were to receive a severe mauling in the aerial offensive over Britain.

version was the first to enter service, equipping a number of *schweren Jagdgruppen* (heavy fighter wings) in the autum of 1938.

Early in 1939 the Messerschmitt Bf 110C-0 pre-production fighters were issued to the newly-formed *Zerstörergruppen* (ex-*schweren Jagdgruppen*); these featured the modified airframe that was to endure throughout the aircraft's lifetime, and were powered by the 12-cylinder, inverted-Vee direct-injection Daimler-Benz DB 601A-1 engines rated at 820 kW (1,100 hp) at 3700 m (12,140 ft). The production Bf 110C-1s were highly effective long-range fighters, and the crews of I(Zerst)/Lehrgeschwader Nr 1, the I/Zerstörergeschwader Nr 1 and the I/ZG 76, who manned the new type, represented the cream of the Luftwaffe's fighter arm. Just before the outbreak of

war, in September 1939, each *Gruppe* had two *Staffeln* with Bf 110C-1s and a conversion unit with Bf 110B-3 trainers. The crews used their heavy mounts well during the short campaign in Poland during September, flying top cover to the Heinkels and Dorniers and conducting sweeps at 6000 m (19,685 ft) and above; they quickly recognised the stupidity of entering turning matches with the nimble Polish PZL P.11c fighters, and adopted climb-and-dive tactics while maintaining good airspeed at all times. Oberst Walter Grabmann's I(Z)/LG 1 (led by Hauptmann Schleif) downed five PZL P.11s over Warsaw on the evening of 1 September while covering the Heinkel He 111Ps of II/KG 1. The centralised armament, aimed by a Revi C.12/C reflector sight, was found to be devastating: one burst of 1-2 seconds was sufficient to blow off a wing of an opposing fighter. But was this enough?

Already it was apparent that the Zerstörergruppen had eschewed what was probably the originally intended role, and were being

A Messerschmitt Bf 110C-2 fighter reveals the slim fuselage and its graceful lines. The aircraft was hard put to stay the pace with single-seat Allied fighters, although many German aces claimed high scores. But its vulnerability has been overemphasised, and it was the mainstay of Germany's night-fighter force from 1940 to 1945.

Ground crew prepare to load an Rb 50/30 camera on to a Bf 110C-5. Operating from Greece prior to the German airborne invasion of Crete, such photo missions failed to reveal the island's hostile terrain.

Messerschmitt Bf 110 variants

Messerschmitt Bf 110 V1: first prototype powered with two Daimler-Benz DB 600A engines; first flight on 12 May 1936
Messerschmitt Bf 110 V2: second prototype featuring some refinements; to E-Stelle Rechlin for service evaluation on 14 January 1937
Messerschmitt Bf 110 V3: armament test prototype with initial flight on 24 December 1936; four 7.92-mm (0.31-in) MG 17 machine-guns fitted in nose
Messerschmitt Bf 110A-0: production models intended for DB 600Aa engines, but considered underpowered and phased out; some with Junkers Jumo 210Da engines
Messerschmitt Bf 110B-1: production version following the redesigned Bf 110B-01, with modified nose for an armament of four 7.92-mm (0.31-in) MG 17 and two 20-mm Oerlikon MG FF cannon; rear gunner had one 7.92-mm (0.31-in) MG 15; powerplant of two Junkers 210Ga engines; entered service with the Luftwaffe
Messerschmitt Bf 110B-2: reconnaissance version with camera installed in place of MG FF cannon
Messerschmitt Bf 110B-3: conversion trainer with armament removed, and improved radio and instruments
Messerschmitt Bf 110C-0: pre-production aircraft with two Daimler-Benz DB 601A-1 engines each rated at 820 kW (1,100 hp)
Messerschmitt Bf 110C-1: armament and engines standardised in this major military version at four MG 17s, two MG FFs and two DB 601A-1 engines
Messerschmitt Bf 110C-2: improved H/F

Lorenz FuG 10 radio in place of FuG IIIa
Messerschmitt Bf 110C-3: improved Oerlikon MG FF/M cannon
Messerschmitt Bf 110C-4: additional 9-mm armour plating for pilot
Messerschmitt Bf 110C-4/B: fighter-bomber version with two ETC 250 racks under fuselage and two Daimler-Benz DB 601N-1 engines each rated at 895 kW (1,200 hp)
Messerschmitt Bf 110C-5: reconnaissance version with reduced armament, and with single Rb 50/30 camera; **Bf 110C-5/N** with two DB 601N-1 engines
Messerschmitt Bf 110C-6: twin 20-mm MG FFs replaced by single 30-mm MK 101 cannon
Messerschmitt Bf 110C-7: basic Bf 110C-4/B with stronger landing gear and two ETC 500 belly racks for increased load
Messerschmitt Bf 110D-0: pre-production long-range fighter
Messerschmitt Bf 110D-1/R1: similar to Bf 110C series but with 1200-litre (264-Imp gal) external belly tank for extended range missions
Messerschmitt Bf 110D-1/R2: similar to Bf 110C but with two 900-litre (198-Imp gal) wing-mounted drop-tanks
Messerschmitt Bf 110D-2: long-range fighter-bomber with two ETC 500 racks, and provision for two 300-litre (66-Imp gal) drop-tanks
Messerschmitt Bf 110D-3: long-range shipping patrol version with either two 300-litre (66-Imp gal) or two 900-litre (198-Imp gal) drop-tanks, a supplementary oil tank, and stowage in tailcone for two-man liferaft
Messerschmitt Bf 110E-1: definitive

fighter-bomber series with additional four ETC 50 racks under wing surfaces, and increased load to 1200 kg (2,645 lb); initially with two DB 601A-1s then two DB 601N-1 engines; updated ancillary equipment, improved armour
Messerschmitt Bf 110E-1/U1: modified to night-fighter work, with infra-red *Spanner-Anlage* sighting device
Messerschmitt Bf 110E-1/U2: night-fighter with additional crew member
Messerschmitt Bf 110E-2 and **Bf 110E-3:** fighter-bomber and reconnaissance versions of standard Bf 110E-1 with updated ancillary equipment
Messerschmitt Bf 110F-1: introduced two 1005-kW (1,350-hp) Daimler-Benz DB 601F-1 engines; close-support aircraft with standard gunnery, two ETC 500 and four ETC 50 racks, and 57-mm armour-glass windshield plus additional armour
Messerschmitt Bf 110F-2: heavy fighter version with deletion of ETC racks
Messerschmitt Bf 110F-3: reconnaissance version
Messerschmitt Bf 110F-4: definitive night-fighter version, with improved UV instrument lighting and radio equipment; optional two 30-mm MK 108 cannon in place of MG-FF/Ms in ventral tray; some later with twin 30-mm *schräge Musik* oblique-firing cannon in aft cockpit area (**Bf 110F-4/U1**)
Messerschmitt Bf 110F-4a: radar-equipped night-fighter with Telefunken FuG 202 *Lichtenstein BC*; 20-mm MG FF/Ms replaced by twin 20-mm MG 151/20 guns
Messerschmitt Bf 110G-1: introduced two Daimler-Benz DB 605B-1 engines rated at 1100 kW (1,475 hp); heavy day fighter with four MG 17s and twin 20-mm MG 151/20 cannon
Messerschmitt Bf 110G-2: revised vertical

tail, strengthened landing gear, and twin 7.92-mm (0.31-in) MG 81Z for rear gunner; fighter or close-support version with ETC 250 and ETC 50/VIII or 300-litre (66-Imp gal) drop-tanks
Messerschmitt Bf 110G-2/R1: bomber destroyer with single 37-mm BK 3, 7 (Flak 18) cannon in belly tray, with deletion of MG 151/20s; the **Bf 110G-2/R2** was similar but with provision of GM-1 power-boosting
Messerschmitt Bf 110G-2/R3: heavy fighter version with twin 30-mm MK 108 cannon in place of the quadruple 7.92-mm (0.31-in) MG 17s, but retaining the MG 151s
Messerschmitt Bf 110G-3: reconnaissance fighter
Messerschmitt Bf 110G-4: definitive radar-equipped night-fighter, with return to four 7.92-mm (0.31-in) MG 17s and twin MG 151 cannon
Messerschmitt Bf 110G-4a: night-fighter with FuG 212 *Lichtenstein C-1* radar; field modification (*Rüstsätz*) **Bf 110G-4a/R1** with one 37-mm BK 3,7 cannon, **Bf 110G-4a/R2** with GM 1 boosting, and **Bf 110G-4a/R3** with twin 30-mm MK 108s in place of the MG 17s
Messerschmitt Bf 110G-4b: night-fighter with new FuG 220 *Lichtenstein SN-2* radar, but with retention of earlier FuG 212 for close-in work
Messerschmitt Bf 110G-4c: night-fighter with improved FuG 220b *Lichtenstein SN-2* radar to overcome short-range AI limitations; various *Rüstsätze* for weaponry, fuel tanks and GM-1 equipment
Messerschmitt Bf 110H: manufactured in small numbers in parallel with the Bf 110G series, differing in use of engines, in this case DB 605Es, with **Bf 110H-2, Bf 110H-3** and **Bf 110H-4** delivered

employed on escort and superiority sorties against enemy single-engine fighters. In theory there was little wrong in the performance parameters of the Bf 110C-1: for its size and configuration it was the finest heavy fighter extant, with a combat weight of 5900 kg (13,007 lb) it attained 540 km/h (336 mph) at a rated altitude of 6050 m (19,850 ft), faster than most Allied contemporary fighters, and only 32-43 km/h (20-30 mph) slower than its next opponents, the French Dewoitine D.520 and the British Supermarine Spitfire Mk I. But in fighter-versus-fighter combat, snappy rates of rolls and swift acceleration win the day, with maximum-rate turns being a factor of power, wing-loading and pilot strength.

Few problems were encountered by the *Zerstörer* pilots over Poland and Scandinavia, and their undoubted ability was awarded with the accolade that suggested to all that the Bf 110C-1 was an outstanding combat aircraft. But staunch fighter opposition over France and southern England in 1940 was to destroy much of the myth. On *freie Jagd* sweeps over Sussex and Kent at heights above 6700 m (21,980 ft) the Bf 110C-1s and Bf 110C-4s were virtually immune throughout the Battle of Britain, with RAF tacticians acknowledging the fact that it out-performed the Hurricane Mk I in all regimes, and that it could out-climb the Spitfire Mk I; the dive-and-climb tactics of

the Bf 110s were effective, and the armament had to be watched with care. The horrendous casualties sustained by I/ZG 76 and Zerstörergeschwader Nrn 2 and 26 during the battle occurred almost without exception during medium-level bomber escort missions. Throttled back and at slow speed the Bf 110Cs were cut to pieces, being wholly unable to out-turn the lighter Spitfires and Hurricanes. The pilots of the Messerschmitt Bf 109E-4s suffered similar disadvantage, but to an extent that was not as disastrous.

In the rain at Haunstetten. Only four Messerschmitt Bf 110A-01 aircraft were built for pre-production trials; powered by twin Junkers Jumo 210Da engines, they started trials in the summer of 1937. The sleek airframe of this large strategic fighter was very advanced for its time.

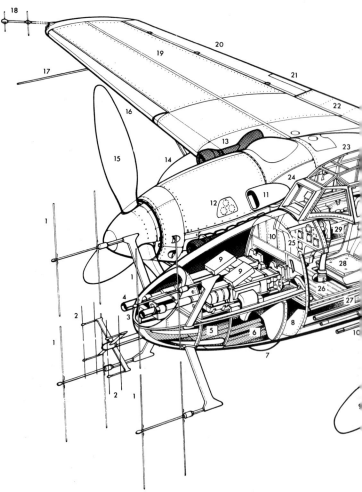

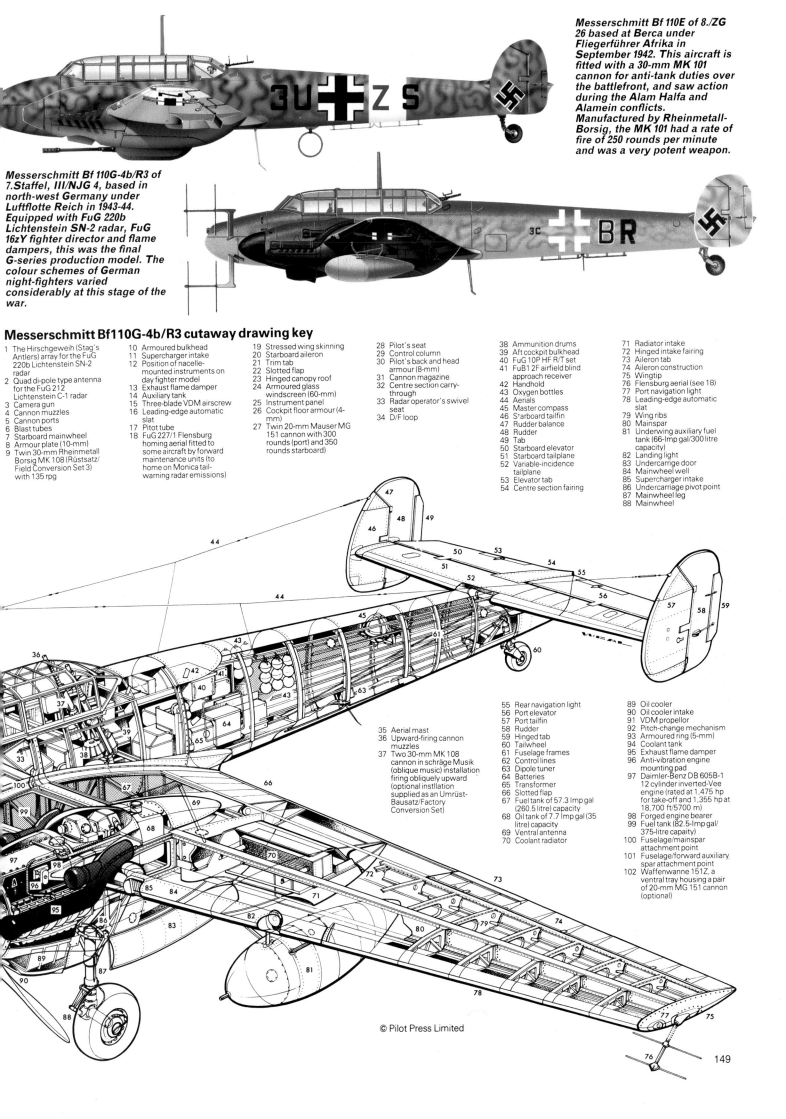

Messerschmitt Bf 110E of 8./ZG 26 based at Berca under Fliegerführer Afrika in September 1942. This aircraft is fitted with a 30-mm MK 101 cannon for anti-tank duties over the battlefront, and saw action during the Alam Halfa and Alamein conflicts. Manufactured by Rheinmetall-Borsig, the MK 101 had a rate of fire of 250 rounds per minute and was a very potent weapon.

Messerschmitt Bf 110G-4b/R3 of 7.Staffel, III/NJG 4, based in north-west Germany under Luftflotte Reich in 1943-44. Equipped with FuG 220b Lichtenstein SN-2 radar, FuG 16zY fighter director and flame dampers, this was the final G-series production model. The colour schemes of German night-fighters varied considerably at this stage of the war.

Messerschmitt Bf110G-4b/R3 cutaway drawing key

1 The Hirschgeweih (Stag's Antlers) array for the FuG 220b Lichtenstein SN-2 radar
2 Quad di-pole type antenna for the FuG 212 Lichtenstein C-1 radar
3 Camera gun
4 Cannon muzzles
5 Cannon ports
6 Blast tubes
7 Starboard mainwheel
8 Armour plate (10-mm)
9 Twin 30-mm Rheinmetall Borsig MK 108 (Rüstsatz/Field Conversion Set 3) with 135 rpg
10 Armoured bulkhead
11 Supercharger intake
12 Position of nacelle-mounted instruments on day fighter model
13 Exhaust flame damper
14 Auxiliary tank
15 Three-blade VDM airscrew
16 Leading-edge automatic slat
17 Pitot tube
18 FuG 227/1 Flensburg homing aerial fitted to some aircraft by forward maintenance units (to home on Monica tail-warning radar emissions)
19 Stressed wing skinning
20 Starboard aileron
21 Trim tab
22 Slotted flap
23 Hinged canopy roof
24 Armoured glass windscreen (60-mm)
25 Instrument panel
26 Cockpit floor armour (4-mm)
27 Twin 20-mm Mauser MG 151 cannon with 300 rounds (port) and 350 rounds starboard)
28 Pilot's seat
29 Aft control column
30 Pilot's back and head armour (8-mm)
31 Cannon magazine
32 Centre section carry-through
33 Radar operator's swivel seat
34 D/F loop
35 Aerial mast
36 Upward-firing cannon muzzles
37 Two 30-mm MK 108 cannon in schräge Musik (oblique music) installation firing obliquely upward (optional instllation supplied as an Umrüst-Bausatz/Factory Conversion Set)
38 Ammunition drums
39 Armoured bulkhead
40 FuG 10P HF R/T set
41 FuB1 2F airfield blind approach receiver
42 Handhold
43 Oxygen bottles
44 Aerials
45 Master compass
46 S*arboard tailfin
47 Rudder balance
48 Rudder
49 Tab
50 Starboard elevator
51 Starboard tailplane
52 Variable-incidence tailplane
53 Elevator tab
54 Centre section fairing
55 Rear navigation light
56 Port elevator
57 Port tailfin
58 Rudder
59 Hinged tab
60 Tailwheel
61 Fuselage frames
62 Control lines
63 Dipole tuner
64 Batteries
65 Transformer
66 Slotted flap
67 Fuel tank of 57.3 Imp gal (260.5 litre) capacity
68 Oil tank of 7.7 Imp gal (35 litre) capacity
69 Ventral antenna
70 Coolant radiator
71 Radiator intake
72 Hinged intake fairing
73 Aileron tab
74 Aileron construction
75 Wingtip
76 Flensburg aerial (see 18)
77 Port navigation light
78 Leading-edge automatic slat
79 Wing ribs
80 Mainspar
81 Underwing auxiliary fuel tank (66-Imp gal/300 litre capacity)
82 Landing light
83 Undercarrige door
84 Mainwheel well
85 Supercharger intake
86 Undercarriage pivot point
87 Mainwheel leg
88 Mainwheel
89 Oil cooler
90 Oil cooler intake
91 VDM propellor
92 Pitch-change mechanism
93 Armoured ring (5-mm)
94 Coolant tank
95 Exhaust flame damper
96 Anti-vibration engine mounting pad
97 Daimler-Benz DB 605B-1 12 cylinder inverted-Vee engine (rated at 1,475 hp for take-off and 1,355 hp at 18,700 ft/5700 m)
98 Forged engine bearer
99 Fuel tank (82.5-Imp gal/375-litre capaity)
100 Fuselage/mainspar attachment point
101 Fuselage/forward auxiliary spar attachment point
102 Waffenwanne 151Z, a ventral tray housing a pair of 20-mm MG 151 cannon (optional)

© Pilot Press Limited

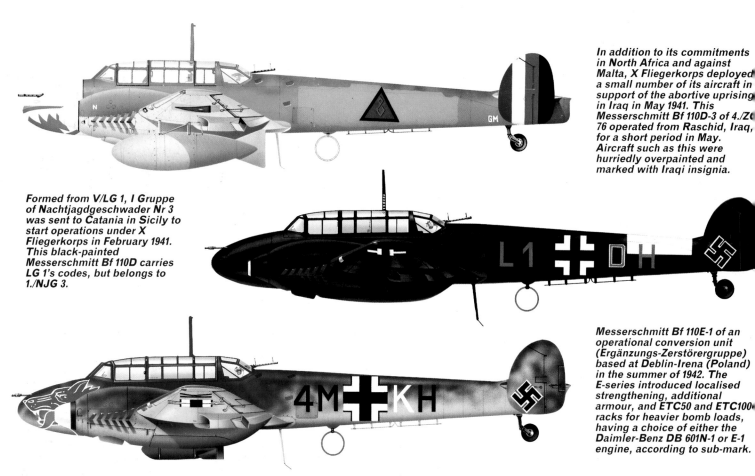

In addition to its commitments in North Africa and against Malta, X Fliegerkorps deployed a small number of its aircraft in support of the abortive uprising in Iraq in May 1941. This Messerschmitt Bf 110D-3 of 4./ZG 76 operated from Raschid, Iraq, for a short period in May. Aircraft such as this were hurriedly overpainted and marked with Iraqi insignia.

Formed from V/LG 1, I Gruppe of Nachtjagdgeschwader Nr 3 was sent to Catania in Sicily to start operations under X Fliegerkorps in February 1941. This black-painted Messerschmitt Bf 110D carries LG 1's codes, but belongs to 1./NJG 3.

Messerschmitt Bf 110E-1 of an operational conversion unit (Ergänzungs-Zerstörergruppe) based at Deblin-Irena (Poland) in the summer of 1942. The E-series introduced localised strengthening, additional armour, and ETC50 and ETC100 racks for heavier bomb loads, having a choice of either the Daimler-Benz DB 601N-1 or E-1 engine, according to sub-mark.

During the Battle of Britain the extended-range Messerschmitt Bf 110D-1/R1 saw service with I/ZG 76 at Stavanger, while the fighter-bomber Bf 110C-4/Bs of Erprobungskommando 210 flew several audacious, and often costly, missions on precision targets in southern England. In the winter of 1940-41 the III/ZG26 took its Bf 110D-3s to Sicily and thence to North Africa: other *Gruppen* of the parent *Geschwader* operated over the Balkans, Greece and Crete during the spring. For the invasion of the Soviet Union on 22 June 1941 (Operation Barbarossa), the II Fliegerkorps controlled the Bf 110C-4 fighter-bombers of Major Karl-Heinz Stricker's Schnellkampfgeschwader Nr 210 (I and II Gruppen), and the VIII Fliegerkorps the Bf 110C-4s of Oberst Johannes Schalk's Zerstörergeschwader Nr 26 (I and II Gruppen); remaining units equipped with the day-fighting Bf 110 were I and II/ZG 6, based at Kirkenes in northern Norway, and at Jever and Nordholz in Germany. Production of the big Messerschmitt had been reduced in favour of its replacement, the Messerschmitt Me 210A-1, while many *Zerstörer-gruppen* had been re-formed as night-fighter units. Upgunned and with increased power, the Bf 110E, Bf 110F and Bf 110G series continued to operate in small numbers throughout the campaigns in the USSR and North Africa. In August 1943 the decimated elements were withdrawn from the USSR and Italy to form I-III/ZG 26 at Wunstorf and I-III/ZG 76 at Ansbach for the daylight defence of the Reich with Messerschmitt Bf 110G-2s: these carried a variety of weapons including 20-mm MG 151/20 and 30-mm MK 108A-3 cannons, 37-mm Flak 18 guns, and 21-cm Werfergranäte (WfrGr 21) rocket mortars. Against unescorted formations of Boeing B-17s and Consolidated B-24D Liberators this new breed of fighter wrought mayhem in its role of Pulk-Zerstörer (formation destroyer) until the appearance of P-47D Thunderbolts with 410-litre (108-US gal) auxiliary tanks. Their slaughter was on a scale that dwarfed the losses sustained in 1940, and by April 1944 the Messerschmitt Bf 110G-2, with the exception of those with II/ZG 76 at Wien-Seying in Austria, was withdrawn from service.

Reformed from SKG 210, Zerstörergeschwader Nr 1 operated in the USSR in 1942, seeing action in the Caucasus and Stalingrad theatres under VIII Fliegerkorps. When the North African crisis developed in October 1942 Gruppen of ZG 1 were posted to Sicily under Luftflotte 2; pictured are a Staffel of the group's Bf 110G-2s.

A Messerschmitt Bf 110G-2/R3 day fighter of 7./ZG 26 serving under Luftwaffenbefehlshaber Mitte in the defence of the Reich in 1943. Liberally equipped with 20-mm and 30-mm cannon and Wfr Gr 21 rocket-mortars, the aircraft was a killer. But the Luftwaffe failed to foresee the introduction of US escort fighters.

Messerschmitt Bf 110

The Messerschmitt Bf 110F-1 was fitted with armoured glass and extra plate around the crew. Two ETC 500 racks beneath the fuselage could carry a pair of SC 250 250-kg (551-lb) bombs.

Without doubt the Messerschmitt Bf 110's most successful service record was that of a night-fighter in the defence of the Reich, a duty that it performed with lethal efficiency for nearly five years. On 20 July 1940 Goering ordered Oberst Josef Kammhuber to form a night-fighter force: the I/Nachtjagdgeschwader Nr 1 (I/NJG 1) was established with Bf 110C-2s at Venlo in the Netherlands towards the end of the month, to form the nucleus of a full *Geschwader*. *Zestörer* crews had already taken up night-fighting, and on the day of Goering's order Hauptmann Werner Streib, of 2./NJG 2, claimed the first official kill of the new night-fighter arm. In the attempt to increase the chances of visual identification a number of aids were used mostly without success: the infra-red sighting device (*Spanner-Anlage*) was fitted to a few Bf 110D-1/U1s. For the most part crews relied on radar-assisted searchlights to illuminate their prey over strictly demarked territorial zones. In addition use of ground radar, the *AN-Freya* (FuMG 80), enabled some interception to be made over the sea.

Night-fighting techniques with the Messerschmitt Bf 110C-2s were enhanced with the introduction of high-frequency *Würzburg* FuMG 62 ground radars: one plotted the approaching enemy bomber following early warning from a longer-ranged *Freya*, while a second kept track of the German fighter. Using a map display the controller gave R/T instructions to the fighter which, hopefully, closed to visual range. The system, known as *Himmelbett* (four-poster bed), was more cumbersome than the British GCI radar system, but nevertheless it worked. By 1942 the system of box-like *Himmelbett* GCI areas stretched from the northern tip of Denmark to the Swiss border, to give early warning and fighter control to counter the depredations of RAF Bomber Command.

Airborne radar was deemed essential, and during 1941 a *Staffel* of I/NJG 1 based at Venlo with Bf 110E-1/U1s experimented with the Telefunken FuG 202 (*Lichtenstein BC*) pre-production AI, which worked on 490 MHz; maximum range was 3.5 km (2.2 miles) with a minimum of 200 m (655 ft). It was not until July 1942, following the series of massed raids on Bremen and Cologne, that AI, in the form of FuG 212 *Lichtenstein*, arrived in the front-line units. By now the standard night-fighter was the Messerschmitt Bf 110F-4 (two Daimler-Benz DB 601F-1 engines) which carried four 7.92-mm (0.31-in) MG 17 machine-guns and two Mauser MG 151/20 cannon; the radar-equipped Bf 110F-4a usually carried two 300-litre (66-Imp gal) drop-tanks, flame-dampers, and night glimmer HE ammunition. The increase in weight to 9275 kg (20,448 lb) and the additional drag of the

radar antennas reduced speed to 510 km/h (317 mph) at 5600 m (18,375 ft). Despite the RAF's recently adopted tactics of streaming in order to swamp a particular *Himmelbett* area, pilots such as Lent, Falk, Strieb, Meurer, Schnaufer and Becker achieved many successes with the Messerschmitt Bf 110F-4 during 1942-3: the aircraft was sufficiently fast, had excellent visibility and retained its gentle flight characteristics. On achieving visual contact the pilot usually throttled back and eased his aircraft some 76 m (250 ft) into a position directly below his quarry, before pulling up into a 50° pitch-up and opening fire into the bomber's belly and fuel tanks with 20-mm or 30-mm HE/I and armour-piercing/incendiary.

Night-fighter developments

During 1943 this technique was broadened to include the use of upward-firing cannon so that the night-fighter merely had to keep station below the target and open fire. Two 20-mm MG-FF/M cannon were installed in the aft cockpit to fire at an angle of 60-70° from the horizontal: the modification was known as *schräge Musik* (jazz), and was highly effective. With the failure of the Messerschmitt Me 210 series the Luftwaffe was forced to retain the Bf 110 in front-line service primarily as a night-fighter, and in 1942 the Daimler-Benz DB 605B-1 engine was installed in the new Bf 110G series. The Messerschmitt Bf 110G-4, equipped first with FuG 212 and, after the introduction of ECM chaff ('Window'), with *Lichtenstein SN-2* (FuG 220) radar, bore the brunt of Luftflotte Reich's night-fighter commitment in late 1943. By June 1944 the Bf 110G-4 equipped the majority of *Gruppen* within Nachtjagdgeschwader Nrn 1, 3, 4, 5 and 6, stationed from Aalborg in Denmark to Reims in France, and from Schleissheim to the Romanian border. They were thus the veritable backbone of the Luftwaffe's night-fighter arm. But the Junkers Ju 88C-6b and Ju 88G-1 night-fighters became preponderant in the course of the last year of the war, and the Messerschmitt became less numerous, although many *Experten* (aces) preferred this type to the heavy Junkers. No one was more successful as an exponent of the Messerschmitt Bf 110G-4 than Major Heinz-Wolfgang Schnaufer, the last Kommodore of NJG 4 and a recipient of the Diamonds to the Knight's Cross, who claimed no less than 121 nocturnal kills in the war. There was no doubt that despite its detractors and the fact that only 6,170 were produced, the Messerschmitt Bf 110 could go down in the annals of World War II as an efficient all-purpose twin-engine combat aircraft, for no twin could stand the test against well-flown single-engine fighters by day; not the Bristol Beaufighter, the de Havilland Mosquito, the Kawasaki Ki-45 Toryu, nor even the excellent Lockheed P-38 Lightning.

A captured Bf 110G-4b/R3 night-fighter displays the **Lichtenstein SN-2 Hirschgeweih** *(stag's antlers) radar array around the smaller dipole* **Lichtenstein C-1** *antenna necessary to defeat RAF 'window' chaff.*

Messerschmitt Bf 110

Messerschmitt Bf 110C-4/B of 9. Staffel, Zerstörergeschwader 26 'Horst Wessel', shown carrying two 250-kg (551-lb) and four 100-kg (220-lb) bombs. This unit was among the first German units to be sent to the Mediterranean, being based at Palermo at the end of 1940.

Messerschmitt Bf 110C-4

Type: two-seat heavy fighter
Powerplant: two 821-kW (1,100-hp) Daimler-Benz DB 601A inverted V-12 piston engines

Performance: maximum speed 560 km/h (349 mph) at 7000 m (22,965 ft); initial climb rate 660 m (2,165 ft) per minute; service ceiling 10000 m (32,810 ft); normal range 775 km (482 miles)
Weights: empty 5200 kg (11,454 lb); maximum take-off 6750 kg (14,881 lb)
Dimensions: span 16.27 m (5 ft 3¾ in); length 12.65 m (41 ft 6¾ in); height 3.50 m (11 ft 6 in); wing area 38.40 m² (413.3 sq ft)
Armament: two 20-mm MG 151 cannon and four 7.92-mm (0.31-in) MG 17 guns in the nose firing forward, and one 7.92-mm (0.31-in) MG 812 twin gun on pivoted mounting in the rear cockpit firing aft

Keith Fretwell

Kawasaki Ki-61

Displaying the unmistakable design legacy of an earlier German-led team, the Japanese Ki-61 fighter was a formidable opponent in the Pacific war. On account of persistent engine problems, however, it never achieved the success and reputation of the radial engine fighters, yet when these engines were hastily fitted at the end of the war, the resulting Ki-100 was one of Japan's best fighters.

Under the terms of the Treaty of Versailles imposed by the Allies after World War I Germany was forbidden to pursue the manufacture of military aircraft, with the result that young up-coming technicians sought employment overseas, just as the manufacturing companies themselves moved lock, stock and barrel out of reach of the invigilating nations. Among the Germans who found employment in Japan was Dr Richard Vogt, under whose direction Kawasaki Kokuki Kogyo KK acquired the manufacturing rights of German liquid-cooled aircraft engines during the early 1930s. Long after Vogt had returned to Germany (where he became the chief designer of Blohm und Voss), this association continued to flourish and in the late 1930s negotiations were conducted by Kawasaki to obtain the rights to build the Daimler-Benz DB 600, and later the DB 601. In April 1940 a Japanese team brought home from Germany a set of design drawings and a number of examples of the excellent DB 601A 12-cylinder inverted-Vee liquid-cooled engine. After adaptation to Japanese manufacturing techniques, the first Kawasaki Ha-40 engine (as the licence DB 601A was designated) was completed in July 1941, and four months later entered production as the 820-kW (1,100-hp) Army Type 2 engine.

Meanwhile, encouraged by the apparent superiority of European V-12 engine-powered aircraft (compared with those using radials), Kawasaki had approached the Imperial Japanese Army with proposals for a number of fighter designs employing the new Ha-40 V-12 powerplant, and in February 1940 the Koku Hombu (Air Headquarters) ordered the company to undertake development of two aircraft; the Ki-60 heavy fighter and the Ki-61, a lighter all-purpose fighter. Although higher priority was initially afforded to the former, emphasis later swung towards a preference for better performance at the expense of cockpit armour and fuel tank protection, with the result that the Ki-61 gained favour. Design leadership was assumed by Takeo Doi, and his assistant was Shin Owada.

The Ki-60 was in effect the basis of the Ki-61, and the reduced weight was achieved by adopting a fuselage of smaller cross-section, and an armament reduced to two nose- and two wing-mounted machine-guns; on the other hand a higher aspect ratio wing was introduced together with increased fuel capacity to meet the 'all-purpose' demands.

Design and manufacture of the prototype progressed swiftly, and this machine emerged from the Kagamigahara plant in Gifu Prefecture, north of Nagoya, in the same week that Japanese aircraft launched their great attack on Pearl Harbor in December 1941. Already a production line was being assembled; this confidence in the aircraft being confirmed by early flight trials with the prototype. Eleven additional prototypes were ordered and these introduced self-sealing fuel tanks which increased the wingloading to around 146.5 kg/m² (30 lb/sq ft), considerably more than Imperial Japanese Army air force pilots had generally experienced. Nevertheless the Ki-61 was popular among service evaluation pilots, who saw in its high diving speed an effective answer to American tactics of using a diving approach to combat. It was only after comparative trials in mock combat with a captured Curtiss P-40E, an imported Messerschmitt Bf 109E-3, a Nakajima Ki-43-II and a Ki-44-I that its superiority prompted the Imperial Japanese Army to confirm a production order.

The thirteenth Ki-61, built from production tooling and delivered in August 1942, differed little from the prototypes, the main distinguishing feature being the deletion of two small transparent panels in the sides of the fuselage immediately forward of the windscreen frames. Production accelerated slowly and by the end of the year 34 aircraft had been delivered under the designation Army Type 3 Fighter Model 1 Hien (Swallow), or Ki-61-I. Among these early aircraft two versions, the Ki-61-IA and Ki-61-Ib, were produced; the former was armed with two 12.7-mm (0.5-in) Type 1 guns in the nose and two 7.7-mm (0.303-in) Type 89 guns in the wings, and the latter with four 12.7-mm (0.5-in) Type 1 guns.

The first service unit to take delivery of the Ki-61 in February 1943 was the home-based 23rd Dokuritsu Dai Shijugo Chutai (independent squadron) for pilot conversion training. The fighter made its combat debut over the north coast of New Guinea a couple of months later with the 68th and 78th Sentais (groups), and proved itself a better match for Allied fighters than the Ki-43 (which it was replacing), principally on account of its superior diving speed. However problems were already being encountered in New Guinea where the hot, humid conditions were causing engine boiling on the ground, necessitating fast taxiing over the inadequate field taxiways.

Although in no way associated with these engine-cooling problems, an experimental Ki-61-I had been produced with the large ventral radiator replaced by a small retractable unit for ground cooling, and wing-mounted surface condensers to achieve cooling in flight by means of steam evaporation. These tests were conducted in preparation for Takeo Doi's radical new Ki-64 fighter, which in the event only appeared in prototype form.

Although outclassed by the North American P-51D Mustang, the Ki-61 provided much to interest American engineers and pilots when captured aircraft were subsequently evaluated (as seen here on 23 June 1945); it is probably the Ki-61-Ib that was flown at Wright Field, Ohio, during the last summer of the war.

Ki-61-I of the home-defence 244th Sentai, Headquarters Flight, commanded by Major Tembico Kobayashi. The widely observed Japanese tail marking convention included white for 1st Chutai, red for 2nd Chutai and yellow for 3rd Chutai. Blue was frequently, though not invariably, used to denote the Headquarters Flight.

In the field of armament the Ki-61 was also undergoing improvement despite the lack of an indigenous 20-mm cannon in production in Japan. Instead later Ki-61-Ias and Ki-61-Ibs were adapted in the factory to accommodate imported Mauser MG 151 20-mm guns in the wings; two such weapons, installed on their sides, replaced the customary machine-guns. Later, when the Japanese Ho-5 20-mm gun became available, Takeo Doi took the opportunity to strengthen and simplify the wing structure, and in the Ki-61-KAIc, which started appearing in January 1944, the Ho-5 cannon also replaced the fuselage machine-guns. Later still, the Ki-61-I KAId featured two 30-mm Ho-105 guns in the wings but a return to 12.7-mm (0.5-in) Type 1 machine-guns in the nose. The KAI versions (this being an abbreviation for Kaizo, or 'modified') also introduced a fixed tailwheel in place of the retractable wheel previously fitted, and underwing store pylons – made possible by the strengthened wing.

Through 1944 production was concentrated on the Ki-61-I KAIc, and production rates, hitherto relatively low, considerably improved, with the result that by January 1945 2,654 Ki-61s had been produced.

When the Hien appeared over New Guinea the Allies temporarily lost their air superiority, and there were even reports among

American pilots that the Japanese were apparently using Messerschmitt Bf 109s. Once the combat tactics favoured by the Japanese pilots had been fully assessed, Allied pilots were warned to avoid diving attacks and in due course the Ki-61, whose top speed was, after all, not spectacular, was mastered. As deliveries of the Hien were stepped up in 1944, the type was encountered in much larger numbers during the Philippine campaign of 1944-5 (when it equipped the 17th, 18th and 19th Sentais), and over Okinawa and Formosa (19th, 37th, 59th and 105th Sentais).

The Ki-61-II

As the Pacific war dragged on, the quality of Japanese manufacturing labour deteriorated, and among the manifestations of this were the falling standards of workmanship in Japanese aero engines, particularly in the Ha-40 of the Ki-61. Faced with demands for better performance, Takeo Doi was urged to adapt his aircraft to accommodate the new 1119-kW (1,500-hp) Ha-140 V-12 engine, and the first prototype Ki-61-II with this powerplant was completed in August 1943. At the same time the new aircraft introduced a wing of increased area and a modified cockpit canopy to provide the pilot with improved field of view. The Ha-140 engine suffered a spate of prob-

A Ki-61-I of the 37th Sentai, a unit that fought in the last stages of the defence of the Philippines before being forced to redeploy in Formosa and Okinawa in the last year of the war.

Pictograph representation of the letters AK on the rudders identify these Ki-61-I KAI as belonging to the Akeno Flying Training School, the principal home-based Hien training unit; the others were the 8th Kyo-iku and the 5th, 7th, 11th, 16th and 18th Rensai Hikotai.

Kawasaki Ki-61

Three Ki-61-I KAIs of the Akeno Flying Training School; the majority of aircraft on this unit were left unpainted, save for coloured spinners (denoting Flights) and black anti-glare panels forward of the windscreens.

The Ki-61-II KAI was dealt its final deathblow on 19 January 1945, when B-29s almost totally destroyed the Akashi engine plant where the Ha-140 engines were being produced, and some 30 other completed aircraft were destroyed on the ground before service delivery. Thus 275 airframes were left without engines, and there the story of the Hien might have ended but for the ingenuity of the Japanese in their desperate hours of misfortune.

The Ki-100

Fortunately, expedients had been examined by which to circumvent the engine problems associated with the Ha-140 engines, studies that had begun as early as November 1944, two months before the catastrophe at Akashi. Clearly with the war going disastrously for Japan, there was insufficient time to evolve an entirely

lems, however, the worst of which was a weak crankshaft causing a number of failures; not even the airframe was free of trouble and there were also several wing failures.

Nevertheless the Ministry of Munitions seemed confident that the engine problems were simply the product of poor quality manufacture, and therefore could be avoided by means of closer quality control, and ordered the Ki-61-II into mass production as the Army Type 3 Fighter Model 2 in September 1944. After completion of 11 prototypes (of which only eight were tested) the rudder area was increased to offset the slightly longer nose, and the Ki-61-II KAI reverted to the Ki-61-I KAI wings, thereby reducing the likelihood of further airframe failures. Provided the Ha-140 engine continued to function smoothly, the new fighter demonstrated a much-improved performance, being capable of a top speed of 610 km/h (379 mph) at 6000 m (19,685 ft), and a climb to 5000 m (16,405 ft) in six minutes.

The Ki-61-II KAI was produced in two versions, the Ki-61-II KAIa with two 20-mm guns in the nose and two 12.7-mm (0.5-in) guns in the wings, and the Ki-61-I KAIb with a total of four 20-mm guns. A total of 374 Ki-61-II KAIs was produced, but owing to persistent engine troubles relatively few of these ever reached operational units and never supplanted the earlier Ki-61-I KAIs. The Ki-61-II KAI was, however, the only Imperial Japanese Army interceptor fighter with adequate armament that could reach the operating altitude of the Boeing B-29 bomber, and was therefore probably responsible for the biggest share in the destruction (by fighters) of these large bombers.

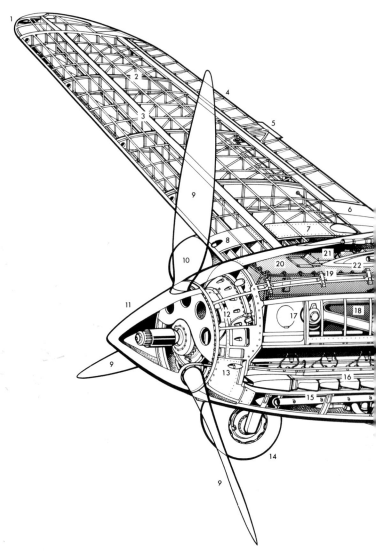

Kawasaki Ki-61-I-KAI-hei Hien cutaway drawing key (KAIc)

1 Starboard navigation light	36 Rearward-sliding cockpit canopy	70 Retractable tailwheel
2 Wing rib bracing	37 Pilot's headrest	71 Tailwheel shock absorber oleo
3 Wing spar	38 Rear-vision cut-out	72 Lower longeron
4 Starboard aileron	39 Aft glazing	73 Radiation bath air outlet
5 Aileron tab	40 Canopy track	74 Adjustable gill
6 Starboard flap	41 Spring-loaded handhold	75 Radiator
7 Wing gun access panel	42 Fuselage fuel tank (36.2 Imp gal/165 litres)	76 Radiator intake ducting
8 Gun port		77 Intake
9 Three-blade constant-speed propeller	43 Fuselage equipment access door (upward hinged)	78 Main spar/fuselage attachment point
10 Auxiliary drop-tank (43.9 Imp gal/200 litres)	44 Radio pack (Type 99-111)	79 Inboard mainwheel doors
11 Propeller boss	45 Aerial mast	80 Mainwheel well
12 Propeller reduction gear housing	46 Aerial lead-in	81 Landing light
	47 Aerial	82 Mainwheel pivot point
13 Air intake duct	48 Elevator control cables	83 Mainwheel leg
14 Starboard mainwheel	49 Upper longeron	84 Oleo shock-absorber section (leather-sleeved)
15 Lower cowling quick-release catches	50 Rudder cable	
16 Exhaust stubs	51 Fuselage join	85 Mainwheel single fork
17 Anti-vibration mounting pad		86 Port mainwheel

18 Engine bearer	52 Starboard tailplane	87 Mainwheel door
19 Upper cowling quick-release catches	53 Starboard elevator	88 Separate mainwheel leg fairing
20 Kawasaki Ha-40 (Army Type 2) engine	54 Tailfin root fairing	89 Gun port
	55 Tailfin structure	90 Machine gun barrel
21 Engine accessories	56 Rear navigation light (port and starboard)	91 Wing-mounted 12.7-mm Ho-103 machine-gun
22 Gun port		
23 Cannon barrels	57 Aerial stub mast	92 Gun access panel
24 Firewall	58 Rudder balance	93 Bomb/tank shackle
25 Cowling panel line	59 Rudder fixed trim tab	94 Port flap
26 Supercharger	60 Rudder post	95 Main spar
27 Supercharger intake	61 Rudder framework	96 Wing ribs
28 Ammunition tanks	62 Elevator tab	97 Auxiliary drop-tank (43.9 Imp gal/200 litres)
29 Ammunition feed chute	63 Elevator fixed trim tab	
30 Two 20-mm Ho-5 cannon	64 Port elevator	98 Pitot head
31 Sloping windscreen	65 Elevator control cable	99 Metal wing skin
32 Gunsight	66 Rudder hinge	100 Aileron tab
33 Control column	67 Rear fuselage frame/tailplane attachment	101 Port aileron
34 Pilot's seat (armoured)		102 Wingtip structure
35 Fuselage frame	68 Tailwheel retraction jack	103 Port navigation light
	69 Tailwheel doors	

Crudely applied green paint was an attempt to tone down the natural metal finish on this **Ki-61-I KAI** of the 3rd Chutai, 19th **Sentai**; this group fought over Leyte Gulf in the Philippines as well as Okinawa and **Formosa.**

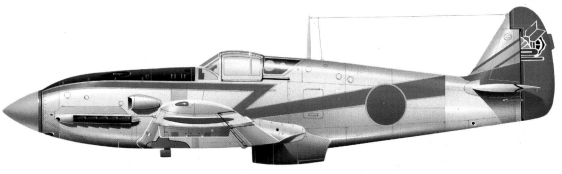

Although serving with the 3rd Chutai, 59th Sentai at Ashiya, Japan, in August 1945, this Ki-61-I Otsu (KAIb) had a replacement rear fuselage and rudder, hence the hybrid tail insignia including those of the 22nd Sentai and the Akeno Flying Training School.

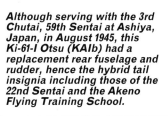

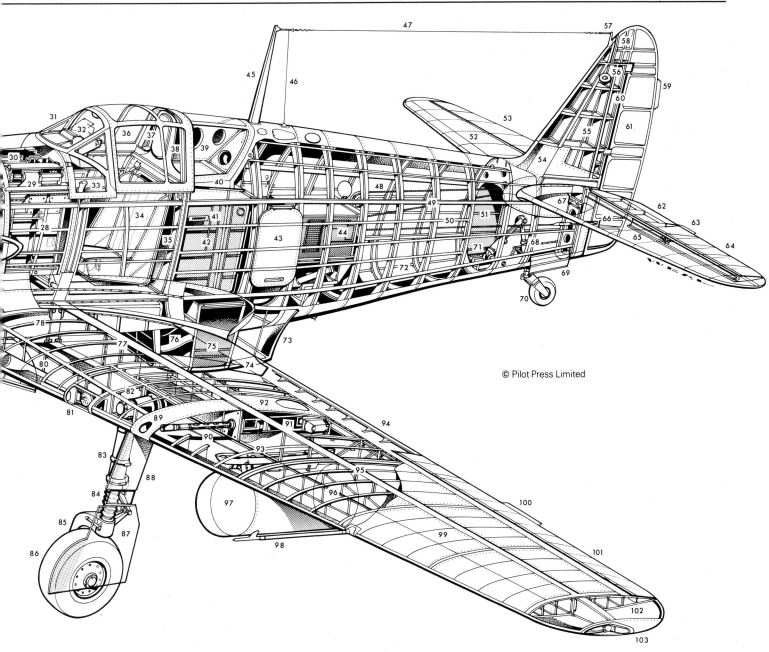

© Pilot Press Limited

157

Kawasaki Ki-61

Specification
Kawasaki Ki-61-I KAIc Hien
Type: single-seat interceptor and fighter-bomber
Powerplant: one 821-kW (1,100-hp) Army Type 2 (Kawasaki Ha-40) 12-cylinder inverted-Vee liquid-cooled engine
Performance: maximum speed 590 km/h (366 mph) at 4260 m (13,980 ft); climb to 5000 m (16,405 ft) in 7 minutes; service ceiling 10000 m (32,810 ft); maximum range 1800 km (1,120 miles)
Weights: empty 2630 kg (5,798 lb); normal loaded 3470 kg (7,650 lb)
Dimensions: span 12.00 m (39 ft 4½ in); length 8.94 m (29 ft 4 in); height 3.70 m (12 ft 1¾ in); wing area 20.00 m² (215.28 sq ft)
Armaments: two 20-mm Ho-5 cannon in nose and two 12.7-mm (0.5-in) Type 1 guns in wings, plus an external load of 240-kg (551-lb) bombs or two 200-litre (44-Imp gal) drop tanks on wing carriers

Kawasaki Ki-61 variants

Ki-61: prototypes (12 aircraft); first flight in December 1941; Ha-40 V-12 engines
Ki-61-I: production, 1,380 aircraft built between August 1942 and July 1944; included **Ki-61-Ia** with two 12.7-mm (0.5-in) nose guns and two 7.7-mm (0.303-in) wing guns, and **Ki-61-Ib** with four 12.7-mm (0.5-in) guns; Ha-40 V-12 engines; both versions also modified with two 20-mm Mauser MG 151/20 guns in wings
Ki-61-I KAI: production, 1,274 aircraft built between January 1944 and January 1945; included **Ki-61-I KAIa** and **Ki-61-I KAIc** with two nose Ho-5 20-mm guns and two 12.7-mm (0.5-in) wing guns; and **Ki-61-I KAId** with two nose 12.7-mm (0.5-in) guns and two Ho-105 30-mm wing guns
Ki-61-II: prototypes (eight aircraft) with Ha-140 inline engine and increased wing area
Ki-61-II: pre-production aircraft, 30 built; Ki-61-I wings and enlarged rudder
Ki-61-II KAI: production, 374 aircraft; Ha-140 engines in only 99 aircraft; included **Ki-61-II KAIa** with two nose Ho-5 20-mm guns and two wing 12.7-mm (0.5-in) guns, and **Ki-61-II KAIb** with four Ho-5 20-mm guns
Ki-61-III: preliminary prototype with Ha-112-II radial and all-round vision canopy; converted from Ki-61-II KAI
Ki-100: prototypes (three aircraft) completed in February 1945; converted from unfinished Ki-61-II KAIs with Ha-112-II radials
Ki-100-Ia: 272 aircraft converted from unfinished Ki-61-II KAIs with Ha-112-II radials
Ki-100-Ib: 118 aircraft built from scratch with Ha-112 radials; included 12 aircraft built at Ichinomiya plant
Ki-100-II: prototypes (three aircraft) with Ha-112-IIRU radials with turbochargers and improved-vision canopy

A drop tank-equipped Kawasaki Ki-61-Ib of the 68th Sentai, one of the first two operational units to introduce the Hien to combat over New Guinea in the spring of 1943. At the outset they wrested air superiority from the Americans' Curtiss P-40s and forced Lieutenant-General George C. Kenney to appeal direct to General of the Army Henry H. Arnold to be allowed P-38s which were otherwise assigned to Europe. In due course the Japanese threat was overcome, although the Ki-61's deteriorating standard of manufacture contributed much to its own failings.

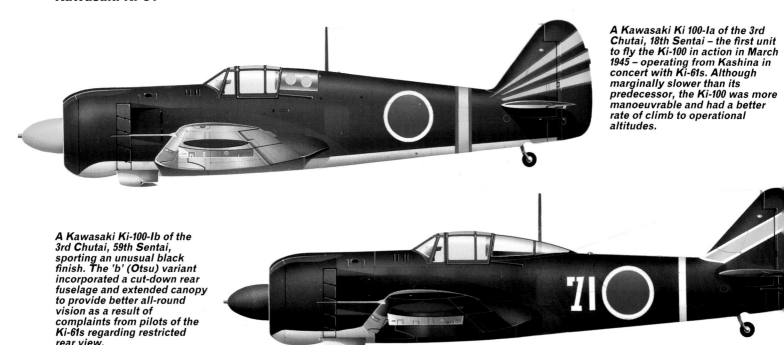

A Kawasaki Ki 100-Ia of the 3rd Chutai, 18th Sentai – the first unit to fly the Ki-100 in action in March 1945 – operating from Kashina in concert with Ki-61s. Although marginally slower than its predecessor, the Ki-100 was more manoeuvrable and had a better rate of climb to operational altitudes.

A Kawasaki Ki-100-Ib of the 3rd Chutai, 59th Sentai, sporting an unusual black finish. The 'b' (Otsu) variant incorporated a cut-down rear fuselage and extended canopy to provide better all-round vision as a result of complaints from pilots of the Ki-61s regarding restricted rear view.

new fighter and Kawasaki was therefore instructed to adapt the Ki-61-II KAI to mount the 1119-kW (1,500-hp) Mitsubishi Ha-112-II 14-cylinder radial. The manner in which this was accomplished in less than 12 weeks amid the depredations of the growing bombing attacks was certainly one of the most extraordinary engineering feats of the war. Despite the need to fit the 1.22-m (4-ft) diameter Ha-112 engine to a fuselage only in 84 cm (33 in) wide, the match was accomplished, largely as the result of Kawasaki engineers being able to examine an imported Focke-Wulf Fw 190 in which a large radial engine had been neatly installed. The new aircraft, a converted Ki-61-II KAI redesignated the Ki-100, first flew in prototype form on 1 February 1945.

For so long an advocate of the liquid-cooled engine, Takeo Doi must have regarded his new creation with bitter irony; for all its bulk the new radial installation, as a result of lower weight and therefore reduced wing and power loadings, produced much-improved handling characteristics and only slightly reduced performance. Moreover, the radial engine had already acquired an excellent reputation for reliability. Accelerated flight tests were followed by an order to adapt all the engineless Ki-61-II KAIs, and 272 Ki-100-Ias were delivered to home-based fighter units between March and June 1945.

In service the Ki-100 was hailed by pilots and groundcrew as the best and most reliable Imperial Japanese Army fighter of the war, simple to handle even for the young, inexperienced Japanese pilots being thrown into the savage air battles over Japan in the last agonising months of the war. Apart from its role as a bomber destroyer, the Ki-100 was at least a match for the US Navy's Grumman F6F Hellcats which now flew in Japan's skies.

As soon as the Ki-100's success was established, Kawasaki started building the new aircraft from scratch, production aircraft first appearing at its Kagamigahara and Ichinomiya factories in May 1945, but heavy raids on these plants severely reduced deliveries and in July production at Ichinomiya was halted altogether.

Ki-100-Is were flown by the 5th, 17th, 111th and 244th Sentais, a total of 390 (including the 272 converted Ki-61s and 12 new aircraft produced at Ichinomiya) being delivered. One more version, the Ki-100-II, was also produced; this featured an Ha-112-IIRU radial with Ru-102 turbosupercharger, and three prototypes appeared before the end of the war prevented the aircraft from entering production.

Giving the impression of strength and sturdiness, this photo shows to good effect the mating of the large-diameter cowling with the narrow contours of the fuselage to incorporate the new radial engine, and the wide track of the Ki-100's undercarriage.

The 5th Sentai based at Kiyosu airfield began converting from the Ki-45 Toryu in May 1945. Units receiving the Ki-100 had no working-up time before commencing operational flying, but nevertheless it was popular with both pilots and ground crews.

Gloster Meteor

The outcome of Project Rampage – the Ministry of Supply's codename covering its three-year plan to introduce a jet-propelled aircraft – the Gloster Meteor was not only the first RAF combat jet fighter, but the first such Allied fighter to enter service in World War II and the only one to serve in both that war and the Korean War.

Design of the original F.9140 twin-jet fighter prototype started in January 1940 under the leadership of Gloster's chief designer, W. G. Carter, some 17 months before the first flight by the Gloster E.28/39 single-jet research aircraft – the world's first pure-jet aeroplane outside Germany. With scarcely any proven design criteria on which to base the new fighter, such a venture was particularly enterprising having regard to the desperate pressures upon the UK and its aircraft industry at that stage in the war. Reflecting the significant contribution by Frank Whittle, for long the leading British protagonist of gas turbine application to aircraft, the 12 prototypes were originally intended to be powered by 'Whittle' engines, but in the event (as a result of ever-widening interest in the development of turbojets among British engine companies) the eight unarmed prototypes which eventually materialised were powered by Rover/Power Jets W.2B/23, Power Jets W.2/500, Metropolitan Vickers MVF.2, Rolls-Royce W.2B/23, Halford (DH) H.1, Halford (DH) H.1b and Rolls-Royce W.2B/37 engines. First to fly was in fact the fifth prototype airframe F.9140H (DG206/G), powered by two Halford H.1 turbojets each giving 10.2-kN (2,300 lb) thrust, flown by Michael Daunt at Cranwell, Lincolnshire, on 5 March 1943; maximum speed of this prototype was 692 km/h (430 mph).

Already, on 8 August 1941, a contract had been awarded for a pilot production batch of 20 aircraft, to be named Meteor Mk Is. The first of these (EE2101G) was flown in January 1944, the first RAF deliveries being made to No. 616 (South Yorkshire) Squadron, commanded by Squadron Leader A. McDowall, DFM, at Culmhead on 12 July that year. Armed with four 20-mm Hispano cannon in the nose and powered by 7.5-kN (1,700-lb) thrust Rolls-Royce/Power Jets W.2B/23 Wellands, seven of these aircraft accompanied the squadron to Manston 10 days

later and flew their first combat sorties against the V-1 flying bombs on 27 July. The first such bomb to fall to a Meteor was destroyed on 4 August: not shot down, but tipped over by Flying Officer Dean's wingtip. Within six weeks No. 616 Squadron had destroyed a dozen flying bombs, and although it was quickly acknowledged that the Meteor Mk I had probably entered operational service prematurely, it had to be admitted that such service was invaluable for the acceleration of development and production. Moreover, the RAF's Meteors provided excellent experience during exercises for American B-17 crews who faced onslaughts by German Messerschmitt Me 262 jets.

The first true production Meteor F.Mk 3s (the Mk 2 with Halford/DH engines did not materialise) were delivered to No. 616 Squadron in December 1944, one flight joining the RAF 2nd Tactical Air Force at Nijmegen the following month. Second RAF squadron to receive Meteor Mk 3s was No. 504 ('County of Nottingham') Squadron in April. There were, however, no authenticated instances of jet-versus-jet combat during World War II.

Not unnaturally, the early Meteors underwent an enormous research programme, but space precludes more than passing mention of some outstanding examples. The first Meteor Mk 1 was sent to the USA for evaluation; the sixth aircraft underwent the world's first reheat (afterburning) trials late in 1944; the 18th aircraft with Rolls-Royce RB.50 Trents and Rotol five-bladed propellers was the world's first turboprop aircraft, being flown by

A rare colour picture of a Meteor Mk 1, EE221, carrying the personal code letters HJ-W of Group Captain H. J. Wilson, commanding the RAF High Speed Flight, summer 1945. The world absolute air speed records were established by later Meteors with lengthened engine nacelles, and EE221 was employed as a flight 'hack'.

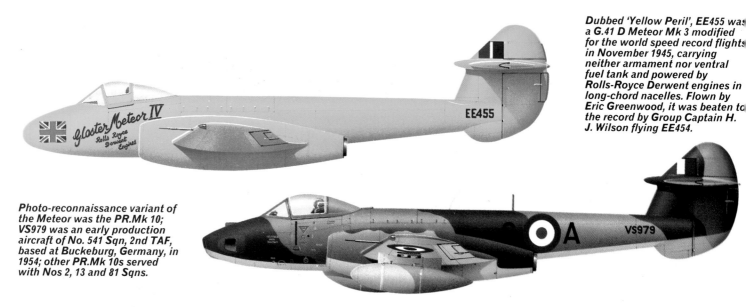

Dubbed 'Yellow Peril', EE455 was a G.41 D Meteor Mk 3 modified for the world speed record flights in November 1945, carrying neither armament nor ventral fuel tank and powered by Rolls-Royce Derwent engines in long-chord nacelles. Flown by Eric Greenwood, it was beaten to the record by Group Captain H. J. Wilson flying EE454.

Photo-reconnaissance variant of the Meteor was the PR.Mk 10; VS979 was an early production aircraft of No. 541 Sqn, 2nd TAF, based at Buckeburg, Germany, in 1954; other PR.Mk 10s served with Nos 2, 13 and 81 Sqns.

Eric Greenwood, Gloster's chief test pilot, on 20 September 1945; a fighter-reconnaissance camera nose was fitted on the ninth Meteor Mk 3; deck landing trials were performed by two Meteor Mk 3s; night-fighter AI radar was fitted in the l9th air-craft; and the first live ejection seat firings in Britain were made by Bernard Lynch of Martin-Baker from a Meteor Mk 3 on 24 July 1946. Two late production Meteor Mk 3s with long engine nacelles were used for high-speed, low-altitude trials and one of them, flown by Group Captain H. J. Wilson, established a new world absolute speed record of 976 km/h (606 mph) on 7 November 1945.

Derwent replaces Welland

As Meteor Mk 3s with Welland turbojets continued to serve with Nos 1, 56, 63, 66, 74, 92, 124, 222, 245, 257, 263, 266, 500, 504 and 616 Squadrons during 1945 and 1946, Rolls-Royce had extended the development of the centrifugal-compressor turbo-jet by replacing the reverse-flow combustion system by a straight-through configuration in the new 8.9-kN (2,000-lb) thrust Derwent 1 turbojet, this engine powering the last 195 Meteor Mk 3s. A combination of the 15,.5-kN (3,500-lb) thrust Derwent 5 in long nacelles with a much strengthened airframe led to the Meteor Mk 4, which first flew on 17 July 1945. To enhance wing stiffness without further major airframe redesign, the wings were each clipped by 87 cm (34 in) from the ninth air-craft onwards, thereby increasing the roll rate but also take-off and landing speeds. Gloster produced 539 Meteor Mk 4s for the

DG206/G was the first of the F.9/40 Meteor prototypes to fly, and was powered by Halford H.1 engines; it was flown by Michael Daunt at Cranwell South airfield on 5 March 1943. Within 16 months the Meteor was entering squadron service with the RAF.

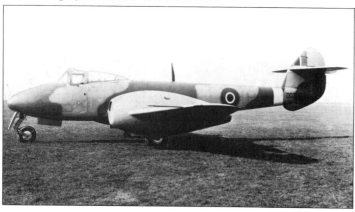

Gloster Meteor Mk III cutaway drawing key

1. Starboard detachable wingtip
2. Starboard navigation light
3. Starboard recognition light
4. Starboard aileron
5. Aileron balance tab
6. Aileron mass balance weights
7. Aileron control coupling
8. Aileron torque shaft
9. Chain sprocket
10. Cross-over control runs
11. Front spar
12. Rear spar
13. Aileron (inboard) mass balance
14. Nacelle detachable tail section
15. Jet pipe exhaust
16. Internal stabilising struts
17. Rear spar 'spectacle' frame
18. Fire extinguisher spray ring
19. Main engine mounting frame
20. Engine access panel(s)
21. Nacelle nose structure
22. Intake internal leading-edge shroud
23. Starboard engine intake
24. Windscreen de-icing spray tube
25. Reflector gunsight
26. Cellular glass bullet-proof windscreen
27. Aft-sliding cockpit canopy
28. Demolition incendiary (cockpit starboard wall)
29. RPM indicators (left and right of gunsight)
30. Pilot's seat
31. Forward fuselage top deflector skin
32. Gun wobble button
33. Control column grip
34. Main instrument panel
35. Nosewheel armoured bulkhead
36. Nose release catches (10)
37. Nosewheel jack bulkhead
38. Nose ballast weight location
39. Nosewheel mounting frames
40. Radius rod (link and jack omitted)
41. Nosewheel pivot bearings
42. Shimmy-damper/self-centring strut
43. Gun camera
44. Camera access
45. Aperture
46. Nose cone
47. Cabin cold-air intake
48. Nosewheel leg door
49. Picketing rings

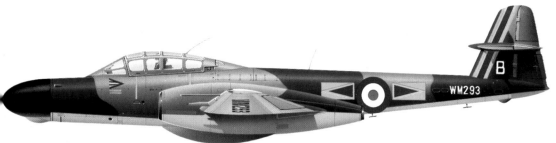

50 Tension shock absorber
51 Pivot bracket
52 Mudguard
53 Torque strut
54 Door hoop
55 Wheel fork
56 Retractable nosewheel
57 Nosewheel doors
58 Port cannon trough fairings
59 Nosewheel cover
60 Intermediate diaphragm
61 Blast tubes
62 Gun front mount rails
63 Pilot's seat pan
64 Emergency crowbar
65 Canopy de-misting silica gel cylinder
66 Bullet-proof glass rear-view cut-outs
67 Canopy track
68 Sea bulkhead
69 Entry step
70 Link ejection chutes
71 Case ejection chutes
72 20-mm Hispano Mk III cannon
73 Belt feed mechanism
74 Ammunition feed necks
75 Ammunition tanks
76 Aft glazing (magazine bay top door)
77 Leading ramp
78 Front spar bulkhead
79 Oxygen bottles (2)
80 Front spar carry-through
81 Tank bearer frames
82 Rear spar carry-through
83 Self-sealing (twin compartment) main fuel tank, capacity 165 Imp gal (750 litres) in each half

84 Fuel connector pipe
85 Return pipe
86 Drain pipes
87 Fuel filler caps
88 Tank doors (2)
89 T.R. 1143 aerial mast
90 Rear spar bulkhead (plywood face)
91 Aerial support frame
92 R.3121 (or B.C.966A) IFF installation
93 Tab control cables
94 Amplifier
95 Fire extinguisher bottles (2)
96 Elevator torque shaft
97 T.R.1143 transmitter/ receiver radio installation
98 Pneumatic system filler
99 Pneumatic system (compressed) air cylinders
100 Tab cable fairlead
101 Elevator control cable
102 Top longeron
103 Fuselage frame
104 IFF aerial
105 DR compass master unit
106 Rudder cables
107 Starboard lower longeron
108 Cable access panels (port and starboard)
109 Tail section joint
110 Rudder linkage

111 Tail ballast weight location
112 Fin spar/fuselage frame
113 Rudder tab control
114 Fin structure
115 Torpedo fairing
116 Tailplane spar/upper fin attachment plates
117 Upper fin section
118 Starboard tailplane
119 Elevator horn and mass balance

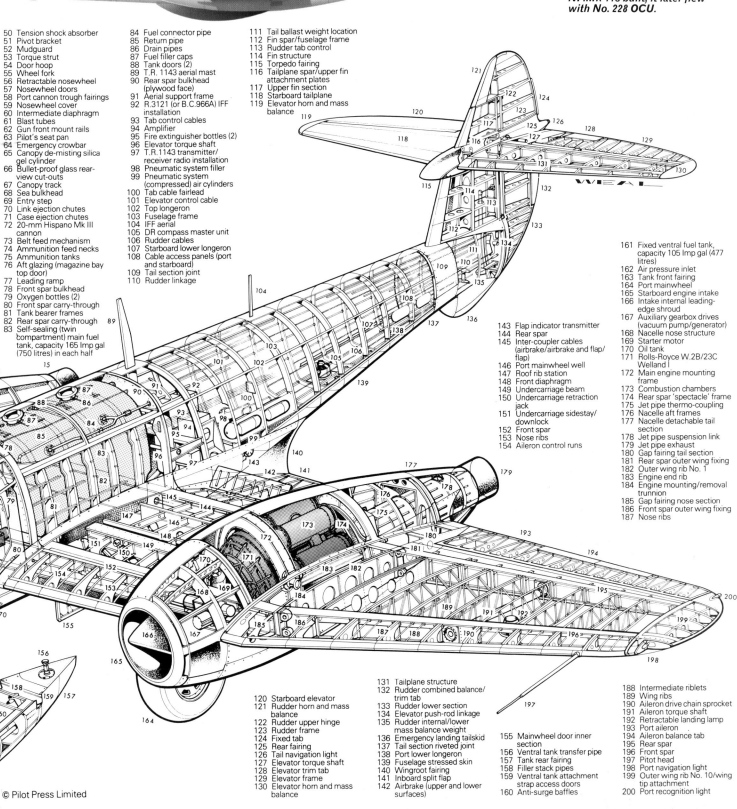

143 Flap indicator transmitter
144 Rear spar
145 Inter-coupler cables (airbrake/airbrake and flap/ flap)
146 Port mainwheel well
147 Roof rib station
148 Front diaphragm
149 Undercarriage beam
150 Undercarriage retraction jack
151 Undercarriage sidestay/ downlock
152 Front spar
153 Nose ribs
154 Aileron control runs

161 Fixed ventral fuel tank, capacity 105 Imp gal (477 litres)
162 Air pressure inlet
163 Tank front fairing
164 Port mainwheel
165 Starboard engine intake
166 Intake internal leading-edge shroud
167 Auxiliary gearbox drives (vacuum pump/generator)
168 Nacelle nose structure
169 Starter motor
170 Oil tank
171 Rolls-Royce W.2B/23C Welland I
172 Main engine mounting frame
173 Combustion chambers
174 Rear spar 'spectacle' frame
175 Jet pipe thermo-coupling
176 Nacelle aft frames
177 Nacelle detachable tail section
178 Jet pipe suspension link
179 Jet pipe exhaust
180 Gap fairing tail section
181 Rear spar outer wing fixing
182 Outer wing rib No. 1
183 Engine end rib
184 Engine mounting/removal trunnion
185 Gap fairing nose section
186 Front spar outer wing fixing
187 Nose ribs

120 Starboard elevator
121 Rudder horn and mass balance
122 Rudder upper hinge
123 Rudder frame
124 Fixed tab
125 Rear fairing
126 Tail navigation light
127 Elevator torque shaft
128 Elevator trim tab
129 Elevator frame
130 Elevator horn and mass balance

131 Tailplane structure
132 Rudder combined balance/ trim tab
133 Rudder lower section
134 Elevator push-rod linkage
135 Elevator internal/lower mass balance weight
136 Emergency landing tailskid
137 Tail section riveted joint
138 Port lower longeron
139 Fuselage stressed skin
140 Wingroot fairing
141 Inboard split flap
142 Airbrake (upper and lower surfaces)

155 Mainwheel door inner section
156 Ventral tank transfer pipe
157 Tank rear fairing
158 Filler stack pipes
159 Ventral tank attachment strap access doors
160 Anti-surge baffles

188 Intermediate riblets
189 Wing ribs
190 Aileron drive chain sprocket
191 Aileron torque shaft
192 Retractable landing lamp
193 Port aileron
194 Aileron balance tab
195 Rear spar
196 Front spar
197 Pitot head
198 Port navigation light
199 Outer wing rib No. 10/wing tip attachment
200 Port recognition light

Gloster Meteor

Specification
Gloster Meteor F.Mk 8
Type: single-seat interceptor fighter
Powerplant: two 15.5-kN (3,500-lb) thrust Rolls-Royce
Derwent 8 turbojets
Performance: maximum speed 953 km/h (592 mph) at
sea level, and 885 km/h (550 mph) at 9145 m (30,000 ft);
climb to 9180 m (30,000 ft) in 6 minutes 30 seconds;
service ceiling 13410 m (44,000 ft); range without wing
drop tanks 1111 km (690 miles)
Weights: empty 4846 kg (10,684 lb); maximum take-off
7122 kg (15,700 lb)
Dimensions: span 11.33 m (37 ft 2 in); length 13.59 m
(44 ft 7 in); height 3.96 m (13 ft 0 in); wing area 32.515 m²
(350.0 sq ft)
Armament: four 20-mm Hispano cannon in the nose
with 195 rounds per gun

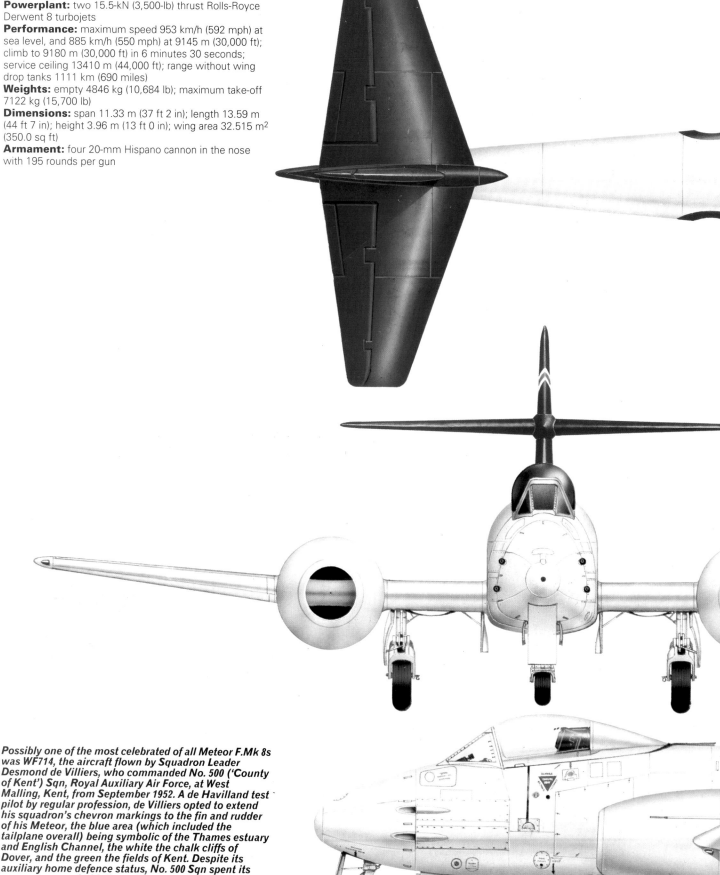

*Possibly one of the most celebrated of all Meteor F.Mk 8s
was WF714, the aircraft flown by Squadron Leader
Desmond de Villiers, who commanded No. 500 ('County
of Kent') Sqn, Royal Auxiliary Air Force, at West
Malling, Kent, from September 1952. A de Havilland test
pilot by regular profession, de Villiers opted to extend
his squadron's chevron markings to the fin and rudder
of his Meteor, the blue area (which included the
tailplane overall) being symbolic of the Thames estuary
and English Channel, the white the chalk cliffs of
Dover, and the green the fields of Kent. Despite its
auxiliary home defence status, No. 500 Sqn spent its
summer camps in Malta and Germany between 1953
and 1956. In common with all auxiliary fighter
squadrons, it fell victim to defence cuts and was
disbanded in 1957.*

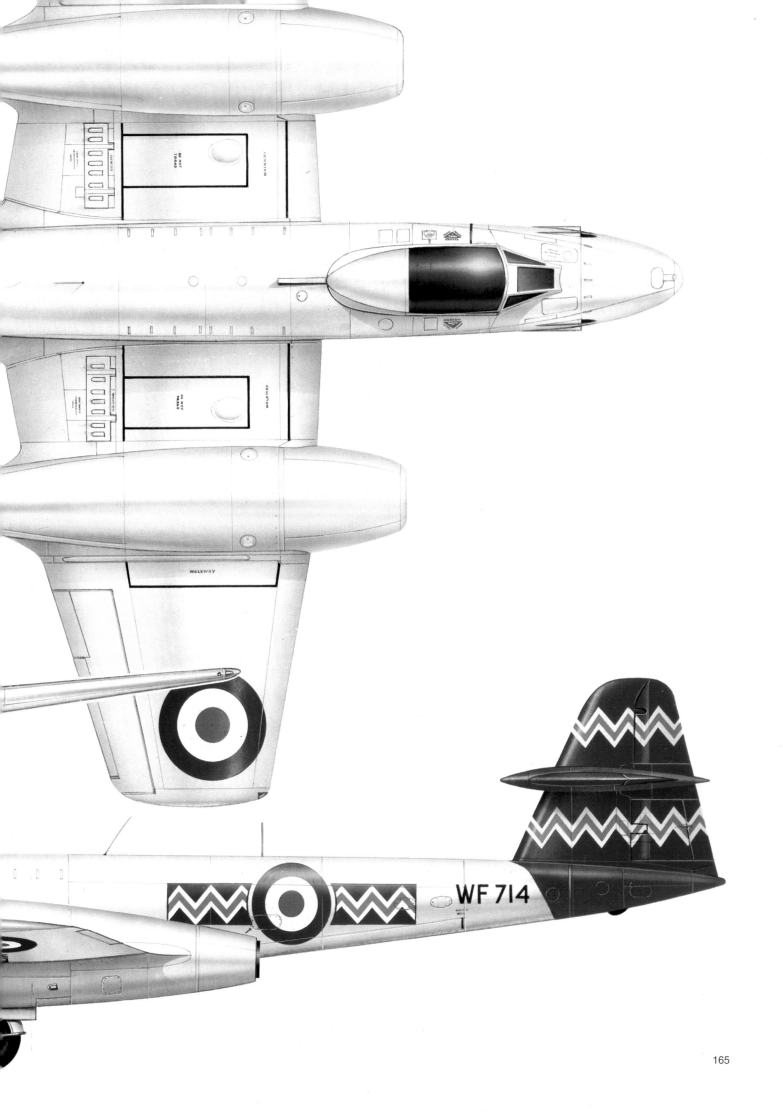

WF 714

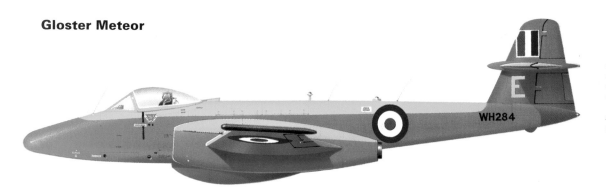

In the twilight of their career many Meteors were converted to become target drones for use at missile ranges; the Meteor U.Mk 16, WH284, a converted AWA-built Mk 8, was delivered to Llanbedr in June 1960.

RAF and Sir W. G. Armstrong Whitworth Aircraft Ltd (AWA), which joined the Meteor programme in 1946, built a further 44. This version was flown by Nos 19, 43, 501, 600, 610, 611 and 615 Squadrons, in addition to those squadrons above equipped with Meteor Mk 3s.

Strong sales abroad

In the year following the earlier world speed record, Meteor Mk 4s were used in a bid to raise the record further, and on 7 September 1946 Group Captain E. M. Donaldson of the RAF High Speed Flight flew EE549 at a speed of 992 km/h (616 mph). Lesser known among the numerous trials with Meteor Mk 4s was a series involving a wing span increased to 15.24 m (50 ft) and tailplane span to 6.10 m (20 ft) in a short-lived project to develop a high-altitude fighter variant. Meteor Mk 4s were sold in large numbers to Argentina (where they were flown in action by both rebel and government forces during the short but bloody revolution of 1955), Belgium, Denmark, Egypt, France (where one was flown as a testbed with SNECMA Atar 101.B21 engines in 1952) and the Netherlands. Engines flown experimentally in British Meteor Mk 4s included the Metropolitan Vickers F.2/4 Beryl, Rolls-Royce Nenes with jet deflectors, Rolls-Royce Avon RA.2 axial-flow turbojets, and Rolls-Royce Derwent 5s and 8s with reheat. Cost of a standard, fully-armed Meteor Mk 4 in 1949 was quoted at £30,468.

There followed the Meteor Mk 5 reconnaissance fighter, in which a nose camera and two vertical cameras aft of the fuselage fuel tank were included; the nose unit could be locked in either the forward-facing or port-facing position. A single Meteor Mk 4 (VT347) was converted as prototype but it crashed on its first flight in 1949, killing test pilot Rodney Dryland. The unbuilt Meteor Mk 6 was intended to employ a straight-tapered tail unit, which was later to feature on the Meteor Mk 8, and Derwent 7 turbojets.

The two-seat Meteor T.7 trainer incorporated a nose lengthened by 76 cm (30 in) to accommodate a second seat in tandem under a single side-hinging canopy; full dual control was included but all armament was omitted. An 818-litre (180-Imp gal) ventral fuel tank was carried as standard. First flight by the prototype was made on 19 March 1948, and it was followed by 640 production aircraft on MoS contracts. Apart from serving on every RAF fighter squadron, Meteor Mk 7s equipped Nos 5, 8 and 12 FTS, Nos 202, 203, 205, 206, 207, 208, 209, 210, 211, 213 and 215 AFS, and Nos 226, 228, 229 and 231 OCU, not to mention almost every station flight in the RAF. They also served with Nos 702 and 759 Squadrons of the Fleet Air Arm. Early aircraft were powered by Derwent 5s but towards the end of production the Derwent 8 was introduced (together with the Meteor Mk 8's tail configuration and spring tab ailerons), giving rise to the spurious 'Mk 7½' appellation. Meteor Mk 7s were sold abroad to Belgium, Brazil, Denmark, Egypt, France, Israel, the Netherlands, Sweden and Syria; the price quoted for the Meteor Mk 7 to foreign buyers in 1950 was £31,540.

Soldiering on with the RAF

For all its pioneering work, the Meteor was by the end of 1947 no longer able to maintain its lead over fighters about to enter service elsewhere, and the Meteor Mk 8 was an attempt to squeeze the utmost performance out of the airframe without

Vic formation of Armstrong-Whitworth Meteor NF.Mk 14s of No. 152 (Fighter) Sqn based at Wattisham and Stradishall between 1954 and 1958. Fuselage bars were yellow, white and green, outlined in dark blue.

extensive modification; the Derwent 8, moreover, gave no appreciable thrust increase and the adoption of a straight-tapered, vertical tail only marginally raised the buffet threshold. Only when the diameter of the nacelle intake apertures was enlarged by 11.43 cm (4½ in) was there any improvement in performance, the 91-kg (200-lb) thrust increase from each engine raising the top speed by about 6.4 km/h (4 mph).

Forced to stay on

The politically-motivated cutback in aeronautical research during 1946-48 had created a vacuum in follow-up RAF fighter equipment, so that no alternative remained but to retain the Meteor and de Havilland Vampire fighters in service well into the 1950s. The first of 1,090 Meteor Mk 8s for the RAF reached the service on 10 December 1949, thereafter serving with Nos 1, 19, 34, 41, 43, 54, 56, 63, 64, 65, 66, 72, 74,92, 111, 222, 245, 247, 257, 263, 500, 504, 600, 601, 604, 609, 610, 611, 615 and 616 Squadrons. None of these squadrons served operationally in the Korean War that started in 1950. Instead it fell to No. 77 Squadron of the Royal Australian Air Force to take its place alongside the United Nations forces in Korea, and after some months flying North American P-51s in combat the squadron re-equipped with Meteor Mk 8s shipped from the UK early in 1951. The first combat sortie was flown on 29 July, but it was not until 29 August that the Meteor's guns were fired at Mikoyan-Gurevich MiG-15s when an Australian pilot was shot down. Continued losses resulted in the Meteor's role being changed to that of escorting Boeing B-29 bombers, and on 1 December Flying Officer B. Gogerely scored the Meteor's first MiG-15 kill (albeit in a combat which cost three Meteors). Early in 1952 the Meteor's task was changed once more, to that of ground attack, armed with eight 27-kg (60-lb) rockets. By the end of the Korean War No. 77 Squadron had flown 18,872 sorties (including those in P-51s), lost 32 pilots in Meteors and destroyed three MiG-15s.

While the Australians had been discharging their rockets over Korea, Gloster had produced a ground attack version of the Meteor Mk 8 as a private venture (known as the G.44 Reaper). Although this could carry up to 24 27-kg (60-lb) rockets or two 454-kg (1,000-lb) bombs, the Meteor remained firmly committed to the air combat role, and remained so until finally replaced by the Hawker Hunter in 1954-55.

The Meteor Mk 8 sold well among foreign air forces: Brazil, Denmark, Egypt, Israel, the Netherlands and Syria all placed orders for the version, which also was selected for licence-production by Avions Fairey in Belgium and Fokker in the Netherlands. Export purchase price was quoted at £42,810 in 1952.

At home, Meteor Mk 8s underwent numerous experiments. Among the interesting powerplant trial installations were those with a 42.2-kN (9,500-lb) thrust Armstrong Siddeley Screamer rocket engine, a pair of wingtip-mounted Rolls-Royce Soar lightweight expendable turbojets, and a pair of 33.8-kN (7,600-lb) thrust Armstrong Siddeley Sapphire turbojets (in the last configuration the Meteor established a number of time-to-height

records). Another Meteor Mk 8 was modified to include an additional cockpit for a prone pilot in the extreme nose, while one aircraft featured a Rolls-Royce RB.108 lift turbojet mounted vertically in the ammunition bay as part of the preparations for the Short SC.1 vertical take-off flying programme. One of the many Rolls-Royce test aircraft was a Meteor Mk 8 fitted with a thrust reverser on its port Derwent 8. Meteor Mk 8s in service with No. 245 (Fighter) Squadron were flown on flight refuelling trials. A proposed but unbuilt version of the Meteor featured no fewer than 12 RB.108 lift engines in two greatly enlarged nacelles.

Profiting from the design experience with the ill-fated Meteor Mk 5, Gloster introduced the fighter reconnaissance Meteor Mk 9 with gun armament retained and a single nose-mounted F.24 camera; ventral and underwing fuel tanks were fitted as standard. The prototype flew on 22 March 1950 and was followed by 126 production examples; they were flown by Nos 2, 8, 79, 208 and 541 Squadrons, and by No. 226 OCU and No. 1417 Flight with the RAF, and 12 ex-Air Ministry aircraft were refurbished by Flight Refuelling Ltd for sale to Ecuador in 1954-55 (remaining in service until the 1970s). Syria also purchased two ex-RAF Meteor Mk 9s in the mid-1950s, at the same time that seven similar aircraft were sold to Israel.

Photo-reconnaissance variants

The Meteor PR.10 photo-reconnaissance aircraft was developed to replace the Spitfire Mk XIX, which had survived with the RAF since World War II. Retaining the original long-span wings of the Meteor Mk 3 for improved high-altitude performance, the Meteor Mk 10 prototype was flown on 29 March 1950, and featured two vertical cameras in the fuselage aft of the main fuel tank, and the FR.9's nose camera installation. The original Meteor Mk 4 tail assembly was also retained. Some 59 production aircraft were delivered to the RAF in 1951-52, and

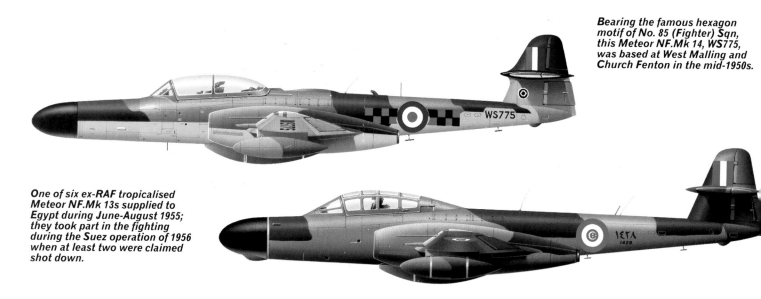

Bearing the famous hexagon motif of No. 85 (Fighter) Sqn, this Meteor NF.Mk 14, WS775, was based at West Malling and Church Fenton in the mid-1950s.

One of six ex-RAF tropicalised Meteor NF.Mk 13s supplied to Egypt during June-August 1955; they took part in the fighting during the Suez operation of 1956 when at least two were claimed shot down.

served with Nos 2, 13, 81 and 541 Squadrons; none was sold abroad. One aircraft was experimentally fitted with a Meteor Mk 7 two-seat nose section.

The remaining production versions of the Meteor were all two-seat night-fighters, and all were built by AWA. The Meteor Mk 11 was developed following the failure by the British Air Staff to agree on a realistic night-fighter requirement in 1946-47 and on account of long delays in the development of the Gloster Javelin. In essence, the Meteor NF.11 was a Meteor Mk 7 with nose AI radar (AI Mk 10, otherwise SCR-720), four 20-mm guns in the outboard sections of the long-span wings, and the rear cockpit's dual controls replaced by the navigator/radar operator's displays. The Meteor Mk 8's straight-tapered tail was adopted and 16.4-kN (3,700-lb) thrust Derwent 8s with large intake apertures were fitted. The first true prototype was flown by Squadron Leader E. G. Franklin on 31 May 1950 and was followed by 335 production aircraft between 1951 and 1954. First RAF squadron to receive the NF.11 was No. 85; others to fly it were Nos 5, 11, 29, 68, 87, 96, 125, 141, 151, 219, 256 and 264 Squadrons. Denmark bought 20 new-build aircraft and ex-RAF machines were sold to Belgium (12) and France (32). Overseas prices varied widely according to equipment fitted, but the Danish price of £60,906, quoted in 1953, was representative. Meteor Mk 11s were used in contemporary de Havilland Fireflash, de Havilland Firestreak and Vickers Blue Boar weapon systems trials on the various service and ministry ranges in the UK and Australia.

Late model night-fighters

The Meteor NF.12 with American APS-21 AI radar in a nose lengthened by 43.2 cm (17 in) was flown on 21 April 1953. Some 97 production aircraft with 16.9-kN (3,800-lb) thrust Derwent 9s were produced for service with Nos 25, 33. 46, 64, 72, 85, 152, 153 and 264 Squadrons. None was sold abroad. This version was in fact preceded by the Meteor NF.13, which was a tropicalised version of the Meteor Mk 11 and first flew on 23 December 1952; only 40 were produced and these served with Nos 39 and 219 Squadrons in the Middle East, six of them being subsequently sold to Egypt.

The Meteor NF.14, which flew on 23 October 1953, featured a fully transparent two-piece blown canopy, and had a maximum speed of 927 km/h (576 mph). A total of 100 production aircraft was built, these aircraft serving with Nos 25, 33, 46, 60, 64, 72, 85, 96, 152, 153, 165, 213 and 264 Squadrons. The last aircraft was delivered to the RAF on 26 May 1955, and the last opera-

tional sortie by an RAF Meteor was flown in an NF.14 of No. 60 Squadron at Tengah, Singapore, in September 1961. A lesser known version was the Meteor NF(T).14 night-fighter trainer.

Considerable conversion of redundant Meteors was undertaken during the 1950s, of which the Meteor TT.Mk 20 involved Meteor NF.14s modified for the target-towing task; Meteor U.15s and U.16s were unmanned target drone conversions of 'single-seat' Meteor Mk 4s and Mk 8s respectively; Meteor U.17s, U.18s and U.19s were similar conversions of two-seat Meteor NF.11s, NF.12s and NF.14s. Meteor U.21s and U.21As were conversions of Meteor Mk 8s undertaken for the RAAF.

For all its maligned antiquity during the 1950s, the Meteor will nevertheless be remembered by countless pilots with affection as the aeroplane that spanned that exciting period between the propeller and jet. It had, moreover, provided the means by which the RAF led the world in fighter aircraft for two short years – a lead that was squandered through no fault of the service or its aircraft. Total Meteor production was 3,875 aircraft.

Gloster G.41/G.43/G.47 Meteor variants

Gloster F.9/40: eight prototypes, various engines (DG202/209)

Gloster G.41A Meteor F.1: 20 pre-production aircraft; Rolls-Royce Welland engines (EE210/229)

Gloster Meteor 2: proposed DH Goblin-powered version, not built

Gloster Meteor F.3: 210 production fighters; first 15 (G.41C) with Welland I; next 180 (G.41D) with Derwent 1 engines in short nacelles; final 15 (G.41E) with Derwent 1 in long nacelles (batches between EE230 and EE493)

Gloster Meteor F.4: 539 fighters built by Gloster and 44 by AWA; first few aircraft with long-span wings (G.41F), remainder with short-span wings (G.41G); Derwent 5 engines (batches in EE, RA, VT, VW and VZ serial ranges); sold abroad to Argentina (100), Belgium (48), Denmark (20), Egypt (12), France (2), the Netherlands (65); two aircraft converted to Mk 7s. and 92 converted to U.15s

Gloster Meteor FR.5 (G.41H): one prototype (VT347) converted from Mk 4

Gloster Meteor F.6 (G.41J): unbuilt project with Derwent 7 engines

Gloster Meteor F.8 (G.41K): 1,090 single-seat fighters built by Gloster and AWA; Derwent 8 engines; straight tapered vertical tail (batches in VZ, WA, WB, WE, WF, WH, WK, and WL serial ranges) sold abroad to Australia (89). Belgium (240, including licence-built in Belgium and the Netherlands), Brazil (60), Denmark (20). Egypt (19), Israel (11),

the Netherlands (160, including 155 built by Fokker), Syria (19)

Gloster Meteor FR.9 (G.41L): 126 Gloster-built reconnaissance fighters; Derwent 8 engines (batches in VW, VZ, WB, WH, WL and WX serial ranges): sold abroad to Ecuador (12), Israel (7), Syria (2)

Gloster Meteor PR.10 (G.41M): 59 Gloster-built photo-reconnaissance aircraft; Derwent 8 engines (VS968/987, VW376/379, VZ620, WB153/181, WH569/573)

Gloster Meteor NF.11 (G.47): three prototypes (WA540, WA547 and WB543); nose AI radar and four 20-mm wing guns; built by AWA

Gloster Meteor NF.11 (G.47): 335 night-fighters built by AWA; four used for Fireflash missile trials; sold abroad to Belgium (12) Denmark (20). France (32)

Gloster Meteor NF.12 (G.47): 97 night-fighters built by AWA (WS590/639, WS658/700, WS715/721)

Gloster Meteor NF.13 (G.47): 40 tropicalised night fighters built by AWA (WM308/341, WM362/367); sold abroad to Egypt (6). France (2), Israel (6). Syria (6)

Gloster Meteor NF.14 (G.47): 100 night-fighters built by AWA (WS722/700, WS774/812, WS827/848); sold abroad to France (1)

Gloster Meteor U.15: 92 Meteor Mk 4s converted to target drones for use by MoA, RAF, RAAF, RAN and RN missile echelons Gloster Meteor U.16: 108 Meteor Mk 8s converted to target drones

Gloster Meteor U.17, U.18, U.19: ad hoc conversion of Meteors NF.11, NF.12 and NF.14 to target drones

Gloster Meteor U.21 and U.21A: target drone conversions of Meteor Mk 8s for RAAF Gloster Meteor TT.20: target-tug conversions of Meteor NF.11 for RAF and RN; also sold to Denmark, Sweden and West Germany

The Mighty Mustang

The greatness of the Mustang is beyond question: the British-inspired, American-built World War II fighter proved itself a potent and versatile weapon operating in roles as varied as long-range escort and close air support. It was a pilot's dream: handy, hard-hitting and very tough, with first-class performance under all combat conditions.

The North American P-51 Mustang was one of very, very few aircraft that fought in World War II to be designed after the conflict had begun. It was purely a private venture (not built to any official US specification), and was carried through with incredible speed for a foreign customer who doubted the company could build a good fighter at all. And when it was given a different engine and even greater fuel capacity, it flew missions far longer than any fighter had ever flown before.

Reichsmarschall Hermann Goering once claimed no enemy bomber would ever fly over Berlin. By 1944 he had got used to intrusions by the Allied bombers, but he was shattered when the US Army Air Force flew fighters all the way to Berlin, and even to Poland and Czechoslovakia. He is reported to have said, "When I saw those Mustangs over Berlin, I knew that the war was lost."

North American Aviation was one of the youngest of the major planemakers; it set up shop in 1934, with just 75 employees. A year later it flew the prototype of what became the world's No. 1 trainer, the AT-6 or Harvard, of which over 20,000 were eventually built. In 1938 this attracted the attention of the British, who placed big orders. Soon after the outbreak of war, in September 1939, the British Purchasing Commission asked NAA whether it could build an American fighter, the Curtiss P-40, for the RAF. The P-40 was a second-rate fighter, and NAA's immediate response was that it had long wanted to build a really first-class fighter and was eager to do so for the UK. The US Army had more new fighter prototypes than it wanted, and was quite uninterested.

In retrospect it seems obvious that the British should have signed a contract then and there, stipulating a US-made Rolls-Royce Merlin engine which was already being planned. Instead the Commission found every possible reason for not letting NAA go ahead. Finally, in late April 1940, it agreed, on the strict understanding that the company wasted $15,000 buying P-40 wind-tunnel data from Curtiss. NAA bought the information, but was far too busy designing the new fighter to waste time looking at it. The contract with Britain, for 320 N.A.73 fighters, was signed on 29 May.

NAA undertook to have the prototype ready in an incredible four months. It beat this target, rolling the N.A.73X out into the Los Angeles sunshine after 102 days. But Allison, suppliers of the 858-kW (1,150-hp) V-1710 engine, were 20 days late with delivery and test pilot Vance Breese finally flew the trim unpainted ship on 26 October.

The new American pursuit was a sleek all-metal stressed-skin machine like the Messerschmitt, but it was considerably larger – about the same size as the old fabric-covered Hurricane. Its aerodynamics were much newer than either. It had one of the new supposedly laminar flow wings with the thickest part much further back than usual. The liquid-cooled engine had its coolant radiator far back under the rear fuselage in the most efficient position, and it was installed in a long profiled duct with a variable-exit shutter so that, instead of causing drag, the heated air could behave like a jet-propulsion unit and help push the fighter along. This leaves the question of why the N.A.73X was so much larger than the Bf 109: it was so that it could carry more fuel, far more than in any European single-engined fighter.

More fuel means not only a bigger aircraft but more weight, and the N.A.73X could have been cumbersome and ineffective. In fact, as Breese soon discovered, it was an absolute winner. It reached 615 km/h (382 mph), much faster than any of the European fighters,

The first of the many: the trim N.A.73X prototype, photographed immediately the Allison engine had been installed and before any markings had been applied. It subsequently received military rudder stripes and civil registration NX19998.

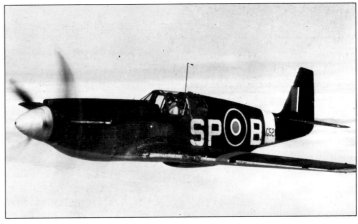

A standard Mustang I (AG528) after arduous service at low level with RAF Army Co-operation Command in 1942-43. One of the 0.5-in (12.7-mm) guns can be seen projecting from the lower front of the cowling.

including even the smaller Supermarine Spitfire, which carried less than half as much fuel. It had devastating armament: four heavy 12.7-mm (0.5-in) guns and four 7.62-mm (0.3-in) guns.

World beater

On the fifth flight Paul Balfour switched the fuel incorrectly, and the engine cut at a crucial moment: the aircraft arrived on the ground upside down and was wrecked, but that was of little consequence. The RAF order for 320 was soon followed by another 300, and the first Mustang I reached Liverpool on 24 October 1941.

With full military load the RAF found the Mustang still reached 603 km/h (375 mph), just 56 km/h (35 mph) faster than a Spitfire V. The Mustang's only shortcoming was that the Allison engine's power faded rapidly as the Mustang climbed, so that above 4572 m (15,000 ft) it was little better than an Allison-engined P-40. But low down it was a world-beater, and by 1942 it was serving with Army Co-operation Command and the Royal Canadian Air Force. It did well on low-level offensive sweeps over Nazi-held Europe, and in October 1942 some RAF Mustangs shot up targets on the Dortmund-Ems canal to become the first British single-engined aircraft to fly over Germany in World War II.

At the start of the N.A.73 programme NAA had been forced to agree to supply two early examples to the US Army at no cost, and Wright Field duly received the fourth and the tenth off the line. The test team tried to be unimpressed by this unwanted 'foreign' machine, but the results were so good that the new fighter was soon on US Army contracts. The first orders comprised 150 P-51s, with four 20-mm cannon; 500 A-36A dive-bombers with six 12.7-mm (0.5-in) guns and two 227-kg (500-lb) bombs (and delivered with dive-brakes which later were wired inoperative); and 310 P-51As with just the four 12.7-mm (0.5-in) wing guns. In 1943 the A-36A was wreaking havoc in the hands of the Army Air Force in Sicily and southern Italy. At first the name Apache was used, but this was soon changed to the British name. Some of the very first in the US Army service were examples of the cannon-armed P-51-1 (converted P-51) designated F-6A, for photo-reconnaissance.

New engine, new power

It seems strange that the idea of putting a high-altitude Merlin into this superb airframe should not have occurred at the outset, and certainly as soon as the need had been shown by tests in Britain in 1941. Yet it was not until well into 1942 that Ron Harker, Rolls-Royce test pilot and an RAF flight lieutenant, did a work-out in a Mustang and immediately wrote a recommendation for the Merlin 61. The Rolls performance engineers calculated this would give a speed of 695 km/h (432 mph) at 7772 m (25,500 ft). Meanwhile Lt-Col. Tommy Hitchcock, US Air Attaché in London, had likewise sug-

The P-51 was swiftly moved to the war zones as soon as it was available. These 31st Fighter Group aircraft are seen over Italy, one of the many theatres in which the aircraft served. No enemy fighter could match its mix of altitude performance and speed.

North American P-51 Mustang cutaway key:

1 Plastic (Phenol fibre) rudder trim tab
2 Rudder frame (fabric covered)
3 Rudder balance
4 Fin front spar
5 Fin structure
6 Access panel
7 Rudder trim-tab actuating drum
8 Rudder trim-tab control link
9 Rear navigation light
10 Rudder metal bottom section
11 Elevator plywood trim tab
12 Starboard elevator frame
13 Elevator balance weight
14 Starboard tailplane structure
15 Reinforced bracket (rear steering stresses)
16 Rudder operating horn forging
17 Elevator operating horns
18 Tab control turnbuckles
19 Fin front spar/fuselage attachment
20 Port elevator tab
21 Fabric-covered elevator
22 Elevator balance weight
23 Port tailplane
24 Tab control drum
25 Fin root fairing
26 Elevator cables
27 Tab control access panels
28 Tailwheel steering mechanism
29 Tailwheel
30 Tailwheel leg assembly
31 Forward-retracting steerable tailwheel
32 Tailwheel doors
33 Lifting tube
34 Fuselage aft bulkhead/break point
35 Fuselage break point
36 Control cable pulley brackets
37 Fuselage frames
38 Oxygen bottles
39 Cooling-air exit flap actuating mechanism
40 Rudder cables
41 Fuselage lower longeron
42 Rear tunnel
43 Cooling-air exit flap
44 Coolant radiator assembly
45 Radio and equipment shelf
46 Power supply pack
47 Fuselage upper longeron
48 Radio bay aft bulkhead (plywood)
49 Fuselage stringers
50 SCR-695 radio transmitter-receiver (on upper sliding shelf)
51 Whip aerial
52 Junction box
53 Cockpit aft glazing
54 Canopy track
55 SCR-552 radio transmitter-receiver
56 Battery installation
57 Radiator/supercharger coolant pipes
58 Radiator forward air duct
59 Coolant header tank/radiator pipe
60 Coolant radiator ventral access cover

61 Oil-cooler air inlet door
62 Oil radiator
63 Oil pipes
64 Flap control linkage
65 Wing rear spar/fuselage attachment bracket
66 Crash pylon structure
67 Aileron control linkage
68 Hydraulic hand pump
69 Radio control boxes
70 Pilot's seat
71 Seat suspension frame
72 Pilot's head/back armour
73 Rearward-sliding clear-vision canopy
74 External rear-view mirror
75 Ring and bead gunsight
76 Bullet-proof windshield
77 Gyro gunsight
78 Engine controls
79 Signal-pistol discharge tube
80 Circuit-breaker panel
81 Oxygen regulator
82 Pilot's footrest and seat mounting bracket
83 Control linkage
84 Rudder pedal
85 Tailwheel lock control
86 Wing centre-section
87 Hydraulic reservoir
88 Port wing fuel tank filler point
89 Port Browning 0.5-in guns
90 Ammunition feed chutes
91 Gun-bay access door (raised)
92 Ammunition box troughs
93 Aileron control cables
94 Flap lower skin (Alclad)
95 Aileron profile (internal aerodynamic balance diaphragm)
96 Aileron control drum and mounting bracket
97 Aileron trim-tab control drum
98 Aileron plastic (Phenol fibre trim tab)
99 Port aileron assembly
100 Wing skinning
101 Outer section sub-assembly
102 Port navigation light
103 Port wingtip
104 Leading-edge skin
105 Landing lamp
106 Weapons/stores pylon
107 500 lb (227 kg) bomb
108 Gun ports
109 Gun barrels
110 Detachable cowling panels
111 Firewall/integral armour
112 Oil tank
113 Oil pipes
114 Upper longeron/engine mount attachment
115 Oil-tank metal retaining straps
116 Carburettor
117 Engine bearer assembly

118 Cowling panel frames
119 Engine aftercooler
120 Engine leads
121 1,520 hp Packard V-1650 (R-R Merlin) twelve-cylinder liquid-cooled engine
122 Exhaust fairing panel
123 Stub exhausts
124 Magneto
125 Coolant pipes
126 Cowling forward frame
127 Coolant header tank
128 Armour plate
129 Propeller hub
130 Spinner
131 Hamilton Standard Hydromatic propeller
132 Carburettor air intake, integral with (133)
133 Engine-mount front-frame assembly
134 Intake trunk
135 Engine-mount reinforcing tie
136 Hand-crank starter
137 Carburettor trunk vibration-absorbing connection
138 Wing centre-section front bulkhead
139 Wing centre-section end rib
140 Starboard mainwheel well
141 Wing front spar/fuselage attachment bracket
142 Ventral air intake (radiator and oil cooler)
143 Starboard wing fuel tank
144 Fuel filler point
145 Mainwheel leg mount/pivot
146 Mainwheel leg rib cut-outs
147 Main gear fairing doors
148 Auxiliary fuel tank (plastic/pressed-paper composition, 90 gal/409 litres)
149 Auxiliary fuel tank (metal 62.5 gal/284 litres)
150 27-in smooth-contour mainwheel
151 Axle fork
152 Towing lugs
153 Landing-gear fairing
154 Main-gear shock strut
155 Blast tubes

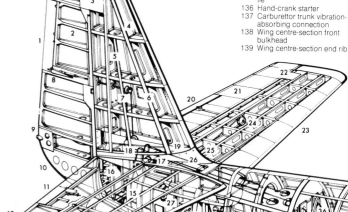

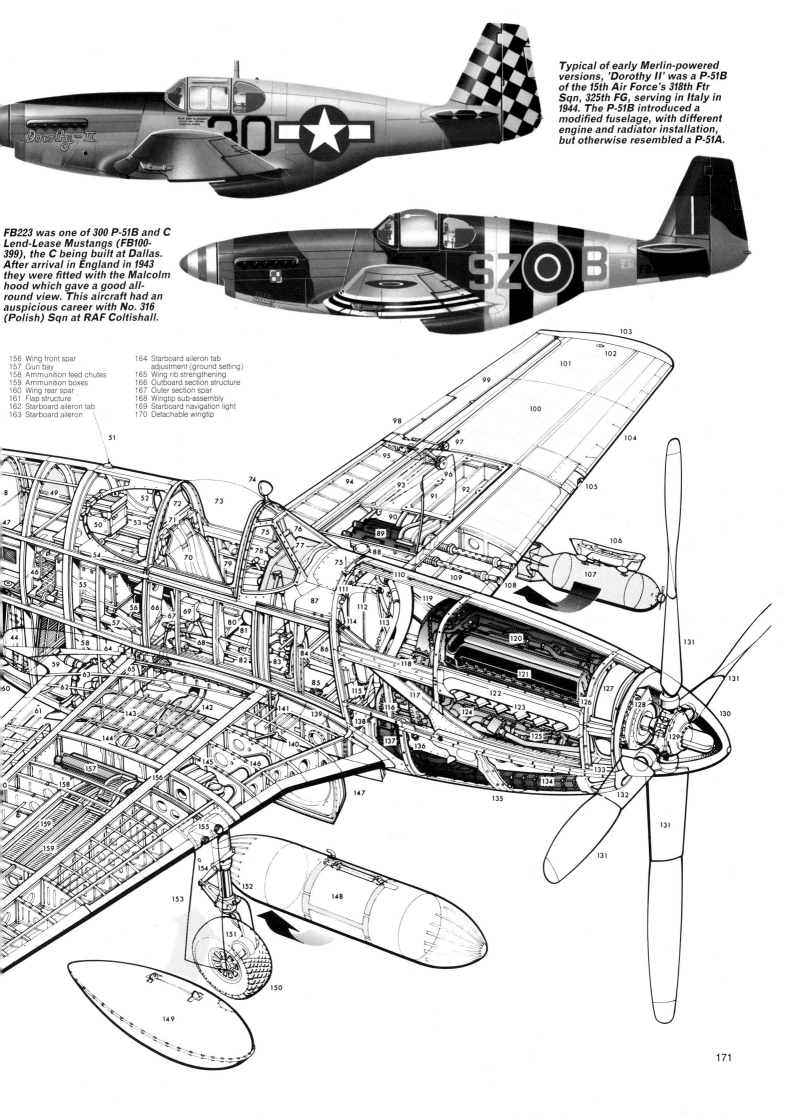

Typical of early Merlin-powered versions, 'Dorothy II' was a P-51B of the 15th Air Force's 318th Ftr Sqn, 325th FG, serving in Italy in 1944. The P-51B introduced a modified fuselage, with different engine and radiator installation, but otherwise resembled a P-51A.

FB223 was one of 300 P-51B and C Lend-Lease Mustangs (FB100-399), the C being built at Dallas. After arrival in England in 1943 they were fitted with the Malcolm hood which gave a good all-round view. This aircraft had an auspicious career with No. 316 (Polish) Sqn at RAF Coltishall.

156 Wing front spar
157 Gun bay
158 Ammunition feed chutes
159 Ammunition boxes
160 Wing rear spar
161 Flap structure
162 Starboard aileron tab
163 Starboard aileron
164 Starboard aileron tab adjustment (ground setting)
165 Wing rib strengthening
166 Outboard section structure
167 Outer section spar
168 Wingtip sub-assembly
169 Starboard navigation light
170 Detachable wingtip

The Mighty Mustang

Though it was in service only in the final 18 months of World War II, the P-51D and basically identical K (different propeller) have since hogged almost all the Mustang limelight and also accounted for most of the 15,586 of all models produced. This aircraft, USAAF 1944-13926, served with the 361st Fighter Group of the 8th Air Force, at Bottisham (England) and in late 1944 at St Dizier (France).

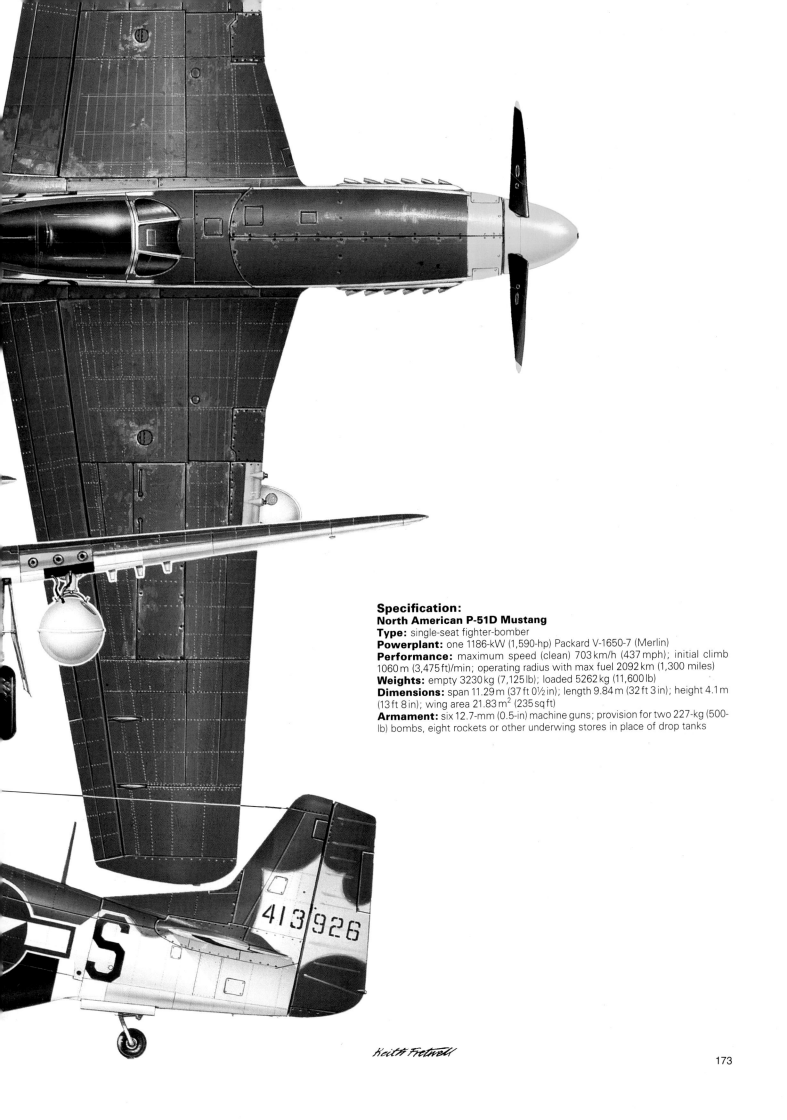

Specification:
North American P-51D Mustang
Type: single-seat fighter-bomber
Powerplant: one 1186-kW (1,590-hp) Packard V-1650-7 (Merlin)
Performance: maximum speed (clean) 703 km/h (437 mph); initial climb 1060 m (3,475 ft)/min; operating radius with max fuel 2092 km (1,300 miles)
Weights: empty 3230 kg (7,125 lb); loaded 5262 kg (11,600 lb)
Dimensions: span 11.29 m (37 ft 0½ in); length 9.84 m (32 ft 3 in); height 4.1 m (13 ft 8 in); wing area 21.83 m² (235 sq ft)
Armament: six 12.7-mm (0.5-in) machine guns; provision for two 227-kg (500-lb) bombs, eight rockets or other underwing stores in place of drop tanks

Keith Fretwell

The Mighty Mustang

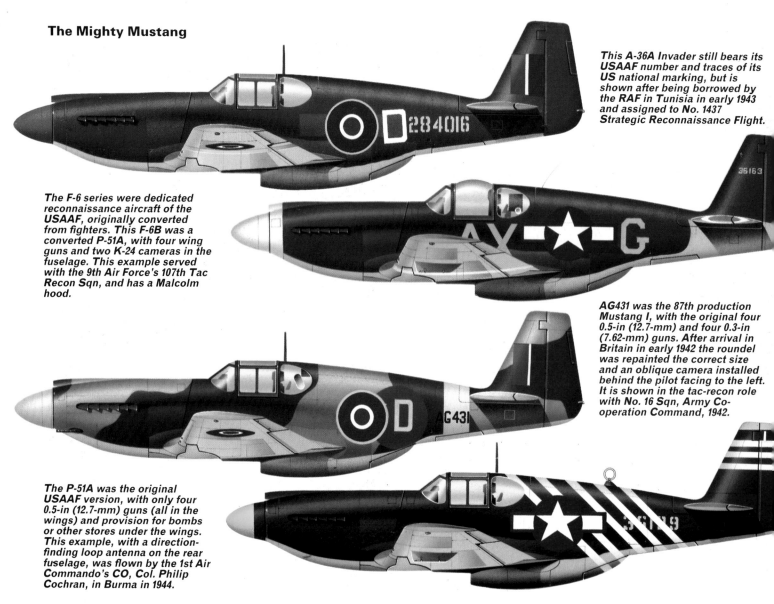

This A-36A Invader still bears its USAAF number and traces of its US national marking, but is shown after being borrowed by the RAF in Tunisia in early 1943 and assigned to No. 1437 Strategic Reconnaissance Flight.

The F-6 series were dedicated reconnaissance aircraft of the USAAF, originally converted from fighters. This F-6B was a converted P-51A, with four wing guns and two K-24 cameras in the fuselage. This example served with the 9th Air Force's 107th Tac Recon Sqn, and has a Malcolm hood.

AG431 was the 87th production Mustang I, with the original four 0.5-in (12.7-mm) and four 0.3-in (7.62-mm) guns. After arrival in Britain in early 1942 the roundel was repainted the correct size and an oblique camera installed behind the pilot facing to the left. It is shown in the tac-recon role with No. 16 Sqn, Army Co-operation Command, 1942.

The P-51A was the original USAAF version, with only four 0.5-in (12.7-mm) guns (all in the wings) and provision for bombs or other stores under the wings. This example, with a direction-finding loop antenna on the rear fuselage, was flown by the 1st Air Commando's CO, Col. Philip Cochran, in Burma in 1944.

gested installation of the Merlin, which by 1943 was in mass production at the Packard company as the V-1650. Rolls got a Merlin conversion into the air on 13 October 1942, but NAA designed the P-51B as a largely new aircraft with an optimised V-1650-7 engine installation planned for mass production. The first XP-51B flew on 30 November 1942.

The new fighter had better lines, and a new propeller with four very broad blades to turn the power into thrust at high altitudes. The carburettor inlet above the engine had vanished, but reappeared in enlarged form on the underside. The radiator was deepened, and an intercooler added in the same duct. The whole aircraft, especially the fuselage, was strengthened. It turned in the remarkable speed of 710 km/h (441 mph) at 9083 m (29,800 ft).

On test the XP-51B behaved like a different animal. Whereas the original Mustangs, then at war all over Europe, were smooth and silky, the new model was more like a sports car. It needed a bit more attention, was noisier in the cockpit, and seemed to splutter and crackle. Such things were mere first impressions; what mattered was that at height it could outperform anything in the sky. The US Army, still looking on the P-51 basically as a tactical attack aircraft, ordered 2,200 of the new model before the first flight. By mid-1943 the new Mustangs were pouring from the Los Angeles plant and from another factory built at Dallas.

Fighter escort over Germany

For more than a year the embattled US 8th Air Force in England had been seeking a superior long-range escort fighter for its heavy bombers. It sent Col. Cass Hough to try the new P-51B; he said it was terrific, but directional stability was poor. NAA switched to the P-51C at Dallas with a sliding bulged hood and six guns, and then to

the P-51D with a teardrop canopy and six guns. Soon after the start of P-51D production a dorsal fin was added to cure the directional problem. Already the Mustang was by far the world's best escort, with fuel consumption half that of the Lockheed P-38 or Republic P-47, and combat capability better than that of either (though the P-47 had eight guns). But back in the USA a massive new fighter, the Fisher XP-75, had been designed specifically to do the long-range escort job.

Col. (later General) Mark Bradley tested the XP-75 and was very worried. Something else had to be found, and quickly. He called

FX893 was a Mustang III retained for armament trials, and is seen here equipped with unusual rocket rails, each carrying a 60-lb (27-kg) RP (rocket projectile) above and below so that the single hardpoint on each wing could serve to launch two pairs of RPs. Like most RAF Mustang IIIs this aircraft was fitted with the Malcolm hood.

NAA's boss, 'Dutch' Kindelberger, the man who had finally convinced the British he could build the Mustang in the first place. Bradley asked for a big 322-litre (85-US gallon) tank to be installed behind the pilot's seat in a Merlin-Mustang, and filled. He knew this would make directional stability almost unacceptable, so that for the first hour or two the pilot would have to concentrate to keep flying the way the nose was pointing. After that time the extra tank would be empty, the pilot could switch to the usual 697 litres (184 US gallons) in the wings and forget about stability problems. With two 284-litre (75-US gallon) drop tanks under the wings, the Mustang could only just stagger into the sky, but with 1586 litres (419 US gallons), ought to go quite a distance. NAA quickly put in the extra tank, and Bradley did the testing. On the first trip he flew to Albuquerque, circled the city and flew back; he had just done the equivalent of England to Berlin!

This ability to put a first-class high-performance fighter anywhere in Europe was something that, a few months earlier, had seemed impossible. It really did mean, as Goering said, that Germany had lost the war. The build-up in P-51 strength was so rapid that over 9,000 reached combat units in 1944 – 1,377 of them being Dallas-built P-51Ks with a different propeller. Mustangs dominated the sky not only over north-west Europe and across to the advancing Russian armies, but also in northern Italy – where among many other exploits, Mustangs smashed the Pescara Dam – and in the Pacific theatre.

Pride of the Eighth

The only aircraft the Mustang could not catch were the new German jets, and even here the Mustang was far more successful than any other Allied fighter. On 7 October 1944 Lt Urban L. Drew of the 361st Fighter Group surprised two Messerschmitt Me 262s taking off and shot down both. On 25 February 1945 Mustangs of the 55th FG did the same to a whole Me 262 squadron and destroyed six. Audacious exploits by Mustangs came almost every day. On at least three occasions, twice by the US 8th AF and once by the famed CO of No. 315 (Polish) Sqn, RAF, Mustangs landed in enemy territory, picked up a shot-down comrade and flew back to base with one pilot sitting on the other.

By far the most numerous Mustangs were the P-51D and P-51K, and though they did not really get into action until 1944 the Merlin-powered models accounted for some 13,600 of the total production of all versions of 15,586. This impressive total includes 266 of the P-51D model built under licence by Commonwealth Aircraft of Melbourne.

By 1944 NAA's main development effort was on two fronts. While recognizing that it was mainly the excellence of the P-51 that stopped the development of America's shoal of unconventional fighter prototypes during World War II, there is never anything so good that it cannot be improved. The chief effort was concentrated on making the Mustang lighter, but a totally different development was the unusual N.A.-120, the Twin Mustang. First flown as the XP-82 in April 1945, the Twin Mustang comprised two lengthened Mustang fuselages joined together by a new rectangular wing centre section and tailplane. The propellers turned in opposite directions, and the main landing gears were new, there being just one under each fuselage retracting inwards. Production Twin Mustangs were post-war aircraft, designated F-82 after 1947. They included heavily-armed night fighters with SCR-720 or APS-4 radar in a large pod on the centreline. Twin Mustangs, which had Allison engines, served in Korea where their few victories – mainly at night – were among the very first to be credited to the US Air Force.

Post-war development

As for the lightweight Mustangs, these began with the XP-51F and XP-51G, moved on to the XP-51J with the Allison engine, and also yielded 555 of a planned 4,100 of the P-51H model, the fastest fighter of World War II (apart from German jets) with a speed of 784 km/h (487 mph). Though it had six 12.7-mm (0.5-in) guns, it had a structure more than 454 kg (1,000 lb) lighter than that of the P-51D, the P-51H's internal fuel capacity was actually greater. The P-51H just got into action in the Pacific in the summer of 1945.

Surprisingly, it was not the P-51H but the mass-produced P-51D

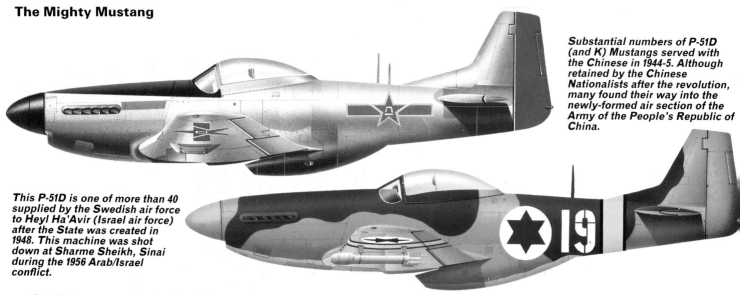

Substantial numbers of P-51D (and K) Mustangs served with the Chinese in 1944-5. Although retained by the Chinese Nationalists after the revolution, many found their way into the newly-formed air section of the Army of the People's Republic of China.

This P-51D is one of more than 40 supplied by the Swedish air force to Heyl Ha'Avir (Israel air force) after the State was created in 1948. This machine was shot down at Sharme Sheikh, Sinai during the 1956 Arab/Israel conflict.

and P-51K that were picked up by air forces all over the world in the immediate post-war era, until the Mustang was probably the world's most widely used combat aircraft. Instead of compiling a list of users, it would be simpler to make a list of the few countries which did not have at least one P-51D or P-51K squadron. Very large numbers saw action in Korea, and many were rebuilt by various companies as tandem two-seaters, either for special liaison or as dual trainers. Others emerged with various kinds of modifications as civilian racers, one of the fastest having its normal radiator replaced by long radiator pods on the wingtips. In a rather similar-looking conversion a USAF machine tested large ramjets on the wingtips, easily exceeding 805 km/h (500 mph).

In the 1950s Trans-Florida Aviation actually marketed a two-seat executive model, and this led to a long series of not only rebuilds but even completely new Mustangs in the 1960s by Cavalier Aircraft. As they were unarmed, most of the Cavaliers had even more fuel than wartime Mustangs, and in 1961 for $32,500 one could buy a variant with tandem seats, full airline avionics and 416-litre (110-US gal) tanks on the wingtips yet fully stressed for aerobatics. By the late 1960s the range of new Mustangs included several for counterinsurgent and Forward Air Control duties with the USAF, as well as lengthened Turbo Mustangs with a Rolls-Royce Dart turboprop. From the latter stemmed the Piper Enforcer of 1971, and anyone who thought that by this time the Mustang must surely have been obsolete should note, that in 1980 the Enforcer was again studied as a light attack machine for the USAF!

North American P-51 Mustang variants

N.A.73 Prototype: 1,100 hp Allison V-1710-39 engine. Provision for four 0.5 in and four 0.3 in guns but these not fitted. US civil registration NX19998 but flown with no markings except US Army style rudder insignia, 26 October 1940

N.A.73X

N.A.73 Mustang I: first production batch of 320 aircraft. 1,150 hp V-1710-F3R (export designation of V-1710-39). Four 0.5 in and four 0.303 in guns; fitted in England with vertical and oblique cameras for tac-recon duties. First aircraft (RAF serial AG345) flown 1 May 1941
N.A.73 XP-51: aircraft Nos 4 and 10 off production line, US Army Air Corps numbers 41-038, -039
N.A.83 Mustang I: second batch of 300, minor changes. RAF serials AL958/AM257 and AP164/AP263. AL975/G became prototype Merlin-Mustang (Merlin 61) and AM121, 203 and 208 became Mustang X (Merlin 65); AM106/G fitted with two 40 mm Vickers S guns

Mustang I

Mustang IA/P-51: lend-lease funds, 150 for RAF with four 20 mm guns; only 93 supplied (serials between FD438/509), rest retained for USAAF after Pearl Harbor with RAF camouflage (serials between FD418/567) and US insignia; 57 later converted to recon (F-6A, P-51-1)

P-51/Mustang IA

N.A.97 A-36: dive bomber, 1,325 hp V-1719-87. Six 0.5 in guns, two 500 lb bombs; wing-mounted dive brakes (later made inoperative). First of 500 flown September 1942, USAAF numbers 42-83663/84162 (83685 to RAF as EW998)
N.A.99 P-51A: multi-role fighter/bomber, 1,200 hp V-1710-81 (export V-1710-F20R). Four 0.5 in guns all in wings (no guns under engine), two wing hardpoints for bombs up to 500 lb or drop tanks up to 125 Imp gal; no dive brakes. Batch of 310, of which 50 being passed to RAF (FR890/939) to replace N.A.91s retained by USAAF for conversion to recon F-6A; 35 USAAF P-51A converted to recon as F-6B
N.A.101 XP-51B: NAA conversions to 1,450 hp V-1650-3, two aircraft (41-37352, 37421) from P-51 batch retained by USAAF. Guns removed

N.A.102 P-51B: productionized N.A.101 with V-1650-3, four 0.5 in wing guns; 400 built at Inglewood 1943 (USAAF from 42-106429)

P-51B, C

N.A.103 P-51C: as N.A.102 but built at new Dallas plant as P-51C-1-NT and subsequent blocks eventually totalling 1,350
N.A.104 P-51B: with wing hardpoints rated at 1,000 lb, and from P-51B-7 onwards with 70.7 Imp gal fuselage tank; total 1,588 including 25 to RAF as Mustang III (FB100/124)
N.A.105: seven experimental aircraft with completely redesigned airframes to reduce weight and increase performance, built 1944. First five designed for V-1650-3, actually built with 1,695 hp V-1650-7, four guns; first three only to this standard (USAAF XP-51F, 43-43332/43334,

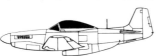

P-51F

one to RAF as FR409) final pair fitted with six guns, more fuel and 1,910 hp RR-built Merlin 145M and British five-blade propellers (USAAF XP-51G, 43-43335/43336, one to RAF as FR410); last two airframes completed with 1,720 hp Allison V-1710-119 as XP-51J (44-76027/76028)

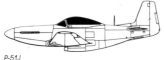

P-51J

N.A.106: first two prototypes of **P-51D** with six wing guns, cut-down rear fuselage and sliding teardrop canopy; taken from P-51B-10-NA (Inglewood) line (USAAF 42-106539/106540)
N.A.109: first production P-51D order, 2,500 aircraft with 1,695 hp V-1650-7, six guns, and from late in D-5 block with added dorsal fin. Some early aircraft retained folding canopy and Dash-3 engine, most later converted, and all with 70 7-gal rear fuselage tank

P-51D, K

N.A.110 P-51D: 100 shipped in kit form to CAC, Melbourne, for assembly with various Australian designations
N.A.111: covered three batches of P-51C, D and K, all from Dallas: 400 P-51C included 275 to RAF as Mustang III (RAF FB125/399) fitted on arrival with Malcolm sliding canopy; 600 P-51D; and 1,500 P-51K similar to D but with Aeroproducts propeller (594 to RAF as Mustang IVA, from KH671)
N.A.122 P-51D: blocks totalling 4,000 aircraft, from Inglewood
N.A.124 P-51D: blocks of 2,000 from Dallas, cut at war's end to 1,000, plus single P-51M (intended as first of large batch) with Dash-9A engine
N.A.126 P-51H: production derivative of N.A.105 lightweight family, six guns, V-1650-9A giving 1,380 hp for take-off and 2,218 hp with water injection for combat at best height; block of 2,400 from Inglewood but terminated at VJ-Day after completion of 555 (USAAF 44-64160/64714)
Note: RAF received 281 P-51D from various blocks as Mustang IV (RAF KH641 onwards); unarmed photo-recon conversions included **F-6B** (35 ex-P-51A), **F-6C** (71 ex-P-51B and 20 ex-P-51C), **F-6D** (146 ex-P-51D, Dallas) and **F-6K** (163 ex-P-51K)

P-51H

Twin Mustangs
N.A.120 two prototypes with V-1650/23/25 (Merlin); USAAF XP-82 (44-83886/83887); No 3 completed as XP-82A with V-1710-119 engines
N.A.123: production version of N.A.120, 500 ordered as **P-82B** but 480 cancelled (20 delivered as 44-65160/65179); No 10 converted as **P-82C** night fighter with SCR-720 radar in external pod, No 11 converted as

F-82Gs of 347th F(AW) Group.

P-82D with APS-4 radar
N.A.144: first post-war procurement, 100 **P-82E** (later F-82E) escorts with attack capability; 1,600 hp V-1710-143/145 engines, bomb/rocket load 4,000 lb, no radar
N.A.149 P-82F: (F-82F) night fighter, 100 with APS-4 radar
N.A.150 P-82G: (F-82G) night fighter, 50 with SCR-720 radar. A total of 14 F-82F and G were given designation F-82H after winterization for Alaskan service
Post-war variants
F-51D, H and K: designations of surviving P-51D, H and K in 1951
RF-51D, RF-51K: post-1951 designations of F-6D, F-6K
TRF-51D: two-seat conversion of RF-51D (there were several

wartime two-seat conversions, some effected by field units but including TP-51D series (ten aircraft) rebuilt by NAA
TP-51D: post-war designation for (a) P-51Ds rebuilt by Temco Aircraft as dual trainers, many having P-51H tall vertical tail, and (b) P-51D single-seaters used as trainers by ANG

Cavalier Mustang: in 1954 Trans-Florida Aviation purchased all rights to F-51 design and began marketing two-seat civil 'executive' and liaison rebuild of F-51D as Cavalier 2000; company changed name to Cavalier Aircraft and from 1961 offered range including Model 750, Model 1200 with extra 40 Imp gal in each wing, Model 1500 with extra 52.5 Imp gal in each wing, Model 2000 with 91.6 Imp gal tip tanks, and Model 2500 as 2000 with extra 50 Imp gal in each wing. Cavalier followed in 1967 with Mustang II family of military aircraft rebuilt from F-51D with civil Merlin 620, tip tanks and six or eight wing hardpoints. In addition the Cavalier F-51D was a remanufactured two-seater with F-51H vertical tail, Dash-7 engine, six guns and eight hardpoints for wide variety of loads (eg two 1,000 lb bombs and six HVAR). Rear seat normally for observer, but one, TF-51D, had dual control. Most supplied under MAP to S American air forces, but two stripped of armament and used by US Army at Ft Rucker as AH-56A chase aircraft

Civil Cavalier with Cavalier F-51D.

Cavalier Turbo Mustang III: single prototype with restressed airframe for increased airspeeds, longer fuselage with Rolls-Royce Dart 510 of 1,740 hp driving Rotol propeller. Civil registered N6167U

Turbo Mustang III

Piper Enforcer: second and third Turbo Mustang IIIs taken over by Piper Aircraft and completed to different standard with Lycoming T55-L-9 turboprop of 2,535 hp in shorter nose with exhaust stack on left side; two seats in second aircraft only, ten wing pylons, tip tanks and large rear ventral fin ahead of tailwheel. First crashed July 1971; second selected by USAF in Pave Coin evaluation for tactical Co-In aircraft

Piper Enforcer (single-seat).

Messerschmitt Bf 110 Night Fighters

The mauling that the Bf 110 received at the hands of the Royal Air Force shook the Luftwaffe's faith in the aircraft, but the strengths (and weaknesses) of Messerschmitt's heavy fighter remained unchanged. Attempts at using it in a new role, that of a night fighter, ultimately proved encouraging and the Bf 110 became the backbone of the Nachtjäger force.

"The spearhead of the Blitzkrieg is my Luftwaffe, and the spearhead of the Luftwaffe is formed by the Zerstörer (destroyer) groups." So proclaimed Reichsmarscall Goering in early 1940, at a time when the German propaganda machine was telling the world that the Zerstörers were invincible. Equipped entirely with the Messerschmitt Bf 110, they had rampaged through Poland in precisely the way everyone had expected, roaming far and wide and destroying every enemy aircraft they came up against.

The Bf 110 was Nazi Germany's entry in a new field of warplane that, though costly, was thought to justify itself. Basically a big fighter with two engines and two seats, it was seen as having the ability to shoot down enemy aircraft while carrying more guns than smaller fighters, and so much more fuel that, despite its two engines, it could fly much further. Early Bf 110s could fly 1600 km, more than twice as far as contemporary single-engined Bf 109s. But the Zerstörergruppen was in for a rude shock. In the campaign against Britain they received such a mauling from Hurricanes and

Spitfires that, on occasion, these fighters themselves had to be escorted by 109s.

It was widely thought that the 110 had proved a failure. Production was cut back, and work was hastened on the Me 210 successor. One role envisaged for the luckless 110 was night fighting, but early experiments were discouraging. On 3 October 1939 Feldwebwel Zimmermann of 10/ZG76 crashed embarrassingly in Holland, while on 6 December Uffizier Fuchs collided with a Wellington near Texel, resulting in the staffel being re-equipped with old Bf 109Ds. During the Norwegian campaign Hauptmann Wolfgang Falck of I/ZG1 became convinced that he could shoot sown RAF bombers at night. He began a campaign which gradually bore fruit, culminating in the great

A pair of late-model Bf 110G-4/R3 night fighters waits for night to fall. Severly outclassed in the day fighter role, the design was well-suited to attacking bombers at night. The type featured good endurance, a capacity to carry radar and other electronic equipment, and was heavily armed.

The Bf 110G-4 was produced by essentially adding FuG 202 Lichtenstein B/C radar to the Bf 110G-2 Zerstörer, and it was to become the basis for virtually all the night fighter variants. All aircraft with this radar retained the small G-2-type fins.

nationwide night air defence Himmelbett (four-poster bed) network commanded by Oberst (later General) Josef Kammhuber. From the start the Bf 110, in its C-2, C-4 and D-1 versions, played a central role in the NJGs (night fighter wings).

The Himmelbett system divided German airspace up into rectangular boxes, in each of which were ground radars and communications which tracked both the bomber and the night fighter and brought the two into proximity by radio instructions. Thus, the fighter hardly differed at all from other Bf 110s, apart from being painted black. Those that had Dackelbauch belly tanks had them removed, and the only other changes were the addition of exhaust flame dampers and cockpit anti-glare shields.

In 1940-42 the NJG pilots were divided into two groups with differing ideas. One lot came from JG and ZG (day fighter and Zerstörer) units, and to a man they preferred the Bf 110. With its speed, manoeuvrability, firepower (two 20-mm MG FF cannon and four 7.92-mm MG17 machine-guns, plus a gun for the backseater), good endurance, reliability and docile handling, it seemed the ideal night fighter. The contrary view was held by crews from KG (bomber) units, who considered that in night fighting manoeuvrability hardly mattered and that the Do 17Z, Do 217 and, above all, the Ju 88 were superior because of their spacious cockpits, third or fourth crew member, autopilot and ability to carry more guns and fly even longer than the 110 could. In the longer term the standard night fighters were to be specially developed versions of the Ju 88 and Bf 110, and there is no doubt that the Bf 110 was to prove far more valuable as a night fighter than in its original role as a day Zerstörer.

The first Bf 110 version specially equipped for night fighting was the D-1/I1, in the nose of which was mounted one of the Spanner series of IR (infra-red) sensors. Produced by AEG, the Spanner I was an active device. An IR searchlight like a bowl electric fire projected a beam of heat ahead and any heat scattered or reflected back from a target aircraft was detected. Spanner II, III and IV were passive, being merely highly sensitive receivers able to detect the exhaust fumes and hot pipes of the enemy bombers (but increasingly the RAF countered this by fitting flame dampers).

A close-up of this 6./NJG 6 shows the antennas for the FuG 202 Lichtenstein B/C radar and the flame-damped exhaust. The underwing tanks held extra fuel, the fitment of them covered under the designation B2. This aircraft force-landed in Switzerland after becoming lost.

Initial experience with the Bf 110G-4 night fighter was favourable, although it was not long before the Royal Air Force developed tactics to defeat the German radars, beginning a long battle involving radars and countermeasurers.

From spring 1941 the RAF four-engined 'heavies' began appearing in numbers, and the Halifax and Lancaster could, when alerted, give most Bf 110s a run for their money, either on the level or in a shallow dive. Accordingly, the Bf 110E received the DB601N and the Bf 110F the DB601F of 1006 kW (1,350 hp), which arrested the previous decline in performance caused by progressive increases in weight. From early 1942, and partly because of severe problems with the Me 210, the importance of the Bf 110 rapidly increased. Apart from the Ju 88 there was no other really suitable aircraft for the night-fighter

Nachtjagdgeschwaders used Bf 110s during the early years of the war, these being the earlier versions lacking radar but armed with heavy 30-mm cannon. Spanner-Anlage infra-red sensors were sometimes fitted to aid the crew find their targets.

The hunter hunted: a Lichtenstein SN-2 equipped Bf 110 gets caught behind an RAF fighter over Germany. The most feared was the de Havilland Mosquito, which could easily outmanoeuvre and outperform the German machine in night combats.

role, and with the increasing scale of RAF attacks the need was growing very urgent.

Accordingly, the Messerschmitt design staff dusted off their old Bf 110 drawings and began planning a completed unexpected further major version, the 110G. Back in 1941 plans had been agreed for eventual testing of a Bf 110 with the DB605 engine (as was also later to be fitted to the Bf 109G), and using this 1099-kW (1,475-hp) engine the 110G was schemed in several versions, of which the G-4 was to be a night fighter. But before production of the G-4 got under way in the summer of 1942 Messerschmitt had begun delivering the F-4, the first really major night-fighter version.

Though still powered by the DB601, this carried considerably more than a ton of extra load. In all except the first few, the MG FF cannon were replaced by the far more powerful MG151/20, with belt feed (300 rounds for the left gun, 350 for the right). Many F-4s had in addition a ventral tray for two 30-mm MK108s, and this necessitated enlarging the rudders to restore handling, especially with one engine out, which had become marginal. The cockpit was rearranged for a crew of three, the third man being essential once airborne radar was fitted. From late summer 1942 the FuG 202 Lichtenstein BC radar was introduced, the aircraft being redesignated Bf 110F-4a. Compared with the day F-2 the F-4a had gross weight increased from about 7200 kg (15,873 lb) to no less than 9287 kg (20,474 lb), with 300-litre (79-Imp gal) drop tanks. Worse, the radar used a large array of dipole antennas fixed to the nose – called Maikäferfüler – which caused a severe drag penalty. Worse still, the exhaust flame dampers seriously affected engine performance, so that not only did maximum speed drop to a bare 500 km/h (310 mph) but engine life

was short (valves lasted around 20 hours) and seized pistons and engine fires were common. Many crews had the flame dampers removed.

By 1943 RAF Bomber Command's attacks were on a massive scale, and the US 8th Air Force was mounting increasingly damaging missions by day. The need for more and better fighters of all kinds was becoming the Luftwaffe's No. 1 priority, and Messerschmitt strove to build up production. The original production lines at Augsburg was augmented by MIAG at Braunschweig and GWF at Gotha and Fürth. Oddly, however, the first DB605-powered versions to come off the assembly lines in May 1942 were for day operations, and the Bf 110G-4 night fighter did not reach NJG units until April 1943. It was identifiable mainly by the bigger propeller spinners, though the new engine cowlings were also different in detail.

The first G-4 batches had the same armament as the F-4, namely two MK108s in a ventral blister, two MG151/20s and four MG17s firing ahead; the aft-firing MG15 was replaced by the neat MG81Z twin machine-guns firing at a combined rate of 3,600 rounds/min (though it was extremely rare for the aft-firing guns to be needed). The extra power of the DB605B-1 engines restored maximum speed to about 540 km/h (336 mph) even with the radar fitted, and the drag of the radar was greatly reduced by fitting the FuG 212 Lichtenstein C-1 set, with a much smaller central antenna array.

For several years previously there had been discussion and experiment, mainly at Rechlin and Tarnewitz test centres, about the pros and cons of guns firing upwards. In May 1943 an armourer serving with II/NJG5, Ofw Mahle, had been intrigued at the upward-firing guns of the 'special' Do 217J of the Gruppe's CO, Oblt Rudolf Schoenert. The Gruppe's Bf 110s had had their MG FF cannon replaced by MG151/20s, and the old guns were piled up doing nothing. Using parts of the old mountings, Mahle fitted upward-firing MG FFs to one of the Bf 110s, in what was called a schräge Musik installation, and within days Schoenert scored a kill with it over Berlin in May 1943. Subsequently, large numbers of such installations were made on Ju 88s and other night fighters, but there was less room in the Bf 110 and the only officially approved installation comprised twin 30-mm MK108s in the front of the rear cockpit, the designation becoming Bf 110G-4/U1. With the FuG 212 radar the designation was G-4/U5. The U6 sub-type had in addition the FuG 221a Rosendaal-Halbe passive receiver which homed on the Monica tail-warning

During the day the night-fighter Messerschmitts hid from Allied bombers under elaborate camouflages involving nets and foliage. This aircraft has the Rustsatz-3 applied, which replaced four forward-firing MG 17 guns with two Mk 108 30-mm cannon.

This front view of a Lichtenstein C-1 Bf 110 shows WfrGr 21 mortars under the wing racks. This weapon was an attempt to hit bombers with a far larger explosive charge than possible with cannon, ensuring the destruction of any bomber.

The Bf 110-G-4d/R3 was the ultimate night-fighting variant of the Messerschmitt twin. The primary sensor was the FuG 220b Lichtenstein SN-2 radar in the nose, which in the G-4d/R3 version had low-drag aerials set diagonally, as opposed to vertically in earlier variants. The SN-2 radar was typified by the hirschgeweih (stag's antlers) aerials, and operated at a different wavelength from that affected by the 'Window' chaff which was carried in large quantities by RAF bombers. Some Bf 110G-4d/R3s mounted the FuG 227/1 Flensburg radar receiver, this equipment being used to home in on the Monica tail warning radars carried by the bombers.

Specification
Messerschmitt Bf 110G-4d/R3

Type: three-seat night fighter

Powerplant: two Daimler-Benz DB 605B-1 12-cylinder inverted-vee engines, each rated at 1100 kW (1,475 hp) for take-off, 1010 kW (1,355 hp) at 5700 m (18,700 ft)

Performance: maximum speed 500 km/h (311 mph) at sea level, 550 km/h (342 mph) at 6980 m (22,900 ft); maximum cruising speed 510 km/h (317 mph) at 6000 m (19685 ft); maximum rate of climb 660 m (2,165 ft) per minute; service ceiling 8000 m (26,250 ft); maximum range with internal fuel 900 km (560 miles), with two 900-litre (198-Imp gal) drop tanks 2100 km (1,305 miles)

Weights: empty 5090 kg (11,200 lb); normal loaded 9390 kg (20,700 lb); maximum loaded 9890 kg (21,804 lb)

Dimensions: wing span 16.25 m (53 ft 3¾ in); length 13.05 m (42 ft 9¾ in); height 4.18 m (13 ft 8½ in); wing area 38.4 m (413.34 sq ft)

Armament: two 30-mm MK 108 cannon in lower fuselage, each with 135 rounds; two 20-mm MG 151 cannon in upper fuselage, starboard weapon with 350 rounds and port weapon with 300 rounds; 7.9-mm MG 81Z twin machine-gun installation in rear cockpit with 800 rounds

Messerschmitt Bf 110 Night Fighters

The Bf 110G-2 was essentially a day fighter version, lacking the radar and other sensors of the G-4. It was issued to night fighter units, as evidenced by this machine of 12/NJG 3 based at Stavanger in Norway, and occasionally used on moonlit nights.

radar carried by RAF heavy bombers from 1943. Later this was replaced by the FuG 227 Flensburg.

Throughout 1943 the NJG Gruppen fielded between 380 and 500 night fighters and, apart from a handful of Ju 88C-6b and Do 217J and N night fighters, the entire force used the Bf 110, mainly of the F-4 type but rapidly replacing this by the G-4. In some ways the NJG crews were getting the measure of the enemy, but in summer 1943 the day fighter defences were augmented by sending out the Bf 110 night fighters against the American B-17s and B-24s, and losses were almost crippling. Quite soon day operations were forbidden, especially to the key experienced NJG crews, though in fact the Bf 110G-4 night fighters were to be found operating by day to the end of the war.

For at least a year after its introduction the G-4 suffered from engine problems at least as severely as the F-4 series. The causes were fundamental, resulting in catastrophic failures of the pistons, crankshafts and other highly stressed parts, usually leading not only to single-engined flight but also to severe inflight fires. Indeed, in June 1943 the Bf 110G-4s were grounded, and engine problems did not really subside until the summer of 1944. Production of the Bf 110 had been more than doubled, and 1,518 were delivered in the course of 1944. Whereas manufacturer of most German aircraft except fighters was stopped in autumn 1944, the seemingly obsolescent Bf 110 continued in production right to the final collapse.

From autumn 1943 most newly built G-4s had their performance improved by fitting the GM-1 installation, in Rüstsatz 2. This added a tank holding 439 kg (968 lb) of nitrous oxide, together with a rather complex and heavy system for injecting the chemical into the cylinders to permit a substantial short-term boost in maximum power. The resulting aircraft were designated G-4/U7. Soon afterwards the G-4a entered production with various detail changes, which included replacement of the four MG17s by twin MK108s, so

The equipment of the Bf 110 night fighters was under continuous development throughout its career. Eventually the short range problems of the Lichtenstein SN-2 were overcome, allowing the Bf 110 to dispense with the C-1 single pole aerial array.

that some aircraft had the powerful forward-firing armament of four 30-mm and two 20-mm guns. A few had a single BK 3,7 or Flak 18 gun slung under the fuselage, while others replaced the radar operator/gunner by a 540-litre (143-Imp gal) fuel tank to give increased endurance (this proved unsuccessful).

In July 1943, in a series of devastating attacks on Hamburg, the RAF had begun using what today is called chaff, billions of small strips of reflective metal foil tailored to the wavelengths of the German radars. Thus blinded, the night fighters did badly, but by the end of the year the Bf 110G-4b was in production with the FuG 220 Lichtenstein SN-2. This set worked on longer wavelengths against which the RAF chaff was useless. At first operating at frequencies from 73 to 91 MHz, this radar later expanded to cover the so-called 'dispersal

A small number of Bf 110s had received the FuG 218 Neptun radar by the end of the war, but their impact was negligible. An excellent radar, the Neptun was distinguished by its single pole mounting. This aircraft is seen wearing RAF markings after capture at the end of the war.

This Messerschmitt Bf 110G-4b/R3 flew with 7 Staffel of III/Nachtjagdgeschwader 4, which defended the skies of northern Germany during 1944. The mottled grey camouflage on the upper surfaces was common, with either black or grey undersides.

The tail of this Bf 110G-4b/R3 shows RAF bomber kills. Flown by Wilhelm Johnen, one of the top scoring night aces, it was flown by accident to Switzerland where it was interned. His unit at the time was Nachtjagdgeschwader 5.

waveband' from 37.5-118 MHz. Unfortunately, not only did it need a massive antenna installation, called the Hirschgeweih, but the set's minimum range was no less than 350 m (1,148 ft) so the C-1 set still had to be retained for guidance over the final, crucial part of the interception to visual contact. Two years earlier Goering, who hated and distrusted things like radar, had exclaimed, "A fighter cannot have things sprouting from its head!" Now the G-4b had two sets of "things sprouting", but in fact by February 1944 the SN-2 was able to

operate at ranges down to 300 m (984 ft) and many aircraft had the C-1 removed.

This was the peak of the NJG force. The venerable Bf 110 equipped 14 of the 22 combat-ready Gruppen, and the toll they exacted upon the RAF heavies was so great that night operations over Germany were tapered off, the attacks instead switching to targets further west in support of the forthcoming invasion. By this time even the night sky over central Germany was becoming perilous because of marauding Mosquitoes and even Beaufighters, but at all times the docile qualities of the Bf 110 were often instrumental in enabling a crew in difficulties to get somewhere safely. The only feature that made it unpopular was the cramped interior (especially if schräge Musik guns were fitted). By 1944 virtually every NJG crew numbered three, and if the gunner was killed or injured the radar operator was completely trapped and could not get out in emergency.

As well as small numbers of the H-4 night fighter, which differed only in details, the final production variants were the G-4c, with C-1 radar omitted, and the G-4d with a reduced-drag SN-2 antenna system. The /R4 sub-types replaced the upper nose MK108s by MG151s. Total night-fighter production amounted to almost exactly half the total of about 6,050 of all versions.

Late Bf 110G-4c aircraft had the antennas of the Lichtenstein SN-2 canted to improve detection capability. This close-up shows the cannon ports for the MG 151 and MK 108 weapons, of 20-mm calibre (lower nose) and 30-mm calibre (upper nose) respectively.

Dornier Do 335

*In its intended role as a bomber destroyer the Dornier Do 335
Pfeil could have spelt disaster for the Allies. Very fast and well
armed, it was another example of the innovative approach of
German aircraft designers. It was also an example of one of the
Luftwaffe's greatest problems in the closing stages of the war:
fielding important new aircraft, too little and too late.*

No-one can accuse the World War II German aircraft designers of conservatism, and while the majority of combat aircraft were of conventional design, there were many others which pushed the forefront of aeronautics. Unhampered by tradition, German designers sought fresh means to solve old problems, and in so doing provided the Allies in both East and West with a wealth of advanced research material following the end of hostilities. One of the most famous of the bizarre shapes which took to the air over Germany was the Dornier Do 335 Pfeil, a brave attempt to provide the Luftwaffe with a potent fighter-bomber, night fighter and reconnaissance platform.

Prof.-Dr. Claudius Dornier was the genius behind the famous company of Dornier-Werke GmbH, and he had established a long line of successful aircraft, notably in the field of flying boats. For most of the late 1930s and World War II, Dornier was primarily concerned with the production of bombers for the Luftwaffe. Since the end of World War I, Claudius Dornier had been interested in the field of centre-line thrust, whereby two engines shared the same thrust line – one pulling and one pushing. Benefits of this system were obvious over a conventional twin layout, with only the same frontal area as a single-engined aircraft, the wing left clean of engine nacelles and attendant structures, and no asymmetric pull if one engine cut out. However, problems did exist in the area of the drive shaft which drove the rear propeller.

Dornier's extensive flying-boat experience gave him a wealth of knowledge in simple centreline thrust arrangements, where two engines were mounted back-to-back over the centreline of many of his designs. By the mid-1930s he saw the possibility of using this concept to power a high-speed fighter, but first the rear engine extension shaft arrangement had to be proved. To that end Ulrich Hütter was commissioned to design a small test-bed for the arrangement. Designated the Göppingen Gö 9, and built by Schempp-Hirth, the test-bed featured a pencil-slim fuselage contained a 59.6-kW (80-hp) Hirth HM 60R engine mounted at the centre of gravity beneath the shoulder-set wing. Stalky main undercarriage units retracted into the wing, while a nosewheel unit retracted forward into the extreme nose. Behind the wing a long and slender tail boom hid the drive shaft which extended past a cruciform tail to a four-blade wooden propeller.

Flying for the first time in 1940, the Gö 9 proved that the rear pusher principle was both efficient and safe, which gave Dornier new impetus to his fighter designs taking shape on the drawing boards. However, the Technische Amt of the RLM decreed that Dornier abandon his work with fighters and return to the main job in hand of producing bombers and flying-boats, despite some initial interest in his radical designs. Nevertheless, in 1942 the Technische Amt issued a requirement for a high-speed unarmed intruder aircraft, and Dornier submitted his Projekt 231 design, incorporating the tractor-

The second production Do 335A-0 wears werk-nr 102 on its tail. To the RLM, the German air ministry, the Pfeil was projekt 231, but its prominent nose saw it dubbed ameisenbär (anteater) by its crews.

The Do 335 V1 differed most obviously from subsequent prototypes in having an extra oil cooler intake underneath. The first aircraft (CP+UA) took to the air on 26 October 1943.

Designed by Ulrich-Hütter, the all-wooden Göppingen G.9 was the testbed for the Do 335's aft-mounted prop design. Its Hirth engine was mounted below the wing and with it the G.9 reached a speed of 220 km/h (37 mph).

pusher engine arrangement. After evaluation, Dornier was awarded a development contract in the face of opposition from Arado and Junkers, and the designation Do 335 was assigned to Projekt 231.

As design got underway, the RLM issued a new directive to re-design the Do 335 as a multi-purpose day fighter, night fighter, fighter-bomber, Zerstörer and reconnaissance platform, which caused a delay in production of the prototype. By the autumn of 1943 the Do 335 was ready for flight.

Dornier's concept had emerged as a fearsome looking aircraft, appearing as purposeful as a fighter could. In the forward fuselage a Daimler-Benz DB 603 featured an annular-ring cowl, while exhaust stubs just aft of the trailing edge belied the position of the rear engine. Underneath the rear fuselage a large airscoop aspirated the second unit, which powered a three-blade propeller mounted behind

*The **Pfeil** was the first production aircraft to be fitted with an ejection seat; however, the system for actually escaping was a complicated one. German pilots told of how, during the test programme, two aircraft crashed and their pilots were found still in the cockpit but with their arms missing. This was supposedly due to too firm a grip being taken on the handles, which first jettisoned the canopy before the seat could be fired out.*

a cruciform tail. Under the centre-section of the wing were doors for a small weapons bay, capable of carrying a single 500-kg (1,100-lb) or two 250-kg (550-lb) bombs. The undercarriage was a tricycle arrangement, with the wide-track main units retracting inwards into the wing and the nosewheel retracting backwards (following a 90° rotation) into the area beneath the cockpit.

Remarkable shape, remarkable performance

The broad wing was set well back, and although the name Pfeil was used semi-officially, the service pilots who became acquainted with this extraordinary machine soon dubbed it 'Ameisenbär', thanks to its long nose. A Dornier pilot was at the controls for the first flight from Oberpfaffenhofen, this taking place on 26 October 1943 with the Do 335 V1 first prototype (CP+UA). After initial Dornier trials, the aircraft moved to Rechlin to begin extensive official trials. Reports from Oberpfaffenhofen and Rechlin were favourable, with only slight longitudinal stability problems encountered. Most pilots were surprised at the speed, acceleration, turning circle and general handling of the type, and development continued smoothly. Further prototypes joined Dornier and Rechlin trials, introducing new improvements such as redesigned undercarriage doors and blisters in the canopy accommodating mirrors for improved rearward vision.

By the fifth prototype, armament was installed, this comprising two MG 151 15-mm cannon in the upper fuselage decking and a single MK 103 30-mm cannon firing through the forward propeller hub. Subsequent prototypes were used for further flight trials and engine tests, culminating in the Do 335 V9 built to pre-production standards. The first Do 335A-0 pre-production aircraft (VG+PG) followed shortly in mid-1944, with full armament and ready to start operational evaluation. In September of that year, the Erprobungskommando 335 was established to conduct tactical development using many of the 10 Do 335A-0s built. Service trials began with the Do 335 V9 with the Versuchsverband des Oberfehlshabers des Luftwaffe.

By late autumn in 1944, the Do 335A-1 full production model appeared at Oberpfaffenhofen, this introducing the definitive DB 603E-1 engine and two underwing hardpoints capable of carrying fuel or 250-kg (550-lb) bombs. Similar in airframe details to the Do 335A-1 was the Do 335A-4 unarmed reconnaissance version. Only one was completed, adapted from a Do 335A-0 with two Rb 50/18 cameras in the weapons bay and increased external fuel. DB 603G engines were to have been fitted with higher compression ratio and more powerful superchargers.

Two-seat night fighter

Next in the line of Pfeil variants was the Do 335A-6 (prototype Do 335 V10) which was the night fighter variant. Armament remained unchanged from the fighter-bomber, but FuG 217J Neptun airborne intercept radar was added, the aerials being located forward of the wing (lateral beam port and vertical beam starboard). To operate the radar a second crewman was needed, and to accommodate him a cockpit was incorporated above and behind that of the pilot. Giving the Pfeil an even stranger appearance than before, the second cockpit also meant a considerable restructuring of the fuel system, with the weapons bay area given over to fuel carriage. The negative effect on performance of the extra cockpit, aerials, weight and other modifications such as flame-damping tubes over the exhaust ports was in the region of 10%, but production aircraft would have offset this partially by being fitted with water-methanol boosted DB 603E engines, instead of the DB 603A units retained by the sole example. Production was scheduled to have been undertaken by Heinkel in Vienna, but this plan was overtaken by events and the tooling never assembled.

The final pair of Do 355A variants were the Do 335A-10 and Do 335A-12, both featuring the second cockpit for use as conversion trainers. The former was powered by the DB 603A engine (prototype Do 335 V11) and the latter by the DB 603E (prototype Do 335 V12). With full controls in the raised cockpit for the instructor, the two prototypes were both delivered without armament, but this was rectified in the pair of Do 335A-12 production aircraft.

After development of fighter-bomber, reconnaissance, trainer and night fighter variants, the role of heavy Zerstörer was next to be developed, as a direct result of the worsening war situation. During the winter of 1944/45, the Do 335 V13 emerged from the

This was the seventh Do 335A-0 fighter to be built and was one of 10 evaluated by Erprobungskommando 335 which was formed in September 1944 to develop operational tactics for the type. The aircraft were armed with a 30-mm MK 103 cannon and a pair of 15-mm MG 151 machine-guns.

Dornier Do 335B-2 cutaway drawing key

1 Upper rudder trim tab
2 Upper rudder
3 Upper tailfin (jettisonable by means of explosive bolts)
4 VDM airscrew of 3.30 m (10.83 ft) diameter
5 Airscrew spinner
6 Airscrew pitch mechanism
7 Starboard elevator
8 Elevator tab
9 Metal stressed-skin tailplane structure
10 Ventral rudder
11 Tail bumper
12 Tail bumper oleo shock-absorber
13 Ventral tailfin (jettisonable for belly landing)
14 Coolant outlet
15 Rear navigation light
16 Explosive bolt seatings
17 Rudder and elevator tab controls
18 Hollow airscrew extension shaft
19 Rear airscrew lubricant feeds
20 Aft bulkhead
21 Coolant trunking
22 Oil cooler radiator
23 Coolant radiator
24 Fire extinguisher
25 Ventral air intake
26 FuG 25a IFF
27 FuG 125a blind landing receiver
28 Rear engine access cover latches
29 Exhaust stubs
30 Supercharger intake
31 Coolant tank
32 Engine bearer
33 Aft Daimler-Benz DB 603E-1 12-cylinder inverted-Vee liquid-cooled engine rated at 1340 kW(1,800 hp) for take-off and 1415 kW (1,900 hp) at 1800 m (5,905 ft)
34 Supercharger
35 Aft firewall
36 FuG 25a ring antenna
37 Fuel filler cap
38 Main fuel tank (1230-litre/270 Imp gal capacity)
39 Secondary ventral fuel tank

Oberpfaffenhofen factory as the Do 335B-1. This aircraft featured the replacement of the weapons bay by a fuel tank, and the replacement of the 15-mm cannon by 20-mm MG 151 cannon. More heavily armed was the Do 335 V14 which, intended for service as the Do 335B-2, featured the same armament and an added Mk 103 30-mm cannon mounted in the wings.

In the event, these were the only B-series aircraft to be completed, although others were on the construction line at the termination of the project. These included more B-1 and B-2 prototypes, and a pair of Do 335B-6 prototypes, these being night fighters similar to the Do 335A-6 but with the heavy armament of the Do 335B-1. Other prototypes would have featured DB 603LA engines with a two-stage supercharger. One other development deserves mention, the B-4, B-5 and B-8 models which featured a 4.3 m (14 ft 10 in)

The nose-mounted Daimler-Benz DB603A-2 engine was provided with an annular nose radiator, while the ventral scoop intake was for the aft powerplant. The tractor propeller was pitch-reversible.

40 Two (45-litre/9.9-Imp gal capacity) lubricant tanks (port for forward engine and starboard for rear engine)
41 Pilot's back armour
42 Rearview mirror in glazed teardrop
43 Headrest
44 Pilot's armoured ejection seat
45 Clear-vision panel
46 Jettisonable canopy (hinged to starboard)
47 Protected hydraulic fluid tank (45-litre/9.9-Imp gal capacity)

64 Ammunition box
65 Forward firewall
66 Breech of nose-mounted MK 103 cannon
67 Engine bearer
68 Forward DB 603E-1 engine
69 MG 151 cannon blast tubes
70 Gun trough
71 Hydraulically-operated cooling gills
72 Coolant radiator (upper segment)
73 Oil cooler radiator (lower segment)

91 Ejector seat compressed air bottles
92 Rudder pedals
93 Ammunition tray
94 Armour
95 Cannon fairing
96 MK 103 barrel
97 Muzzle brake
98 Ammunition feed chute
99 Starboard MK 103 wing cannon

100 Mainwheel retraction strut
101 Oleo leg
102 Starboard mainwheel
103 Mainwheel door
104 Forward face of box spar
105 Stressed wing skinning
106 Starboard navigation light
107 Wingtip structure
108 Starboard aileron
109 Aileron trim tab
110 Starboard wing fuel tank

111 Aileron control rod
112 Trim tab linkage
113 Oxygen bottles
114 Starboard flaps
115 Starter fuel tank
116 Flap hydraulic motor
117 Starboard mainwhell well
118 Boxspar
119 Compressed air bottles (emergency undercarriage actuation)
120 Mainspar/fuselage attachment points

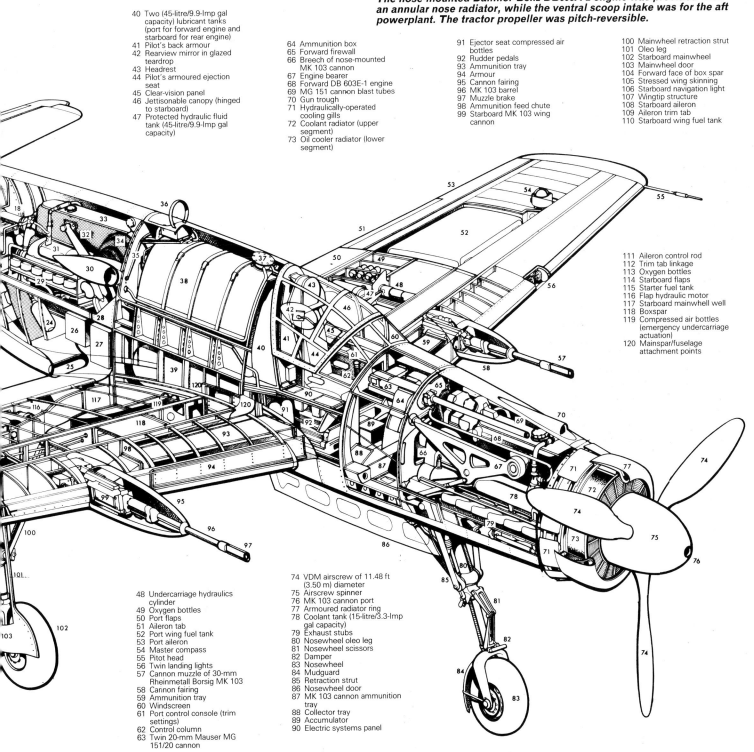

48 Undercarriage hydraulics cylinder
49 Oxygen bottles
50 Port flaps
51 Aileron tab
52 Port wing fuel tank
53 Port aileron
54 Master compass
55 Pitot head
56 Twin landing lights
57 Cannon muzzle of 30-mm Rheinmetall Borsig MK 103
58 Cannon fairing
59 Ammunition tray
60 Windscreen
61 Port control console (trim settings)
62 Control column
63 Twin 20-mm Mauser MG 151/20 cannon

74 VDM airscrew of 11.48 ft (3.50 m) diameter
75 Airscrew spinner
76 MK 103 cannon port
77 Armoured radiator ring
78 Coolant tank (15-litre/3.3-Imp gal capacity)
79 Exhaust stubs
80 Nosewheel oleo leg
81 Nosewheel scissors
82 Damper
83 Nosewheel
84 Mudguard
85 Retraction strut
86 Nosewheel door
87 MK 103 cannon ammunition tray
88 Collector tray
89 Accumulator
90 Electric systems panel

V11 was the prototype for the Do 335A-10 two-seat trainer. Both this and a second example (V12) were delivered unarmed, but the intention was to equip production models with the armament of the Do 335A-1.

increase in wing span for greater altitude performance. The development of these new outer wing panels had been undertaken by Heinkel, but they remained on the drawing board. Derivative designs included the Do 435 night fighter, with side-by-side seating, cabin pressurisation and long-span wings, the Do 535 mixed-power-plant fighter with the rear DB 603 replaced by a jet engine and the Do 635 long range reconnaissance platform which aimed to mate two Do 335 fuselages together with a new centre-section. At the termination of production, 37 Pfeils had been completed, with others awaiting final assembly and components for many more finished.

As far as is known, the Pfeil never entered into combat, although US pilots reported seeing the strange aircraft in the sky during forays over Germany. In it single-seat version it was one of the fastest piston-engined fighters ever built, with a claimed top speed of around 765 km/h (475 mph). Despite this high performance, it was the much slower two-seat night fighter version which would prob-

ably have proved the most effective if the war had continued. Equipped with excellent radar and powerful weapons, and blessed with good visibility, combat persistence and performance, the night fighter would have been excellent against the RAF bomber streams.

A complicated escape

Flying the Pfeil was an experience thanks to its high performance and unusual configuration. While the performance provided an exhilarating ride for the pilot, the configuration gave him a few consternations. His main concern was the ejection seat, the Do 335 being only the second production type to feature this. Before firing the seat, explosive bolts which held the upper vertical tail surface and rear propeller on were fired to clear a way for the egressing pilot. Despite the ejection seat he had to jettison the canopy manually. As another safety feature, the lower vertical tail surface was jettisonable in case a wheels-up landing was undertaken.

To conclude, the Pfeil proved to be a sound design with no major pitfalls. If development had been allowed to continue at a steady pace, the teething problems which remained with the type could have been ironed out at an early stage, and the Pfeil could have emerged as a warplane of major importance to the Luftwaffe. However, as the military situation facing Germany darkened during 1944/45, so development was rushed through at great speed. Also hampering development and production attempts was the state of Germany industry, which could not provide the sub-contracted components such as propellers, engines and radios fast enough.

No matter what the problems, the aviation enthusiast has been left the experience of witnessing one of the world's most exciting warplanes, and another chapter in the story of 'Might Have Been . . .'

The Do 335A-1, the initial production version, started to appear in the autumn of 1944. Emphasis soon switched to the Do 335B, the more heavily armed Zerstörer single-seat heavy fighter.

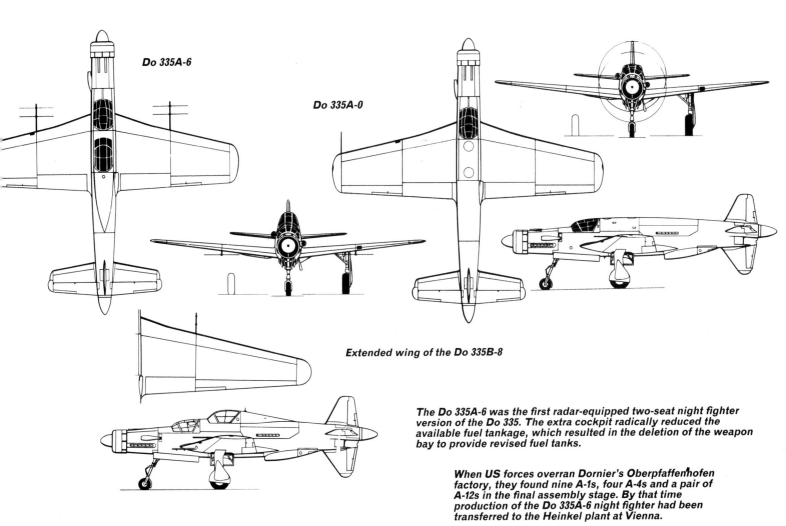

Do 335A-6

Do 335A-0

Extended wing of the Do 335B-8

The Do 335A-6 was the first radar-equipped two-seat night fighter version of the Do 335. The extra cockpit radically reduced the available fuel tankage, which resulted in the deletion of the weapon bay to provide revised fuel tanks.

When US forces overran Dornier's Oberpfaffenhofen factory, they found nine A-1s, four A-4s and a pair of A-12s in the final assembly stage. By that time production of the Do 335A-6 night fighter had been transferred to the Heinkel plant at Vienna.

INDEX

Note: page numbers in italics refer to illustrations